Business Logistics Management
Theory and Practice

Business Logistics Management
Theory and Practice

JJ Vogt, WJ Pienaar, PWC de Wit

with contributions by
P Linford, G de Villiers

OXFORD
UNIVERSITY PRESS

OXFORD

UNIVERSITY PRESS

Great Clarendon Street, Oxford OX2 6DP

Oxford University Press is a department of the University of Oxford.
It furthers the University's objective of excellence in research, scholarship,
and education by publishing worldwide in

Oxford New York

Auckland Bangkok Buenos Aires Cape Town Chennai
Dar es Salaam Delhi Hong Kong Istanbul Karachi Kolkata
Kuala Lumpur Madrid Melbourne Mexico City Mumbai Nairobi
São Paulo Shanghai Singapore Taipei Tokyo Toronto

with an associated company in Berlin

Oxford is a registered trade mark of Oxford University Press
in the UK and certain other countries

Published in South Africa
by Oxford University Press Southern Africa, Cape Town

Business Logistics Management: Theory and Practice
ISBN 0 19 578011 6

Editor: Danelle Scholtz
Designer: Chris Davis

Published by Oxford University Press Southern Africa
PO Box 12119, N1 City, 7463, Cape Town, South Africa

Set in 9.5 pt on 12 pt Adobe Caslon
Typesetting by Global Graphics
Imagesetting by Castle Graphics
Cover reproduction by The Image Bureau
Printed and bound by Clyson Printers, Maitland

Contents

Preface

Logistics management rose to prominence during the previous decade. Many manufacturing enterprises have developed their production processes to a point of maximum productivity. Technological innovations, including sophisticated computer systems, have enhanced the efficiency of production processes to such an extent that in future significant cost savings are unlikely in this area.

Effective logistics management is now the one remaining management function of an enterprise where significant cost savings can be achieved and where the effectiveness of the enterprise can be increased substantially. The whole business world is currently gaining because of developments in logistics. Modern computer systems make it possible for enterprises to continuously improve all their logistics activities.

Enterprises can now hold smaller inventories and transport systems are effectively linked to the operations of enterprises. Modern computerised warehouses and handling equipment are being used and improved procurement systems are developed to enhance the flow of materials from the raw material stage through the logistics chain to the final consumer. The same principles apply to trading enterprises. Advanced logistics activities make it possible for these enterprises to manage their incoming and outgoing goods more efficiently. This has a positive effect on consumer service and ultimately on consumer satisfaction.

South Africa, as an economy in transition that became a role player in the global village when a democratic government was elected in 1994, should benefit from the developments in the logistics field. Many southern African enterprises have realised that they can become more competitive by improving their logistics systems. This has led to a need for a handbook of logistics management that will serve as a useful guide to the theoretical and practical characteristics of the field. Business Logistics Management was written against this background and it is suitable for graduate students in their second and third year as well as managers who wish to learn more about logistics.

The handbook has nineteen chapters. Each chapter contains a comprehensive discussion on a specific logistics subject. Supplements at the end of certain chapters illustrate the quantitative approaches to the applicable logistics activities. The last chapter is a case study covering all the work in the book. This should provide students with an example of how to solve practical problems by using the theoretical background provided in the previous chapters. The 'Test yourself' questions in the chapters serve to assist students in their academic development, while self-evaluating questions at the end of each chapter guide students in obtaining the most possible knowledge in this field.

An Instructor's Manual is provided, containing the answers to all the 'Test yourself' questions as well as a number of multiple choice questions and their answers.

We are pleased to dedicate this book to our respective spouses, Anne, Isabel and Yvette, for their patience, encouragement and support; and to Anne for her assistance during the editing.

John Vogt
Wessel Pienaar
Piet de Wit

1

1 Introduction to business logistics

Contents

Learning Outcomes

After you have studied this chapter, you should be able to:
- explain the origin of and define logistics;
- define and explain the difference between efficiency and effectiveness;
- discuss the four principles of logistics taken from the definition;
- give an example of two competing supply chains and describe why one is preferred in the logistics process;
- explain in which ways logistics may be viewed as the linkage between the source of goods and the consumer;
- understand the supply and delivery logistics concept and link this to a supply chain which incorporates a number of sequential stages in the manufacturing and/or distribution process before the final delivery stage;
- describe the impact logistics has on the marketing effort of a business by reference to the 4 Ps of marketing;
- discuss the management of a logistics chain with a consumer and service providers and explain:
  - how to translate consumer needs into measurable parameters for the overall chain,
  - how interfaces influence the supply chain and the method to manage them, and
  - how service providers are managed and on what criteria they are chosen;
- give one performance measurement which a service provider may use and explain why this may not be suitable in a logistics chain.

Introduction

Logistics became a formal function hundreds of years ago in the military context where troops had to be provisioned, looked after, and supported during a military campaign. Logistics in the commercial world has become increasingly important over the last twenty years. Logistics today is different from the original concept utilised by commercial enterprises and the logistics manager has a much more complex and challenging position in the business world than ever before. He or she must be able to manage both the flow of supplies into the enterprise and the delivery of all its products. The position requires the manager to be able to co-ordinate the activities of internal departments as well as external service providers. The co-ordination should include the suppliers, transporters, warehouse facilities, shipping lines, purchasing, manufacturing, delivery transport, air cargo, information systems, financial aspects, and a host of other functions required to make a logistics chain work effectively (see Figure 1.1).

Figure 1.1 Logistics functions conceptualised

The position is exciting and challenging to logistics managers who understand the fundamentals of logistics and can utilise these in a practical and sensible way to add value to their enterprise.

There are still many enterprises that claim to perform logistics without offering the integrated capability which logistics truly requires. Logistics is not a 'wheels and warehouse' capability (see Figure 1.2). While the transport and the storage capability are part of the logistics capability, the extent of logistics is far wider.

Figure 1.2 Wheels and warehouse view of logistics

Logistics is both a strategic commitment to support the marketing effort of the business and an operational quest for excellence. It incorporates the total supply chain and the focus is on satisfying the consumer. While the above sets right some of the misconceptions of logistics, the remainder of this text explains the capability of logistics to add a competitive advantage to the enterprise as well as the functions which must be mastered in order to understand and practice logistics.

> **Test yourself**
>
> 1.1 Name five activities that are part of the logistics chain.

Origins of logistics

Military

Logistics grew from the military function of supplying troops in the field.[1] The term is derived from the Greek word *logistikos*, meaning skilled in calculations. This skill in factual calculations remains a tenet for today's logistics capability. Initially, logistics was simply the provision of lodging, food and water for the soldiers. As the troops moved further away from the home base, the complexity of the supply problem grew. Soldiers now had to carry their own shelter and the food they could carry was only enough for a few days. In areas where food was not available in the quantities required, the supply lines had to provide the food and goods necessary to maintain the fighting capability of the army. As soldiers acquired more sophisticated weapons, which required supplies that were not available from the surrounding countryside, the complexity of the logistics increased. A cannon required ammunition and horses to move the carriage into firing positions. Horses required fodder, as they could often not survive in countries with completely different vegetation from their natural pastures. (Horses raised in England and fed on fodder could not adapt to the South African veld immediately. Prime English cavalry regiments struggled to perform because of this problem during the Anglo Boer War.)[2]

Logistics in the military context grew rapidly during the 19th century in Europe, as the continent was involved in numerous campaigns. Logistics as a formal study evolved with the work of Antoine Henri, Baron of Jomini, who served as a brigadier-general in Napoleon's army. He first used the word logistique in his work *Precis de l'art de la guerre (Summary of the art of war)*.

The following facts illustrate the growing complexity of military logistics:

The artillery ammunition expended in one month during World War I was twice the total amount of artillery ammunition expended in the entire American Civil War (lasting four years). By World War II, this had risen even further with an estimated ten tons of supplies and equipment required to place a soldier in the field; and a further two tons per month required to maintain the soldier in battle readiness.

To support the Zulu War in 1879, Lord Chelmsford had 16 800 soldiers with over two million rounds of ammunition in the field.[3] He had 113 two-wheeled carts, 612 wagons, and 7 626 dray animals shuttling goods from depots to the soldiers. Several hundred additional wagons brought supplies to the depots. Recent conflicts, for example the Gulf War in the 1990s, also reflected this trend. Enormous amounts of cargo were delivered into the area to supply aircraft and soldiers. Weapons and support equipment for continual aircraft sorties were supplied in a major build-up of materials and munitions before the

conflict commenced. The health of the soldiers was even considered to the point where the drinking water was brought into the area in bottled form to maintain peak physical fitness. The result of this was a war that lasted forty-three days, and with an air force delivering on average an enormous 2 555 sorties per day.[4]

Logistics in the modern army is not just about the supply of ammunition, equipment and food to troops, aircraft and ships. It includes training facilities, rest and recreation movements, and even medical facilities for the wounded, the evacuation of wounded and dead from the battlefield, and burial details.

Commercial

The commercial world has paralleled the military world as far as logistics is concerned. Many businesses have grown from the small operation that satisfies the needs of a community into larger ones whose products are distributed throughout southern Africa and often around the world. There is a need to compete with other producers of goods and services who have a competitive advantage due to the economies of scale derived from larger enterprises. This need drives the growth of small and medium enterprises into larger enterprises. As an enterprise grows beyond serving its immediate environment, the distance and complexity of delivering or sourcing products increases the need for logistics. Raw material must be sourced in the most effective way possible. This motivates enterprises to look at a myriad of suppliers, not just locally but also throughout the world. The finished goods or services can be distributed in the local market or into international markets. To achieve this effectively, the goods must be delivered at the right place and at the right time. The latter is the cornerstone of logistics. An example may illustrate this.

Example: Repair of a taxi

A taxi needs to be repaired. The livelihood of the owner is vested in the vehicle. The owner takes the vehicle to a garage. The mechanic does the repairs and replaces three parts. The taxi is returned on the same day. However, the complexity behind this simple service is significant.

The three parts required for the repair were scheduled for manufacture in Japan four months before. The parts were made three months ago. The motor manufacturer purchased the parts two months ago and arranged for them to be shipped to South Africa. This voyage to the car assembler's warehouse took nearly a month. The parts were ordered by the repair facility and placed into their own stock two weeks ago, from where they were used for the repairs. Any delay in scheduling the manufacturing of the parts, or in ordering the parts, or any part that was incorrectly ordered, would have had significant consequences for the owner of the vehicle. The repairs would have been delayed until the correct part was found and delivered to the repair facility. This could have taken days or even months if the part had to be manufactured. In the meantime, the vehicle would not have been earning money for the owner. In this example, logistics is the provision of the parts, the mechanics and the repair facility in a convenient location and at an acceptable price and time scale.

The above example shows that logistics is not just about moving goods. It is about providing an integrated service or product in the most effective manner possible. The enterprise that masters logistics has a competitive advantage. The enterprise that cannot get the logistics standard to the point where it is acceptable to the customer (the owner of the vehicle in the above example) will not get new or retain current business.

International competition

Smaller economies cannot exist in isolation from the rest of the world, even if they wanted to. All countries trade with other countries and the enterprises in these countries. Whether there is a need for oil products to fuel commercial jet aircraft or foreign exchange to purchase new equipment made outside the country – international trade must take place. This means that enterprises which can move goods to the country effectively can trade in the country. These international enterprises compete against the local enterprises. The enterprises that are able to provide their goods at the right time and at the right place to satisfy the consumer – so that the consumer not only purchases the goods, but wants to continue to purchase additional goods from the enterprise – will prosper.

Defining logistics

It is important to define logistics for two reasons: The definition provides the scope of logistics. Lack of this scope often gives rise to confusion in the enterprise as to what logistics actually incorporates. It also provides the focus of logistics, which is very different from traditional views of the enterprise. The scope and focus will be explained later as the definition is explored.

There are a number of definitions of business logistics management available. The following definition, which will be applied throughout the book, is that utilised by the Council of Logistics Management (URL/Web reference www.clm1.org):

> Logistics is the process of planning, implementing and controlling the efficient, effective flow and storage of goods, services, and related information from point-of-origin to point-of-consumption for the purpose of conforming to customer requirements.[5]

The above definition is a comprehensive one and needs to be clearly understood to conceptualise logistics as it is today. Let us break this definition into components to determine what the scope and the focus of logistics are.

There are four fundamental issues forming the definition.

The processes associated with flow and storage

Logistics is about the processes associated with the flow and storage of goods and services. The key to this is the concept of processes. It is not functional issues of transport or a warehouse, nor even the inbound side of receiving goods into the warehouse. It is the total ability to move and store goods and provide services as an integrated process. Enterprises that run segregated operations (such as a separate warehouse and an independent transport department) cannot achieve efficient (doing actions right the first time) or effective (doing the right actions at the right time for the right reason) logistics.

Efficiency and effectiveness

The processes must be efficient and effective. Efficiency means doing all the activities in the process using the least possible resources, whether these are people, equipment or the inventory. Achieving effectiveness is far more onerous. To be effective, the processes must also add the most value possible by either increasing revenue or reducing costs or both. This latter concept is important to understand. Logistics impacts directly on the ability of an enterprise to market its goods. This marketing effort is often described as incorporating the four Ps:[6]

Product
Place
Promotion
Price

Logistics focuses on the right goods in the right place at the right time. It therefore plays an important role in the place portion of marketing. Its impact does not stop there. The product quality is intimately affected by the logistics function (who would buy a television in a badly damaged box?). The logistics capability can affect the promotional opportunities of the product. An enterprise that can deliver the product faster and more reliably to the consumer has a competitive advantage which it can use as a further aspect of product promotion. The market determines the price at which the product can be sold. However, logistics partly determines the cost of making and delivering the product. It therefore has a direct effect on the profitability of the product.

To achieve efficiency and effectiveness, appropriate information in the form of physical and financial data is required. The following example illustrates this.

The example of Dell Computers

Dell Computers, in the high volume personal computer market, came up with a way of delivering PCs to consumers within twenty-four hours of the order – fitted with the hardware the consumer wanted and loaded with the appropriate software. The consumers had to supply the exact specifications for their hardware and software configuration to Dell. In exchange, they got a fast delivery of a new PC which merely needed to be plugged in to allow operation. Dell eliminated all the repetitive set-up problems for the enterprise's IT people and secured a large portion of the market through a new, unusual application of logistics.

From point-of-origin to point-of-consumption with information

The scope of logistics is from the point of the origin of the process to the point of the process where the goods or services are consumed or utilised by the consumer. It is not just the simple delivery of a product. It is the entire chain linking the raw material, inventory, and ultimately the final delivery and hand-over to the consumer in a manner that satisfies the consumer. Thus logistics encompasses all physical movement and storage, and all services offered in the total process from the source of the product or service until the consumer has been satisfied. To expedite movement, to manage inventory, and to be able to choose between chains and improve existing chains, accurate information is required. This information includes the appropriate physical parameters associated with the goods as well as the financial impact of the movement or storage costs of the goods. The old adage of 'if you can't measure it, you can't manage it' remains true for logistics.

The purpose is to conform to consumer requirements

The entire aim of logistics is to conform to consumer requirements. By so doing, the focus of the enterprise is to satisfy the consumer – thereby enhancing the marketing effort of the enterprise, and drawing the maximum profit from the operation. Logistics supports the marketing effort directly (place) as well indirectly (through the other three Ps of marketing). It requires an understanding of the consumers' needs or requirements, so that the process is efficient and effective. This means that one standard offering or a common approach to the total market is not feasible. The planning, implementing and controlling of all the processes must be directed towards satisfying the consumers' needs.

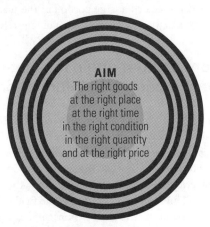

AIM
The right goods
at the right place
at the right time
in the right condition
in the right quantity
and at the right price

Figure 1.3 Aim of logistics

As a result of the focus on the consumer, the enterprise is focused on the end of the chain and the processes are altered to pull product through the chain. This is significantly different from the traditional push system of stocking product in warehouses and trying to match supply and demand from large reserves of stock. The pull system of logistics, correctly applied, results in faster movement of goods through the chain, using less inventory, and achieving higher levels of consumer satisfaction.

More definitions of terms

In this book, some terms are used extensively and consequently need some clarification:

- Logistics management is the management of the logistics activities.
- Business enterprise is the party who creates or instigates the logistics chain.
- Consumers, sometimes called end customers, are the party who buys the final goods or services. They may be either clients or customers.
- Clients are the party who buys services.
- Customers are the party who buys goods, i.e. physical products and/or raw materials.

Test yourself

1.3 The scope of the logistics chain forms part of the definition of logistics. The logistics chain is from the _____ to the _____. It includes the related _____.

1.4 The marketing of a product can be defined as encompassing the four aspects of _____, _____, _____, and _____.

1.5 Logistics is characterised as a _____, not a function.

1.6 The purpose of logistics is to conform to _____.

Logistics initiatives

While the concept of logistics has been discussed in some detail, there are other concepts with which the logistician should be familiar. These are briefly described here.

Supply chain management

Supply chain management is the operation associated with one chain of movement of the goods. For example, there could be two alternative supply chains to move goods from Johannesburg into Malawi. In the one supply chain, the goods could be moved by road through Zimbabwe and Zambia to Malawi. In the alternative supply chain, the goods could be moved by road to Durban, then by sea to Northern Mozambique, and further by rail to Malawi. Each of these is a supply chain. Logistics includes reviewing alternative supply chains to ensure that the most effective one is utilised. It also includes designing the chain to maximise the benefit to the consumers and putting it into operation.

Efficient consumer response

Efficient consumer response (ECR)[7] is a movement, predominantly in the grocery industry, that is focused on the total supply chain (suppliers, manufacturers, wholesalers, and retailers). It encourages trading partners to work closely together to satisfy the changing demands of the grocery industry and to fulfil consumer wishes better, faster, and at less cost.

The concept of logistics in business

As logistics is an integrated process of operation, logistics personnel should not think in terms of individual functions. They should rather find ways of co-ordinating and integrating the functions to be efficient and effective.

It is necessary to look conceptually at the scope of logistics. Every enterprise has different capabilities and different consumers. Logistics differs from one enterprise to the next, as each enterprise focuses on its unique circumstances and specific consumer needs. For logistics to add value, the enterprise must seek to differentiate its service offering from that of its competitors. The longer the logistics chain, the greater the scope for the logistics capability to achieve efficiency and effectiveness.

The start of any transactional process is the action of arranging to buy raw materials or goods for later sale by the enterprise. The completion of the process is when the consumer agrees to purchase the finished goods (the final transaction where any value is added). Logistics supports this process by linking every part of it: from the raw materials and goods (inbound logistics) to the delivery of the finished goods to the end customer (outbound logistics). This linkage bridges the decision to buy and the sale acquisition or consumer acceptance. The bridge concept focuses on the flow of processes and the inherently integrated nature of logistics.

The concept of business logistics is similar to the military concept, where logistics bridges the strategy and tactics of fighting a battle.

Rugby posts supply another conceptual view of logistics. The uprights or posts represent the purchase decision and the sale conclusion. Logistics, as the crossbar, links them. With logistics, there is a purpose for these goals – without it, there is none.

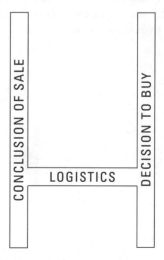

Figure 1.4 Concept of logistics

Supply and distribution logistics

The concept, scope, and focus of logistics have been discussed. The origin and consumption in the overall process still need to be explored. For an individual enterprise, determining the origin and the consumption is fairly simple. Logistics is not about the performance of a single enterprise but about the total capability of the logistics chain – from the raw material to the final product delivered to the consumer.

Supply and delivery logistics for an enterprise

The concept of supply to a process and delivery from a process can be depicted as in Figure 1.5.

It is important to realise that goods are supplied to the manufacturing or the value adding process; and the products from this are delivered to the next process link of the supply chain. This continues until the consumer is served. The logistics chain can therefore consist of a number of the supply and distribution logistics elements in Figure 1.5, one feeding the other until the final element feeds the consumer.

Point-of-origin to point-of-consumption of a logistics chain

Consider the tyres that motor cars use. The initial product is a particular sap derived from trees. This is the raw material for rubber. (There are now synthetic products, in addition to natural rubber, that are used to improve tyre wear and other characteristics.) The sap is processed into rubber compound and then moulded into tyres. Thus the process is as follows:

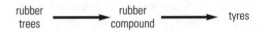

Figure 1.6 Process of supply and delivery

There are a number of customers in the process. The principal one is the consumer or end customer, who defines the requirements of the total chain. This may be the person who purchases tyres. However, the chain can be extended to include another sector – for example the vehicle assembler who adds the tyres to a different finished product (in this case the motor vehicle). The market for new vehicles is different from the market for the sale of tyres.

In this example, making the enterprise that grows the trees or the enterprise that converts the sap from the trees into rubber compound the most efficient and cost-effective operation has limited value. It may even be detrimental and lead to some

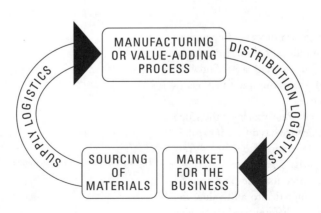

Figure 1.5 Supply and delivery logistics

enterprises being inefficient and the cost of the tyres increasing.

An example is the business which processes sap into rubber compound. Assume the sap is obtained primarily during the six-month growth season for the trees. The cheapest rubber compound process (i.e. the most efficient) can only support one type of sap. It is very expensive to stockpile the rubber compound for the additional six months, when no sap is available. The process of the compound manufacturer is as efficient and effective as possible. However, the overall chain will be more expensive. The appropriate logistics process is for the rubber compound production to operate all year using different types of sap. The increase in the cost of the plant is much less than the cost of holding six months of inventory. The whole logistics chain rather than only one element of the chain should be made as efficient and effective as possible.

Test yourself

1.7 For a business, the logistics chain can be broken into _____ logistics and _____ logistics.
1.8 The point of origin for a logistics chain is the source of the _____ that starts the logistics chain for the business.

Ideally, an enterprise will have direct influence over the entire logistics chain, in order to derive the maximum benefit from the advantages logistics provides. This may not be possible, as different businesses may operate and own the various sectors. The ownership of all the sectors is, however, not a prerequisite for logistics to be applied. The aim of logistics is to view the chain in totality and to ensure that it is optimised in the interest of all parties. The importance of this concept is confirmed in the Efficient Consumer Response (ECR) methodology where a fundamental principle of the process is to 'work closely together'.

Test yourself

1.9 The objective of the business is to satisfy the needs of its _____.

Business enterprise, logistics management and service providers

We have discussed how consumers drive the logistics process and should be the focus of the entire enterprise. Each enterprise has a strategy and the various functions of production, marketing and logistics. We have seen that logistics can be conceptualised as the bridge which links the entire process – from the point-of-origin (or purchasing of raw materials) to the point-of-consumption (or consumer). How does the enterprise interact with the logistics management capability and the service providers, suppliers, and consumers? Figure 1.7 puts this into

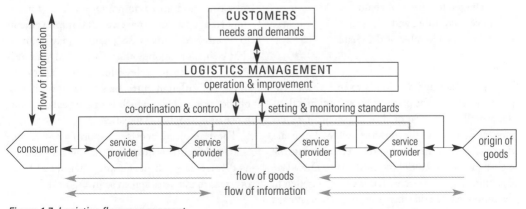

Figure 1.7 Logistics flow management

perspective and explores the process of establishing a logistics management capability.

The flow of goods is from the origin of goods to the consumer. The flow of information in Figure 1.7 is vertically from the service providers to the logistics management to the business enterprise and vice versa. It must be emphasised that there is a two-way information flow at all levels.

Business Enterprise

The business enterprise in Figure 1.7 is any enterprise or group of enterprises that create a logistics chain to provide the right quantity of the right goods to the right place – at the right time, in the right condition, and at the right price. The business enterprise is the source of the strategy which logistics will support. The parameters which guide the logistics capability are derived from the strategy. These parameters include the mix of products and the targeted consumers.

The needs and demands of business enterprises

The strategy needs to be defined in terms of measurable parameters that will ensure that the logistics chain or chains satisfy the needs of the consumers. The measures will define the focus of the logistics chains.

The criteria from the business enterprise must deal with the total chain and should address three primary issues. These are:
* time taken for the total chain;
* allowed deviation; and
* total cash cycle value of the chain.

Time

The time taken for the goods to move from the point-of-origin to the point-of-consumption reflects the overall service standard of the chain. The less time the demands of the consumers allow, the greater the inventory of finished goods required and the higher the overall cost of the total chain. The adage that 'time is money' is one that is often forgotten in the commercial world where the goods are in storage or in transit. The time taken from the goods being ordered to the delivery to the consumer will directly influence the total inventory in the chain. The inventory of goods in the pipeline represents a significant cost to the enterprise. In a country such as South Africa, where the lending rate for money (in the fifteen per cent to twenty per cent range) is significantly above the rates in major economies (three to five per cent), this is an even more significant figure.

Allowed deviation

No logistics system can deliver the products on time every time (i.e. a hundred per cent perfect record). The prohibitive cost of this would render it commercially ineffective. The acceptable deviation is therefore specified. For example, say on two per cent of the occasions the delivery may arrive up to two hours late (allowed deviation), while ninety-eight per cent of the time the truck will arrive within fifteen minutes of the given time (on-time standard).

Cash cycle value

The cash cycle is the period from the initial disbursement of cash to the receipt of the final payment from the consumer. The cost of maintaining the service described above is incurred by having a certain amount of spare capacity in the system. The spare capacity will be stand-by transport, equipment, and inventory ready to supplement the existing requirements. The total cost of achieving the agreed standard needs to be known and understood if value adding improvements are to be made. Measuring the chain by breaking it down into time and cost components allows for the important areas to be reviewed and improvements to be effected. Otherwise, changes may be made that cost more money than the improvement is worth. The cash cycle value also assesses the impact of different currencies on the overall cost of the supply chain, which is of particular importance in international logistics.

For example, the costs of exporting a semi-finished product (this holds in principle for products as diverse as steel, paper, and chemicals) to an overseas market, are spread as in Figure 1.8.

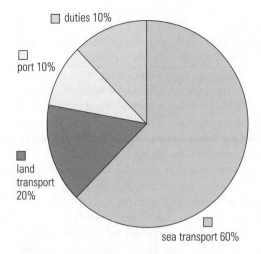

Figure 1.8 Approximate charges for exporting a product

The dominant value is the shipping cost, which overshadows the port charges. The port costs can be increased by, say, one per cent overall (a ten per cent cut in the terminal change), if the resultant shipping charge drops by more than one per cent overall. The cost of a more efficient terminal is often less than the savings that can be made from the reduced loading time for the vessel.

Logistics management role

The logistics capability may exist within the business or may be outsourced to a third party. The logistics management capability in effect translates the strategy into objectives – and into measurable parameters to monitor the performance against these objectives. With an eye on these objectives, logistics supply chains are designed to continually ensure the logistics process is as efficient and effective as is possible. This is achieved via the two roles of co-ordination and control and the setting and monitoring of standards. For the illustration of this process, assume that a sequence of the services necessary in the logistics chain is as follows: receipt of finished goods into the manufacturing warehouse; packaging before dispatch; delivery; and receipt into the distribution warehouse.

Co-ordination and control

Co-ordination and control are applied to the interface between service providers. These service providers form the supply chain. They do, however, need to be co-ordinated and controlled to ensure the overall chain is effective. Each service provider, in the absence of the logistics co-ordination and control, will try to maximise its opportunities for efficiency and effectiveness. The transporter is paid to move goods, and so its vehicles are only really effective while carrying goods. The distribution warehouse is responsible for the goods it receives. The warehouse personnel want to inspect the goods carefully before allowing the truck that brought them to depart. This is a dichotomy of purpose – the vehicle wants to leave as soon as possible to earn revenue while the warehouse needs the vehicle to remain at the warehouse while the goods are checked and unloaded. Part of the logistics process of planning and implementing is to define the interface measurements that are needed to make both parties, and the entire chain, as efficient and effective as possible. In this example, the issue might be resolved by agreeing on a procedure to deal with problems with the goods received, so the vehicles are not delayed. As the trust between the two parties improves, so the need to inspect the goods in the driver's presence decreases, and the inspection can be done after the vehicle has left, thereby making both parties more effective. Trust must be an objective for the logistics management.

In simple terms, the need of the individual service providers to make the most profit possible needs to be subjected to working closely with the other service providers in the chain for the benefit of the overall chain. This is achieved by the logistics management setting the parameters for co-ordination and control.

Setting and monitoring standards

While co-ordination and control affect the management of the interfaces, the service provider must be managed on the service it agreed to provide. The standards required from the service provider are recorded and measured, or monitored. Any chain is as strong as its weakest link and the logistics management must monitor the performance of the service provider continually to ensure the chain operates at optimal performance.

Assume the delivery standard for the transporter suggested previously (ninety-eight per cent of the deliveries within fifteen minutes and the remaining two per cent within two hours of the agreed time) is in place. The transporter's performance on these values should be measured daily and the long-term trends of the service provider's performance can be monitored. The logistics management will then be able to prevent the problems of poor performance and will have a supply chain which consistently operates at the desired standard.

Test yourself

1.10 In linking the service providers into the logistics chain, two aspects must be in place. These are the _____ and the _____ of the interfaces; and the _____ and _____ of standards.

Service provider chain

Each of the service providers is chosen to fulfil an integral function in the chain. Service providers may come from departments within the enterprise or may be external – or a combination of these. The choice of the service providers must be made as a part of the logistics planning capability.

In choosing the service providers, the total time for the chain and its cost must be balanced. Interfaces between service providers cost time and hence money. The fewer the interfaces, the easier it is to align the service providers to the aims of the total chain. It is therefore preferable not to break the service providers into the smallest elements possible, but rather to utilise a discrete capability. The latter is a single capability of, say, a customs clearing function. It would not be sensible to break the customs clearing function into smaller elements of, for example, document preparation and then delivery and payment. This would merely add interfaces

within one capability in the chain, which adds complexity without achieving the presumed reduction in the overall effectiveness of the chain.

Some larger businesses offer 'integrated services'; but these are often functional entities within the business that are co-ordinated by a manager of the supply chain. This merely adds to the complexity and requires an unwanted level of logistics management. The introduction of more levels of suppliers – where one supplier offers a service and utilises other subcontractors, whether internal or external to the enterprise – introduces further levels of communication and increases the potential for problems. As far as possible, these need to be eliminated. For logistic processes to work effectively, the information must flow directly to the logistics manager. The latter must manage the operation and report to the business enterprise regarding the critical success factors agreed upon, so that the chain can be continually improved and strengthened. The following example illustrates the dangers of not defining the service properly.

Dangers of having no critical success factors

An enterprise receives an order. The correct goods are taken from stock and sent to a dispatch section which packs the goods into containers for delivery to consumers. There are three sales entities working for the business, with sales to the American, the European, and the local market respectively. No service standards are applied. The sales entities release orders as they receive them. The goods are taken from storage and sent to the dispatch department as the orders are received. The sequence for this specific day is that the local market is fed first and then work on the European container is started. Due to the work-load, the American container is ready only the next day and the transport of the containers to the ship is delayed until the following day. However, the ship to America sails before the container is delivered. The consequences are severe in this example, as the next ship to America is a week later. The order is delivered late, for which the purchaser charges the business a penalty.

In addition to the above, on some days, no orders are received while on others, all three sales departments require large quantities of garments to be dispatched. The dispatch department cannot cope with the volume of garments on days of major dispatch requirements, and on other days has no work.

What should have been done was that the sales departments should have been provided with critical success factors like the following:

+ Determine if stock is available in the warehouse before committing to an order.
+ Each department will advise the dispatch department four days prior to the required delivery of the container to the ship.
+ The warehouse will make the garments available to dispatch within four hours from request.

The dispatch department then has a clear and defined target for when containers must be delivered to the ship. There is time for the dispatch department to plan the work so that the workload is acceptable to the dispatch department and the warehouse. The end date does not refer to the completion of the loading, but to the delivery of the goods to the ship – in other words, the completion of an element of the process. This completion of a process element is important, as each service provider must take responsibility for completing an element before handing it to the next service provider. This minimises communication problems and places responsibility directly on the service providers so that their performance can be measured and monitored.

Test yourself

1.11 Logistics management is tasked with the design or planning of _____ logistic supply chains to continually ensure the logistics process is as _____ and _____ as is possible.

Strategic issues in logistics

The topic of strategic issues in logistics will be covered extensively in a later chapter. This section deals only with the strategic issues enterprises face in utilising logistics to their maximum advantage.

Logistics is a competitive advantage, if used cleverly, which requires the enterprise to be different from the traditional functional enterprise. First, it should have a different perspective on business: It should focus on a strategy for satisfying customers. To support this strategy, three elements must work in tandem – marketing, logistics, and production or service provision. These three are inextricably linked. For example, a new marketing initiative is doomed to failure if the production or logistics elements cannot support it. These elements need to be supported by financial systems and information systems. The latter are enabling functions, not of themselves the competitive advantage. An enterprise may have the most advanced warehouse management system, but the consumers see the product at the end of the chain and not the elements of the chain. While the warehouse operates more effectively, the chain is only slightly improved until the technology of the entire chain reaches a similar standard. Technology and information are essential to the enterprise. They must, however, be integrated with the ability to market, make, and deliver the finished goods to the right consumer, at the right place and time, and in the right quantity.

To support the consumer-focused strategy, any decision must be agreed upon by all three of the above functions. As new marketing initiatives occur, or as new products, new methods of delivery, or new standards are introduced, the three entities must adapt to these changes together and in unison. Businesses regularly experience the consequences of not working in this integrated manner. For example, a new marketing initiative occurs. However, the initiative requires special warehouse operations to package two items together. The warehouse is not involved in the planning and does not prepare for the added volume of work. The goods are shipped late because of this and the marketing initiative loses impact.

To enforce this understanding, the logistics, marketing, and production or service provision processes are shown in Figure 1.9 as interdependent functions in the level immediately adjacent to the strategy. These functions are focused via a strategy on the consumer, and supported by the financial and information systems.

Figure 1.9 Strategic focus of logistics, marketing, and production

This perspective does not necessarily advocate a new organisational structure. Strategy, and not just the focus of an enterprise, influences the structure. What is required, is that the culture changes so that the three functions of the enterprise are focused on supplying the chosen market faster, more accurately and with better goods or services than any competitor. To achieve this change in culture requires recognition of a process based orginisation (logistics), driven to measure the elements of the total supply chain, to choose the most efficient and effective supply chains, and to strive for continual improvement.[8]

The application of the principles discussed here will enhance the processes essential to the financial and competitive health of the enterprise. This is a change from the traditional functional view of the enterprise and one must take care that the traditional functional way of thinking does not override the process manner of viewing the organisation. If this happens, the competitive advantage for the enterprise is lost and logistics will only deliver occasional improvements as special projects highlight current opportunities. The continuous improvement will fall away and the focus will be internal to support functional disciplines and not the customers.

Value of logistics

The value of logistics is reflected in two ways.

The first is difficult to measure. Logistics drives processes to be efficient and effective across the total chain or total system. The value of logistics is not the same for different businesses as they introduce logistics strategies. It is furthermore difficult to measure the value of logistics over a period, as improvements may come from such diverse changes as a new system or a different outsourcing partner.

The impact of logistics can also be seen in the value of the shares of businesses. In the USA, the effects of problems in the supply chain on the share price were studied over a ten year period.[9] The conclusions were that the share price dropped on average almost nine per cent when a supply chain problem was announced to the market. In the months preceding the formal announcement, the share price also dropped up to nine per cent as soon as consumers and the market realised that a problem existed. The reasons for the supply chain problem were not important. Whether the problem was caused by suppliers, software, or by late delivery of a new facility, the share price was affected significantly and for roughly similar amounts. Even if the enterprise was not directly responsible, consumers became dissatisfied and the market reacted. Very few businesses can afford to have up to a twenty per cent decline in their share value!

Logistics is linked to the value the business creates. It provides the focus and the method to make all the processes efficient and effective in order to satisfy consumers. In so doing it creates long-term financial gain for the business.

Conclusion

Logistics is not solely about trucks, warehouses, ships, information systems, or even the consumers' needs as isolated elements. Logistics is the integration of the elements of the chain to supply the goods required by the customers in the most efficient and effective manner possible, together with accurate and appropriate information. The aim is to have the total chain perform to a given standard at the lowest possible cost commensurate to supporting the standard. The focus is on the total chain and not the individual elements alone.[8]

The means to achieve this objective is through the logistics management process described in this chapter. It requires a process approach to achieve the flow of the correct goods, rather than a functional management approach. The elements of logistics must all be in place, together with the strategy for logistics management, in order to provide the potential benefits of this approach.

Questions

1 Describe the steps – from the consumer to the choice of input providers – for setting up a new supply chain.
2 If the origin of logistics is military, why has logistics been adopted by the commercial world and what has made it so pertinent in today's business world?
3 Why is the point-of-origin of a supply chain the decision to purchase goods and not the delivery of the goods into the first production facility?
4 Create a figure of the logistics chain where:
   ◆ goods are purchased overseas and moved to this country;
   ◆ a manufacturing process takes place;
   ◆ the goods are moved to a warehouse and then sold to a customer.
Describe the method of managing each of the interfaces between the service providers in the logistics chain.
5 What length of supply chain does logistics require to be most effective?
6 How does one choose between two competing supply chains? Assume the two chains involve different modes of transport, for example the movement of goods to Europe either by sea container or by means of air containers.

Notes

1 Colliers, P.F. 1993: 739–743.
2 Morris, D.R. 1966: 500–501.
3 Morris, D.R. 1966: 295.
4 FAS Military Analysis Network: Operation Desert Storm. www.fas.org/man/dod-101/ops/desertstorm.htm
5 Council for Logistics Management. 1993: 3.
6 McCarthy, E.J. and Perreault, W.D. 1984: 4–9.
7 PricewaterhouseCoopers 1999: 12.
8 Bramel, J. and Simchi-Levi, D. 1997: 3.
9 APICS 2001 (b): 10–11.

Contents

Learning Outcomes

After studying this chapter, you should be able to:
- identify the ultimate goal and the immediate objectives of the business logistics process;
- describe how value is created by logistics;
- understand the concepts of consumer service and consumer satisfaction;
- describe the most pertinent logistics performance determinants;
- describe how logistics can help to create wealth within a firm; and
- identify and briefly describe the variety of activities involved in the flow of goods, services, and information between the place of origin and the place of consumption or application.

Introduction

The ultimate goal of employing business logistics management throughout the supply chain of products (i.e. goods and services) is to increase the long-term wealth of all the member firms within this chain. In order to achieve maximum wealth in the long run, the immediate objective of business logistics practice is to be efficient and effective across the entire supply chain and to conform to the requirements of customers and clients.

An important characteristic of logistics is that it is not demanded in its own right. It is a means to ensure that the right goods, services, and information are made available at the designated place and time, in the required condition and quantity, and at an acceptable cost or price. If a firm can consistently provide its customers or clients with the quality of logistics service they require, it can gain a competitive advantage in the market.

This chapter is devoted to exploring how logistics management principles can assist the firm to obtain a competitive advantage in the market.

Logistics linkages with the value chain

The definition of business logistics used in this book is the one utilised by the Council of Logistics Management (CLM). In 1991, the CLM defined logistics as

> the process of planning, implementing, and controlling the efficient, effective flow and storage of goods, services, and related information from the point-of-origin to the point-of-consumption for the purpose of conforming to customer requirements.

The CLM stresses that 'this definition includes inbound, outbound, internal, and external movements, and return materials for environmental purposes'.[1] The CLM's 1991 definition of logistics is the generally accepted description of the concept in contemporary business logistics management literature around the world.

This definition is explicit about the fact that the logistics process should be efficient and effective across the entire system. The objective is to minimise system-wide costs, from line-haul transport and short-distance distribution to inventory of raw material, semi-finished goods and finished goods. Thus, the emphasis is not simply on the cheapest or the fastest transport or on reducing inventories, but rather on an integrated and co-ordinated systems approach to the logistics process.[2] The acceptance of the total-cost logistics concept has changed the relative importance of the different logistics activities. For example, the total-cost approach has led to logistics cost trade-offs between transport services provided and the operating costs of facilities assuming greater importance.

Although the CLM's definition of logistics incorporates the notions of efficiency and effectiveness, it does not address the reconciliation of these elements. Attempting system-wide minimum cost while conforming to consumer requirements is a laudable objective, but it should be dealt with in the context of a common goal. From the viewpoint of the firm, the goal is the maximisation of its long-term wealth.

Cost minimisation ought, therefore, to be confined only to eliminating waste, and should not include pruning costs at the expense of greater revenue. Reducing logistics costs makes sense only if the foregone profits are smaller than the cost reduction. Similarly, the acceptance of additional logistics costs is justified only if net revenue increases as a result. For example, an air freight delivery may be chosen for this reason instead of delivery with a cheaper but slower mode of transport, but only if the former is offset by lower inventory carrying cost or other logistics cost savings that lead to increased net revenue.

The optimal level of logistics expenditure occurs where marginal expenditure (i.e. the expenditure attributed to the last unit of output) equals marginal revenue (i.e. the revenue attributable to the last unit of output). To reflect this, the 1991 CLM definition of logistics management can be adjusted to read as follows for business logistics management:[3]

> Business logistics management is the process of planning, organising and controlling the efficient, effective flow and storage of goods, services and related information from the place of origin to the place of consumption or application for the purpose of optimally meeting customer and client requirements in order to help maximise the long-term wealth of the firm.

Test yourself

2.1 Reducing logistics costs makes sense only if the foregone profits are _____ than the cost reduction.

Value-added role of logistics

Value-added utilities

Four types of utility can add value to a product. They are form, place, time, and possession utility. Form utility is created by manufacturing activities, place and time utility by logistics activities, and possession utility by marketing activities.

Form utility

Form utility results when raw materials are combined in the production and/or manufacturing process to make a finished product for which demand exists.

Place utility

Place utility can be seen as the value of the availability of goods at places where they are wanted to satisfy consumers' needs. Logistics creates place utility by moving goods from places where they occur in a form that cannot be utilised or where they are in surplus (i.e. in over-supply) to places where they are processed into a useful form or where they are relatively scarce in relation to the demand which exists. For example, certain types of raw material may be sparsely distributed and

geographically separate from production facilities. In order to process them, they need to be conveyed to points of concentration in the proximity of these facilities. Manufactured goods are furthermore in over-supply at their place of manufacture. Through physical distribution, they are delivered to places where demand for them matches their supply volume. In short, place utility is the value added to goods by transporting them from a place where they are not needed to a place where they are needed.

Time utility

Logistics creates time utility by storing and then delivering goods at the place of demand at a time desired by the customer.

Possession utility

Possession utility is created through marketing activities related to the promotion of goods. Logistics supports and enhances possession utility, because place and time utility are prerequisites to affording the physical availability of goods to consumers and therefore the disposal of goods where and when required.

Consumer surplus

Consumers' willingness to pay reflects the monetary value placed by them on a product. The difference between what consumers are willing to pay and the price that they actually pay for a product is known as consumer surplus. The maximum amount of money that consumers are willing to pay is subjectively derived from the utility that a product is expected to offer them. The utility per unit is perceived to decline from consuming additional units of a product in a given period. Given this, the consumer surplus arises because consumers are willing to pay for these additional units up to the point where the value derived from the utility of the last unit is equal to the unit price of the product. Business clients of the firm who are downstream within the logistics chain could reveal a declining willingness to pay for additional units of a product in a given period. For example, capacity constraints within warehouses and other facilities may limit the volumes of inventory a business entity can handle. Surplus inventory bears an opportunity cost and huge production volumes may simply not be compatible with efficient logistics practice.

Perceptions of value

Consumer value must be defined from the customer's perspective, based on the relative importance to the customer of the various elements of perceived price, perceived total cost of acquisition and use, and perceived benefits of owning or using the goods or service.[4]

Zeithaml identified four different perceptions of value among consumers:[4]

- *Low price*
  For those who equated value with low price, the most significant dimension of value seemed to be the small amount of money they had to pay.
- *Whatever demanders want in a product*
  For the demanders (potential customers) who equated value with whatever they wanted in a product, benefits seemed to be the critical element in their perception of value. This might equate to a utility approach to value.
- *The quality demanders get for the price they pay*
  For demanders who viewed value as the quality received in exchange for the price paid, value was perceived as the trade-off between a single benefit (quality) and a single sacrifice (price).
- *What demanders get for what they give*
  Those who viewed value as what you get for what you give seemed to consider all the relevant benefits as well as all the relevant sacrifices or costs.

If a firm can consistently provide its customers and clients with the desired quality and quantity of products (i.e. goods and services), where and when needed, at an acceptable cost, it can gain market share advantage over its competitors. Competitive advantage consists of cost leadership and effective product differentiation. It occurs when a firm implements a value-creating strategy and other firms are unable to duplicate the benefits thereof or find it too costly to imitate. The firm might be able to sell its products at a lower cost as a result of logistics efficiencies, or provide a higher level of customer and client service as a result of logistics effectiveness, or both – thereby gaining a competitive edge in the market.

The efficiency with which resources are used and organised to achieve their stated objectives will have a direct effect on the competitiveness of the firm. In competitive conditions, the lower the cost of output per unit – without sacrificing the quality of service in relation to the value or price of the delivered product – the greater the efficiency of the logistics process. Technically, efficiency refers to the combination of the following:

- the best and most modern production, marketing, and logistics techniques;
- prudent management;
- a highly skilled workforce; and
- organisation of the firm to allow its logistics function to operate at a scale or size where economy is achieved.

Economy means that resources are used optimally, so that the maximum benefit is gained from any given input. In logistics, economies of scale may result from increasing vehicle sizes and successfully utilising their carrying and distance capacity, increasing fleet sizes and successfully utilising fleet capacity, and intensifying the use of infrastructure and facilities (e.g. warehouses, distribution centres, and terminals) whenever these are owned. Achieving economies of scale in transport is dependent on the attainment of any or all of the following three subgroups of economies: economies of density, economies of scope, and long-haul economies. These efficiency concepts are discussed in Chapter 12.

Test yourself

2.2 Four types of utility can add value to a product. These are _____, _____, _____, and _____ utility.

2.3 Consumers' willingness to pay reflects the _____ placed by them on a product.

2.4 Competitive advantage consists of _____ leadership and effective product _____

Consumer service

Consumer service acts as the unifying force for all of the logistics activities. Consumer satisfaction occurs when the firm's manufacturing or service provision, marketing, and logistics efforts are successful, thus adding sufficient value to prevent the demander from procuring the product in an alternative way. Consumer satisfaction is the demander's positive reaction to the goods or service, based on an excess of the perceived value of the goods or service over some standard that represents the demander's expectations of the goods or service.

Each element of a firm's logistics system can affect whether a consumer receives the right goods, services, and information at the right place and time, in the right condition and quantity, and at the right price. Optimal consumer service requires well-managed logistics in order to provide the necessary level of customer and client satisfaction (i.e. effectiveness) at the lowest possible total cost (i.e. efficiency). This level of consumer retention is also known as consumer responsiveness. Consumer responsiveness is the positive reactions by demanders as a result of satisfaction with the value of goods and services. These reactions can contribute to a greater market share or improved profitability for the firm. Examples of consumer responsiveness are repeat purchases, consumer loyalty, and positive word of mouth communications about the product.

The most pertinent determinants of logistics service performance are suitability, accessibility, goods security, transaction time, reliability, and flexibility.

Suitability

This refers to the ability to provide the equipment and facilities that the carriage, handling, and storage of a particular commodity or item requires. Examples of suitability are storage facilities that can provide controlled temperatures or humidity, special handling equipment, and vehicles which can carry abnormal loads.

Accessibility

This is the ability to provide service between particular facilities and to physically gain access to such facilities.

Suitability and accessibility determine whether the provider can physically perform the desired logistics services.

Goods security

This involves goods being delivered in the same physical condition and quantity as when tendered for storage and conveyance. Insecure logistics service results in opportunity costs of forgone profits or productivity because the goods are not available for sale or use, or have to be sold at a lower price than intended.

Transaction time

This is also known as order delivery time. It is the total time which elapses from when an order is received to when the goods are delivered to the customer. This includes the time for order processing, pick-up and delivery, and handling and movement between origin and destination.

Reliability

This refers to the consistency of the transaction time provided. It is the proven record or reputation of a provider to consistently maintain punctual delivery lead times in terms of pre-arranged order processing, pick-up, and delivery times.

Flexibility

This is the proven ability, readiness, and willingness to effectively handle variations in order and inventory quantities, freight consignment volumes and mass, delivery times, and delivery locations, without any significant loss of overall efficiency.

Shorter transaction times, higher reliability, and greater flexibility lead to lower inventory levels and lower stockout costs, the latter being a source of competitive advantage.

Generally, the most important value-adding service criterion is reliability. The impact of reliable and consistent transaction time on inventory levels, stockout costs, and consumer service is more important than the length of the total transaction time.

Consistency of service is a more comprehensive concept which is concerned with the punctuality and time variability in service offered. Perhaps the biggest reason for consumers considering consistency of service more important than transaction time is that service consistency is vital to logistical planning. For example, a customer would prefer a consignment to arrive at a specific time every time that product is ordered, rather than have it delivered early one time, late the next, and on time the next. Therefore, if an enterprise provides a short transaction time, but is inconsistent in delivering that level of service, a consumer is likely to choose a service provider with longer transaction time, but with more consistency. The many benefits resulting from providing a consistently punctual service include improved goodwill, marketing (and sales) advantages, the ability to plan more precisely, fewer product stockouts, and inventory cost savings.

Studies dealing with the role of logistics management in creating competitive advantage and wealth within supply chains have indicated the following:[5]

- The objective of logistically managing a product's supply chain is to enhance the competitive advantage of the entire chain, rather than to improve the competitive advantage of any single member in the chain.
- The means to achieve competitive advantage is through creating value for downstream member clients in excess of that offered by competitors.
- Consumer value is created through co-operation and co-ordination to improve cost efficiency and/or service effectiveness in ways that are most valuable to key consumers.
- Willingness to pay as related to value is not inherent in products only, but is rather determined by the perceptions of customers and clients.
- To compete through adding consumer value, a firm must clearly understand its consumers' value perception and the product attributes demanded by them.
- Value perceptions differ among consumer segments. A firm must therefore identify the consumer segments that are important for its long-term success and adjust its capability correspondingly to deliver the value important to them.
- The competitiveness of several chain members can improve even if only one chain member becomes more cost-efficient and/or more service-effective.
- Delivering consumer value in dimensions that are important to consumers better than the competition leads to consumer satisfaction and competitive advantage.
- By satisfying consumers' needs and achieving competitive advantage, firms in a supply chain influence consumers to make choices and respond in ways which improve the financial performance of all the members in the supply chain.

Test yourself

2.5 Consumer responsiveness is the _____ reactions by demanders as a result of satisfaction with the _____ by goods and services.

2.6 The most pertinent logistics service performance determinants are suitability, _____, _____, _____, _____, and flexibility.

Wealth creation through logistics

Drivers of wealth creation

Business logistics strategy, tactics, and operations can enhance the long-term wealth of the firm in four areas. These are revenue growth, operating cost reductions, working capital efficiency, and fixed capital efficiency.[6]

Revenue growth

Logistics of consumer service can significantly influence sales volume and customer retention. Although it is not generally possible to determine the exact correlation between service level and sales volume, several studies have indicated a positive relationship between the two variables. Superior consumer service (in terms of reliability and responsiveness) increases the probability that consumers will remain loyal to a supplier. Experience indicates that higher levels of consumer retention lead to increased sales: Customers are likely to place increasing proportions of their orders with a vendor who consistently supplies superior service.

Operating cost reductions

There exists significant potential for operating cost savings through logistics. A large proportion of costs in many firms is driven by logistics operations. Savings in transport costs, warehousing costs, lot quantity costs (i.e. the costs associated with purchasing and manufacturing in different lot sizes), information systems costs, and the opportunity cost of carrying inventory, all potentially represent increased net operating profit. Logistics innovations that can reduce costs, such as time compression in the supply chain, must be recognised by top management. Enterprises must be made aware of how these savings enhance their competitive advantage.

Working capital efficiency

Logistics can have a significant influence on working capital requirements. By their nature, long supply chains accumulate substantial volumes of inventory. The time span of transactions and the accuracy of order processing and invoices can directly affect the ability to collect timely payments. Faster collection of payments and lower inventories make funds available for other investment opportunities. Working capital requirements can be lowered through time compression in the logistics chain and the associated improvement in

cash-to-cash cycle times (i.e. the time from the payment for purchased materials until the sale of the finished product and collection of its transaction payment). The cash-to-cash cycle time can exceed six months in many manufacturing industries. By concentrating on decreasing the amount of time in the logistics chain when no value is added, reductions in working capital can be achieved.

Fixed capital efficiency

Logistics is capital intensive and in many firms the opportunities for asset reductions are substantial. Investments in vehicles, handling equipment and facilities (such as workshops, terminals and warehouses) can be significant. Whenever the reduction of a firm's investment in fixed assets is considered, the feasibility of and the expected value created by pursuing an alternative strategy should be assessed.

Example of a wealth-creating strategy

An owner-driver scheme is an example of a wealth-creating strategy within business enterprises. When implemented successfully, an owner-driver scheme has the potential to add value within a firm through all of the above-mentioned drivers of wealth creation.

The scheme involves the outsourcing of a firm's transport activities to vehicle owner-drivers who are not employees of the firm. In many cases, these individuals are ex-employees who are now acting as independent hauliers (third-party carriers).

The primary goal of an owner-driver scheme is to enhance a firm's long-term profitability through improved productivity. Greater productivity can be achieved through cost savings and increased returns. Cost savings are achieved by conducting the transport function more efficiently. Increases in returns may result from the fact that the firm gets the opportunity to concentrate on its primary or core business functions and the fact that owner-drivers are being rewarded for greater output and for more effectively conforming to customer service requirements. Secondary objectives of an owner-driver scheme can be to reduce labour problems and to empower the workforce.[7]

Financial aspects of logistics are discussed in Chapter 17.

Test yourself

2.7 Business logistics strategy, tactics, and operations can enhance the _____ wealth of the firm in four areas. These are _____ growth, _____ reductions, _____ efficiency and _____ efficiency.

Logistics activities

The flow of products and information between the point of origin and the point of consumption or application involves the following activities: demand forecasting, facility site selection and design, procurement, materials handling, packaging, warehouse management, inventory management, order processing, logistics communications, transport, waste disposal, return goods handling, and parts and service support.

Demand forecasting

Demand forecasting refers to the process of determining the amount of product and related information which consumers will require in the future, be it in the short or long run. This information is important for marketing, manufacturing, and logistics.

Marketing forecasts of future demand determine promotional strategies, allocation of sales force effort, pricing strategies, market research activities, and manufacturing scheduling and sizing.

Manufacturing schedules determine acquisition strategies, plant inventory decisions, and right-sizing production capacity in line with marketing forecasts.

Logistics management forecasts determine how much of each item manufactured by the firm

must be transported to the various markets it serves. Logistics management must also determine where the demand will occur so that appropriate volumes of goods can be made available in each market area. Knowledge of future demand levels enables logistics managers to plan for the activities needed to service that demand.

Aspects of forecasting and planning are covered in Chapters 3 and 4.

Facility site selection and design

The type, layout, location, number, and capacity of facilities are of strategic importance.

The first consideration in selecting a site is the location of the firm's various resources and markets. The placement of sales facilities near the firm's markets can improve customer service. Proper facility location can also allow lower total transport costs from the location of raw materials or primary producers through the logistics chain to the consumer. The needs of consumers and the location of raw materials and other resources are important when considering the inbound movement, storage of materials, and outbound flows of a firm. Other important factors of site selection include:

- labour costs;
- transport costs;
- land and construction costs;
- property rates and taxes;
- availability and cost of utilities, services, and infrastructure;
- security;
- legal concerns; and
- local factors, such as the attitude of the community towards new industry.

Facility site and design considerations are addressed in Chapters 3, 9, and 11.

Procurement

Procurement is the acquisition of goods, services, and information to ensure that the firm's manufacturing and marketing processes operate effectively. The procurement function includes:

- the selection of resources and suppliers;
- determination of the form in which the inputs are to be acquired;
- timing and co-ordination of the arrival of incoming goods;
- price negotiation; and
- quality control of incoming goods.

Procurement management is discussed in Chapter 5.

Materials handling

Materials handling is concerned with the (off-road) movement or flow of raw materials, semi-finished goods, and finished goods at premises and within a facility. Successful materials handling contributes towards smooth manufacturing operations; reduced inventory; lowered processing, storage, and transhipment costs; and increased productivity within facilities.

Materials handling as a function within warehouse management is dealt with in Chapters 7, 9, and 10.

Packaging

Packaging performs two functions – marketing and logistics. As a marketing function, the package acts as a form of promotion and advertising. Its size, mass, colour, appearance, and printed information can attract attention and convey knowledge about the product. From a logistics perspective, packaging serves a dual role. Firstly, the package protects the product from damage and sometimes prevents potentially hazardous products from damaging other goods. Secondly, packaging can make it easier to store and move products, thereby lowering materials handling and distribution costs.

Packaging is the subject of Chapter 8.

Warehouse management

Warehousing entails the activities related to managing the space needed to hold or maintain inventories. Goods must be stored for later sale and consumption unless customers need them immediately after production. Generally, the greater the time lag between production and consumption, the larger the quantity of inventory required. Specific warehouse management decisions include:

- warehouse location, capacity, and design;
- whether the storage facility should be owned or rented;
- the level of mechanisation or automation;
- goods mix considerations;
- security and maintenance;
- personnel training;
- productivity measurement;
- operational standards; and
- range of services offered.

Warehouse management is discussed in Chapter 10.

Inventory management

Inventory management is a critical issue. The requirements for both manufacturing and marketing have to be met continuously. However, large volumes of inventory occupy capital-intensive warehouse space, while possession of the inventory itself requires financial sacrifice. The cost of warehouse space and the value of the inventory both have an opportunity cost. An optimal trade-off must be reached between this opportunity cost and the harmful effects which will emanate from a stockout situation. This illustrates again that accurate demand forecasting is important when striving to satisfy customer needs without sacrificing efficiency.

Inventory management is the topic of Chapter 6.

Order processing

Order processing refers to those activities associated with filling consumers' orders. These include:

- transmission of the order details to the sales section;
- verification of consumers' creditworthiness;
- transmission of the required packaging details to inventory control staff for delivery to the dispatch section;
- preparation of the consignment documentation; and
- communication of the order status, method of payment, and delivery details to customers.

The time span and accuracy of a firm's order processing are important determinants of the level of its customer service. Advanced automatic systems, such as electronic data interchange and electronic funds transfer, can reduce the time between order placement and delivery. Such systems, although initially expensive, can substantially improve both order processing accuracy and response time. Savings in other logistics expenses (for example, inventory control, transport, and warehousing) or increased sales from improved customer service often justifies the investment cost of the system.

Value creation through effective order processing is addressed in Chapters 6 and 15.

Logistics communications

Successful logistics requires the effective management of information and communications systems. Effective communication must take place between:

- the firm and its customers and clients;
- the firm and its suppliers;
- the major functional components of the firm – for example, marketing, manufacturing, and logistics;
- the various logistics activities, such as procurement, warehousing, order processing, inventory control, and transport; and
- the various components of each logistics activity.

Accurate and timely communication is the cornerstone of successfully integrated and co-ordinated logistics management.

The flow and importance of information are discussed in Chapters 13, 15, and 16.

Transport

The movement of goods is a key activity and usually the largest cost component of logistics. It includes decisions such as:

- operating one's own transport versus hiring transport;
- mode, carrier, and service selection;
- method of freight consolidation;
- vehicle routing and crew and trip scheduling; and
- equipment selection, replacement, and acquisition (i.e. purchase, lease, or rent).

Within the logistics chain, the transport system is indispensable in determining whether customers receive goods as and when required. The elements of the transport system and its stakeholders are discussed in Chapter 11. The most pertinent decision-making and management actions which ensure that the logistics requirements are met, are discussed in Chapter 12. Aspects of international transport are dealt with in Chapter 13.

Waste disposal

Waste is a side-effect of manufacturing and consumption. Whenever waste can be reused or recycled, the handling, storage, and carriage to plants is the responsibility of logistics management. If it cannot be recycled, it must be properly disposed of. In the case of hazardous material, one needs to conform to special disposal standards and environmental regulations. Waste disposal will assume increasing importance as recycling and environmental considerations gain greater significance.

Waste disposal is discussed in Chapter 14.

Return goods handling

Handling returned goods is an integral part of the logistics process. Customers may return goods to the seller due to defects, excesses, or because they received the wrong items. Logistics systems are often not established for or incapable of handling goods movement on return or contra-flow trips. Whenever customers return items for warranty repair, replacement, or recycling, costs may be high. Returned goods can often not be transported, stored, and/or handled as easily as new goods. Return goods handling promises to become even more important as consumers demand more flexible and lenient goods return policies, especially whenever effective product competition exists.

Return goods handling is addressed in Chapter 14.

Parts and service support

A part of the marketing activity is often to provide consumers with after-sale service. This includes providing replacement parts when products malfunction. The logistics function is responsible for ensuring that parts are available where and when the customer needs them. Product failure can be costly to the customer if it results in a production interruption. In order to ensure customer satisfaction, the firm supplying the replacement part must be able to respond promptly.

After-sales service usually requires that faulty items be returned to the supplier. Whenever this occurs, it forms part of reverse logistics, which is discussed in Chapter 14.

Test yourself

2.8 The need to know how much product will be demanded is important for _____, _____, and logistics.

2.9 Packaging performs two functions: _____ and logistics.

2.10 Order processing relates to those activities associated with _____ consumers' _____.

Conclusion

An important characteristic of logistics is that it is not demanded in its own right. It is a means to an end, a way of ensuring that the goods, services, and information are made available as and when needed. If a firm can consistently provide its customers and clients with the quality of logistics service they require, it can gain a competitive advantage in the market.

Consumers' willingness to pay reflects the monetary value placed by them on a product. The maximum amount of money that consumers are willing to pay is subjectively derived from the utility that a product is expected to offer them. The most pertinent logistics service performance determinants are suitability, accessibility, goods security, transaction time, reliability, and flexibility.

Business logistics strategy, tactics, and operations can enhance the long-term wealth of the firm in four areas. These areas are revenue growth, operating cost reductions, working capital efficiency, and fixed capital efficiency.

The following variety of activities guides the flow of products and information between the place of origin and the place of consumption or application:

- demand forecasting;
- facility site selection and design;
- procurement;
- materials handling;
- packaging;
- warehouse management;
- inventory management;
- order processing;
- logistics communications;
- transport;
- waste disposal;
- return goods handling; and
- parts and service support.

Questions

1 Describe why successful business logistics management is a value-creating process.
2 Discuss the various types of utility that can add

value to a product. Refer to the contribution of logistics in this process.

3 Describe how perceived utility is related to a consumer's willingness to pay for effective logistics services.

4 Discuss the concepts of consumer service and consumer satisfaction.

5 Why should customers and clients be made aware of the value of a logistics service provided to them?

6 Discuss the most pertinent determinants of logistics performance.

7 Describe how logistics can help to increase a firm's wealth.

8 Identify the range of activities which can form part of a business logistics process and briefly describe the function(s) of each activity.

Notes

1 Council of Logistics Management 1998: 4.
2 Bramel, J. and Simchi-Levi, D. 1997: 3.
3 Pienaar, W.J. 2001: 3.
4 Zeithaml, V.A. 1998: 2–22.
5 Nix, N.W. 2001: 62.
6 Christopher, M.G. and Ryals, L. 1999: 3–4.
7 Spamer, J.S. and Pienaar, W.J. 1998: 171.

Contents

Learning Outcomes

After you have studied this chapter, you should be able to:
- understand the role of strategic planning in logistics;
- prepare a logistics strategic plan;
- understand the importance of channel strategy and network design in logistics;
- use the systems analysis process for the development of a new logistics channel selection strategy to:
  - identify the socio-economic environment and the effect it has on the logistics strategy;
  - define the objectives and state the problems;
  - identify appropriate alternative solutions;
  - analyse the different alternatives and evaluate these against total logistics costs; and
- recognise the importance of performance management.

Introduction

Due to the competitiveness of the business environment, businesses are forced to focus on those matters that will allow them to maintain or gain a competitive advantage. The four Ps of marketing are price, promotion, product, and place. These direct the focus of the organisation towards adding value for the consumer. Because of global competition, the effectiveness of price as a long-term competitive advantage is restricted. Promotion is utilised effectively by many businesses and is therefore not generally a major source of competitive advantage. In our fast developing, globally competitive world, dynamic product innovations which provide sustainable competitive advantage are rare.

The fourth P – place – remains as a likely source of competitive advantage. It includes the ability to make the product available at the right time and the right place, as required by the consumer. In order to maximise this advantage, it is necessary to plan the strategic direction of the business. This enables the business to anticipate change rather than react to it. Planning the strategic direction also assists in the identification of risk when choosing alternative strategies. The development of viable logistics strategies is focused on the consumer service needs and the costs of providing for these needs, within the framework of the business's corporate goals.[1]

The logistics strategy is set at a conceptual level in this chapter. The subsequent two strategic aspects of network design and channel selection are also explored.

Logistics strategy planning

The logistics strategy forms part of an integrated business plan. The overall business plan has a goal or mission which clearly expresses the focus of the business. Three primary criteria must be addressed in the mission:

◆ the goods that will be manufactured, or the services that will be offered;
◆ the technology and the processes that will be used to create these goods and/or services; and
◆ the geographic area where the goods or services will be marketed.

The strategic plan can specify objectives based on these criteria for each of the areas of the business. The objectives for logistics must be developed to support this strategy. For example, the overall strategy may translate into an objective to deliver a new range of goods, which are critical products for the consumer, within five hours. The logistics strategy then determines how a new channel for these goods will be created. In addition, the network and channel design necessary in order to give effect to these are addressed.

The logistics strategic business plan focuses on what the logistics capability must be able to deliver in order to add value to the business in the long, medium, and short term. The primary objectives of the business are defined in terms of strategy, tactics, and operation for the logistics capability. There are four levels in the strategic hierarchy as shown in Figure 3.1 below. These form part of three plans within the logistics strategy:

◆ the logistics strategic plan;
◆ the logistics tactical plan; and
◆ the logistics operational plan.

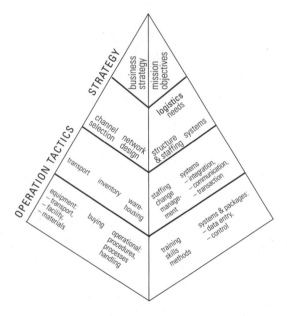

Figure 3.1 Strategic hierarchy

The business strategy and the logistics strategic plan focus on long-term objectives and look at both the strategy and the structures necessary to carry these out. The structures include the channels for distribution of finished products, the network design, and the channels for sourcing materials required to manufacture the finished products.

The tactical plan focuses on issues of a medium term nature and, within the framework of the strategic plan, puts in place the objectives which will guide the operations. This plan includes aspects such as the transport, warehousing, inventory, and systems necessary to manage the business effectively.

The operational plan addresses immediate or short-term issues that ensure that consumers are satisfied on a day-to-day basis. These issues often include management of the processes in the operation, transport decisions such as vehicle allocation, decisions necessary to overcome any problems encountered in the operation, and the implementation of change management.

The logistics strategy should be in a written format and it should be communicated to all the stakeholders who will be affected by it. The content of the written information may differ from what was discussed because of the need to keep parts of the strategy as a competitive advantage, and therefore confidential. It is essential, however, that the people who will make the strategy a reality both understand and are in agreement with it. If there is a division between any part of the strategy and parts of the business (or even external stakeholders), change management processes need to be utilised to align all the parties with the strategy.

The following aspects need to be addressed when formulating a strategy:[2]

- a management overview, describing the logistics strategy in general terms and its relationship to other important business functions;
- the financial and physical value of the logistics strategy to the business, and how this will be measured;
- a description of how the logistics objectives are related to the service levels to be offered to consumers;
- a statement of the logistics objectives to make

the service offered the most efficient and effective possible;
- a description of the individual consumer service, inventory, warehousing, order processing, and transport capabilities necessary to support the overall plan;
- a detailed outline of the most important logistics programmes or operational plans, documenting plans, related costs, timing, and their business impact;
- a forecast of the workforce and capital requirements; and
- a logistics financial statement detailing operating costs, revenues, capital requirements, and cash flow.

At the tactical level, the strategic plan should cover at least the following:[3]

- Inventory strategy: service level policy, replenishment strategy, differential deployment (ABC concept), stock-turn targets, and stock location.
- Warehousing strategy: number of stockholding points, location of depots, use of public warehouses, warehouse design and layout, and materials handling methods.
- Transport strategy: own account/third-party split, lease/buy decisions, customer pickup/direct delivery/other options, vehicle utilisation targets, routing flexibility, and modal split.
- Consumer communications strategy: order cycle time policy, differential consumer response strategies, order processing systems, damages/claims/returns strategy, and order status reporting.

When writing the logistics strategic plan, the focus should be on the conceptual level (strategic and structural) as indicated in Figure 3.1. It should, however, include sufficient detail to be able to specify appropriate strategies on the tactical level. Operational detail should not be included except for where it has a direct impact on long-term issues.

Figure 3.2 proposes another way of looking at this process, with the logistics strategy shown together with the supply chain and marketing considerations.

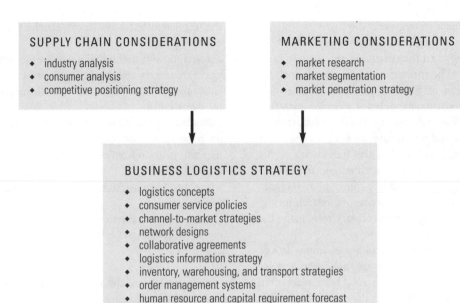

SUPPLY CHAIN CONSIDERATIONS

- industry analysis
- consumer analysis
- competitive positioning strategy

MARKETING CONSIDERATIONS

- market research
- market segmentation
- market penetration strategy

BUSINESS LOGISTICS STRATEGY

- logistics concepts
- consumer service policies
- channel-to-market strategies
- network designs
- collaborative agreements
- logistics information strategy
- inventory, warehousing, and transport strategies
- order management systems
- human resource and capital requirement forecast

Figure 3.2 Logistics strategy

Finally, it is important to consider the realities of new organisational paradigms when developing the logistics strategic plan. These realities include the following transformations:[4]

- from functions to processes;
- from products to customers' needs;
- from inventory to information; and
- from transactions to relationships.

These paradigm shifts directly impact on the design of the new network, and in particular on the development of the logistics channel strategy.

> **Test yourself**
>
> 3.1 What should be addressed in a logistics strategic plan?

Distribution channels

Distribution channels refer to the outbound parts of the supply chain, with specific emphasis on who is responsible for the many activities involved in the distribution function.

> A distribution channel is the route along which a product and its title (i.e. the rights of ownership) flow from production to consumption.[5]

The activities performed by a distribution channel fall into three categories:[5]

- activities concerned with changes in ownership, such as negotiation, buying, and selling – called the trading channel (sometimes referred to as the commercial channel);
- activities concerned with the physical supply of the product, including transport and storage – called the physical distribution network; and
- activities that are ancillary to or facilitate either of the above, such as collecting and disseminating information, financing, and promotional activities.

Figure 3.3 shows the trading or commercial aspect which runs parallel to the physical movement of goods.

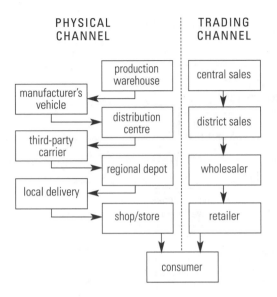

PHYSICAL CHANNEL	TRADING CHANNEL

Figure 3.3 Physical and trading channels

The objective of developing a channel strategy is to determine who should be responsible for the activities in the channel. This decision is similar to the make-or-buy decision in the financial area. The question in the distribution channel is whether the service should be provided by the business itself or by a third party. As the services offered in a distribution channel vary significantly, it is important to consider the following control aspects:

- exclusivity of the service offered;
- the range of managerial activities offered/ required;
- continuity of relationship, commitment, and reliability;
- performance measurement;
- cost control through pricing agreement;
- commercial and financial security;
- consumer relations; and
- industrial relations.

The physical aspects affecting the decision include:

- throughput potential and variability;
- operational flexibility;
- service level;
- geographical coverage; and
- product or market specialisation.

Outsourcing is contracting with a vendor of a service (or service provider) to perform a function in the logistics chain.[6]

The benefits of outsourcing can include:[7]

- spreading the risk;
- exploiting logistics to gain competitive advantage;
- the ability to focus on core activities ('stick to the knitting');
- off-balance sheet financing; and
- gaining access to sophisticated technology (specialisation).

The disadvantages of outsourcing can include:[7]

- loss of control;
- inflexible systems;
- poor representation of the business by the third party;
- inter-organisational conflict;
- adverse employee relations; and
- change in management.

A number of different types of distribution channels can be identified:[8]

- from manufacturer directly to retail outlet (full truckloads, for example, beverages);
- from manufacturer via manufacturer's warehouse to retail outlet (e.g. the brewery industry);
- from manufacturer via retailer's warehouse to retail outlet or store (e.g. large, multiple retail businesses);
- from manufacturer to wholesaler to retail outlet (wholesale trade);
- from manufacturer to cash and carry wholesaler to retail outlet (independent shops collecting from regional warehouses);
- from manufacturer via distribution service to retail outlet (third-party distribution);
- from manufacturer via small parcels carrier to retail outlet (third-party courier distribution);
- from manufacturer via broker to retail outlet (trading channel with broker acting as intermediary);
- mail order (catalogue shopping directly from home); and
- from factory directly to home (direct selling, for example, construction materials).

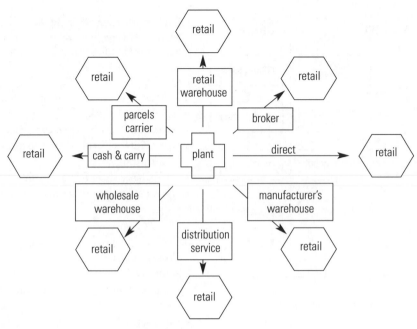

Figure 3.4 Examples of channels of distribution

Third-party logistics (3PL) provides the business with effective physical and information capabilities supplied by external service providers. These may include warehousing, transport, and similar functions. Fourth party logistics (4PL) is a new concept which has emerged in the last few years. It is the provision of an enabling system which assists with reducing intermediation and allows many parties to offer services to the business. This capability offers co-ordination and control as well as the potential for reduced costs due to the increased competition.

The following characteristics distinguish 4PL from 3PL:[9]

- The 4PL organisation is often a separate entity established as a joint venture (JV) or engaging in a long-term contract between a primary client and one or more partners.
- It acts as a single interface between the client and multiple logistics service providers.
- All aspects of the client's supply chain are managed by the 4PL organisation.
- It is also possible for a third-party logistics provider to form a 4PL organisation within the existing structure of the supply chain.

Test yourself

3.2 What is a channel of distribution?
3.3 What are the potential advantages of outsourcing?
3.4 What are the potential disadvantages of outsourcing?

Logistics networks

The physical channel in a logistics network assumes the existence of distribution centres, warehouses, and/or depots – collectively referred to as storage facilities. These facilities are important components of any logistics system. Most channel strategies rely on some form of consolidation, intermediate unloading, and/or storing between producer and retailer or consumer.[10] Storage facilities perform the following functions:

- accommodate buffer stock of long production runs;
- accommodate seasonal stock;
- allow for consolidation of loads;
- prepare for promotions;
- keep safety stock; and

◆ facilitate high service levels by being closer to customers.

The decisions related to network strategy, which include warehouse location, could be split into the following categories, which are similar to the planning hierarchy in Figure 3.1:

◆ strategic decisions which are long-term, per-haps reviewed every three to five years – e.g. number, size, and location of storage facilities;
◆ tactical decisions which are medium-term, per-haps reviewed annually – e.g. transport con-tracts, customer service levels, and inventory policies; and
◆ operational decisions, which are reviewed often – e.g. daily load planning, routing and schedul-ing, and staff deployment.

These decisions can be very complicated. Detailed analyses are required to establish the cost trade-offs, as are quantitative techniques to determine the best location for storage facilities. One such technique, and probably the most powerful tool for designing a new network using quantitative data, is the centre-of-gravity analysis. It enables enterprises to do an objective assessment of the actual centres for demand and supply.

The analysis is based on the differential trans-port costs from production facilities to distribu-tion centres (primary), and from distribution centres to destinations such as retail outlets (secondary). The result of the analysis provides a theoretical indication of the most cost-efficient location for a storage facility. The centre of gravity is calculated using the vectors of flow and the distance from a given point for every flow. The point where the sum of all the vectors is the lowest is the theoret-ical optimal centre of gravity. It is also called the Grid Technique[11] in some publications.

The quantitative analysis allows networks to be analysed for individual channels of movement. The most favoured networks can then be compared. However, networks cannot be chosen solely on the quantitative issues. A centre-of-gravity analysis pro-vides the locations that are theoretically the most suitable. Qualitative factors are used to further refine the decision-making process and these may alter the

choice of the final network. Typical qualitative issues influencing the location include the following:[12,13]

◆ availability of skilled labour;
◆ affordability of labour rates;
◆ productivity of local labour;
◆ local management–trade union relations;
◆ access to main markets;
◆ access to manufacturers;
◆ access to production/manufacturing plants;
◆ utilisation of existing infrastructure;
◆ availability of ready built factories or other facilities;
◆ rental, rates, and taxes;
◆ availability of fully serviced sites;
◆ public transport for staff;
◆ local technical education or support facilities;
◆ attractiveness of local environment for trans-ferred key workers and management; and
◆ local authority co-operation.

Test yourself

3.5 Explain the concept of centre-of-gravity analysis.
3.6 Give examples of decisions taken on strategic, tactical, and operational levels.
3.7 List five qualitative location factors.

Channel selection: systems analysis process

Once networks have been identified, the strategy for selecting individual channels needs to be addressed.

Methodology

Developing the strategies for individual logistics channels is not simple. It is a complex challenge and many aspects – e.g. current and future demand, service level requirements, and existing and future capacities – need to be considered. The following method, which is recommended for developing channel strategies, can be used in the analysis process:[14]

- Establish channel objectives.
- Formulate a channel strategy.
- Determine channel structure alternatives.
- Evaluate channel structure alternatives.
- Select a channel structure.
- Determine alternatives for individual channel members.
- Evaluate and select individual channel members or service providers.
- Measure and evaluate channel performance.
- Evaluate channel alternatives when performance objectives are not met.

With a business strategy in place and a broad logistics strategy – based on the business objectives – defined, the process of defining a channel strategy may be summarised into the following steps.

1 Determine the market environment.
2 Define the objectives to satisfy the needs.
3 Generate technically feasible alternative strategies.
4 Analyse (quantitative) alternative strategies.
5 Evaluate (qualitative) alternative strategies.
6 Select and implement a new channel strategy.
7 Manage performance.

Each of the above steps is discussed in the following sections.

Determine the socio-economic environment

The market environment provides the background against which the logistics channel strategy is planned, and is often referred to as the 'situation analysis'. In this phase, external factors such as the consumer profile have to be defined and agreed upon and all potential target markets identified and evaluated. Internal factors such as the resources of the business have to be objectively

assessed in line with the corporate objectives and business strategy.

The assessment of growth potential is of significant importance to ensure that the logistics channel strategy allows for current as well as anticipated product profiles, demand, and sourcing constraints. The following important market parameters affect the decisions when developing logistics strategies:[15]

- market characteristics;
- product characteristics;
- channel characteristics;
- competitive characteristics; and
- business resources.

Data on the above parameters has to be collected and transformed into meaningful information. The collection process is undoubtedly the most time-consuming part of the analysis process, due to challenges such as the need for manual record keeping, or incompatible electronic data formats.

Detailed flow diagrams, which indicate all inbound and outbound product flows for both the current and the anticipated growth scenarios, have to be prepared. These can be done manually, but should preferably be based on a geographical information system (GIS). A GIS will allow further intelligent manipulation of the data and provide a future framework for structured data collection.

Define objectives

It is very important that a logistics strategic plan should be developed to address specific needs. The perceived need should be carefully assessed to ascertain that it is the core problem and not a symptom of the actual problem. For example, when deciding whether or not to rationalise multiple production facilities, the logistical implications for the total supply chain, rather than the optimisation of production processes at only one facility, should be considered. Different logistics functions impact differently on total logistics costs and a holistic approach should be taken when defining objectives.

Issues which may need to be addressed by objectives include:[16]

- maximisation of sales opportunities;
- achieving high levels of product availability;
- achieving high levels of consumer service;
- minimising costs;
- gaining timely, accurate, market intelligence; and
- ensuring smooth integration of trading and physical aspects. This could include order size requirements and unit-load characteristics.

It is important to get general buy-in at this stage, as the deliverables of the systems analysis process should be compared with what the original objectives were. This ensures compliance with the objectives and sufficient credibility for the process.

Test yourself

3.10 List five issues which may need to be addressed when defining objectives for logistics channels.

Generate and select technically feasible strategies

Once the needs have been determined and the objectives formulated, potential solutions should be generated. One solution is to change nothing – sometimes called the 'null alternative' or maintaining the status quo. This serves as the basis with which the alternatives can be compared to record any improvements which may flow from the new channel.

The selection of alternative strategies should not be restricted by current procedures or habits. All technically feasible practical solutions should be considered. To assist in lateral thinking, the following main determinants of channel structures should be considered:[17]

- requirements of the consumer;

- capabilities of the originating firm; and
- availability and willingness of appropriate intermediaries (if needed) to participate in the channel.

The availability of intermediaries can simplify the structure of a logistics channel significantly. If two suppliers send goods to four customers, there are eight channels of movement. If an intermediary is used, the two suppliers send goods to the intermediary. The intermediary then distributes to the four customers, so that there are now only six channels of movement. As the number of suppliers and customers increases, the difference becomes even more noteworthy. For four suppliers and ten customers, there are forty movement channels without an intermediary and only fourteen with an intermediary.

Centre-of-gravity analyses – similar to those used for the location of depots or distribution centres, as discussed under network design – are often used to determine the location of possible intermediaries.

The following factors should be considered in selecting alternative channels:[18]

- Market coverage objectives:
  - consumer buying behaviour;
  - type of distribution;
  - market concentration;
  - channel structure; and
  - control.
- Product characteristics:
  - value;
  - technicality;
  - market acceptance;
  - substitutability;
  - mass;
  - perishability;
  - seasonality; and
  - volume.
- Consumer service objectives:
  - availability;
  - order cycle; and
  - communication.
- Profitability.

Once the potential alternative solutions have been generated, it is necessary to identify the data and information required for the quantitative and qualitative analyses.

Techniques which may be considered when generating alternatives include the following:[19]

- Differentiated distribution: A strategy which incorporates different channels of distribution to achieve the desired service levels.
- Mixed strategy: A mixed distribution strategy will be more cost-effective than a single channel strategy where service requirements vary. A mixed strategy allows for an optimal channel to be established for each separate product group, instead of employing a single, global strategy which must average across all products.
- Postponement: The configuration or customisation of goods is delayed as far as is possible in the distribution channel to minimise the stock which is carried. An example is the colour pigmentation of paint on demand in the hardware store, which eliminates the need for keeping stock of many different colour paints. This is a classic 'pull' system.
- Speculation: This is the opposite of postponement, with the channel initiator assuming the risk rather than passing it to the downstream members of the channel. As much of a specific product as possible is made and 'pushed' into the market, in order to capitalise on economies of scale in production and sales opportunities.
- Consolidation: Creating large shipments from potentially small ones is a powerful economic tool in logistics planning. Potentially reduced consumer service (due to increased delivery time) must be balanced with the cost benefit of order consolidation.
- Standardisation: Standardisation in production is achieved by creating interchangeable parts, modularising products, and labelling the same products under different brand names.

After carefully selecting different alternative logistics strategies, the next step is the quantitative analysis.

Test yourself

3.11 What affects a channel structure?
3.12 What is the difference between postponement and speculation?

Analyse alternative strategies

The analysis of alternatives for the logistics strategy, and more specifically the distribution strategy, should be done according to the Total Logistics Cost concept.[20] This concept recognises that many more costs are incurred in the process of making a product available than just transport and warehouse costs. The least total cost does not necessarily occur where the transport, inventory, or order-processing costs are at their minimum. Efficient and effective logistics encompasses the entire chain; therefore managing transport, inventories, and order-processing activities collectively could be substantially more efficient than managing them separately.[21] This can be expressed in the equation shown in Figure 3.5:

$$TLC = TC + DC + FC + CC + SC + IC + HC + PC + RC + MC + XC$$

Where:

TLC	=	Total Logistics Costs
TC	=	Transport cost: long distance (operating and capital)
DC	=	Transport cost: local delivery, short distance (operating and capital)
FC	=	Facility cost (warehouse, depot etc.)
CC	=	Communication cost (invoicing, administration etc.)
SC	=	Information system cost (tracking and tracing etc.)
IC	=	Inventory cost (carrying cost, risk etc.)
HC	=	Materials handling cost
PC	=	Protective packaging cost
RC	=	Cost of reverse logistics (returned goods)
MC	=	Logistics management cost
XC	=	Direct and indirect taxes

Figure 3.5 Total logistics cost formula

It is not easy to collect the data pertaining to these cost items. Although most of the source information is readily available, it usually has to be converted to standard units and, as a rule, is not available in compatible electronic data format. Consequently, considerable time is spent on the recording and manipulation of the data.

To make the analysis more efficient, only those costs which vary between the alternatives under consideration should be compared. This reduces the time and effort of acquiring the data and of performing the analysis.

The following cost items should be calculated at the very least:

+ long distance transport costs;
+ short distance transport costs;
+ storage costs;
+ facility costs;
+ inventory carrying costs; and
+ process costs, including systems and administration costs.

Test yourself

3.13 List five of the six most important logistics costs.

Evaluate alternative strategies

Once the different alternatives have been costed and compared quantitatively, the evaluation can start. The alternative logistics strategies should be evaluated against the business strategy, while taking cognisance of practical considerations. For example, it might be important for a business to operate two production facilities to prevent total shutdown in the case of industrial action, even if the cost analysis indicated that one facility would be more efficient.

Consequently, the evaluation should not be based only on a quantitative comparison, but should also include qualitative issues. The costing comparison might give an indication of the financial implications of each strategy, but the business has to consider strategic, social, and political issues from a policy perspective. The quantitative analysis assists management in making informed decisions on these qualitative issues.

The strategies under comparison can be compared to the benchmarks in the industry, if available. The benchmark of a distribution channel can be obtained in many cases. However, care must be taken when comparing these numbers because volume, distance, and other factors may vary, thereby radically affecting the validity of the comparison.

Test yourself

3.14 Both _____ and _____ analyses should be utilised to choose the correct channel.

Select and implement new strategy

With the quantitative and qualitative evaluation completed, the business can make a selection and recommend the most suitable alternative. Implementation must be carefully planned.

It is important not to underestimate the challenges of implementing new logistics strategies, as the process imposes demands on both the staff and the operations. Cultural issues and change management, as well as their impact on the strategy, must be recognised as factors when implementing the strategy in order to shape and successfully deliver rewarding strategies. The Strategic Alignment Model can be used as a framework for aligning the formulation and the execution of strategy.[22]

It is sometimes difficult for operational personnel, used to traditional methods and faced with day-to-day operations, to handle the complex behavioural aspects of change. There are four prerequisites for fast and efficient change management:[23]

+ visible pressure for change;
+ a clear vision for change;
+ capacity for change; and
+ primary actions.

Primary actions include the following:

+ Align the culture with the strategic response.
+ Appoint a process owner to manage and promote the new channel.

- Reshape performance measures to focus on the new, desired channel.
- Develop and train the workforce.
- Communicate and demonstrate top management commitment to the new channel.
- Involve stakeholders and gain commitment to change.
- Implement a system to track benefits.
- Communicate progress with all stakeholders.
- Create an integration map.

People provide the route to fast and effective change. They need to know what to do, when to do it, why to do it, and how to do it. They also need the resources to do it and they need to be motivated and guided. The manager of the supply chain must be able to reconcile the paradoxical demands of managing costs, time, benefits, and quality with team building, managing stakeholders and their emotions, communication, commitment building, risk management, and people development.[24]

Test yourself

3.15 What are the first actions which need to be taken to ensure successful change management?

Manage performance

Measurements have to be introduced to ensure that the new process is correctly managed. When no measurements are introduced to effect management, poor performance occurs. Sub-optimal operation occurs when the measurement parameters are defined to measure functional rather than process performance.

Objectives for developing and implementing performance measurement systems include:[25]

- monitoring historical performance;
- controlling ongoing performance; and
- motivating personnel.

Consumer service – both from the view of the actual service (effectiveness) and the costs of its provision (efficiency) – is a suitable focus for a performance monitoring system.[26] The following sequence may be used to introduce a performance measurement system:

1. Identify all the important parameters of logistics costs, along with inputs of physical measurement, which are needed to provide the desired consumer service.
2. Institute systems and procedures for the collection of this cost data.
3. Identify and collect output data that reflects the critical parameters for the control of the process.
4. Prepare a set of desired measures by which the overall channel logistics activities should be evaluated.
5. Set up a mechanism for the regular presentation of status reports.

The best measure of channel performance in terms of business goals and objectives is profitability analyses of the various channels of distribution. The size of the net segment margin will determine which structural alternative is financially the best option. This information, combined with estimates of future growth for each structural alternative, permits the channel designer to select the most desirable alternative.

This last phase of the systems analysis process should include a structured review process to allow revisiting of the original objectives and checking for compliance. The systems analysis process should not be seen as a once-off exercise, but rather as a tool for continuous improvement.

Test yourself

3.16 How would you measure performance inside a business?

3.17 What are typical performance measurements outside a business?

Conclusion

Logistics strategies should be generated within the framework of the integrated business strategy.

The logistics strategy focuses on what is required from the logistics capability in the long, medium and short term to support this business strategy. The process of generating a logistics channel strategy involves conceptualising a strategy, deciding on network design, and selecting a channel. In this chapter, a format for the written strategy was presented. The process of generating a strategy was described. The aspects of network definition and alternative channel selection were laid out in detail. The method of generating alternative channels, and of selecting channels with the help of quantitative and qualitative analysis, was presented.

Questions

1 List the different planning hierarchies and give an example of decisions taken at each level.
2 Discuss typical channels of distribution and give examples of each.
3 Why would depots be provided in a logistics network?
4 The centre of gravity provides a quantitative method for establishing the ideal location of a storage facility. Which qualitative factors should be considered?
5 Discuss the systems analysis process for the development of a logistics strategy.
6 Compare and contrast speculation and postponement. Which concept represents a 'pull' strategy, and which one represents a 'push' strategy?
7 What are the most important prerequisites for fast and efficient change management?
8 Why is it important to manage performance?
9 Discuss a typical procedure for establishing a performance monitoring system.
10 What is a logistics master plan and what should be included in such a plan?

Notes

1   Christopher, M. 1990: 145–149.
2   Christopher, M. 1990: 724–726.
3   Christopher, M. 1990: 149.
4   Christopher, M. 1990: 259–271.
5   Gattorna, J.L. 1998(a): 30–39.
6   Gattorna, J.L. 1998(b): 417.
7   De Villiers, G. 1997: 3–6.
8   Gattorna, J.L. 1998(b): 416–418 and Chapter 27.
9   Rushton, A. and Oxley, J. 1989: 52–56.
10 Fawcett, P., et al. 1992(a): 31–33.
11 Coyle, J.J. et al. 1996: 457–463.
12 Bowersox, D.J. and Closs, D.J. 1996: 407.
13 Lambert, D.M. and Stock, J.R. 1993: 314–315.
14 Lambert, D.M. and Stock, J.R. 1993: 88.
15 Rushton, A. and Oxley, J. 1989: 58–60.
16 Fawcett, P. et al. 1992(a): 31–33.
17 Gattorna, J. 1998(a): 30.
18 Gattorna, J. 1998(a): 90–100.
19 Ballou, R.H. 1987: 345–349.
20 Adapted from Christopher, M. 1990: 6–8.
21 Ballou, R.H. 1987: 31.
22 Gattorna, J.L. 1998(b): 4–7.
23 Gattorna, J.L. 1998(b): Chapter 28.
24 Gattorna, J.L. 1998(b): 467.
25 Bowersox, D.J. and Closs, D.J. 1996: 670.
26 Christopher, M. 1990: 150–154.

Contents

Learning Outcomes

After you have studied this chapter, you should be able to:
- identify logistics concepts that are typical of certain industries;
- draw a basic goods flow diagram, using the three elements depicting a primary activity, buffer inventory points, and movement;
- identify the impact of poor forecasting on consumer order lead times; and
- identify four levels of the logistics planning hierarchy, and explain the time horizons and typical review periods of each level.

Introduction

At a glance, the logistics environment appears to be very varied. The logistics processes adopted by one business do not seem to suit the next business in the same industry. When one analyses the market, it looks as if one could identify a logistics concept for each type of industry. However, this is not really the case, as the principles of logistics apply to all industries. It is the application of these principles which is adapted for each industry to provide for the needs of consumers. Each business tries to tailor its logistics processes to give it a competitive advantage.

To supply the demands of the market and at the same time provide a differentiated offering to consumers, the logistics chain needs to be co-ordinated and controlled. This requires that the activities and focus of the total chain, as well as the individual parts of the chain, are well-planned. This chapter focuses on how to plan logistics processes which minimise the impacts from the environment and which allow the chain to operate efficiently and effectively.

> Logistics planning is the integrated process whereby the resources of the entire supply chain are planned, using current and forecast demand, in order to achieve the desired consumer service levels.

Basic logistics structures

A basic logistics structure consists of specific elements added together to form a logistics chain. These elements are primary activities, inventory holding buffers, and the movement of goods between the primary activities and inventory holding buffers. The most widely used ways of depicting the elements of a logistics structure are described below.

The elements of a basic logistics structure

Primary activities

Primary activities or processes include manufacturing processes and/or transactional processes. Manufacturing processes could be production activities or transformation processes (as found in the various processing industries). Primary activities are usually depicted as rectangular blocks, as in Figure 4.1.

primary activities

Figure 4.1 Primary activities

Inventory holding buffers

Inventory holding buffers (depots, warehouses etc.) are necessary to protect or buffer the process from an excess or shortage of inventory. The shortage may be caused by late delivery of inventory (such as raw materials or sub-assemblies) due to uncertainties in supply or demand. Excess can be caused by process restrictions or problems downstream which restrict throughput. Buffers decouple processes. Excessive buffer stock is inefficient, while shortages cause delays in production.

Inventory holding buffers are usually depicted as a triangle pointing downward, as in Figure 4.2. The downward pointing triangle resembles a drawing pin, which symbolises the pain incurred if too much buffer inventory is carried.

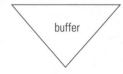

Figure 4.2 Buffer inventories

Movement

Movement can be both intra-plant (material handling within a plant) or inter-plant (transport between plants). It is usually indicated by means of an arrow, to indicate direction and movement across distance, as in Figure 4.3.

Figure 4.3 Movement

The goods flow

The individual businesses which form part of a supply chain need input materials, which they convert into finished goods and then distribute to consumers. The output or finished goods from one business may be the input materials of the next business, and so forth. This flow of goods constitutes a supply chain. The goods flow can be illustrated as indicated in Figure 4.4.

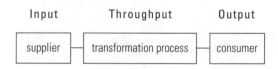

Figure 4.4 The basic goods flow

Because of uncertainties in demand and/or supply – caused by disturbances in the macro and micro environments, special promotions, product launches, seasonality etc. – it is necessary to carry buffer inventory. Figure 4.5 depicts a basic goods flow which includes buffer inventory.

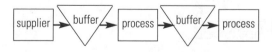

Figure 4.5 The basic goods flow including buffer inventory

The goods flow and the creation of utility

A business process (such as the goods flow process illustrated above) adds utility or value to the total supply chain. As mentioned in the discussion of the value-added role of logistics in chapter two, there are essentially four types of utility: form utility, place utility, time utility and possession utility. These various utilities are created by different functions in an enterprise, as shown in Table 4.1.

Utility type	Created by
Form utility	Operations
Place utility	Logistics
Time utility	Logistics
Possession utility	Sales

Table 4.1 Types of utility

Form utility

This is created by the operations or production function. Form utility is added to the supply chain when input materials, including raw materials and semi-finished goods, are converted from one form to another. This is the throughput part of the goods flow where, for example, iron ore and other materials are converted into steel, or where steel sheets are converted into body panels for vehicles.

Place utility

This is created by the logistics function, and more specifically by the transport function. Moving goods from a point where they are in surplus to a point where demand for them exists creates place utility. For example, fuel is cheaper at the coastal refineries, but has little value to the inland consumer if it is not available nearby. Customers are therefore prepared to pay more for fuel inland than at the coast. Hence, transporting the fuel from the coast creates place utility.

Time utility

Being able to provide goods or services to consumers when they need such goods or services creates time utility. This is also created by the logistics function, and then more specifically by the distribution function. Distribution consists of transport, warehousing, and the replenishment of the stock in the warehouse. The transport function, which creates place utility, therefore also contributes towards time utility.

The location and size of the warehouse is integral to the time utility. Warehouses are located strategically to ensure that the time required for distribution matches the needs of the consumers. Warehouses add the buffer of stock necessary to provide for demand fluctuations. The availability of the right stock in the right quantity in the warehouse contributes to the time utility.

Warehouses also deal effectively with load mismatching, i.e. where the received order quantity is large compared to the consignment size that can be distributed. This may happen when, for example, an order of steel is moved to the port warehouse by road. Each vehicle can only carry a limited tonnage, but to be economical, the ship must carry a large quantity of the product. The warehouse provides a buffer to ensure the time utility.

Possession utility

Possession utility is created once the ownership transfers from a supplier to a consumer. This is achieved through the interaction between the consumer and the sales function of the business.

Without form, place, and time utility, Sales cannot create possession utility.

Test yourself

4.1 The _____ function creates place utility and contributes towards _____ utility.

Managing the goods flow

In the previous section, the flow of goods in a logistics chain was discussed. It is important to be able to manage the goods flow, to know what systems are used for managing it, and what impact the management of the goods flow has on the logistics environment.

In Figure 4.6, a customer order starts the logist-

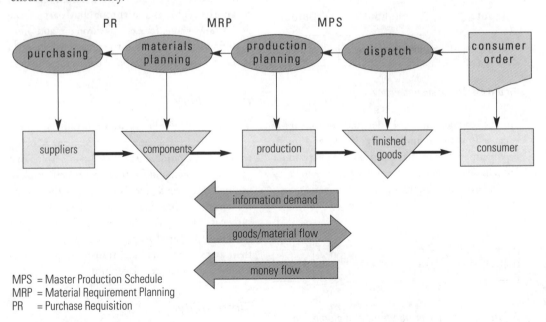

MPS = Master Production Schedule
MRP = Material Requirement Planning
PR = Purchase Requisition

Figure 4.6 Managing the goods flow

ics planning system via the sales function. If the finished goods are available in the finished goods store, the dispatch function distributes the finished goods to the customer. (The customer in this case is not necessarily the final customer but could be the next party in the supply chain.)

If the finished goods are not available, the customer demand forms part of the Management Planning System (MPS). Production planning then places a works order on the production function. The production function picks the components from the component store, manufactures or assembles the items required and forwards the finished products to the finished goods store, ready for dispatch.

If the components are not available in the components store, the materials planning function acts via the Materials Requirements Planning (MRP) system to generate requisitions on the purchasing function. The purchasing function (as part of Purchase Requisition) in turn places purchase orders with suppliers of raw materials for the delivery of raw materials, so that the products for the components store can be manufactured.

It is important to understand the impact of the above on the logistics planning environment.

In Figure 4.7, the values in the circles are lead times. If the customer order is picked from the sub-assembly store, the reaction lead time is ten time units. (A time unit can be hours, days, weeks, months or even longer units of time.)

If the customer order is picked from the component inventory store to produce sub-assemblies for the sub-assembly store, the reaction lead time is extended by seventeen time units (four time units for the processing of the MPS requirements, plus thirteen time units for the production of the sub-assemblies).

If the customer order cannot be picked from the component inventory store, a further twenty-two time units are added to the reaction lead time (two time units for the processing of the MRP and another twenty for the production of the components).

Therefore, in the above example, the total reaction lead time of an unexpected, unplanned customer order could amount to forty-nine time units (two time units to process the order, four to process the MPS if the sub-assemblies are not available, two to process the MRP if the components are not available, twenty to produce the components, thirteen to manufacture the sub-assemblies, and eight for final assembly). This means that, in order to guarantee customer service levels in this example, the sales need to be forecast accurately forty-nine time units in advance.

It is impossible for any sales forecast to be accurate foty-nine time units in advance. Logistics systems therefore need to be in place to accommodate the situations in the above example. In the next section, the logistics concepts that can alter reaction lead times and introduce flexibility are discussed.

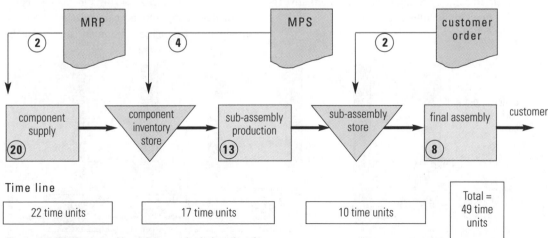

Figure 4.7 The impact of lead times on logistics planning

Logistics supply processes

Problems within logistics systems usually manifest themselves in poor consumer service, unsatisfactory financial results, and high capital expenditure due to high inventories. In some cases, the poor results are caused by ignorance and misunderstanding of the logistics supply process.

Japanese workers are regarded as being highly efficient. Part of this efficiency can be attributed to the organisation of their logistics concepts. They have fixed and stable demand patterns, long planning horizons, high volumes, and thus high economies of scale, high asset utilisation, and high efficiency, but low flexibility.

Different approaches are necessary in different industries and in different economic circumstances. The approaches vary primarily as to where the customer order decoupling point is located. A customer order decoupling point determines how far upstream in the logistics chain the customer order penetrates.

The location of customer order decoupling points is described in the following section, and is illustrated in Figure 4.8. Each of the alternatives is described in the following sections.

Assemble and ship to stock

The customer order decoupling point is located at the distribution centre. This is typical of the fast moving consumer goods (FMCG) industry, where the finished goods inventory must be available on the shelves at all times. If the product is not available, the consumer is likely to buy a substitute product, or to go to an alternative location to purchase the specific product.

The main challenge facing this process is demand management and more specifically the forecasting of independent demand. The major risks in this concept lie in the inventory levels. Shortage of inventory will result in poor consumer service. Surplus of inventory might result in obsolescence, either through the product shelf-life expiring or the demand falling away.

Make to stock

The customer order decoupling point is located at the finished goods store. This is typical for consumer goods such as home appliances. Relatively few products are kept for display and demonstration purposes in showrooms, but back-up inventory is kept in a central finished goods store. The customer order triggers the delivery of the goods from the location of the finished goods, either to the customer or to the sales outlet for replenishment.

The main challenge of this logistics concept is to manage demand, and particularly to forecast independent demand. The main risk lies in the management of inventory levels.

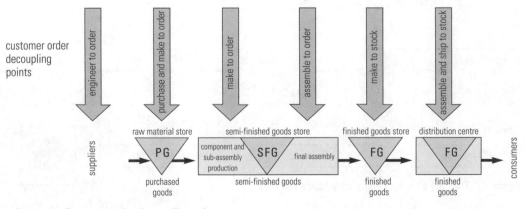

Figure 4.8 Customer order decoupling points

Assemble to order

The customer order penetrates into the final assembly line, where sub-assemblies and semi-finished goods are picked and assembled to the customer's desired configuration. All permutations of the various possible configurations must be offered, but these cannot all be kept in the finished goods store. It will inflate finished goods inventory levels and total logistics cost.

This customer order decoupling point is typical of markets where mass customisation is essential. An example is the lap top computer industry. Many motor vehicle manufacturers also utilise this process. In the manufacturing process, they allow and make provision for orders for specific options on vehicles. The inventory must be controlled at the sub-assembly level. The manufacturer has to forecast the independent demand for the sub-assemblies.

This process can satisfy the customer's needs for a specifically configured item. The challenge is to keep the assembly lead times short in order for this to add value for the customer. Capacity constraints should not cause the final assembly to extend the delivery time. The major risks are excess stocks and subsequent obsolescence of sub-assemblies and/or components due to changes in market demand.

Make to order

The customer order decoupling point is located at the component and sub-assembly production point. This is typical of industries that produce items such as custom-made furniture. The manufacturer utilises unique components or sub-assemblies to make the furniture. This process is far more extensive than in the motor vehicle industry, where the sub-assemblies are standard and only the choice of the sub-assemblies makes the car unique to the customer.

The forecasting here is focused on replenishing the sub-assemblies to maintain the semi-finished goods store inventory. The assembly process of the basic item is only started once an order is received.

Therefore, the independent demand for components and sub-assemblies needs to be forecast. One of the major challenges is to balance the capacity of the logistics pipeline. The people employed in this type of environment are usually multi-skilled.

Purchase and make to order

The customer order decoupling point is located at the raw material store. This process is typically used in industries where the components and/or sub-assemblies are very expensive, or where the components are not used frequently. In the manufacturing process, this is the traditional job-shop process. The business does not carry the inventory, but orders the components once the customer order has been received.

The Bill of Materials (BOM) for the components is of critical importance. An incorrect BOM will result in delays, which will impact on the delivery time of the entire process.

Engineer to order

The customer order decoupling point is located at the supplier level. This process is typically used to supply unique products or services, and is very often undertaken as a special project. The design and manufacturing of an oil rig or a harbour quay is one example.

There are no repeat orders and no economies of scale. There is also no predetermined BOM. The cost and the lead times are determined for each individual project.

Test yourself

4.3 The preferred logistics concept determines how far upstream the _____ penetrates into the logistics process, and determines the customer order _____.

The planning hierarchy

The purpose of the planning hierarchy, which was introduced in chapter three, is to address the logistics needs of a business enterprise – and to provide an integrated platform to do so. The planning hierarchy should also take supplier integration and consumer relationship management into account.

Figure 4.9 reflects four planning levels:

- the strategic planning level;
- the master planning level (also called the sales and operational planning level);
- the master scheduling level; and
- the order processing level.

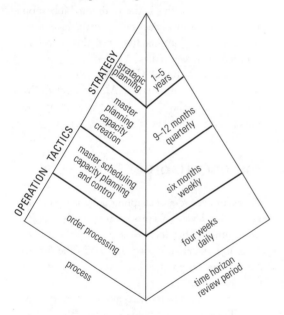

Figure 4.9 The planning hierarchy

The installation of a central heating system in a building can be used as an example. The decision to have central heating or not will be on the strategic planning level. The capacity of the installation (i.e. whether only some of the rooms are going to be supplied, or the whole building) will be decided upon on the master planning level. On the master scheduling or capacity planning level, decisions about the temperature control strategy (for example, which rooms are to have independent control, and which ones are to be on a floor by floor control

system) are made. Decisions about the valves inside the rooms and the furnace are made on the fourth planning level, the order processing level.

The above analogy illustrates how various levels of planning and control are required for most systems. These levels are also valid for a logistics management system. Each of the different planning levels has different planning horizons or time spans for which the plans are made, as well as review periods. It is very important to allow sensible time frames for the planning and review processes. It is inappropriate to revise one's business strategy on a weekly basis, and unrealistic to expect to control the productivity of the pickers in a warehouse every six months.

Figure 4.9 provides approximate planning horizons and review periods for the various planning levels. In times of rapid change, these periods may well be reduced. In times of stability, the periods can increase.

Strategic logistics planning

As mentioned before, the logistics strategy plan is derived from the corporate strategy of the business. The strategic planning process determines the broad direction which the business will follow.

It is also critically important to align the strategic logistics plan, the strategic marketing plan, and the manufacturing or supply plan.

The planning horizon for logistics strategic plans is of the order of two to three years. The review period is six to twelve months.

Master planning

Master planning has as its purpose the creation of capacity. The master plan does not focus on detail. A supplier may determine the volume of business that can be expected during, say, the next twelve to eighteen months. The supplier then uses this information to plan and create the capacity to supply the required volume. The detail of the production process is not determined on this level. For example, this would be the level where a bicycle manufacturer translates the quantity of bicycles to be manufactured into the capacity which is required for manufacturing to match the expected sales.

When master planning deals with the supplier interface, it serves to manage the strategic purchasing function which serves as the basis for contract negotiations. When master planning deals with the consumer interface, it forms part of the business plan.

Master scheduling

The capacity that was created on the previous level is planned in more detail on this level. Master scheduling involves the functional planning done between a business and its suppliers. In the example of the bicycle manufacturer, the major product categories (such as women's, men's, mountain, and racing bikes) would be dealt with on this level.

Customer order processing

This is the level where operational activities, such as works order scheduling, are prioritised. In our example, this is the level where a materials requirement plan provides specifications for manufacturing the wheels, tyres, seats, frames, and handlebars of the bicycles.

> *Test yourself*
>
> 4.4 The planning hierarchy consists of four levels. Name them.

Integration with the logistics elements

Logistics planning is required to co-ordinate and integrate the various functions performed in a logistics chain to make it both efficient and effective. Planning should also be done to help logistics managers cope with changes in the environment. If the logistics plan allows for flexibility, it will be possible to react to changes in a cost-effective manner.

At the master planning level, for example, volume flexibility can be achieved by planning for sufficient excess capacity. The functional managers responsible for the individual logistics elements cannot work or interact – and react to changes in the market and so on – without an integrated plan, which is the master schedule. In the customer order processing procedure, rescheduling or introducing postponement can allow for flexible product mixing.

> *Test yourself*
>
> 4.5 Volume flexibility can be achieved by _____ at the master planning level, whilst product mix flexibility can be achieved in the customer order processing procedure by _____ or _____.

Conclusion

The logistics plan is essential for co-ordinating and controlling the elements of the logistics chain, and thus for making the overall chain optimally efficient and effective. Planning involves working with the business plan to create capacity for the processes to be carried out. The sequence and the throughput of each process are also determined and planned. This planning guides the operations.

In this chapter, we have also discussed how to introduce flexibility and reduce lead times by varying the point where the customer order enters the process.

Questions

1 Draw a flow diagram to depict the basic goods flow, indicating buffer stock, primary processes, and material movement.
2 Discuss the impact of poor forecasting on delivery lead times.
3 Discuss the four levels in the planning hierarchy, as well as the planning horizons and typical time span of each level.
4 List the six logistics supply processes and describe the typical industry with which one would match these concepts.

Contents

Learning Outcomes

After you have studied this chapter, you should be able to:
- explain the difference between purchasing and procurement;
- discuss the strategic role of procurement;
- define and describe the nature of procurement management;
- describe the five procurement management tasks;
- discuss the nature of goods that can be purchased;
- discuss the ways in which suppliers can be managed;
- discuss the activities that ensure an efficient logistics channel; and
- discuss the methods to be used to curb procurement costs

Introduction

Any business enterprise purchases its materials, services and assets such as machinery and equipment, motor vehicles, furniture, and fittings from other firms. These materials, services, and assets are used in the production, marketing, logistics, and other operations of the enterprise. The process of purchasing these items and services is known as procurement.

Procurement and purchasing are often mistakenly regarded as synonymous. Purchasing is the buying of materials, services, and other assets. Its focus is only on the buying activity. Procurement entails much more than purchasing. It includes purchasing, transporting, packaging, warehousing, and all the other activities related to receiving inbound materials.[1] Purchasing is a subset of procurement management.

Procurement management is also known as supply management. We refer to it as procurement management because of its wider scope. It includes the planning, organising, leading, co-ordination, and control of many activities such as choosing the right suppliers, negotiating prices, negotiating payment and delivery terms, and assessing supplier quality.

In this chapter, we give attention to the strategic role of purchasing, the nature of procurement management, the nature of goods purchased, managing suppliers, activities ensuring an effective logistics chain, and procurement cost management.

> **Test yourself**
>
> 5.1 Explain the differences between purchasing and procurement in your own words.

Strategic roles of procurement

Procurement can be regarded as one of a firm's most important functions. It contributes to the profitability of a firm, which leads to an increase in the wealth of its owners. Procurement brings the firm in touch with the outside world, nationally as well as internationally. Procurement has two important strategic roles: it provides access to external markets, and it has an integrated relationship with the other management functions of a firm.

Access to external markets

The world has changed into a global village – a change which reveals new business horizons for firms. Firms now have the opportunity to become internationally competitive and can enlarge their market through exposure to a broader international public. The firm can gain contact with the external market by selecting suppliers both from abroad and locally. (Local suppliers are within the borders of the country in which the firm is situated.) The external contacts can supply the firm with information regarding new kinds of materials, new technology, potential suppliers, and other important factors.

The firm can select and develop the external suppliers in such a way that they will contribute to its effectiveness. The suppliers can be incorporated into the activities of the firm, which may lead to substantial cost and time savings in the development of new products.

An example of this is the motor vehicle manufacturing industry, where the computers of the manufacturers are linked to those of their suppliers. When the designer at head office designs a new vehicle, the designers of the different components are connected to the computer system of the designer. They can design the new brake system, steering system, engine, and gearbox at the same time the main designer is designing the vehicle. This leads to a tremendous saving in the designing and development time. A new vehicle can be designed and developed in less than half the time spent on it before.[2] All this can happen without the designers of the components being present in the main designer's office.

Relationship to the other management functions

The procurement function has an integrated relationship with the following management functions of the firm:

Top management

Top management relies on the procurement function for the buying, renting, and leasing of all its materials, services, and assets. The procurement department should have properly trained experts of the law and other sciences to assist the firm in buying the best quality items at the lowest possible prices.

Production and operations management

Production and operations management relies on the procurement department for buying its machinery, equipment, and tools. The procurement department also ensures that services, such as after sales services of machinery, are supplied.

Human resources management

Human resources management relies on the procurement department to supply them with their furniture and items such as stationery and printing equipment. Procurement management relies on the human resources department to train suitable personnel for them.

Financial management

Financial management relies on the procurement department for buying its furniture, stationery, and equipment such as computers and air conditioners. Procurement management relies on the financial department for financing the purchases which go through the procurement department.

Information management

Information is a very important component of logistics management. The procurement department needs accurate and timely information regarding inventory levels, lead times, and suppliers to function effectively.

Marketing management

The marketing department is the last link in the supply chain. Information about the demand for a product is fed into the logistics system to determine what quantity of the product needs to be manufactured to meet the demand. The whole logistics operation, and therefore also the procurement process, is based on the figures of the marketing department.

Nature of procurement management

The procurement management tasks in the context of logistics management are the planning, organisation, leading, co-ordination, and control of the activities related to the procurement of all inbound items such as raw materials, components, sub-assemblies, services, and final products. Procurement management links all the members in the supply chain and ensures the quality of the final product.

Test yourself

5.2 Define procurement management in your own words.

Planning

Planning is a basic management task which involves the visualisation, even amidst uncertainties, of what a business enterprise wishes to achieve in future.

The formulation of objectives forms the basis of planning. Specific objectives regarding time frames and quantitative terms can be derived from the overall objectives. Objectives can be formulated at strategic, tactical, and operational levels.[3]

Strategic procurement planning

Strategic procurement planning should take place at top management level as it involves long-term planning. Long-term planning carries a high risk, so that it is the responsibility of the procurement manager to plan pro-actively. The strategic procurement objectives should enable the firm to:

- ensure the availability of raw materials, components, sub-assemblies, and other input items at competitive prices;
- keep inventory levels as low as possible in order to ensure minimum investment in inventory;
- search for new suppliers; and
- develop the existing suppliers.

Tactical procurement planning

Tactical procurement planning involves planning for the medium term. These plans should be executed at middle management level. The strategic plans formulated by top management must be implemented by middle management. The tactical procurement objectives should be to:

- study the different inventory control systems available in the market and implement the one most appropriate for the enterprise;
- study the most appropriate materials flow systems within the business enterprise and implement the best one;
- develop the current as well as the new suppliers; and
- enter into long-term contracts with the reliable suppliers.

Operational procurement planning

Operational procurement planning involves short-term planning and it is done by lower management. The operational objectives are based on the tactical planning done by middle management. These objectives are usually stated in concrete and quantitative terms. The operational procurement objectives should be to:

- conduct inventory analyses;
- reduce inventories;
- improve the relationships with suppliers;
- develop and assist suppliers by supplying technical and other support;
- order on time and pay the suppliers' accounts on time; and
- adhere to the contract clauses of the suppliers.

Test yourself

5.3 Objectives can be formulated at _____, _____, and _____ levels.

Organisation

The main decision to be made here is where the procurement function should be positioned in the broad organisation structure. Usually, there is a purchasing manager on the middle management level who reports to the purchasing director. The trend in many American companies is to place a logistics manager on middle management level. The production operations manager and the purchasing manager report to the logistics manager. The logistics manager has direct access to top management.

Two kinds of organisation structures can be found in business enterprises: centralised and decentralised organisation structures. When one person or one department in a group of companies is responsible for the procurement of the group's products and/or services, the procurement organisation structure is centralised. When each of the departments or each of the subsidiaries of the company is allowed to buy its own products and/or services, the procurement organisation structure is decentralised.

Leading

Leading (command) is the management task where the action is. Effective leadership affects the motivation of the workers as it involves the personnel directly. Leading includes giving workers instructions to perform certain tasks. The purchasing manager may, for example, instruct the buyers to draft a list of alternative suppliers.

Co-ordination

The procurement function is a support function. The procurement activities support and supplement the activities of the other functions and the procurement department gets its instructions from the other departments. Procurement activities have advantages for the procurement as well as the other functions in a business enterprise. The procurement department also acts in an advisory capacity. For example, the procurement personnel can advise the production personnel on where to buy the equipment which will suit their needs; or they can advise the finance department on where to buy the new computer software needed for new financial systems.

Control

Control refers to the efforts of management to achieve the set objectives. Certain parameters between which the business enterprise can operate are determined. The moment the business exceeds the parameters, management must find reasons for these deviations and rectify the problem. For example, usually only a certain percentage of orders in a procurement department may be back-orders. The moment the number of back-orders exceeds the stated maximum, management must determine the cause and solve the problem.

Test yourself

5.4 The procurement management tasks include _____, _____, _____, _____, and _____.

Nature of goods purchased

A variety of goods can be bought by the procurement department. The main categories of goods are raw materials, components, sub-assemblies, services, capital goods, and final products.

Raw materials, components, and sub-assemblies

Raw materials

Raw materials are those materials that are found in nature and that are transformed to final products through the production process. These materials include ore, milk, iron, sugar cane, carrots, gold etc. Final products of one business enterprise can serve as raw materials of the next. For example, Iscor manufactures steel plates. These plates are used for building car bodies in the motor vehicle manufacturing industry. Milk supplied by a farmer is a raw material for a dairy which uses it to manufacture cheese or butter.

Components

Business enterprises store components, or parts, and use them to repair and maintain equipment. Components are also used in the production process. A manufacturer of television sets purchases certain components, such as electronic components, to build into the television sets.

Sub-assemblies

Sub-assemblies, or semi-finished goods, are products in the production process on which work still needs to be done. They are also known as work in process. An example of this is the electric transformers in big cities. It takes a long time to build such a transformer. At any stage before the completion date, it is regarded as a semi-finished product.

Services

Services have certain characteristics that differentiate them from the other goods:[4]

Services are intangible and perishable

Services are usually intangible and perishable. In cases where service industries, such as banks, offer service packages, the services have both tangible and intangible characteristics. In the case of a current bank account, the bank offers a cheque book (tangible) and the convenience of the bank account (intangible). The service has a limited lifetime and hence is perishable.

Services cannot be kept in inventory

Unlike physical products, services cannot be prepared beforehand and then be kept in inventory. Inventory can absorb the fluctuations in demand in the case of physical products, but services must be supplied in accordance with the demand.

The client is part of the service process

The client is present in most cases when the service is provided. Examples are patients who visit a doctor, clients who visit a hairdresser, and pet owners who take their animals to a veterinary surgeon.

A small service centre is used for providing a service

As services are not manufactured, kept in stock, and then distributed, a small service centre is used for providing a service. In the case of business enterprises that manufacture physical products, big factories can be built to benefit from the economies of scale. A service facility usually supplies the market in its immediate vicinity. This means that the business enterprise must be situated near its potential clients. In the case of physical products, factories can be situated far from the customers as the products can be transported.

Services are labour-intensive

Service business enterprises are usually labour-intensive. In many cases, however, technological development has resulted in a change to machines. Examples of this are automatic teller machines and automatic car washing machines which perform tasks that were previously performed by people.

Services have a short response time

In the case of physical products, there is lead time (i.e. the time that elapses from the time the product is ordered up to the time that it is delivered). This lead time can be expressed in quantities of hours, days, weeks, and even months. In the case of a service, the response time is short because of the fact that a service cannot be kept in stock. Clients standing in a queue in a bank will lose their temper if they have to wait for too long to be served – especially when the subsequent service is slow and poor.

Service quality is difficult to measure

The quality standards of physical products are specified and the quality of these products can be checked against the set specifications. In the case of services, this is not such an easy task. It is difficult to set quality specifications for services, as the quality of a service is relative: One person may regard a service as good while the next may think it is bad. One customer in a restaurant may enjoy it when the service is slow because it gives more time to relax. Another person may see this slow service as bad service.

The quality specifications of the intangible part must be set properly to enable proper quality control.

Patent rights for services

It is difficult to exercise a patent right on the intangible component of a service.

Capital goods

Capital goods, such as machinery and equipment, are used in the manufacturing of products and/or services. These machines are usually expensive and in many cases they must be specially made according to the buyer's specifications.

It might take some time for such a machine to be manufactured and delivered, especially in the case of specialised machines. After sales service is important: A machine must be installed properly and tuned until it operates to the satisfaction of the buyer. Continuous contact with the supplier after ordering the machine is necessary to ensure that the manufacturing of the machine is on schedule.

As capital goods are generally expensive, businesses need to do careful financial planning through capital budgets. This ensures that the needed capacity is available and that the business enterprise has sufficient funds available to finance the goods when needed.

Final products

Final (finished) products are the products that come out of the production process. They are ready for sale and are stored by the business enterprise for distribution to the customers.

As seen earlier in this chapter, finished products of one business enterprise can be the raw materials, components, or sub-assemblies of another. Gold, the final product of a gold mine, is sold to a jeweller who makes jewellery from it. The gold is a raw material from the jeweller's perspective.

Managing suppliers

Suppliers are present throughout the supply chain – from the manufacturers of the components to the customers. These suppliers form very important links in the supply chain as the effective functioning of the business enterprises in this chain is in their hands.

It is necessary for the business enterprises in every supply chain to manage the suppliers in their chain properly. This can be done by selecting, evaluating, and choosing the right suppliers. The business enterprise can then develop the chosen suppliers properly and it can form healthy relationships with them.

Steps in the selection process

The following steps can be followed in the selection of suppliers:[5]

1 Survey.
2 Investigate.
3 Select.
4 Form relationships.

Survey

This is the phase where potential suppliers must be identified. The research department of the procurement department should be responsible for this as it can be a time-consuming and expensive exercise. In many cases, the right suppliers must be found overseas – especially where high-tech products such as machinery and vehicles are concerned.

The following sources can be used to find information on potential suppliers:

◆ trade journals;
◆ the Internet;
◆ the Yellow Pages;
◆ representatives of suppliers; and

◆ catalogues, price lists, and advertisements.

A business enterprise can also make use of the open tender system, which allows suppliers to tender in response to advertisements and open invitations in the media and on the Internet. After obtaining all this information, a list must be drafted with the names, addresses, and other information available on the suppliers.

Test yourself

5.7 Name five sources which can be used to find information on potential suppliers.

Investigate

The investigation phase follows the survey phase. During this phase, the procurement department investigates the suppliers on the list to select the most suitable ones. The following factors can be considered in this investigation:

Suppliers' retail prices

The retail price of the supplier is the purchase price of the purchaser. The cheaper purchasers can buy their goods, the higher their net profit will be. The purchaser always endeavours to get high quality goods at low prices. The purchaser must therefore be able to bargain with the supplier and convince the supplier to absorb some of the costs. The suppliers must also be consistent with their prices in order to prevent losses for the purchaser. Suppliers who are conscious of costs generally offer lower retail prices.

Reputation of the supplier

Investigate in the market place whether the potential supplier has a good reputation. Other customers of the supplier will be able to provide this information. Ask them the following important questions about suppliers: Do they always deliver on time? Do they adhere to the contracted prices? Is the quality of their goods high? Is the supplier's administration of a high standard?

Management quality of the supplier

It is difficult to investigate the quality of the business management of a potential supplier. Companies that are quoted on the Johannesburg Securities Exchange are easier to investigate as they must provide financial reporting. These financial reports are of a high standard and supply information on the results of management's efforts. In the other cases, visits to the supplier's business should give the investigators an insight into the quality of management. Talks with the personnel of the supplier can be an excellent source of information.

Supplier's labour relations

The supplier's labour relations are of great importance as poor labour relations can lead to late deliveries and quality fluctuations. Investigate the strike record of the supplier. A visit to the premises of the supplier may also be insightful.

Financial strength of the supplier

A supplier who battles financially will most probably not be able to guarantee future production of their products. The purchaser also runs the risk of the supplier becoming insolvent at an inconvenient time. The purchaser can analyse suppliers' financial statements to ensure that their financial position is sound.

Ability to supply support services

A supplier, especially the supplier of capital goods, must be able to provide support services. This should form part of the purchase. Support services include installation, maintenance, training, and advice. The costs of these support services must be included in the tender or selling price. These costs should exclude the maintenance after the guarantee of the product has expired.

Consistent and timely delivery of products

It is important that products are delivered consistently and on time. Failure to do so may lead to interruptions in the production process. In the case of wholesalers and retailers, it may lead to stock-out situations. Information on the supplier's ability to do this can be obtained from other customers of the supplier or from the printed media.

Select

During the selection phase, interviews are held with the potential suppliers in order to select the most suitable ones. Choose one of the suppliers who conforms to the requirements stated in the investigation phase, as they should be able to provide the goods and services of the required quantity and quality.

Form relationships

The relationship phase is one of the most important phases in the selection process. The procurement department must build long-term relationships with its suppliers to motivate the suppliers to provide the goods as and when required. It is desirable for a supplier to be in a long-term relationship with its customers as this will ensure a prosperous future for all the parties involved.

Test yourself

5.8 Name four steps that can be followed when selecting suppliers.

5.9 Name seven factors that can be considered in the investigation of possible future suppliers.

Activities ensuring an efficient logistics channel

There are a number of activities which ensure that a logistics chain is efficient. The most important ones are:
- The 'just-in-time' (JIT) system
- Value analyses
- Managing inbound transport
- Total Quality Management (TQM)

The 'just-in-time' (JIT) system

The 'just-in-time' system is common in business enterprises. The activities in the JIT system are geared towards providing the business enterprise with raw materials just before they are needed in the production process. The effect of this is that minimum inventory is held and that waste is reduced. In the case of wholesalers and retailers, the JIT system reduces the amount of money invested in inventory.[6] The JIT system therefore improves the effectiveness of the entire logistics channel.

Value analysis

Value analysis is the examination of the design, functioning, and cost of products and raw materials. The purpose of value analysis is to reduce costs. This can be done by changing the design of the product, by replacing a component with another kind of component, by eliminating a certain component, or by changing the source of supply. The quality and reliability of the final product should, however, be the same or better than what it was before the change.

Value analysis is done by a committee consisting of members of the following departments: procurement, marketing, design, operations management, and finance and costing. Personnel from the supplier's design and production departments should also serve on this committee. The committee members work together to formulate the best design for a product. Only certain products should be chosen for value analysis. These must be products:
- on which a substantial amount of money is spent annually;
- of an intricate design;
- of which large quantities are purchased;
- with a high percentage of waste and remanufacturing costs; and
- which form part of other components.

The technique of value analysis

Questioning forms the basis of value analysis. The so-called 'ten tests for value' consist of the following ten questions:
- Does the use of the product or component have any advantages for the business?
- Does the cost of the product or component equal the value it has for the business?

- Must the product or component have all the existing features?
- Isn't there a better component than the existing one which can be used for the same purpose?
- Can't the business enterprise use a better product than the existing one?
- Can't a cheaper, standardised component be used?
- Is the best manufacturing process being used?
- Does the cost of materials, labour, overheads, plus a reasonable profit equal the value of the product or component?
- Isn't there another reliable supplier who can supply a similar item at a lower price?
- Is there another buyer who buys the same item at a lower price?

Managing inbound transport

The inbound transport system refers to the transport facilities that are used to bring goods to each business enterprise in the logistics chain. The mode of transport used has a direct effect on the lead times of the different orders. Every business enterprise in the logistics chain should manage its inbound transport system properly to ensure a constant flow of goods and to ensure that they arrive at the specified dates and time.[7]

Total Quality Management (TQM)

We have emphasised before that inventories must be reduced to minimum levels. To achieve this, while at the same time ensuring sufficient inventory, the lead times must be reduced. The emphasis therefore shifts from quality in the production process only, to quality in all areas of a business enterprise. Special attention is paid to the service areas interfacing with the customer. This concept is called Total Quality Management (TQM). Strategically, TQM deals with the following elements of total quality:[8]

An obsession with quality

Quality should be an obsession with all the personnel of a business enterprise. The personnel must be motivated to meet the stated quality levels and to continually improve on that quality. The result is higher quality products and services at lower prices, which should ensure greater consumer satisfaction.

Unity of purpose

Unity of purpose means that management and the rest of the personnel all realise the importance of competitiveness and long-term survival. They support the implementation of TQM to ensure the effectiveness of the logistics activities.

Employee involvement and empowerment

Employee involvement means that employees are engaged at all levels of the thinking processes in a business enterprise. The result is that employees are responsible for what they do or fail to do. The knowledge that they are responsible for the decisions they make should motivate them to make better, more informed decisions.

Employee involvement must be accompanied by employee empowerment. Employee empowerment adds to the responsibility of the employee the authority to identify problems and to seek and implement solutions.

The advantage for the logistics chain is that empowered employees continually endeavour to find ways to improve current systems and to solve problems immediately and effectively. This leads to greater consumer satisfaction.

Consumer focus

All the employees of a business must be focused on the consumer. Employees should know the consumers of the business and should treat them as if they were their own customers or clients. It is important to remember that the final product of a supplier might be the raw material of its customer. Should the supplier provide low quality products or provide them late, there may be serious consequences for the customer's business.

Scientific approach

Statistical models should be used to measure and control quality performance and improvements. These quantitative models are exact and are essential in managing total quality.

Long-term commitment

Total quality is a way of living. It is a new paradigm for management which may only produce workable results after a long period. It is also a long-term commitment between the business enterprise, its suppliers, and its customers and clients. Synchronising all the activities of a business to achieve the standards specified for TQM in the ISO 9000 (ISO 9000 to 9004) is a big task which may take years.

Freedom through control

Employees are free to concentrate on the implementation of new production and other processes. Once these processes function properly, the employees can concentrate on the continuous improvement thereof.

Teamwork, education, and training

TQM works best when all the employees work as one team. Employees must take pride in their work and in their employer. It is also desirable that they form alliances with the employees of suppliers and consumers. This ensures a culture of team-work.

Employees need to be skilled to deliver high quality work and to be valuable members of the team. Education and training is therefore essential. This is one of the reasons why the South African government has a global policy on the development of workers' skills.

Continuous improvement

TQM cannot function properly in a static environment. The quality of products and services needs to be improved continually. Continuous improvement in the skills of employees and the development of better processes and environments form part of the TQM process.

Procurement cost management

Many business enterprises spend large amounts of money on the procurement of goods and services. Saving money through effective cost control has a lever effect: the net profit of the business increases. The best ways to reduce procurement costs are cost reduction programmes, speculative buying, forward buying, price change management, volume contracts, and stockless purchasing.[9]

Cost reduction programmes

Cost reduction programmes should form part of the business policies formulated by top management and are implemented by lower management. Top management must support these programmes. The results of the programmes must be controlled continuously to ensure that the goals are met. There are many methods for reducing costs. The most important ones are value analysis, supplier development, volume buying, reduction of waste, and standardisation.

Speculative buying

Speculative buying takes place when goods that are not meant for internal consumption, are purchased with the aim to resell them at a big profit at a later date. For example, a sales representative of a liquor distributor makes the following offer on a certain kind of brandy to liquor stores: The liquor stores get one free case for every five bought. The cost price of the brandy will increase the following month. This special offer ends one week before the price increase.

The management of a liquor store may decide to buy hundred boxes of brandy. When the price increases, a substantial profit can be made. The business enterprise will only do this speculative buying if the money to be made through the price increase and the special discount is substantially more than the additional warehousing and transport costs.

Forward buying

Forward buying is done when a business enterprise anticipates future shortages – which may lead to production interference and price increases – of its raw materials. A furniture manufacturer may be aware of a possible strike at the sawmill factory that provides it with timber. It may then decide to buy the timber needed for a specific period in advance. Businesses that use the 'just-in-time' system are more inclined to buy forward as a shortage of raw materials can have disastrous complications for them.

Price change management

Procurement managers should continuously challenge supplier price increases to ensure lower prices. Long-term and medium term contracts must be negotiated thoroughly. Suppliers must be informed of the negative effect that exorbitant price increases will have on the finances of their customers. Sales may also be affected negatively by price increases. Price increases can be limited through shorter delivery lead times, by using better technology, and by using inventory management models such as 'just-in-time' and Materials Requirements Planning (MRP).

Volume contracts

Volume contracts can limit price increases over a period. The different divisions or branches of a business enterprise can combine their purchases in order to reduce the purchase prices and administrative costs. The buyer can negotiate with the supplier for cumulative volume discounts on the successive purchases through the year. Businesses using JIT systems can also benefit from these discounts, despite the fact that they buy smaller volumes at a time.

In the case of non-cumulative discounts the price is based on the monetary value of each order. Suppliers can quote annually or they can fix the future prices through contracts. Bigger orders lead to lower prices as they bring about savings in the transport, administrative, and order costs.

Stockless purchasing

Stockless purchasing reduces materials-related costs such as transport, inventory, and administrative costs, as well as the purchase price per item. The business enterprise does not carry inventories of purchased materials. This is especially suited for frequently bought, low-priced materials of which the administrative and carrying costs are relatively high in comparison with the unit prices. Contracts are drawn up between the suppliers and their customers. A predetermined volume of items is purchased over a specified period. The items must be delivered as required by the purchaser for consumption, so that the carrying of stock by the purchaser is eliminated.

Integrated supply is an important part of stockless purchasing. A business enterprise may decide to order all its stationery from one supplier. That supplier must buy all the stationery from its suppliers and then send the acquired stationery to the customer. Better prices can often be negotiated with the single supplier than when dealing with many suppliers at the same time. In the case of the single supplier, the purchasing costs are reduced in time.

Conclusion

In this chapter, we discussed the strategic role of procurement and the nature of procurement management. We distinguished between the different kinds of goods. Managing suppliers effectively is an important task and we discussed the process of selecting suitable ones. The activities ensuring an efficient logistics channel were explored and the different forms of procurement cost management were identified and described.

Questions

1 Discuss how procurement provides access to the external markets of the business enterprise.
2 Discuss the relationship of procurement with the other management functions of a business enterprise.
3 Define procurement management in the context of logistics management.
4 Discuss the different management tasks of procurement management.
5 Describe the nature of the different categories of goods that can be purchased.
6 Discuss the characteristics of services that differentiate them from other products.
7 Define capital goods in your own words.
8 Define final products in your own words.
9 Discuss the process of selecting, evaluating, and choosing the right suppliers.
10 Discuss the activities that ensure an efficient logistics channel.
11 Discuss Total Quality Management (TQM) and pay attention to the strategic elements of total quality.
12 Explain the best ways of reducing procurement costs.

Notes

1 Lambert, D.M., Stock, J.R. and Ellram, L.M. 1998: 185.
2 Bentley, J. 1995: 100–103.
3 Hugo, W.M.J., Van Rooyen, D.C. and Badenhorst, J.A. 1997: 66–84.
4 Adendorff, S.A. and De Wit, P.W.C. 1997: 319–321.
5 W.M.J. Hugo et al 1997: 162–174.
6 See chapter six for more information on the JIT system.
7 See Chapter 12 for an in-depth study of transport management.
8 Goetsch, D.L. and Davis, S. 1995: 6.
9 Lambert, D.M. et al 1998: 365–371.

6 Inventory management

Contents

Learning Outcomes

After you have studied this chapter, you should be able to:

- discuss the reasons for holding inventory;
- discuss the impact of demand on inventory management;
- define and describe each functional class of inventories in your own words;
- explain what measurements you will use to measure inventory management effectiveness;
- discuss each of the different inventory carrying costs;
- discuss the different systems that can improve the flow of materials; and
- put any of the subjects discussed in this chapter in perspective.

Introduction

Inventories are present in all business enterprises. In manufacturing industries, certain minimum quantities are needed to ensure that the production process is not interrupted. In wholesale or resale enterprises, sufficient inventories are needed to ensure that no inventory shortages occur.

Management has the difficult task of calculating how many items of each kind of inventory should be in stock at any given moment. Inventories should be kept at minimum levels to prevent over-stocking and over-investment. Inventory appears in the income statement and in the balance sheet of the business. Too many dead and slow moving inventories lead to a higher closing stock figure, which increases the net profit and thus the income tax payable by the business. The balance sheet figure will also be inflated. This means that the value of the assets will be inflated (i.e. a higher value is placed on the assets than what they are really worth).

In this chapter, the following aspects of inventory management will receive attention:
- the reasons for holding inventory;
- impact of demand on inventory management;
- classification of inventories;
- measurements of inventory management effectiveness;
- inventory carrying costs; and
- systems to improve materials flow.

The terms inventory and stock are used interchangeably as they are synonymous.

The reasons for holding inventory

Holding inventory is important for the following reasons:
- achieving economies of scale;
- minimising uncertainties in the demand and order cycle;
- balancing supply and demand;
- ensuring stable employment; and
- buffering.

Achieving economies of scale

Holding inventory enables an enterprise to reap the benefits of economies of scale. An enterprise can sometimes buy raw materials or other merchandise in bulk and thus obtain large price discounts. One must realise, however, that the inventory costs will be higher because of the larger volumes of stock. Larger inventories should be kept only up to the point where the increase in inventory costs exceeds the discounts received on the purchases.

Transport costs are very high and they often form a significant part of the cost price of the inventory. An example of this is building sand, which is stockpiled by contractors on their building sites. The transportation cost is usually higher than the purchase price of the sand, depending on what distance the sand has to be transported. Many firms import raw materials and other inventories from abroad. The high transportation cost of this encourages firms to import their inventories in bulk by truck, train, or ship in order to get discounts.

Many of these inventories are not expensive to store. Crushed stone, which hardware shops often stockpile for builders, cannot be damaged. It can be stored on an open piece of land. It is only necessary to fence it in to prevent theft. Other inventories may be high in value and need to be stored in warehouses. This increases the inventory cost and may force the firm to reduce its inventories.

Minimising uncertainties in the demand and order cycle

When forecasting sales, enterprises should be prepared for future uncertainties. A rise in interest rates or in taxes may put a damper on sales. A decrease in these expenses may lead to an increase in demand, causing out-of-stock situations for the firm. The firm should be flexible in increasing or decreasing its inventory levels to keep up with future changes in demand.

The future supply of raw materials is also uncertain. Strikes put pressure on order cycles. A strike at a steel manufacturing plant can have a negative effect on the motor vehicle manufacturers if they have not acquired additional stocks to last them through the strike. A strike by truck drivers can bring an enterprise to a standstill if they have made no provision for such an event.

Balancing supply and demand

Many products are only available on a seasonal basis. Examples are agricultural products such as maize, wheat, sorghum, and potatoes. Maize is harvested during the winter months but demanded all year round. This is why co-operatives build large silos. They fill these silos during the harvesting months and maize can be supplied to customers through the year.

There is a substantial increase in the demand for rifles and ammunition during the winter months, when it is the hunting season. Gunsmiths build up extra stock before the high season in order to meet the demand during the busy months.

December is a very busy month for many business enterprises. Wholesalers and retailers should prepare for the holiday season by building inventories during the last months of the year. In this way, they ensure that they have sufficient stock to meet the extra demand for products such as toys and gifts.

Ensuring stable employment

It is not always feasible for a manufacturing enterprise to lay off workers after the high season or when the demand is low, and to then increase their worker component when the demand increases. Many skilled workers may be lost in this way, which will have a negative effect on the productivity. Training costs will also increase, because new workers will have to be trained.

During a long-term decrease in demand, however, employment levels cannot be sustained. The large inventory build-ups, which are detrimental to the business, may force an enterprise to reduce its workers.

Buffering

Inventories act as a buffer to ensure that products are available at all times. Out-of-stock situations result in lost sales.

The longer the distance between the store and its suppliers, the larger the buffer inventory that must be held, because the longer lead times complicate the holding of sufficient inventories.

Test yourself

6.1 Name the five most important reasons for holding inventory.

Impact of demand on inventory management

A fluctuation in demand affects the inventory levels of a business enterprise. Efficient inventory management entails ensuring that the enterprise has sufficient inventories to meet the demand during high seasons and that the inventory levels are lowered afterwards. Inventory management also involves keeping the surplus inventories as near to zero as possible. The 'just-in-time' system, which was discussed in the previous chapter, is often used for this purpose.

The forecast of future demand for physical products should be as accurate as possible to ensure minimum inventories. Demand forecasting is usually done by the marketing department as it has the closest contact with the customers. The other departments get the projected sales figures from the marketing department.

Demand forecasting

Demand forecasting entails estimating the future medium and long-term demand for products and services. Demand forecasting is done for a specific kind of product and service, in a particular area, for a certain period, and in the context of a particular marketing effort.

The production and operations manager uses long-term demand forecasting for aggregate planning. In the case of motor vehicle manufacturers, it is used for planning the long-term production capacity.[1] This means they plan for the total expected amount of vehicles to be manufactured, without taking the different models into consideration. These aggregate figures are then broken down into medium term figures that do take into account the expected manufacturing figures of the different models and colours of motor vehicles.

As mentioned before, demand forecasting is also important for inventory management. The inventory levels can only be kept low if the business can fairly accurately forecast the future demand for its products.

There is a number of demand forecasting techniques, which can be divided into three categories: qualitative techniques, time series analysis, and causal methods.[2] We describe the different techniques only briefly below, as the logistics manager does not have to be able to do the forecasting.

Qualitative forecasting techniques

Qualitative forecasting techniques are not based on mathematical calculations. The analysis of the data is mainly based on the subjective judgement of the forecaster. The forecaster's experience of the business and its sales therefore determines the accuracy level of the forecast to an extent. The more experience the forecaster has of the business, the more accurate the results should be.

A well-known qualitative technique is the Delphi technique. A number of experts in different fields gather around a table. A facilitator asks them numerous questions, both as a group and individually. In this brainstorming session, fairly accurate estimated figures can be deduced from the different viewpoints of the participants.

Time series analysis

Time series analysis entails manipulating mathematical data to forecast the demand for a pro-duct or service or a group of products or services. There are two kinds of times series:

multi-period pattern projections and single-period patternless projections.

Multi-period pattern projections

Multi-period pattern projections produce forecasts for more than one period (a week, a month, a quarter etc.). For example, the average monthly sales of the last six months can be used to forecast the demand for the next six months. The circumstances for the next six months must, however, be the same as those for the last six months – which means that no trend or seasonal component may be present in the demand pattern.

A second method is to take trends into account. The trend may be a one per cent increase per month. The mean of the previous month is then taken and that figure is increased by one per cent per month in order to forecast the sales for the following months.

Single-period patternless projections

Historical data is also used in this case, but just for the next single period. Only the most recent demand quantities are used. Examples of these projections are the moving average and exponential smoothing.

Causal methods

Causal methods aim to explain the reasons for changes in demand patterns. The object of these methods is to find a cause–effect relationship in the historical demand patterns in order to do a more accurate forecast of the demand. Causal techniques include regression analysis, multiple regression, and econometric models. These techniques are complicated but they give very accurate results.

Test yourself

6.2 The _____ department is responsible for doing the demand forecasting for a product.

6.3 Time series analysis may consist of _____ and _____ projections.

6.4 The object of the _____ methods of demand forecasting is to find a cause–effect relationship in the historical demand patterns.

Functional classification of inventories

Inventories can be classified as follows: cycle stock, safety or buffer stock, in-transit inventories, speculative stock, promotional stock, seasonal stock, and dead stock.[3]

Cycle stock

> The cycle stock is that portion of a business enterprise's inventory which gets depleted through normal sales or through the usage of these stocks in the production process. Cycle stock is replenished through the routine ordering process.

A grocery store which sells Coca-Cola orders a certain quantity of Coca-Cola once a week, twice a week, or once a fortnight – depending on the order cycle of the business. The quantity per order depends on the sales. During summer or the festive season, more units are ordered because of the bigger demand. The cycle stock should meet the demand for the product whenever the demand can be estimated fairly accurately and the lead time is certain.

In the case of raw materials, the cycle stock depends on the demand for the final product. This demand is reflected in the production volumes. A motor vehicle manufacturer should buy more steel when the demand for its motor vehicles increases. The steel is ordered on the usual, predetermined ordering dates. This ensures that the plant does not run out of stock.

Safety or buffer stock

> The safety or buffer stock protects the business enterprise against uncertainties in the demand rate and/or the length of the lead time. A business enterprise should hold safety stocks in addition to cycle stocks as a safety net in the event of unforeseen situations caused by, for example, late deliveries or a rapid change in demand.

A store which buys its inventories from suppliers who are situated 100 km away must keep more safety stock than a store which is situated near the suppliers. The lead time of the former business is longer and the business will not be able to respond immediately to a sudden change in demand. This might lead to out-of-stock situations, which can be harmful to the business.

In-transit inventories

> Inventory in transit are those inventories that are in the process of being transported to a buyer.

In-transit inventories are sometimes regarded as part of the inventories held – depending on the terms of the purchase. The result is an increase in the current assets on the balance sheet, which affects the net profit of the business.

In other cases, in-transit inventories are not regarded as part of the firm's assets up to the point where they are delivered at the premises. These inventories are therefore not reflected on the balance sheet.

In-transit inventories must be properly insured by the owner. It is important to choose the most appropriate form of transport to ensure safe and timely delivery.

Speculative stock

> Speculative stock is stock which protects the business enterprise against price increases and constrained availability.

Speculative stock is important for manufacturing companies that rely on the consistent delivery of raw materials and semi-finished goods. A manufacturer of television sets will buy more screens if there is a chance of a strike in the factories of the suppliers of the screens. These extra screens will ensure that the manufacturing plant does not run out of stock.

If the sales representative of a supplier informs a store that the price of a product will increase soon, they may order a large quantity of the specific product because they know that it can be sold at a higher price in the near future. Although the inventory costs increase in the short term, the store is ensured of higher profits in the medium term.

Promotional stock

When businesses have special promotions, they must be able to meet the higher demand. Motor vehicle tyre retailers have special promotions during the festive season when they sell various brands of tyres at special prices. They must be able to cope with an increase in demand on short notice to enhance the efficiency of such promotions.

Seasonal stock

Seasonal stock is the stock that a business enterprise keeps to accommodate the seasonal harvesting of products that will be sold throughout the year. It can also be the stock that a business accumulates before a season to accommodate the increase in demand during high season.

Fruit is harvested at certain times of the year. Fruit canneries must have sufficient storage capacity to store the fruit during high season. As the fruit is perishable, it is also necessary to use refrigerated storage facilities. This can be a costly exercise. The canning and distribution is not a seasonal bound operation, which means that production can be kept at the same levels throughout the year.

Doctors and pharmacists order large quantities of influenza vaccines and medicines against colds before winter to ensure that ample inventory is available when the cold weather causes outbreaks of these diseases.

Dead stock

Dead stock is stock that has no value for a business. It can be products that do not sell or raw materials, semi-finished products, and components that are not needed in the production process anymore.

Motor vehicle manufacturers are an example of businesses in which model changes and technological innovations are part and parcel of the industry. Many components become redundant as the years go by and eventually lie on the shelves as dead stock. The business can then try to send them to retailers who may need them, they can advertise them and sell them at reduced prices, or they can even sell them to scrap metal dealers for recycling purposes.

A retailer may find that a certain product is nearing its expiry date. The product can be sold at a reduced price or it can be handed out to regular customers as gifts.

It is important to remove dead stock from the existing stock as it inflates the balance sheet figures and has a detrimental effect on the net profit and the income tax payable by a business.

Test yourself

6.5 Name seven categories for classifying inventories.

Measuring the effectiveness of inventory management

Inventory should be managed in such a way that only the smallest possible quantity of each inventory item is in stock at all times. This minimises the investment in inventory. The lower the value of the closing stock, the lower will be the value of the net profit and the current assets in the balance sheet at the end of the year.[4]

There are many ways to measure the effectiveness of the inventory management system. The most important of these are the extent of consumer satisfaction, the extent of back-ordering and expediting, inventory turnover, inventory to sales ratio, and inventory to cost of sales ratio.

Extent of consumer satisfaction

Manufacturers, wholesalers, and retailers must ensure that they have sufficient amounts of inventory at all times to ensure customer satisfaction. Remember that a manufacturer's customer is the wholesaler – and the wholesaler's customer is the retailer, who sells to the final customer. Stock shortages at the wholesaler will also cause stock shortages at the retailer. This snowball effect can affect business negatively.

If the supplier runs out of stock, sales may be lost. Customers may adjust their needs and buy a different product, or buy from another supplier. Suppliers can make use of more efficient transportation methods to prevent damage to stock and thereby enhance customer satisfaction.

Extent of back-ordering and expediting

Increases in back-ordering and the expediting of orders are indications that something is wrong with the inventory management. This problem may damage the relationship with the suppliers. Back-ordering and expediting also involve higher overheads because of longer working hours, additional telephone calls etc.

The implementation of an ABC inventory system, which is discussed later in this chapter, can solve the problem.

Inventory turnover

The rate of the inventory turnover provides a measurement to assist the business enterprise in reducing its inventory to more manageable levels. The annual turnover must be divided by the value of the average inventory on hand. Take care that both these values are determined either at cost or at selling prices. A higher turnover rate means that the whole inventory is sold more times per year. This reduces the investment in inventory and it should ensure higher profits for the business. If the business generates a gross profit percentage of ten per cent every time the inventory is turned over, a turnover rate of seven times instead of five times per year translates into a substantial increase in the total gross profit. The reduction of inventories is very good for investment purposes but one must be careful that it does not lead to stock shortages.

Inventory to sales ratio

An increase in sales should lead to a decrease in inventory, as more products leave than enter the inventory. At times when sales are low, businesses should try to reduce their stocks. This will enhance their cash flow and will make the product items more manageable.

Gross profit to cost of sales ratio

The gross profit to cost of sales ratio is one of the most important ratios in the management of inventories.[6] This ratio represents the mark-up of the business's products – in other words it represents the percentage that is added to the cost price of its products to determine their selling price. This percentage should not change dramatically through the year. Should it fluctuate beyond the set limits from time to time, it means that there is something wrong with the stock control. For example, if this percentage is thirty per cent at the end of a specific month while it was on average thirty-five per cent per month for the previous twelve months, management must take immediate steps to find the reason for this discrepancy. One or a combination of the following factors may have caused it:
- Closing stock items were valued lower than the cost price of the items.

- Stock items were stolen.
- Products were sold at lower prices than the determined selling prices.
- Some of the stock items were not counted during the physical stock count.
- The calculations on the stock sheets were not done properly.

Use computers to ensure that the calculations are done correctly. Theoretical stock figures can be obtained from a computer at any time and these figures can be checked through physical stock counts.

Inventory carrying costs

The inventory carrying costs are all the costs involved in holding inventory. Management must decide whether it will be cheaper and more efficient to hold more or less inventory. Should they decide to hold more inventory, the carrying costs will be higher and the ordering costs will be lower. Less inventory will lead to higher ordering costs as more orders will be placed more frequently.

The most important inventory carrying costs are:

- capital costs;
- inventory risk costs;
- storage space costs; and
- inventory service costs.

Capital costs

The capital cost is the interest on the money used to buy the inventory, or the interest lost from other potential investments that were forgone to buy inventory. Capital costs are the so-called opportunity costs, a term indicating that an investment opportunity is not taken in order to allow, in this case, for an investment in inventory. The capital costs are usually calculated as a percentage of the total investment in inventory.

A wise entrepreneur will borrow money or use existing investments to buy inventory up to the point where the rate of return on the investment in inventory equals the rate of return available from alternative investments or the interest paid on the money borrowed. At times when prices are expected to increase, the enterprise should invest more money in inventory as it can generate higher profits out of the stock in future.

Inventory risk costs

Inventory risk costs are those costs associated with the obsolescence, shrinkage, deterioration, and damage of inventory. Dead stock is a common occurrence in the clothing industry where fashion changes from season to season. Clothing retailers can be stuck with thousands of stock items at the end of the year. These are sold at special prices to customers who place more value on low prices than on fashions.

Shrinkage, or theft, can be minimised by properly locking up small stock items or items of high value. Deterioration refers to the reduction of the quality of stock due to damage during the storage and the handling processes. Maize meal, for example, may be damaged by insects if it is stored over a long period.

Damage can also be caused by forklifts, leaking roofs, or fire. These damages can have a very negative impact on the inventory carrying costs.

Storage space costs

Inventory is usually stored in warehouses or in stores on the sites of business enterprises. The costs involved are calculated by multiplying the cost per cubic metre (i.e. the space occupied) with the amount of time the inventory is stored. Storage costs can also be measured in terms of weight. Should a business enterprise own its own warehouses, the depreciation on the buildings, machinery and equipment, air conditioning, lighting, and wages paid to the staff working in the warehouses will form part of the storage space costs. Should it lease the warehouses, the rent, instead of the depreciation, is part of the storage space costs.

Inventory service costs

Inventory service costs include costs such as insurance and taxes. Insurance is taken out to safeguard the enterprise against theft or other damages. Take care that the warehouses are properly protected by burglar proofing in order to minimise risk and to keep the insurance premiums low.

If the enterprise has branches in the US, a tax is imposed on the closing value of the inventory every year. In many states, it is levied on a monthly basis. It is important to store inventory in states where there is no or less tax.

Test yourself

6.7 Name the most important inventory carrying costs.

Systems to improve materials flow

The most common systems for improving materials flow are the "just-in-time", Materials Requirements Planning, Manufacturing Resource Planning, and Distribution Resource Planning systems.

"Just-in-time" (JIT)

"Just-in-time" has been discussed briefly in the previous chapter. The name implies that inventories are available exactly when a business enterprise needs them. JIT systems are used to keep the lead times of the inventories as short and consistent as possible and to eliminate waste. Business enterprises often use contracting to ensure safe, fast, and consistent service. With this system,

inventory levels are kept as low as possible, defects are minimised, quality is high (zero defect principle), and waste is eliminated.

Operation of a JIT system

A JIT system operates with two bins. One bin is used to fill the demand for the part, while the second bin supplies the part. Production cards (*kan* cards) are used to authorise the volume of units that must be manufactured. The requisition cards (*ban* cards) authorise the withdrawal of the components and/or materials from the feeding system. In the case of a motor vehicle factory, every component that is used in the manufacturing of the vehicles has its own *kan* and *ban* cards, i.e. its own *Kanban* system. For example, a box contains a steering wheel. When the steering wheel is taken from the box, a card is placed in the box. This card is then replaced by another steering wheel. This is a very simple system that can even operate without computers.

The *Andon* or light system is used in factories to inform the staff if production problems occur. A yellow light represents a small problem and a red light represents a big problem. These lights are placed in every section and can be seen by all the staff in the factory.

Differences between JIT systems and traditional systems

The following differences between the JIT systems and the traditional systems can be identified:

Short and consistent lead times
The JIT system uses short, consistent lead times to ensure timely deliveries of inventory items. This is why manufacturers of motor vehicles demand that suppliers establish their factories and/or warehouses within a certain radius from the production plants. Many of these motor vehicle manufacturers build warehouses, which are integrated into the production process, next to their manufacturing plants. Every item that is requested is invoiced by the supplier at the moment of delivery.

Shorter production runs

A successful JIT programme will ensure short production runs. This means that the set-up of the machines can be changed frequently to manufacture different kinds of products. A business does not have to use lengthy production runs anymore.

Lower inventory levels

JIT systems eliminate surplus inventory for the business enterprise and its suppliers. The final products are manufactured only according to demand (pull system). This leads to lower stock figures at the premises of both the business and the suppliers.

Long-term involvement with suppliers

Special attention is given to the selection and appointment of suppliers. The contract between the business enterprise and a supplier is the beginning of a long-term relationship. This relationship ensures that the supplier delivers to the satisfaction of the business enterprise. Doing anything that may jeopardise this contract might lead to the cancellation thereof and may cause bad publicity for the supplier.

Improved quality

An efficient JIT system ensures final products of a high quality. The system requires total quality management (TQM). Delivering low quality raw materials may also jeopardise the long-term relationship between the supplier and the business enterprise.

Materials Requirements Planning (MRP)

MRP is an inventory and scheduling system in which the supply of materials and components depends on the demand for the final product. If the demand for the final product decreases, the demand for the manufacturing materials also decreases.

A materials requirements planning system consists of a set of logically related procedures, rules for making decisions, and records. These procedures, rules, and records are designed to translate a master production schedule into time-phased net requirements. The coverage of each inventory item needed to implement this production schedule must be planned properly. The net requirements for each of these inventory items are determined and the system ensures that these items are received on time.[7]

The MRP system functions by first determining how much of the final product consumers wish to buy and when they require it. Sales budgets are important tools in determining the estimated future demand. The key elements used in the operation of a MRP system are the master production schedule, the bill of materials file, the inventory status file, the MRP programme, and the outputs and reports.

Master production schedule

Sales budgets form the basis of demand forecasts. These budgets, together with the actual orders received, are used to draft the master production schedule. This schedule specifies what quantities of the final products an enterprise has to manufacture in order to meet the demand.

Bill of materials file

The master production schedule has to be broken up to determine the exact amounts of components, parts, and sub-assemblies that are needed to manufacture the final products. The bill of materials specifies when each item must be received to ensure a constant flow in production. It also states how the different input items relate to each other and what role each item plays in the production of the final product. These input items all have different lead times and the bill of materials indicates how these different lead times need to be integrated to complete the final product successfully.

Inventory status file

The inventory status file documents the amount of inventory on hand. As the stock on hand must be deducted from the actual quantities needed, these inventory records assist the manufacturer in determining the quantities of materials and other items to be ordered. An accurate inventory status file will assist the bill of materials file in minimising the inventory on hand.

Materials Requirements Planning programme

The MRP programme involves transforming the information supplied by the master production schedule and the bill of materials into gross requirements for the individual input items. The inventories are then taken into account and the net requirements for the input items are determined. Orders are now placed for the needed input items to ensure a constant flow in the production of the final product. One needs to take the different lead times of the different input items into account when ordering to ensure that the items are received on time.

Outputs and reports

Management relies on reports and other outputs to ensure the efficiency of the logistics system. These reports are reviewed on a daily basis for various reasons: the exact quantities of products the business must order need to be determined, arrival dates of these input items must be rescheduled if necessary, certain orders may need to be expedited, and other orders may need to be cancelled if the demand for the final product diminishes.

Advantages of an MRP system

An MRP system offers the following advantages:
- An MRP system is the most suitable one for intermittent (as a result of changes in the product or process or both) production processes.
- It can help to identify potential supply chain disruptions and allows management to take the necessary steps to prevent these.

- Inventories are kept at a minimum. Safety stock is available but is also kept at the lowest levels possible.
- Production schedules contain information regarding both the actual and estimated demand.

Limitations of an MRP system

An MRP system has the following limitations:
- The system can become very complicated and might as a result not perform as expected.
- Attractive opportunities for bulk purchases or new suppliers cannot always be considered, resulting in the loss of quantity discounts and other price savings.
- It can only function with the assistance of a computer system which is able to handle a variety of functions. As such a system is very expensive, it is difficult to make changes once it is in operation. This might result in the costs of related materials activities (such as transport, materials handling, and storage) not being optimised.
- The fact that the master production schedule dictates the quantities and the rate of delivery may put strain on the suppliers. Unless suppliers are very reliable, out-of-stock situations may occur.
- An MRP system is complex and may take long (often several years) to implement. Extensive data preparation, training, and changes of the internal organisation must take place. It is a costly operation and requires a large capital investment.

Manufacturing Resource Planning (MRP II)

MRP II is an improvement on the MRP system. It enables a business enterprise to integrate the financial planning with the operations and logistics.

> MRP II is a comprehensive planning and control system for a business enterprise as a whole. It makes use of the master production schedule to

schedule tool changes, cash flow, machine and working hours, maintenance services, and other resources.[8]

MRP II functions as a closed loop. The traditional MRP method is used when planning the production tasks. Net requirements are determined in accordance with the estimated and actual demand for the final product. In this planning phase, MRP II brings the production, finance, and marketing departments of a business enterprise together. The other departments, such as Human Resources, Communications, Purchasing etc. get involved in the operations phase.

Characteristics of MRP II

The following characteristics of an MRP II system can be identified:
- It is a comprehensive business system. It draws from all the facets of the business enterprise, as well as all the departments and working documents, to supply management with the figures necessary to manage the business.
- All the different systems, such as the operations and financial systems, are integrated into one system.
- The MRP II system has a 'What if' facility, which means that different solutions to a problem can be generated.

Advantages of a MRP II system

The MRP II system offers the following advantages:
- It improves the productivity of capital, labour, purchasing, marketing, and production activities. It brings about lower inventory levels, less administration, less labour, better consumer service, better cash flow, and better co-ordination between the production and other departments.
- The working conditions of the staff improve as they have clear schedules that lead to less confusion and uncertainty.
- Lead times are reduced, which makes short response times possible. This increases adaptability.

Distribution Resource Planning (DRP)

DRP uses MRP principles to handle and store the final products that are to be delivered to the market place. DRP works from the customer demand backwards through the existing system to establish a realistic and economically justifiable system for handling the ordering of the final products. It involves developing a plan for distributing the final products from the different plants and warehouses to points where the customers can buy them. It uses the push approach, i.e. it operates by allocating final product inventories to meet estimated market place demands.

ABC analysis

The ABC analysis forces an enterprise to focus its attention on those inventory categories that constitute the largest part of the total inventory. This should ultimately improve the movement of all the categories of inventories.

The ABC analysis is based on Pareto's law, which involves the 80–20 rule. In inventory terms it means that a relatively small number of items (approximately twenty per cent) accounts for the largest part (approximately eighty per cent) of the total value of the inventory held. The ABC analysis can also be based on the turnover, utilisation, lead times, and cash flows of the different categories of inventories. A liquor store may find that beer, which constitutes approximately twenty per cent of its total inventory, is responsible for approximately eighty per cent of the total turnover.

Illustration of the ABC analysis

Figure 6.1 illustrates the ABC analysis as it applies to inventory management.

Figure 6.1 illustrates that twenty per cent of the items in stock constitute eighty per cent of the total value of the inventory. The items that make up this twenty per cent are referred to as the A items because of their high value. The B items are

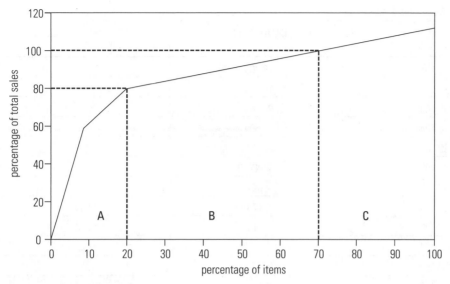

Figure 6.1 ABC Inventory Analysis

the fifty per cent of the items that account for approximately an additional fifteen per cent of the total value. The C items are the remaining stock items, which make up thirty per cent of the total amount of stock items and account for approximately five per cent of the total value.

Management must take care not to spend all their time and attention on the A items while ignoring the B and C items.

Practical example of the use of the ABC analysis

The components warehouse of a bus transportation company can be used as a practical example for explaining the ABC analysis. The components for the buses can be broadly categorised as follows:

Category A components

Examples of category A components are engines, gearboxes, and differentials. These items are highly priced and should be locked up in a safe, separate space where they can be easily controlled. When one of these items is withdrawn from the warehouse, another one is ordered to maintain stock levels.

Category B components

Examples of category B components are starters, alternators, and fuel injectors. These items are also expensive but not as expensive as the category A items. They are also replaced as they are used so that it is easy to assess how many of each should be kept in stock.

Category C components

Items such as bulbs, bolts, nuts, washers, and split pins form part of this category of components. They are inexpensive and reasonably high quantities are stored in accordance with the high demand. A minimum quantity for each of these items is determined and items are ordered as soon as the minimum levels are reached. These items can be controlled effectively with the use of computers.

The ABC analysis in practice

High Voltage Globes Limited distributes fifteen kinds of stock items to businesses throughout the country. The computer printout reproduced in Table 6.1, listing the different stock items, their quantities and selling prices, is submitted to you. The ABC analysis can be done as follows:

Step 1: Calculate the total price of each item

Table 6.1 Stock printout

STOCK ITEMS	QUANTITY	SELLING PRICE PER ITEM
GB 101	16 200	1,85
GB 102	10 000	7,50
GB 103	35 700	3,50
GB 104	32 600	11,50
GC 101	494 200	0,85
GC 102	1 000	22,00
GC 103	2 580	7,00
GC 104	2 470	44,50
GC 105	6 910	13,75
GD 101	2 391 305	0,23
GD 102	96 000	1,25
GD 103	3 115	17,67
GD 104	30	767,50
GD 105	9 400	7,45
GD 106	1 000	4,40

Table 6.2 Step 1: Calculate sales value and percentage of total demand

STOCK ITEMS	QUANTITY	SELLING PRICE PER ITEM	PRICE × QUANTITY = SALES VALUE	PERCENTAGE OF TOTAL DEMAND
GB 101	16 200	1,85	29 970	1,4
GB 102	10 000	7,50	75 000	3,6
GB 103	35 700	3,50	124 950	6,0
GB 104	32 600	11,50	374 900	17,9
GC 101	494 200	0,85	420 070	20,1
GC 102	1 000	22,00	22 000	1,1
GC 103	2 580	7,00	18 060	0,9
GC 104	2 470	44,50	109 915	5,3
GC 105	6 910	13,75	95 013	4,5
GD 101	2 391 305	0,23	550 000	26,3
GD 102	96 000	1,25	120 000	5,7
GD 103	3 115	17,67	55 042	2,6
GD 104	30	767,50	23 025	1,1
GD 105	9 400	7,45	70 030	3,3
GD 106	1 000	4,40	4 400	0,2
15 items			2 092 375	100,0

Table 6.3 Step 2: Stock classified as A, B, and C category items

STOCK ITEMS	PRICE X QUANTITY	PERCENTAGE OF THE TOTAL DEMAND
CATEGORY A ITEMS		
GD 101	550 000	26,3
GC 101	420 070	20,1
CATEGORY B ITEMS		
GB 105	374 900	17,9
GB 104	124 950	6,0
GD 102	120 000	5,7
GC 104	109 915	5,3
GC 105	95 013	4,5
GB 103	75 000	3,6
CATEGORY C ITEMS		
GD 105	70 030	3,3
GD 103	55 042	2,6
GB 101	29 970	1,4
GD 104	23 025	1,1
GC 102	22 000	1,1
GC 103	18 060	0,9
GD 106	4 400	0,2
15 items	2 092 375	100,0

and determine what percentage of the total demand each item constitutes (see Table 6.2.).

Step 2: Classify items as A, B, and C category items respectively (see table Table 6.3).

Category A items = 13 % of 15 items
= 46,4 % of R2 092 375

Category B items = 40 % of 15 items
= 43 % of R2 092 375

Category C items = 47 % of 15 items
= 10,6 % of R2 092 375

Conclusion

This chapter dealt with various aspects of inventory management. We explored the reasons for holding inventory and the impact of demand on inventory management. The functional classification of inventories was described to show the differences between the various kinds of stock. We discussed the variuos measurements as well as the importance of inventory management effectiveness. The various inventory carrying costs and the systems to improve materials flow were explained.

Questions

1 Discuss the reasons for holding inventory.
2 Explain the impact of demand on inventory management.
3 Classify inventories according to their different functions and discuss each classification.

4 Discuss the various methods of measuring inventory management effectiveness.
5 Name and discuss the various inventory carrying costs.
6 Discuss the various systems that can be used to improve materials flow.

Notes

1 Adendorff, S.A. and De Wit, P.W.C. 1997: 97.
2 Adendorff, S.A. and De Wit, P.W.C. 1997: 98–104.
3 Coyle, J.J., Bardi, E.J. and Langley, C.J. (Jr) 1996: 167.
4 See Chapter 17.
5 Coyle, J.J., Bardi, E.J. and Langley, C.J. (Jr) 1996: 181–184.
6 See Chapter 17 for the calculation of the gross and net profits.
7 Coyle, J.J., Bardi, E.J. and Langley, C.J. (Jr) 1996: 92.
8 Schonberger, R.J. and Knod, E.M. 1992: 909.

Contents

Learning Outcomes

After you have studied this chapter, you should be able to:

- identify the most important types of equipment that are encountered in logistics;
- understand the advantages and disadvantages of each type of equipment;
- evaluate and make the correct choice of equipment for a specific need; and
- be conversant with the principles of the operation of the equipment in the logistics chain.

Introduction

This chapter introduces the various types of equipment that a logistics professional may encounter in the facilities within a logistics chain. Only the broad types of equipment are presented, but there are many variations of equipment available from different manufacturers. These variations need to be investigated once the requirements for the equipment have been determined. This can be done by exploring the information provided by the various manufacturers. A number of Internet sites have been included at the end of this chapter for further reference.

You will need to be familiar with the following definitions:

> Picking or order picking is the process of assembling items from a storage location or locations in response to an order.

> The pick face is the location from where orders that require less than full pallets are taken or picked. Pick faces are designed to make goods readily available to the picker and are therefore located where access is simple and easy (such as floor level).

Selection of equipment

The selection criteria for equipment are discussed in the various sections in this chapter. When choosing equipment, one should always have a clear understanding of the needs of the facility. The needs should be expressed in terms of simple criteria with measurable values. The equipment may, for instance, need to be able to lift two tons or travel at 30 km/h. Each criterion must be assigned a priority, i.e. one must decide whether the need is:

+ a prerequisite;
+ required but not a prerequisite; or
+ liked but not required.

While different or even additional criteria can be used, it is important to prioritise them when doing all assessments. The market can be tested against these needs and priorities. Suppliers can be rated according to their compliance with the criteria. Only those who satisfy the 'prerequisite' criteria are considered. When there are suppliers who satisfy both the 'prerequisite' and 'required' criteria, the impact of the 'liked' criteria is used to make the final decision. This method is by far the best to ensure the most appropriate equipment is obtained from the best supplier. Gut feel or choices made solely on suppliers' recommendations or because the 'new' equipment has a high profile are rarely as successful. A logistics professional must analyse purchases with the aid of measurable criteria.

Risk of equipment purchases

A business enterprise does not purchase equipment every day. Identifying needs and obtaining the appropriate equipment is a project. The risks of each such project reach a peak on two occasions. The first peak is when the decision is made to purchase equipment. This decision commits the facility to a specific technology and supplier and to spending a large amount of money. If the equipment is not suited for the facility, a large amount of time, effort, and expense will have been wasted. The second peak is when the equipment is tested against the purchasing criteria and accepted. The testing must be done and recorded in detail to ensure it performs to satisfaction. Failure to do so may result in the facility paying money to modify or replace the equipment, or working with inappropriate equipment that makes the operation inefficient.

> *Test yourself*
>
> 7.1 The _____ of every project reach a peak on _____ occasions.

Storage methods for small items

The smaller products in many industries cannot be stored on or picked from a pallet. The range of products that fit into this category includes such diverse items as boxes of toothpaste, torch batteries, electronic components, and even mechanical parts that are small or fragile. For these items, different forms of storage, such as shelves and bins, are needed.

Shelving

Smaller products can be arranged on shelving (Figure 7.1), which provides ample small storage space that makes access to the product easy. The size of the space created by shelves can be adjusted simply and quickly to suit the products. With careful planning, the box in which the product is transported can be placed onto the shelf and used as the storage container. This simplifies the storage of the product and makes it unnecessary to unpack boxes.

Because the products stored in shelves are generally lighter, the shelves can be multi-tiered (high rise shelving, as it is sometimes called, can be up to 15 m high) or have long spans to create more storage space.

Bins

Smaller items can be stored in small containers called bins (Figure 7.2). These containers are designed so products can be stored safely and accessed easily for counting and picking. Bins are

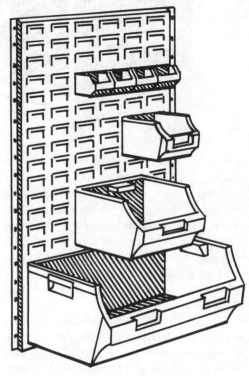

Figure 7.2 Bins

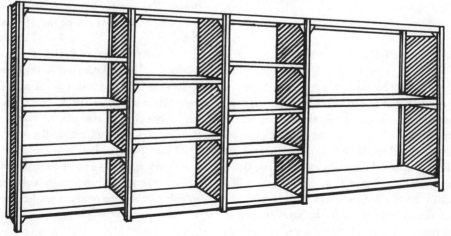

Figure 7.1 Shelving

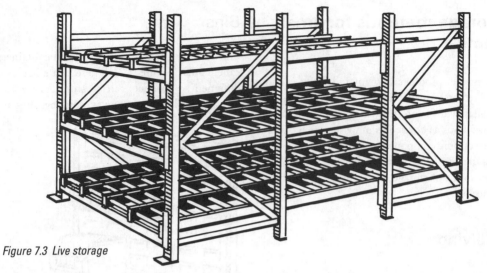

Figure 7.3 Live storage

often colour coded to make it easier to identify products. Bins vary in shape and size, and are made from a variety of materials, although mostly from plastic. These plastic bins are generally lightweight, easy to stack and transport, robust, and durable. The more common bins range in size from units with a face that is 30 to 40 mm wide and high to units that are 500 mm wide and 400 mm high[2] and have a capacity of around 50 000 cm^3.

The bins may be inserted into shelves or hung from a vertical back panel. These panels are made with special supports that allow the bins to hang anywhere on the panel. The panel can thus be fitted with the size and number of bins suitable for storage and picking.

Live storage

Some products have a fast turnover, or require a larger stockholding or strict stock rotation. If these products are in boxes or containers, they can be stored effectively in live storage systems (Figure 7.3). The shelves of live storage systems are inclined and fitted with wheels or rollers. Boxes placed into the live storage move down the rollers towards the front of the racks until they rest on boxes already in the racks. As the boxes can only be removed in the sequence they are inserted into the live racking, stock rotation is ensured. The density

of storage is also higher than that of basic shelving.

This storage method is particularly suitable for perishable items in containers, pharmaceutical products, and high movement products.

Test yourself

7.2 Discuss which items are particularly suited for live storage.

Mobile shelving

Shelving requires aisles for accessing goods. These aisles occupy space, which reduces the density of storage. One way to increase the density of storage is to use shelves that can be moved, manually or powered, on rails (Figure 7.4). The shelves are moved apart to create the aisle from which the product can be picked. In this way, a number of shelves can be fitted into a much smaller area. If the shelves are powered and are operated by remote control, the aisle can be created while the picker moves from one pick to the next.

This storage method is suitable for products that do not need to be accessed frequently. As the frequency of access increases, the delay in opening an aisle to reach the products renders this method less efficient.

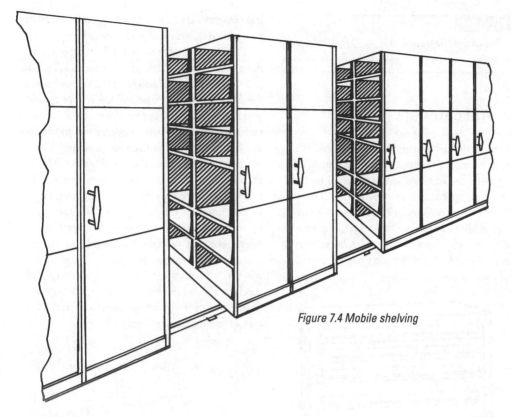

Figure 7.4 Mobile shelving

Carousels

Small items are difficult to store and pick. When using bins or shelves, the picker continually needs to get up and walk to the shelves. This is time-consuming and increases the risk of fatigue and boredom, so that identification of the items may become a problem. A carousel (Figure 7.5) may be a good solution to these problems. It is a series of trays that are connected to a moving mechanism. The trays may be divided into sections to produce a row of storage locations within each tray. These multiple compartments are housed in a cabinet. As a particular item is required, the trays are rotated until the appropriate tray is available through a working or access slot. The rotation may be done automatically or manually.

The carousel represents a high density storage facility for small items. As the cabinet can be locked, it also provides excellent security for expensive items.

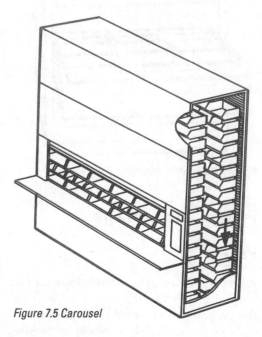

Figure 7.5 Carousel

Test yourself

7.3 The carousel represents a _____ storage facility.

Storage cabinets

Small to medium-sized goods can be stored effectively in cabinets fitted with drawers (Figure 7.6). The drawers are arranged as in a filing cabinet and may have compartments of various sizes. The system increases storage density and allows for secure storage as the drawers can be locked. The size of these units may be extended vertically to give more drawers. Access is limited to one drawer at a time in an operating area.

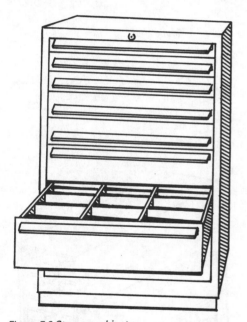

Figure 7.6 Storage cabinets

Pallets and storage

Pallets

Pallets provide a simple and efficient means of consolidating goods into a unit on a single base that can be moved and stored effectively. Products can often not be handled individually by mechanical equipment, but as a consolidated unit they can be handled quickly and with common equipment.

The design and materials of pallets vary. The most basic pallet is made of wood and is 1,2 m long and 1 m wide, with a height of 0,2 m, as shown in the figure below. The ease and low cost of the construction make this a popular form of pallet. Wood pallets get damaged with continual use and are not as robust as those made from plastic or metal. These are more durable than the wood pallets. Metal is the more durable, but is heavy to manoeuvre and transport. Plastic is probably the best compromise, as it is reasonably lightweight. Goods are stacked on the pallets up to the height of approximately 1,6 m. For each product, a standard configuration of boxes is chosen so that one can see at a glance whether all pallets carry the same quantity of the product. The boxes chosen are generally suitable to fill the base of the pallet and then to be stacked one on top of another (see Figure 7.7).

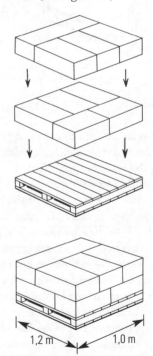

1,2 m   1,0 m

Figure 7.7 Stacking goods on a pallet

Test yourself

7.4 The most basic pallets are _____ m long and _____ m wide.

Block stacking

Boxes can be stacked one on top of another. The weight of the box and the contents, as well as the strength of the box, determines the height to which the boxes can be stacked. Pallets can also be stacked in this way, but only when the boxes are strong enough to support the weight. The weight generally limits this stack to two pallets high.

General racks

Racks provide access to goods from the front and allow one to stack higher than with block stacking. Whereas the goods support the stack in the block stacking method, here the structure of racks supports the goods. Racks are a reasonably dense way of storing goods. However, the aisles that allow access to the goods take up a significant amount of floor area. In the following sections we discuss various configurations of racks which increase the density of storage at the expense of the unlimited access which static storage racks provide.

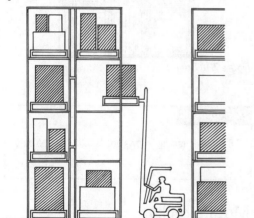

Figure 7.8 Racks with handling equipment

Static storage racks

Storage racks (Figure 7.8) can be erected and altered with relative ease and speed. Two rows of racks are usually assembled back to back. This allows access only to the front of each row, but

reduces the aisle space, thereby increasing the storage density. The height of racks may vary, but practical considerations limit it to approximately 9 m (or six pallets).

This type of rack is particularly useful when the storage density of palletised goods needs to be improved. The bottom shelves of racks are ideal for pick faces. The reach stackers needed for storage or removal are relatively inexpensive, so capital costs are low.

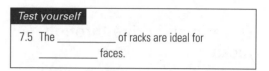

Narrow aisle racks

As the name implies, these racks have a much narrower aisle than general static racks. Narrow aisle racks (Figure 7.9) increase storage density, while still allowing access to all the goods. Narrow aisle trucks

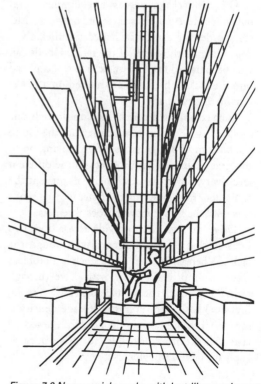

Figure 7.9 Narrow aisle racks with handling equipment

or stacker cranes service the racking. Because the aisle is too narrow for the equipment to turn, the truck or crane moves laterally along the aisle. To prevent the aisle being blocked, pallets are placed in, or collected from, an area outside the aisle. A narrow aisle truck can reach up to 12 m high. This specialised piece of equipment is much more expensive than a reach stacker and runs on rails. It also requires more rigid and sturdy racks. A stacker crane is used to reach higher than 12 m.

Drive-in and drive-through racks

To increase the density of storage, racks can be placed three or more deep. These racks have side supports for pallets that are inserted into the racks with a fork-lift or similar equipment. Drive-in and drive-through racks (Figure 7.10) do not cost more than general racks, but access to the goods is limited.

Drive-in racks give access to equipment from only one side. As there is therefore only one aisle, storage density can be increased significantly – depending on the depth of the racks. Goods can only be extracted from the same side it was placed into the racks. The goods are rotated on a LIFO (last in, first out) basis.

Each column of the racks should store only one product, as pickers remove goods from the top to the bottom of one column before moving on to the next column. If the products on the different levels vary, slower moving stock will prevent the equipment from accessing the faster moving products until the slower moving stock is removed.

Drive-through racks provide access from two sides so that equipment can drive through the racks. Whereas the rotation of stock is a problem when using drive-in racks, with drive-through racks the goods can be rotated on a FIFO (first in, first out) basis. However, the storage density is somewhat reduced due to the need for the second aisle. All the other principles for drive-in racks apply for drive-through racks.

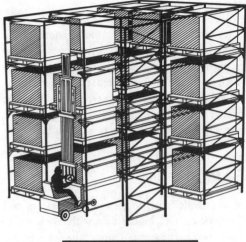

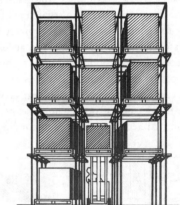

Figure 7.10 Drive-in racks

Test yourself

7.6 Drive-in racking allows goods to be rotated on a _____ basis.

Mobile racks

Two rows of racks are on a solid base that moves on rails in one direction (see Figure 7.11). There should be space for one or more aisles between the mobile racks, so that the racks can move to open an aisle between any two racks. This can be automatically controlled with a remote control on equipment travelling towards the racking. The aisle provides access that is restricted only when

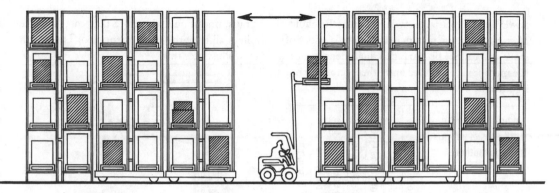

Figure 7.11 Mobile racks

two pieces of equipment concurrently require access to seperate racks. This can be overcome by introducing two aisles. Mobile racks are not suitable for pick faces. Rotation of stock is feasible. The storage density increases significantly as the number of aisles are reduced, but the capital costs are high.

Live storage racks

The racks are fitted with rollers in the slots where the pallets are inserted (see Figure 7.12). The rollers are inclined from the front to the back so that the weight of the pallet carries it from one side to the other. Access is needed on both sides, necessitating two aisles. The advantage is that the pallets are always presented to one (the lower) side of the rack. Each level – and not each column as per drive-in racking – should contain one product. Goods are available on a very strict FIFO basis so

that the lower side is used as a pick face. Live storage racks are very useful where particular lines require increased storage density, or where there is a need for strict stock rotation. The moderate capital cost and standard handling equipment make them an attractive addition to standard racks.

Test yourself

7.7 Live storage provides increased _____ and allows for strict stock _____ on a _____ basis.

Comparison of racks

A number of factors may influence the choice of the storage for palletised goods. These factors are listed below with a rating of 1 to 4, where 1 is the lowest and 4 is the highest. In any installation,

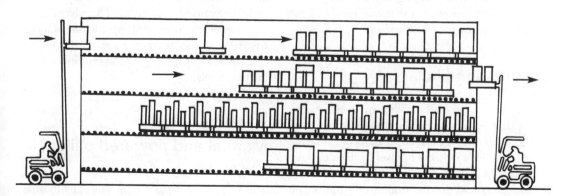

Figure 7.12 Live storage racks

however, other variables will influence the choice of storage. If, for instance, a facility is short of space and cannot be expanded, high density storage methods are required and other factors are not significant.

Comparison of the attributes of various storage methods ranking: 1 is the lowest, 4 the highest	capital cost	storage density	rotation of goods FIFO	access to all goods	handling equipment cost	used for pick face	speed of throughput
block stacking	1	3	1	1	1	2	3
racks	2	2	2	4	2	4	3
narrow aisle racks	3	3	2	3	4	1	3
drive-in racks	3	3	3	2	2		2
mobile racks	4	4	2	3	2		2
live racks	3	4	4	1	2	2	2

Table 7.1: Comparison of storage methods

Note: The ranking is relative to the other methods of storage compared in the table.

Hanging rail systems

Certain goods are best moved on a rail or a suspension system. The prime example of this is clothing, but some food products may also be moved in this way. The following description is orientated towards clothing, but the principles are applicable to any product that must be moved and stored in a hanging configuration.

Hanging rails

This is a rail on which trolleys move (see Figure 7.13). It contains equipment to push trolleys up an incline or control them down an incline. The rail may also have switches to divert trolleys to other rails. The rail is supported from one side and underneath, so that the trolleys only operate on one side of the rail. When designing the merging

of rails, one should therefore take care that the trolleys all have the same orientation. The sketch below illustrates this.

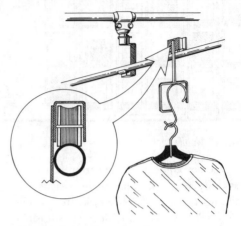

Figure 7.13 A trolley on a rail

Trolleys

Trolleys (Figure 7.13) can be used for one or many garments. In automated facilities, the trolleys have bar codes and the garment or garments are scanned and attached to a specific trolley. In this way, the trolley is known to contain particular garments. The trolleys also have designated storage areas. The retrieval can thus be done automatically. Large throughput facilities can be very efficient and effective with this type of system.

Manual facilities often use the trolleys for a number of similar garments that must be moved quickly and efficiently from a truck into storage and from storage into trucks. The advantage is rapid movement, without lifting, and ease of identification. It also allows the use of the vertical space in a facility, as the garments can be stored on multiple levels.

Moving loads
Manual and powered pallet trucks

The most common piece of equipment for moving pallets quickly is the pallet truck (Figure 7.14), sometimes also called a fork-lift truck or even a pallet taxi. Two forks, which fit into the pallet base, are attached to it. The forks can be raised to lift the load up to approximately 120 mm above the floor. The optimal load is 1 600 kg to 2 000 kg.

The operator supplies the lift effort for the manual truck. A DC power battery is used for powered trucks. Because the operator may ride on the pallet truck, his or her effort and risk of fatigue are reduced. The choice of equipment is primarily based on the speed at which the pallet needs to be moved. The speed of the manual pallet truck depends on the walking speed of the operator. The powered pallet truck can attain speeds of up to 10 km/h (or 3 m/s).

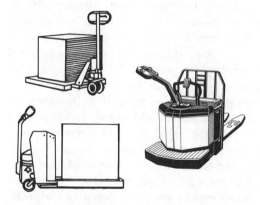

Figure 7.14 *Manual and powered pallet trucks*

Fork-lift or counterbalance truck

The fork-lift or counterbalance truck (so called because the load is raised on one side of the truck and counterbalanced by a fixed weight in the truck) is used for lifting pallets and moving them at a high speed. This piece of equipment (see Figure 7.15) can attain speeds of up to 15 km/h.[1] It can lift pallets to a height of up to 3,5 m, and with special masts this height can be extended to approximately 5 m.[1] These trucks can lift loads that are significantly heavier than two tons.[3] They often have long forks to move two pallets at a time. This saves time and ensures that the services of both the equipment and the operator are

utilised more efficiently – especially if the pallets need to be moved far.

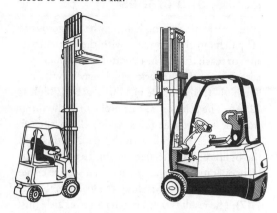

Figure 7.15 *Fork-lift or counterbalance truck*

Reach trucks

Reach trucks (Figure 7.16) are designed to perform the specialised tasks of lifting and lowering pallets with greater ease and speed than counter-balanced trucks. The vision through the lifting mast is improved to increase the ease with which pallets are handled while elevated. Nowadays, there is very little variation in the more advanced units where the best functions – lifting power and speed – are combined. These multi-purpose units are expensive, but the versatility is often worth the additional cost.

Figure 7.16 *Reach truck*

Turret trucks, narrow aisle trucks, and cranes

When racks are very high, it may be dangerous to lift pallets to the top racks with the counterbalance or reach truck. The operator on the floor cannot see up to the top rack, which may be well over 6 m high. (Narrow aisle racking may be as high as 12 m.)[1] The solution to this problem is the turret truck or narrow aisle truck, which allows the cab for the operator to lift with the load. In this way, the operator has excellent visibility of the complete operation. The equipment can service either side of the aisle by swivelling the load (see Figure 7.17). The result is that a much narrower aisle (just larger than the pallet) is needed than when general purpose fork-lift or reach trucks are utilised. The narrow aisle equipment requires very smooth and level floors to maintain stability. The turret truck is ideally suited for long, high racks with narrow aisles. Movement can be sped up by using rails or guide wires that automatically centre the truck in the aisle.

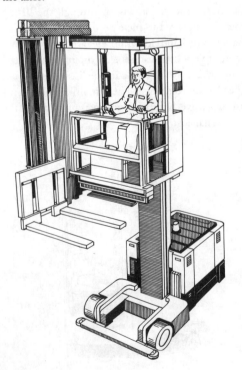

Figure 7.17 Turret truck

Turret trucks running on rails or overhead cranes also service racks higher than 12 m. These racks often support the roof of the building and are built to be an integral part of the facility. This is more common in Europe, where the high volumes and high land costs make such high racks economically viable.

Moving and sorting

Mechanical transport systems move goods without operator intervention. In this way, products can be sorted and the mass and the dimensions determined without touching the goods.

When choosing equipment, the level of sophistication needed must be determined carefully. Some large facilities in which high volumes of goods are moved and stored are fully automated and computer controlled. This is rare in the global economy; and in economies in transition, volumes are generally too low to justify the investment. In these countries, unfavourable exchange rates increase the capital cost and the cost of replacement parts for sophisticated technology.

The combined effects of very high land costs, high throughputs, and the availability of skilled labour explain why many European companies opt for this type of operation. American operations generally do not adopt such sophisticated technology. The Federal Express main hub in Memphis, for example, handles approximately two million parcels between 22:00 and 01:30 every night. While mechanical handling equipment is present, approximately 8 000 employees scan and (in a limited area) sort parcels during these hours. The lower cost of land and quality of labour allow this facility to operate efficiently and effectively with such a system.

Conveyors: belt and roller bed

The continuous movement of boxes or even pallets down a specific route lends itself to the use of mechanical transport methods such as belt conveyors and roller bed conveyors (Figure 7.18).

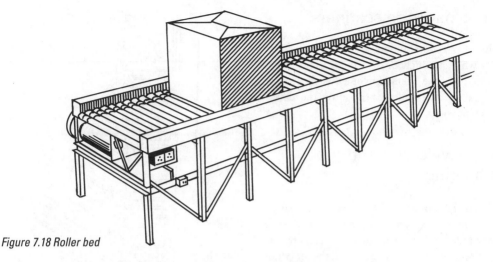

Figure 7.18 Roller bed

Belt conveyers are used where the goods need to move in straight lines, upwards, or downwards; and when speed varies.

Roller beds are a series of rollers that turn in one direction and consequently move the goods. With these conveyors, goods can be diverted by installing bends or equipment between the rollers. The disadvantages are that goods may slip on the rollers and that goods may move at different speeds.

Accelerator belts

Goods that must be sorted, measured, or massed, need to be spaced in order to allow the operator to make accurate measurements. To obtain a specific minimum distance between goods on a conveyer without slowing the goods throughput, an acceleration belt is used. The goods are first fed onto the feeding belt. The acceleration belt, which moves faster than the feeding belt, catches the first box and accelerates it to a higher speed than that of the feeding belt. The second box moves at the slower speed of the feeding belt until the acceleration belt catches it. The first box is therefore a specific distance – proportional to the difference in speed between the two belts – ahead of the second box. The throughput remains stable because the faster speed of the accelerator belt compensates for the space introduced between the boxes.

Test yourself

7.8 An accelerator belt produces a specific _____ between boxes.

Merge systems

Where two or more conveyors feed into one conveyor, a merge occurs (Figure 7.19). The two conveyors cannot feed onto the merge conveyor simultaneously, as the boxes would fall off the conveyor or jam it. To merge successfully, one of the conveyors must be able to delay the feeding in order to take turns with the other conveyor.

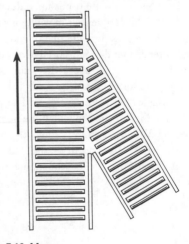

Figure 7.19 Merge

In-line bar code scanners

In-line bar code scanners are able to read bar codes while products pass through the scanner, irrespective of the orientation of either the item or the bar code. This facilitates the automatic identification of goods.

In-line weighing and measuring

Scales, which can accurately measure the weight of an item passing over them, can be fitted to the belt or roller bed. Provided that the belt is travelling at a known and constant speed, the length of the item can be determined by measuring for how long the item blocks a beam. Beams reflected from the item can also determine its height, width, and depth.

Diverters and sorters

Items can be sorted by diverting them from one path onto another (see Figure 7.20). Light items that travel at slow speed can be sorted with an arm which swings across the line and diverts the item to the new path. In some installations, the arm does not move the item, but it moves blocks on the side of the conveyor into a 45° angle across the conveyor. The item is then pushed sideways by these blocks. This is a gentler move than striking an arm which moves into the line of travel. This type of sorter cannot do high-speed diversions.

An alternative is to use a diversion system called a pop-up sorter. A pop-up sorter has wheels that are installed between the rollers. The wheels are driven in the direction to which the item must be diverted. When the item is above the pop-up sorter, the wheels rise and drive the item in the required direction – hence the name pop-up sorter.

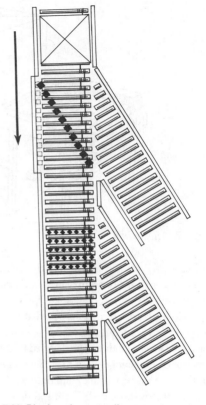

Figure 7.20 Block and pop-up diverters

Containers

The ability to consolidate a load into a container (Figure 7.21) which can be shipped anywhere in the world is probably the greatest advance the shipping industry has seen in the last fifty years. Cargo – from furniture to motor vehicles to rolls of paper – is now transported around the world in a standard, economical way. Containers come in two sizes: 20 feet (approximately 6 m) long and 40 feet (approximately 12 m) long. All containers can be lifted either from the four corners of the container or from the base. This makes it possible to use additional equipment to cope with heavy loads – a 20 feet container can carry a load of approximately 22,5 tons. Table 7.2 below provides the standard sizes, volumes, and payload weights for common containers.

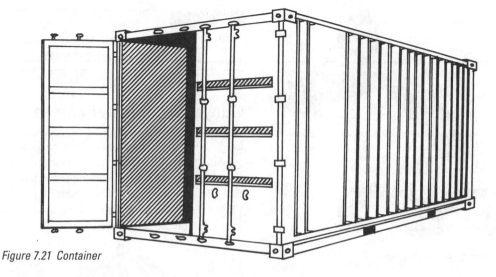

Figure 7.21 Container

Approximate container sizes and weights

Container	Measurement	20 feet	40 feet
Length	m	5,9	12
Width	m	2,3	2,3
Height	m	2,4	2,4
Cubic capacity	m³	33	67
Tare weight	tons	1,9	3,1
Payload weight	tons	22,5	27,4

Table 7.2

Test yourself

7.9 Containers come in two sizes: _____ m long and _____ m long.

Spreaders and twistlocks

An attachment called a spreader is used to connect containers with other equipment. This attachment spreads the load from the mast of the reach stacker to the couplings at the four corners of the container. A twistlock (Figure 7.22) couples the spreader with the container. This device on the spreader extends a rectangular pad through a matching rectangular hole in the container structure. The rectangular pad is then twisted 90° so that it connects with the structure of the container and is locked in position. It is easy and quick to engage or disengage.

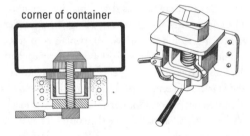

Figure 7.22 Twistlock

Reach stackers

The ordinary reach stacker (Figure 7.23) can handle single 20 feet containers. Larger ones can handle 40 feet or even two 20 feet containers. Reach stackers can stack containers up to six high. It can also place a container in a rear stack by lifting it over another container. The reach stacker lifts the container via a spreader attached to the top of the container.

Straddle carriers

A straddle carrier (Figure 7.24) is a special type of mobile crane which has been developed for con-

Figure 7.23 Reach stacker

tainers. The larger version is also called a straddle crane. This device carries the container within the structure of the crane, thus straddling the container. The carrier lifts the container using the spreader and twistlocks and then moves the container to other locations. The straddle carrier has wheels on each of the four corners of its frame. It is a versatile mover and stacker of containers. The straddling allows it to move containers at higher speeds than the reach stacker, which has to balance the container against a counterweight while moving. The limitation of the straddle carrier is that containers need to be stacked in such a way that the frame of the carrier can move over the container stack, so that an aisle is needed between every stack.

Figure 7.24 Straddle carrier

Test yourself

7.10   The straddle carrier can move the container _____ than a reach stacker can.

Quayside container cranes

Large container cranes situated on rails on the quayside generally handle the movement of containers onto and off ships. The cranes can traverse along the rails to service different parts of the ship. They lift the containers from the quayside and stack them on the ship, and vice versa.

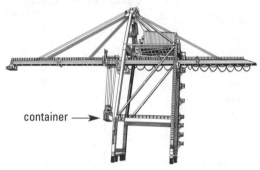

container →

Figure 7.25 Quayside container crane.

Bar codes and scanners

Speed and accuracy are fundamental requirements for the successful operation of many of the tasks in any logistics chain. Identifying a particular item or box is one such task. One way of facilitating identification is to write a product number or code in large letters on the packaging. This, however, requires that a person compares the code on the paperwork with that on the box. This is not only time-consuming, but also leaves room for errors.

Bar codes

Bar codes were designed to eliminate the problems mentioned above. They provide a fast, easy, and accurate method of reading information. There are two types of bar codes: one-dimensional and two-dimensional.

One-dimensional bar codes

A one-dimensional bar code is a series of bars and spaces of varying width. These bars and spaces depict a series of numbers or characters. The characters can be read with a special reader which translates the bars and spaces into the number they depict. This is an extremely accurate method of identification, as the reader scans the bar code numerous times in one second to check that it knows all the characters and that it recognises the number.

The one-dimensional bar code is commonly used to identify items in stores and in industry in one of two ways. The first is as a simple identification code which is unique to the product. In essence, the bar code number is used to find the appropriate records in a computer system. When the code is read, the system uses this unique identification number to look up the information relating to the product. This is very similar to a person's personal identification number: The number itself has no meaning, but it is assigned to a single person and allows institutions to check records, issue licences, and so on.

The second way of using a one-dimensional bar code is to combine a number of ID codes into a single bar code. This is sometimes called an intelligent bar code. It is used where additional information is required to identify individual products and their associated processes. This type of bar code could typically be used to identify the product code, the order number, and a delivery address code. These three ID codes are combined into a bar code. When it is read, the matching records become available for printing or for instructions to the operations.

Two-dimensional

The second type of bar code is two-dimensional. The two-dimensional bar code is a high-density non-linear code. It consists of dark areas and white spaces in a complex pattern. A substantial amount of information can be contained in the code.

The two-dimensional bar codes in driver's licenses contain all the information available about the license and the holder. There is sufficient information capacity in the code to encode personal details, license details, a summary of the driving record, and even a photograph.[4] This can all be recorded in a space approximately 75 mm by 20 mm big.

Figure 7.26 One- and two-dimensional bar codes

Scanners

The scanner system comprises a scanner and associated decoder, as well as the computing memory or storage space to record the scanned information.

The bar code is read as follows: A focused light sweeps across the bar code. The light is either absorbed or reflected, depending on whether it passes over a dark bar or a white space. The scanner measures this light and translates it into the corresponding information. The light sweeps across the bar code a number of times to see if there are any discrepancies in the repeated readings. This is done to prevent reading errors. Each sweep is done in fractions of a second so that the human eye just sees a beam of light which covers the bar code for an instant.

The beam or light from the scanner needs to cover the bar code at each sweep. The length of the bar code is increased if the code is long or if it will need to be read from a distance. The height of the bars carries no information. The bars simply need to be high enough for the scanner to read it without the operator having to align the bar code and the scanner perfectly.

There are three types of scanner systems –

fixed, portable batch, and portable transmission.

Fixed scanners

This type of scanner merely reads the bar code and transmits the information to the computer. The scanner is connected directly to the computer via either the keyboard or the serial sockets. This is sometimes also called a wedge scanner as it gets 'wedged' between the keyboard and the computer. The bar codes can be read directly by the computer, without any need for special software, as it simply appears to the computer as if a very fast typist has recorded the data. Multiple scanners can feed into one computer when they are connected to serial ports in the computer.

Portable batch scanners

Portable batch scanners read information and record it to a portable computer which is attached to the scanner. The information in the portable computer gets moved to the host computer later on. To download the information, the scanner is inserted into a cradle and the batch of information is sent to the host computer. The portable computer usually has a display which allows the system to interface with the operator. This system is cost-effective when the data can arrive in batches and does not need to be sent to the host computer immediately.

Portable transmission scanners

Portable transmission scanners record the information from the scan and immediately transmit the information to the host computer. This type of scanner is used where information is required as soon as it is read. An example of this is the delivery of a product into a manufacturing process on a JIT scheme. If there are delays in capturing data, the entire manufacturing process will be delayed until the system advises the product is available. Transmissions are generally done with wireless transmission processes, although alternatives such as infrared transmission are available.

Test yourself

7.11 Bar codes are a _____ and highly _____ method of reading information.

Resources

The logistics professional will encounter various types of equipment. Each manufacturer has developed its equipment to focus on particular market niches and to offer specialised capabilities that are needed in particular industries. Below are some of the web sites of some well-known providers of equipment. These are not recommended equipment, but only a reference for further information.

Warehouse: sorting and moving
www.egemin.co.uk
www.cartercontrols.com/
www.sld.ch

Lifting and moving equipment
www.linde.com
www.hyster.co.uk
www.crown.com
www.boss-gb.co.uk

Cranes and heavy lifting on the quayside
www.noellcranesystems.com
Twistlocks
www.william-cook.co.uk

Reach stackers and straddle carriers
www.fantuzzi.com
www.hyster.co.uk
www.boss-gb.co.uk
www.catracom.com

General news on cargo handling in ports
www.worldcargonews.com

Conclusions

It is important to choose the most appropriate equipment. Euipment is expensive and should be used intensively in order for the investment to be financially justified. The cost of inappropriate equipment includes not only the capital sum, but also the consequent reduced efficiency and effectiveness. In most cases, there is one piece of equipment which is the most appropriate, and the procedure to identify this has been discussed.

Questions

1 The choice of equipment is made after the choice of racks. Comment on this statement and motivate why you agree or disagree.
2 What are the advantages and disadvantages of a sorting system that automatically sorts the products into lanes, compared with a manual sorting system? If the volume of products to be sorted increases by hundred per cent and the number of customers who need to be serviced also increases by hundred per cent, what are the implications for the manual and automatic systems?
3 Modern facilities utilise a vast array of equipment. Assume a specific facility has chosen racks (not narrow aisle) and that this is the most appropriate storage method. What will the primary problems be when the equipment ages and if the volume handled doubles?
4 On which primary criteria should a firm planning a new warehouse for the following range of products choose the storage, which storage method should be chosen, and how does it satisfy the primary criteria?
   - groceries such as corn flakes and other dry products;
   - toiletries such as shampoos etc.;
   - household items such as brooms and dustpans; and
   - spices.
5 A container is delivered to a facility on a trailer. The container needs to be removed from the trailer, placed inside a warehouse for unloading, and the goods stored in racks six levels high. The container is filled with palletised goods. Which equipment would you use for the operations, and why?
6 Conceptually, a sea container, an air container, and a pallet perform the same functions. Comment on this statement.

Notes

1 Crown Product Information. Crown, Munich Germany.
2 Braziers (Pty) Ltd, Durban. Systems for un-palletised loads.
3 Daewoo Product Catalogue. Daewoo, Inchon, Korea.
4 Symbol Technologies Inc. *Bar coding for beginners*, page 3. Also see page 117 for a more detailed description of bar codes and scanners.

Contents

Learning Outcomes

After you have studied this chapter, you should be able to:

- define packaging in your own words;
- define and discuss the different functions of packaging;
- discuss the different types of packaging;
- explain the impact of packaging on the most important logistics costs;
- discuss the impact of packaging on the other logistics activities;
- discuss the various packaging design considerations; and
- explain the importance and working of labelling and bar coding.

Introduction

Packaging encloses and protects the product. It also makes the physical handling of the product much easier. Although packaging often does not add any value to a product, it has a substantial impact on the efficiency and effectiveness of a warehouse. It also has an impact on the layout, productivity and design of the warehouse. It plays a role in determining the choice of internal as well as external transport methods and the choice of handling equipment.

This chapter deals with the various logistics functions which packaging performs, the types of packaging, the impact of packaging on costs and on other logistics activities, packaging design considerations, and labelling.

Logistics functions of packaging

Packaging is the material (for example, carton, wood, and steel) in which a product or a group of products are wrapped to physically protect the products, to enhance the handling and appearance of products, and to convey important information to the customer.

Packaging performs six important functions pertaining to logistics: containment, protection, apportionment, unitisation, convenience, and communication.[1]

Containment

Containment is the function of packing products into boxes or other containers, and of packing these boxes or containers into bigger containers, in order to transport the products effectively.

Instant coffee can be packed into tins or bags of different sizes. The tins or bags can be packed into boxes, say twenty per box. These boxes can then be packed into a container, say a thousand per container. By doing this, the coffee can be transported effectively.

Protection

Protection refers to the function of protecting the product from damage or loss caused by external factors such as contamination, moisture, and dust.

Sugar needs to be protected against moisture. The paper packets in which it is packed protect it. The boxes in which the packets are packed protect the packets. It is important that the packets are also protected, as they draw the attention of the customers in the retail outlets.

Apportionment

Apportionment is the function of dividing the original volume of manufactured goods into smaller and more manageable units.

Instead of selling sugar in 50 kg bags, it is packed into 500 g, 1 kg, or bigger packets. Customers can then buy the sugar in more manageable packaging sizes. Customers who buy sugar in bulk can buy the bigger bags to meet their needs.

Unitisation

Unitisation is the function of bundling primary packages (i.e. packages that wrap the products) into secondary packages (i.e. containers that hold the primary packages) such as cardboard boxes. The secondary packages can then be grouped into one wrapped pallet. These individual pallets can, in turn, be loaded into a container with several other pallets.

Unitisation reduces the number of times a product needs to be handled. A whole pallet can be placed in an open space on the shop floor of a wholesaler or a retailer. The boxes that are stacked onto the pallet can be opened at the top to enable customers to pick the product, for instance a tin of instant coffee.

Convenience

> Convenience is a characteristic of packaging which refers to the effective handling, storage, and transportation of products.

Mineral water is sold in glass or plastic bottles. These bottles make it easy to handle the product. Some of these bottles can be disposed of easily, while others can be returned for a deposit payback.

Information

> Information refers to the function of communicating with the outside world through the packaging. This can be done by attaching labels or by printing information onto it.

Instructions such as 'handle with care' (for fragile items) or 'store in a cool place' (for perishables) can be printed onto the packaging or onto the labels attached to it.

Test yourself

8.1 Packaging performs six important logistics functions. Name them.

Types of packaging

Packaging can generally be divided into consumer (interior) packaging and industrial (exterior) packaging.[2]

Consumer packaging

The marketing department should be involved with consumer (interior) packaging as this packaging provides information that encourages the consumer to buy the product. Consumer packaging also has the potential to set the product apart from other products on retailers' shelves which are competing for the attention of customers. The brighter the colour of the label on, for instance, the tin of coffee, the more likely it will attract the attention of the customer.

When designing consumer packaging, one should consider retail shelf utilisation, protection of the product, customer convenience, and cost. The result is that packaging often does not comply with logistical requirements such as density of storage. Low-density packaging brings about higher transport rates and greater warehouse space requirements.

Industrial packaging

Industrial (exterior) packaging groups products or components into cartons, barrels, bins, bags etc. It provides protection against shocks, moisture, heat, and other factors that may damage the products. Industrial packaging originates from logistics principles: Besides protecting products, it also enables a business to use its transport and warehouse facilities effectively. It is an effective means of providing information and of conveying and handling products.

It is important to be aware that consumer and industrial packaging sometimes overlap. When consumer packaging is designed to protect the interior product, the exterior packaging should also be considered. It serves no purpose to pack ten 1 kg packets of sugar into one 10 kg bag if the latter does not protect the interior products properly. If the small packets break in the transport process, the bag gets filled with sugar from the broken packets and the purpose of using smaller bags is defeated.

Test yourself

8.2 Packaging can be divided into _____ and _____ packaging. These are also known as _____ and _____ packaging.

Impact of packaging on costs

As the packaging is seen as part of a specific product, packaging costs form part of the total cost of that product. Plastic, steel, wood, carton, and soft materials used for industrial packaging also add to the cost of a product. Some of these materials, such as plastic and carton, are relatively cheap. These materials are also light, which reduces handling and transport costs. Packaging impacts on transport costs, handling costs, and warehousing costs.

Transport costs

The heavier or bulkier the packaging material, the higher the freight charges and handling costs. Products with a higher mass need bulkier handling equipment and more energy (electricity or fuel) is required to move them.

Transport trucks are designed to carry a certain number of containers that fit perfectly onto it. More products can be loaded into one container when using square or rectangular packaging, as these take up less space. An example of the reduction of transport costs through better and more efficient forms of packaging is the stacking of beer cases onto pallets that fit perfectly onto a beer truck. A certain quantity of cases of beer cans, dumpies (340 ml bottles of beer), pints (375 ml bottles of beer) and quarts (750 ml bottles of beer) can be loaded onto the respective pallets. These pallets are designed in such a way that the maximum amount of beer can be loaded onto a truck for each trip. This reduces the cost per load.

Handling costs

The handling of products can be improved by packing them into boxes or crates which are stacked onto pallets. Forklifts load the pallets onto trucks or move them through the warehouse. The products can even be stored on the pallets.

By using more protective packaging methods, damages are reduced to a minimum during handling. The plastic beer crates that are used for pints and quarts are durable and can take the rough handling. They prevent the bottles from knocking against each other or against hard surfaces.

Damage has a negative effect on the costs of a manufacturer, who is responsible for replacing or fixing the products should the damage occur because of poor packaging methods.

Warehousing costs

Warehousing costs are calculated in terms of the amount of cubic metres of space used. The greater the density of the products that can be packed into a certain space, the lower the warehousing costs per cubic metre will be. Boxes and bags can be stacked, and fluids such as paraffin and paint can be stored in large cans or drums. Items such as hosepipes and other plastic pipes are coiled around spools. These spools can hang against the walls of the warehouse or the retailer's shop. In this way, they take up less space but are easily accessible.

Test yourself

8.3 Packaging has an impact on the _____, _____, and _____ costs.

Impact of packaging on other logistics activities

Packaging has an impact on most of the other logistics activities, such as procurement, warehousing, production, transport, and marketing.

Procurement

The packaging used for raw materials and other components can have a positive effect on the procurement of these items.

A liquor store owner can procure beer efficiently by ordering a full truck of beer loaded onto pallets, in quantities that meet the requirements for the store. The packaging informs the owner how many cans or bottles are in each case and how many cases of each kind of beer can be loaded onto each pallet.

Owners of filling stations can also replenish their stock efficiently if they know how many cans of oil and brake fluid go into the respective cases. In this way, they can order according to the quantities set out in their stock control systems.

The purchasing department can easily check the quantity and quality of the raw materials and other products delivered to a business if the quality specifications are mentioned on the exterior packaging. Appropriate packaging also protects the product against damage.

Warehousing

The size, shape, and type of packaging determine not only how much of each product can be stored in the available space, but also how easily and how often the product will be handled. The packaging can safeguard the product against damages during handling and storing. Items can be identified much easier if information, such as the type and quantity of the product, is displayed on the packaging. Different types of products can be stored separately but in such a way that they can be found easily.

Instructions printed onto the exterior packaging enable the warehouse manager to store the product in an appropriate place. A warehouse worker in a very humid area will store a product in an air-conditioned space if the words 'keep in a dry place' are printed on it.

Production

The production and operations manager has an interest in the packaging of both inbound and outbound products.

The packaging of inbound products proves that nobody has tampered with the goods. A manufacturer who builds television sets needs to know that the components bought from suppliers are packed properly and that nobody else has had access to them. The quantities inside a box can easily be checked against the quantities printed on the box. Other information, such as voltage and other technical specifications, should also be printed on the packaging. This enables the manufacturer to use the items with the appropriate specifications in each television set.

The packaging of outbound products should ensure that the products are protected and can be handled properly. It is the task of the production department to put the final products into their respective packages. The shapes, sizes, and types of packaging are important to the production department as these indicate whether packages should be filled by machines or manually. For example, machines usually perform the tasks of canning or bottling beer and of putting soap into boxes.

Transport

Suitable packaging and packaging materials ensure more efficient transport. Breweries use trucks that are designed to suit the shapes and sizes of the beer cases and crates they must carry. The cases and crates are stacked in such a way that they cover the available space in the most efficient way. This ensures that the maximum amount of beer is loaded onto each truck.

A business enterprise gets a bad name if it regularly delivers damaged products. It sends out a message that the business does not care about its customers. Appropriate packaging protects products against damage while being transported. Certain motor vehicle components, for example, are packed in sealed plastic bags. These bags protect the goods against water damage.

Marketing

Packaging plays an important role in marketing a product. It supplies information such as the ingredients or nutritional value to the customer. The packaging of a product can be used to differentiate it from other brands. This will draw the attention of customers should the product be packed between other brands on retailers' shelves.

The packaging can prove to the customers that the manufacturer cares and that all is done to protect the product against damages. Information such as the expiry date of a carton of milk ensures that the customer gets value for money. This is very important for all perishable products.

> **Test yourself**
>
> 8.4 Name five other logistics activities on which packaging has an impact.

Packaging design considerations

When designing interior and exterior packaging, cognisance must be taken of the five locations where a product will be found during its lifetime.[3] These five locations are the plant, the warehouse, the transport unit, the retail outlet, and the consumer's place of use. One must always keep in mind what function the product will have in each of these locations.

The five most important factors that must be taken into consideration when developing an appropriate interior or exterior packaging design are the sales functions, the protective functions, the different packing materials, protection of the environment, and recycling.

The sales functions of packaging

The sales functions of packaging are especially important to the plant manager, the retail outlet, and the consumer.

The plant manager

The plant manager works closely with the marketing manager as far as the sales functions of packaging are concerned. The plant manager is responsible for the packing of the final products. He or she has to ensure that the quality of the labels (colour, adhesiveness, and durability) complies with the set quality specifications. This enables the customer to identify the product much easier and quicker.

The retail outlet

Retailers take the form of packaging into account when they plan the layout of their shelves. The storage space that a shoe retailer reserves for each kind and size of shoe depends on the size of the box in which each pair of shoes is packed.

A grocery retailer needs to pack the products in groups in such a way that they are visible to the customers as they move down the aisles. Different boxes of tea are packed onto one shelf but brands are grouped together.

Sometimes manufacturers want retailers to sell products on promotions. If Coca-Cola wants to sell special cans of soft drinks at reduced prices, the retailer can easily identify these cans by the printing on the labels. The cans are then displayed prominently in special areas where customers can easily recognise them.

The consumer

Consumers rely on the packaging to identify the products they wish to buy. They recognise the shape and colour of products that they buy often. A trusted brand of coffee will be observed immediately when the consumer reaches the coffee shelf. A consumer who wants to buy a two litre container of low fat milk will find the required container by reading the labels and/or by spotting the colours and size of the low fat milk cartons.

> **Test yourself**
>
> 8.5 The sales functions of packaging are specifically of value to the _____ manager, the _____ and the _____.

The protective functions of packaging

The protective functions of packaging are also important to the plant manager, the retailer, and the consumer.

The plant manager

The plant manager uses the information on the packaging to determine how inbound materials and components must be stored (shelves, drums, spools) and under which conditions (temperature, humidity). The quality specifications are often also printed on the packaging. These ensure that the right components are used in the manufacturing of final products.

The plant manager must ensure that the correct materials are used for the packaging of outbound products. Should the business buy or manufacture its own packaging, the plant manager must check if the quality complies with set standards. This ensures that the final products will not be easily damaged and that they can be handled and stored with ease.

Pharmaceutical drug manufacturers use packaging that will show if the sealed product has been opened. This is important because most of these products carry a health risk and tampering can have dire legal consequences for such a business enterprise.

The retailer

The design of the packaging should enable the retailer to display products safely. Some products may need to be stacked (bags of dog food), packed on shelves (toothpaste, toilet soap, breakfast cereals), coiled (garden hoses) or displayed in cages (bottles of wines). The packaging should allow the retailer to use these storage methods without damage to the product.

The design should suit handling requirements. Packets of sugar, boxes of washing powder, bags of cement etc. need to be packed without tearing.

The consumer

The consumer relies on the packaging to identify dangerous products such as caustic soda and poison. The labels of these products contain cautions. The packages of pharmaceutical products often warn that the products must be stored in a safe place, outside the reach of children.

The protective function of packaging is very important for people who stay in rural areas where products need to be carried over long distances. Roads in these areas are often bad and the bumpy rides can damage the products if they are not packed appropriately.

Test yourself

8.6 The protective functions are important to the _____ manager, the _____ and the _____.

Materials

Before the introduction of plastic (ploymers such as polystyrene, polyurethane, and polyethylene), wood and steel were mainly used as packing materials. These materials were strong and durable but their volume or weight placed a burden on transport costs.

Plastic revolutionised packaging. Cardboard boxes are now stuffed with plastic foam to protect products such as televisions and hi-fi components from damage caused by rough handling. These materials are light and the use thereof reduces transport costs substantially.

Many businesses wrap plastic (cling wrap) around pallets of products. The retailer can then remove the wrapping and store the whole pallet of goods on the sales floor without unpacking the goods. This saves shelving space and more open floor space can be utilised.

When choosing materials for the packaging design, end users should also be considered. They can reuse the packaging after the product has been consumed (empty boxes of expensive cigars can be used for storing small items such as jewellery) or throw the packaging away (empty cigarette boxes). Other forms of packaging can be returned for a deposit (soft drink bottles). These returnable items are used again after they have been washed and sterilised. Some items (cardboard boxes) can be recycled and used in other forms.

Protecting the environment

The protection of the environment is an increasingly serious problem worldwide. Millions of plastic bags cover the surface of many countries and pollute the earth at an ever-increasing rate. Besides the plastic bags, many other materials, such as plastic and glass bottles, paper bags, steel and aluminium cans, and cardboard boxes are strewn all over our cities and towns. Some of these items, such as paper and cardboard, are degradable – which means that they will be broken down and will disappear in time. Items such as glass and plastic, however, pollute the earth for a long time.

Most governments are introducing stringent laws against polluting the environment and polluters face heavy fines.

The production and operations manager must take these issues into consideration when packaging is designed. Paper and cardboard should be used in cases where the packaging will be discarded after the products have been consumed. Non-degradable materials should be avoided. Deposits can be paid on all bottles and crates. Consumers are then refunded when returning these bottles and crates for reuse. A positive spin-off of this practice is that unemployed people can earn an income from collecting these items and selling them back to the retailers. Every business is responsible for ensuring a clean environment.

Recycling

Recycling refers to the process in which used materials such as glass, paper, steel, and aluminium are turned into new raw materials that can be used to produce other products.

Raw materials are becoming scarcer as consumption and waste increases. The business sector realised this long ago and they started recycling aluminium, steel, glass, and other containers. Recycling helps to save our raw materials and reduce pollution. In the long run, it will keep the prices of these raw materials at acceptable levels because of better availability.

Test yourself

8.7 The five most important factors that must be taken into consideration when designing interior or exterior packaging are the _____ functions of packaging, the _____ functions of packaging, the different _____ used, protection of the _____, and _____.

Labelling and bar coding

All the activities pertaining to packaging must be executed in such a way that they will assist and enhance all the other logistics activities. We have already discussed the importance of labelling as a part of packaging. Labelling also accommodates the bar coding.

Labelling

Labelling is the fixing of labels onto a product and/or the packaging of a product. These labels contain information that is of importance to production plants, transport companies, wholesalers, retailers, and customers.

The trading colours of products, information about the ingredients of the products, precautionary information, and the bar code are printed on the label. The label may also inform the customer about the storage requirements and the handling of the product.

The labels on the containers and packaging of medicine provide information such as the ingredients, dosage instructions for children and adults, and storage instructions. Without this information, the product is potentially dangerous and the quality may be reduced if it is not stored at the right temperature.

Test yourself

8.8 Labelling is the fixing of labels onto the _____ and/or the _____ of a product. These labels contain information that is of importance to _____ (name five).

Bar coding

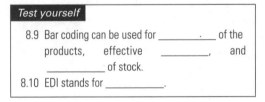

A bar code is a set of coded symbols that can be read by an optical scanner. It consists of a series of parallel vertical black and white bars. These bars vary in width and represent specific letters or numbers.

Bar codes, which have been discussed in the previous chapter, can supply information such as the manufacturer's name, the name of the brand, and the (cost and selling) price of a product. An optical scanner reads all this data. The information on bar codes can be used to price products, effectively keep stock, and automatically order stock to replace sold products.

Pricing products

When a business receives new stock, the quantity and cost of the goods are recorded on a computer. The required percentage of price mark-up of products is also fed into the computer, enabling it to automatically calculate the selling price. All this information is linked to a bar code and kept in the central computer network. Every item passing the cash register at the sales point will be charged at the correct selling price once the scanner has identified the product.

Effective stock keeping

The quantities of goods received are recorded on the computer. As products are sold and pass the cash register's scanner, the computer deducts the number of items sold from the cumulative figure stored. A copy of all the products in stock can be printed from the computer at any moment. A physical stock count can be done and these figures can be checked against those of the computer.

Replenishing stock

Most of the computer programmes available enable the business to capture information such as lead times, re-order points, economic order quantities, safe stock quantities, and other relevant information. By using EDI (Electronic Data Interchange), the computer system of a specific enterprise can be connected to the systems of its suppliers. This enables the enterprise to order the required quantities of stock on time, ensuring that the business will not run out of stock. The computer system can order the items automatically when the volume of the items reach their re-order points.

Test yourself

8.9 Bar coding can be used for _____ of the products, effective _____, and _____ of stock.

8.10 EDI stands for _____.

Conclusion

In this chapter, we defined packaging and discussed consumer and industrial packaging. We explored the impact of packaging on logistics costs and on the other logistics activities. The most important packaging design considerations received attention. The functions of packaging and the importance of labelling and bar coding were also explained.

Questions

1 Define the concept of packaging in your own words.
2 Name and discuss the two general types of packaging.
3 Define and discuss the six logistics functions performed by packaging.
4 Name the different kinds of logistics cost on which packaging has an impact and discuss each.
5 Name the different important logistics activities on which packaging has an impact and discuss each one.
6 Name the five types of locations where a product may be found.
7 Discuss the various packaging design considerations.
8 Discuss the importance of labelling.
9 Discuss the role of bar coding in efficient stock keeping, and the role of computers in bar coding.

Notes

1   Lambert, D.M., Stock, J.R. and Ellram, L.M. 1998: 331.
2   Coyle, J.J., Bardi, E.J. and Langley, C.J. (Jr) 1996: 307–308.
3   Coyle, J.J., Bardi, E.J. and Langley, C.J. (Jr) 1996: 311.

Contents

Learning Outcomes

After you have studied this chapter, you should be able to:

- explain how to use vertical height to achieve cost-effective storage;
- define the purpose of the facility;
- realise the importance of planning for growth;
- define a Product Process Category (PPC) and give an example;
- identify and define the PPCs in a facility;
- plan and design the storage and handling areas of the building for each PPC;
- define and allocate the times of operation for different PPC areas;
- assemble the PPCs into a composite building that is efficient and cost-effective;
- calculate the total floor area required for a storage facility, including aisles and racks;
- define the loading and unloading requirements in terms of floor space and doors for the transport;
- understand the requirements for security and the limitations thereof;
- understand the primary requirements for fire protection and the legal requirements for building protection; and
- specify the overall building shape and orientation to suit the logistics requirements (not the civil requirements).

Introduction

The design of the building structure falls within the sphere of expertise of the architect and building professionals. The orientation of the building and the space allocation within the building are the domain of the logistics professional. Poor orientation and space allocation will cause the operation to be inefficient and costly throughout the life of the facility. Spending time and effort on designing the building to suit the logistics requirements holds future benefits.

Initial requirements

Cross-dock is the process, or operational technique, whereby the goods are received, allocated and sorted for dispatch, and dispatched in one area of a facility, without storing the goods or removing goods from storage in the facility.

Two aspects determine the initial requirements for the design.
- The first is the purpose of the facility. This includes whether the facility is to be a storage facility or a cross-dock facility or both, and whether the service promised is next-day or same-day delivery.
- The second aspect is the growth forecast for the facility over its lifetime. In other words, a forecast of the future storage and handling requirements for the facility is required. The facility can then be sized and orientated to allow for these future needs. It is not sufficient to merely allocate space or additional land for expansion.

There are restrictions on the design of any facility. The size of the land may restrict the orientation, and slopes may restrict truck access. The design should accommodate these restrictions. However, it is of primary importance to stick as closely to the ideal design as possible, and to then amend the design to deal with the restrictions. The restrictions should not be introduced before the basic

needs are identified and translated into design aspects. The design should be focused on enabling the facility to service the needs of the customers, and not on the restrictions.

Test yourself

9.1 The two aspects that determine the requirements for a facility design are the _____ of the facility and the _____ for the facility.

Purpose of the facility

The needs of the customers must be translated into the functions required from the facility. These functions are grouped according to activities and handling requirements. The products in each such group is called a Product Process Category (PPC). A PPC is a product or group of products that are stored in a similar manner and/or require the same handling processes. A new PPC may be created where the handling processes or the storage requirements differ sufficiently from other products. For example, there may be different PPCs for different temperature zones, and for different storage and cross-dock facilities.

As each PPC requires different processes and areas to operate in, it will be extremely difficult and costly to expand in future if the requirements for expansion are not considered when designing the warehouse.

Growth forecast for the facility

The future needs (for the next five or more years) for each of the PPCs must be estimated. Each PPC has different growth rates and will impose different requirements on the facility. Part of a responsible design process is forecasting what is required over the lifetime of the facility. This forecast will not be entirely accurate, as the market may alter in ways that were not foreseen. However, the design will be considerably better if the forecast is used.

Sizing the warehouse

A warehouse is not just the building. It incorporates the transport area, as well as the access to roads and to other essential services. A good rule of thumb is that the building itself should occupy only forty to fifty per cent of the land, with the remainder used for transport manoeuvring, parking, and access.

The cost of a warehouse is significant in the total logistics chain. The warehouse needs to be designed to be cost-effective. The cost, once the land is acquired, lies in the base of the building, the floor, and the roof. The cost of the walls makes up a small percentage of the total cost. It is estimated that the floor and the roof account for eighty per cent of the building cost. It is therefore significantly cheaper to expand storage space vertically than to create additional floor area. Storage in racks is a very cost-effective means of increasing the volume of goods in a given floor space.

Operations and Warehouse Management Systems (WMS)

As part of the design process, it is necessary to choose and define the principles of operation and the capabilities of the WMS. The principles of operation that influence the design are the following:

• *Method of receiving goods*
  The partial receipt of a load of goods reduces the size of the receiving bay dramatically. For partial receipts to be effective, there must be the capability to move the goods quickly from the receiving bay, while unloading continues and the receipt is recorded into the WMS at the same time.

• *Use and control of equipment in the warehouse*
  The appropriate equipment must be chosen to transfer the goods from the storage area and to move them to the dispatch assembly area. The size of the warehouse and the operational processes must be taken into account when choosing equipment.

• *Picking capability*
  If an order is big enough that full pallets are required, these are taken from where they are stored. The remaining products needed to fulfil the order are taken from the pick face. The full pallets taken from storage as part of an order are moved directly to the order assembly area and not to the pick face. As the product in the pick face is removed, it must be replenished by moving a full pallet from storage to the pick face. Pallets should be moved 'Just in time' (JIT) to comply with the two needs of replenishing the pick face and of delivering full pallets for an order to the dispatch area.

One must have a clear understanding of what needs to be achieved with the proposed operation and WMS. Every step in the operation requires equipment or storage/rest areas that must be considered in the design.

Design process

Assumptions

As soon as the number of PPCs, their requirements, and their growth forecast have been determined, the design can be done in detail.

In all cases, it is assumed that the transport is operated as one fleet for all products from a facility. It is not efficient or effective to maintain fleets for each PPC in the facility. One fleet is the most cost-effective and efficient manner of utilising transport.[1]

The detailed design must include the space and capabilities required to handle each PPC. The design should be centred around three operational processes: receiving, storage and pick, and dispatch. The principles of these are discussed in the following sections.

Test yourself

9.4 The design centres around _____, _____ and _____.

Process

Various methods are suggested for approaching a design. Some texts recommend that the design start with the storage area, then look at operational flows and then at the receive and dispatch areas. Others recommend this process in reverse. The best is to consider all of these in an iterative process (i.e. the process is repeated until it is sufficiently refined). The demands for each area impact on other areas. One should seek the appropriate balance between the number of PPCs and the storage areas, operating areas, and the flow into and from the warehouse. Each aspect should therefore be considered and one should determine the best combination to suit the current and future needs of the customers.

The iterative process is simple. After each PPC is identified, the design should define the following aspects:

- storage requirements;
- handling and moving areas;
- assembly areas for transport loading and unloading; and
- receiving requirements.

The next stage of the process is to combine the requirements for each PPC into a common facility that is efficient and cost-effective. This is done in three stages; by deciding

- which areas are unique to each PPC;
- which areas can be shared with other PPC

operations, and what the increased traffic will do to the size of the common areas; and
- the periods when the various PPC operations will take place.

If one PPC operates in a completely different period from another operation, all the areas (except the storage) can potentially be used as common areas. This immediately presents an opportunity for saving space. Where PPCs share a space such as a moving area, the storage areas need to be located near one another. Storage for each PPC requires specific space that cannot be shared with any other PPC. Moving areas, loading and unloading areas, and assembly areas can potentially be shared. Each such possibility must be assessed on the basis of the requirements for individual PPCs.

The above reflects the process of the design. An example towards the end of the chapter will illustrate how to apply this information practically.

First, however, we need to explore the use of calculations to assign the appropriate areas to each operation. To make this information more accessible, one PPC will be discussed in detail – starting with storage.

Test yourself

9.5 If the operation times of a PPC differ from those of other PPCs, only the _____ may not be shared with the other PPCs.

Storage

The storage can done in one of the basic modes:[2]

- block stacking;
- racking;
- drive-in racking; and
- mobile racking.

For our example, we chose a PPC that is stored in racks, but the calculations that follow can be adapted for other methods of storage.

As discussed in Chapter 7, the use of racking increases the storage density of the warehouse.

Storage density refers to the amount of goods per square metre of floor space. In addition to the space taken up by the racks, the design must include space to allow access to the racks. The equipment chosen to move the pallets to or from the rack slots determines the aisle width. The equipment must be able to travel up and down the aisle and turn to place the pallet in the rack. Most warehouses use reach trucks for placing pallets and these require an aisle of approximately 2,8 m wide. Narrow aisle stackers require approximately 1,5 m but cost significantly more than reach trucks. This is a design trade-off: One has to determine whether the cost-effectiveness of the increased number of racks per square metre offsets the price of the narrow aisle stacker.

Once the choice of equipment is made, the aisle width is determined. The equipment must also be able to move from one aisle to another. The outer space required for this is shown in Figure 9.1, with the outer working perimeter marked in a dotted line.

Example

An enterprise wants to have storage for one thousand pallets. Racks are the most economical storage method. The warehouse is therefore designed to have ten rows of racks. Each row of racks is five spaces high and twenty spaces long. The racks are placed with two rows adjacent (back-to-back) to each other. The pallets are placed in the spaces with a reach truck, which requires a 2,8 m wide aisle. To provide the storage space, the area that is required is determined as follows:

Each rack (a single space for a pallet of goods) occupies:
1,2 m from front to back (depth)
1,4 m from side to side (length)
1,8 m from top to bottom (height)

Four aisles are needed between the racks. Two aisles are needed to service the outer racks, and aisles are needed at both ends to move the reach stacker from one aisle to another (see the outer working perimeter in Figure 9.1).

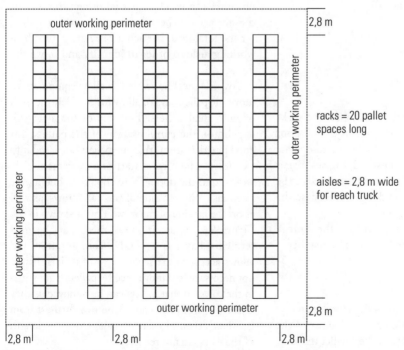

Figure 9.1 Layout of the rack storage in a warehouse

Floor area of the racks
floor area per rack = length of the racks x depth of
the racks
= 1,4 m x 1,2 m

floor area for row of racks = number of racks in the
length x floor area per rack
= 20 x 1,4 m x 1,2 m
= 33,6 m^2 per rack

floor area for ten rows of racks = 336 m^2

Total floor area
length of the storage area = rack length + outer
aisles
= (length of a rack x number of racks per row) +
(aisle width x 2)
= (1,4 m x 20) + (2 x 2,8 m)
= 33,6 m

width of the storage area = width of racks + width
of aisles
= (width of racks x number of racks) + (aisle
width x number of aisles)
= (1,2 m x 10) + (2,8 m x 6)
= 28,8 m

total area = length x width
= 33,6 m x 28,8 m
= 967,68 m^2

It is important to note that, although the racks
cover only 336 m^2 of floor space, the total floor
area needs to be approximately 968 m^2 to operate
equipment in this area – nearly 2,9 times bigger
than the rack area itself. The floor area needs to be
calculated correctly in the design, otherwise the
operations will be inefficient.

Any storage area, irrespective of the storage
method, must be evaluated in the same manner.

Design tip

The density of the storage is directly dependent
on the width of the aisle and the height of the
racks. The higher the racks or the smaller the aisle,
the greater the density.

Receiving

The size of the largest truck commonly received is
used as the basis for the design of the receiving
area. If larger trucks are occasionally received, the
operation needs to be adapted to handle it.

Two important steps dominate the process of
receiving a truck. The first step is to identify the
goods, and the quantity and quality thereof (where
possible). The second step is to record the receipt
into the warehouse.

The size of the area required for the receipt is
equal to the size of the largest load that must be
placed on the floor to determine the quantity and
the quality of the goods. If the WMS and the
processes can handle a partial receipt, the size of
the area needs to be only a portion of that required
for the total load. In such a case, there must be a
working aisle in order to identify and move the
items.[5]

An aisle must be created to allow equipment to
move the pallets and to allow for the identification
of individual pallets. The size of the aisle will
depend on the configuration of the pallets, but
good practice deems that the pallets be placed into
two rows. These rows start one movement aisle
width from the door. There should be one movement aisle on each side of the pallet rows, as well
as on the far side of the rows. This is shown in the
Figure 9.2, where it is assumed that the next
receiving bay has a similar configuration and
allows access to the second row of pallets. If it is
not necessary to remove specific pallets from within the rows, so that pallets can be removed as they
arrive (i.e. from the end of the row furthest from
the door), then movement aisles along the length
of the rows are not required.

Example 1

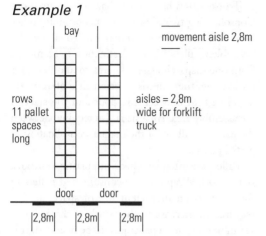

Figure 9.2 Layout of the receiving bay for a truck size of 22 pallets

The largest truck commonly received is 15 m long and can hold twenty-two pallets of goods. This is used to size the receiving bays, as the WMS and the operation of the warehouse do not allow for the receipt of partial shipments. The receiving bay therefore needs to be bigger than the area of the pallets. Two rows of eleven pallets each are made. A forklift truck is used to move the pallets and it requires a width of 2,8 m to operate in.

pallet area = number of pallets x area of a pallet
  = 22 x (1,2 m x 1,4 m)
  = 36,96 m^2

aisle area = length of row of pallets x operating width
  = (11 x 1,4 m) x 2,8 m
  = 43,12 m^2

Bay area for rows and adjacent movement aisle = 80,08 m^2

Example 2

The WMS may also allow for the immediate receipt of each pallet from a truck the same size as above. This can be done if the pallets are inspected manually and the goods do not require detailed inspection or withdrawal from the rows in the bay.

As it is highly probable that no pallet truck will be available at times to move the pallets, some pallets will be placed on the floor. A suitable design will include an area big enough for approximately fifty per cent of the pallets, with a walk isle of 1 m between pallet unloading areas for successive doors. As there are twenty-two pallets, each row should be at least five pallets long.

area of pallets = 2 rows of 5 pallets
  = 5 x 2 x (1,4 x 1,2)
  = 16,8 m^2

aisle = 5 pallets long x width of aisle for walking between stacks
  = 5 x 1,2 x 1
  = 6 m^2

total area = 22,8 m^2

Design tip

The second example above allows for a more effective use of the floor area, which results in a far more cost-effective warehouse. These decisions are important. If the warehouse is laid out for less effective WMS and operations (as in the first example), the introduction of more effective WMS and operations will improve the floor utilisation. However, if the design assumes very effective systems and operations, and these are not in place, the warehouse will have inadequate space and will be highly inefficient due to congestion.

Test yourself

9.8 The pallets unloaded from the transport should be placed on the warehouse floor in _____ rows.

Pick area

If items are picked manually from storage, the picking is done in the aisle between the storage areas. As space is already allocated for the reach stacker or similar equipment to move in the aisle, no additional space is required for picks that are not full pallets. Where a pick requires one or more full pallets plus additional items, the pick occurs from the pick face (at ground level) and the reach truck takes the full pallet or pallets from storage or reserve stock (generally in the upper racks).

If the reach truck takes the pallet to the dispatch bay, no additional space is required. However, reach trucks are specifically designed to move pallets vertically. They are not made for fast movement of the pallets to distant dispatch bays.

If the reach truck remains in the aisle and the picked pallets are moved to the dispatch bays with faster equipment such as pallet trucks, a handover area is required near the aisles. The reach truck places the pallets in the handover zone and the high-speed pallet truck picks it up and takes it to the dispatch bay.

Test yourself

9.9 An improved WMS assists in _____ the floor space required.

Dispatch area

The transport usually constitutes the largest cost of the land-based part of the logistics chain. The goods must be transferred to the transport as fast as possible to reduce the cost of the transport waiting time. The goods must therefore be assembled, as they are picked, to create a truckload. The full load, which consists of goods from different parts of the warehouse, needs to be assembled in one area.

The various sections in the warehouse pick the items and build these into full pallets. An order rarely comprises full pallets only. Partial pallets can be consolidated once the pallets are in the assembly bay (or dispatch area). This is done by moving items from one partially filled pallet to another, until no more than one partially filled pallet remains for the total load. It is therefore recommended that the assembly area is approximately ten per cent bigger than the area covered by the largest truckload. As the truck size determines the limits, the size of the assembly area is determined by the transport needs and not directly by the number of PPCs.

Trucks often have more than one destination. Consolidating two or more destinations into routes is an efficient use of transport. To allow the assembled pallets for one destination to be moved from one dispatch assembly area to another door for loading, there needs to be an aisle of approximately 2,8 m between the door and the start of the assembly area. An aisle is also required between the pallets to allow for the manual consolidation of partial pallets.

Pallets are often wrapped with plastic to make a stable load. Wrapping the consolidated pallets in the aisles is an inefficient use of space, as this requires an increase in the width of the aisles to 1,5 m to allow for a pallet jack to be operated. It is better to wrap the full pallets before they are placed in the assembly area. The consolidated pallets are wrapped in the space between the assembly areas and the loading door. No real delay occurs if the consolidated pallets are moved to one side in the movement aisle between the door and the beginning of the assembly area rows and wrapped while the full, wrapped pallets are checked and loaded onto the truck.

The size of the total assembly area is then determined as follows:

- The length of the rows of pallets in each bay is determined by the largest truck capacity.
- The number of routes of delivery at a time determines the number of bays.
- A variation is to have two rows of pallets of different length, based on the largest and the average truck size. It does reduce the area needed for assembly, but it also introduces a restriction on the use of larger trucks. In some cases, this may be justified. In general, this limitation causes future problems.

Movement zones

The movement of a pallet from the pick area to, say, the dispatch area must be done via a clear floor area. These movement aisles should be twenty to twenty-five per cent wider than what is needed for the largest piece of equipment. If the aisles carry one-way traffic, they need to accommodate only the largest machine. If they carry two-way traffic, they must be wide enough for two machines to pass each other at speed. There must not be a continual need to slow down when two machines approach each other in a movement aisle.

With careful planning, the movement aisles can serve various PPC areas. While the traffic density will make the common aisle slightly wider than an aisle for a single PPC, considerable space is saved using common aisles. The common aisle also facilitates better management of the warehouse.

Flows

Separate PPCs may result in separate storage areas, separate movement areas, and separate processes. In a warehouse where there will be continual and fast movement of goods by machines, the places where intersections of traffic flow occur must be planned carefully. Movement at intersections is restricted, as equipment must slow down and in some cases give way to other equipment. The number of intersections must be minimised with careful design. When they occur near racks and in doorways that have curtains over them to protect temperature zones, it reflects a poor design. The visibility at intersections must be good so that the impact on equipment movement is reduced. This means that, at the most, one vehicle

speeds up or one slows down slightly. One must also demarcate wide turning areas so that the equipment can negotiate the intersection and the changes in direction without delays.

It is important to chart the flow of goods to prevent cross-flows that will reduce the efficiency of operations in future. The simplest way to do this is to draw the flows on a plan of the proposed building and to see where the flows intersect. The movement aisles can be characterised with lines, the thickness of which is proportional to the density of the traffic. The traffic can be scaled as light, medium, or heavy, with three lines of different thickness. Each line is to indicate movement in one direction only. Movement in the opposite direction must be indicated with a second line. In this way both the density and the direction of the traffic are represented. Different colours can be used for different PPCs where necessary. Once these lines are drawn on the plan, it will be much easier to identify the appropriate aisle widths and layout changes to minimise common intersections.

Example

Two different PPCs exist in a warehouse. Both are stored in pallet racks. One is stored at ambient temperature, and the second is stored in a temperature-controlled environment. Figures 9.3 and 9.4 represent two different designs:

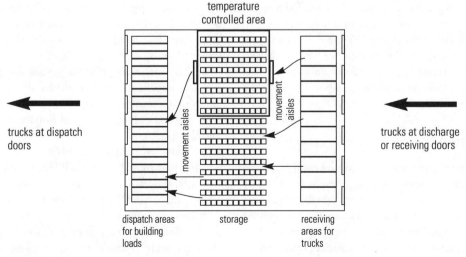

Figure 9.3 Good orientations of storage areas and flows

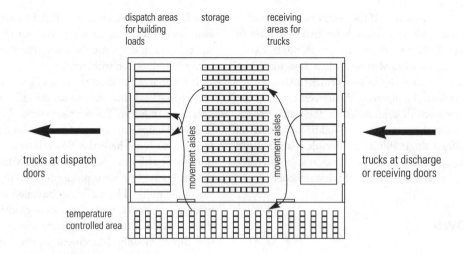

dispatch areas for building loads

storage

receiving areas for trucks

trucks at dispatch doors

movement aisles

movement aisles

trucks at discharge or receiving doors

temperature controlled area

Figure 9.4 Poor operational design of storage areas and flows

In Figure 9.3, the temperature-controlled partition is built around the racks, without changing the flows in the warehouse. The flow is still from receiving to dispatch and the only restriction the temperature-controlled section has added is the two doors into and out of the area.

In Figure 9.4, the temperature-controlled section is built against the walls of the warehouse to reduce the building cost. The indicated flows reflect the problems. An additional movement aisle is required within the temperature-controlled portion to allow for movement in both directions. The doors are placed in the best possible location, facing the existing movement aisles. Even so, on average the goods need to be moved further than in the alternative design (Figure 9.3). The design in Figure 9.4 also leaves room for fewer doors and fewer receiving and dispatch assembly areas, even though there are the same number of racks in the temperature-controlled area.

Design tip

It is very important to consider all the flows in the facility. A cheaper building design must not be accepted without checking whether this will introduce operational inefficiencies. The savings in the capital invested in the building must be balanced against the costs of inefficient operations.[4]

As additional PPCs are introduced, the potential for poor flows is increased. The flows of each new PPC must be charted and the best areas allocated for storage, dispatch assembly, receiving areas and, of prime importance, for movement aisles. In this way, the operation as a whole can be planned.

Loading doors

The warehouse is designed to interface with transport in some form, be it trucks, rail, containers, or even individual pick-ups. These interfaces must be operated in a disciplined and efficient way. The discipline must be imposed to ensure there is a steady flow of work in the facility. Peaks and troughs of work reduce efficiency, make the queue of trucks impatient, and delay the handling of the goods to be received or sent.

The loading doors may need to have the following facilities:

- The door must be easily accessible for transport.
- The door must have a dock leveller on it to match the level of the floor of the warehouse with the level of the floor of the truck or other transport medium.
- The door often has a foam seal around it for temperature-controlled products. The trailer

gets backed against the seal and the temperature is preserved both in the truck and in the warehouse while goods are transferred.

- Whenever products that can be adversely affected by water are moved through a door, a canopy must be erected over the building edge of the door to protect the products at the interface.

More doors mean greater flexibility for handling trucks and transport. Doors are, however, relatively expensive when the price of the door, canopy, dock levellers, and the space needed for movement are added up. The number of doors must at least equal the number of loads received or dispatched at a time. However, this design does not take into account the inefficiencies of having to move loads from the assembly area to a distant door. A more realistic minimum is the greater of one door for every two assembly bays, or the minimum number of routes to be serviced at a time.

Test yourself

9.10 _____ and _____ of in the workload reduce efficiency.

External areas

When a truck arrives at a warehouse, two checks must be done: Make sure that the truck is indeed destined for the facility and that it carries the desired goods. Well-managed warehouses give scheduled time slots for specific trucks to be unloaded. Where this is the practice, the time slot is checked when the truck arrives. If the truck is early, a parking area may be required. If the truck is late and cannot be received by the facility, the truck leaves without discharging or it waits until all other scheduled trucks have discharged. Trucks that need to discharge must be able to reverse up to the door without restrictions and delays.

The total area of good quality roadway needed for this is calculated by determining the following:

- length of the truck and trailer from the door;
- turning circle; and
- boundary area.

The approximate turning circle of some standard trucks and trailers are shown below:

Type	Turning diameter (m)	Length (m)
3 axle truck, 2 axle trailer	21	18
2 axle truck, 3 axle trailer	17	18
Truck and trailer	24–30	15
Articulated pantechnicon van	24–30	15
Rigid body – long (not articulated)	24	8
Rigid body – short (not articulated)	15	6,5

Table 9.1 Approximate turning circle diameter and length of various truck and tractor-trailer combinations

For layout purposes, the width of the roadway should be approximately 2,5 m (one direction) and the maximum height not less than 3 m.

In addition to the roadway for moving and loading/unloading trucks, a parking area is required for waiting tractors and trailers. The parking area, if managed well, should take up only a small space. Leaving trucks waiting on a continual basis is not cost-effective. However, as tractors are far more expensive than trailers, additional trailers are often used. The parking space needs to be sized to contain the total number of trailers and tractor-trailers expected to be on the premises of the facility at any time.

Trucks used for dispatch are treated in a similar manner. They first pass a checkpoint before being loaded. The above specifications for doors and external areas also apply for dispatch trucks. If loading and unloading take place at different times, only one area is required.

Combining areas

We have defined the requirements for individual PPCs. These determine the ideal sizing and shape of the areas designated to each PPC without restrictions and preconceived notions. We have also discussed the process of defining the methods of operation in accordance with the WMS capability across all of the PPCs.

We now need a method to combine these PPCs into a composite warehouse. Very complex mathematical models exist, but the use of these is only justified in very large and very complex facilities. As these are not often built in the southern African market, we recommend the following simple procedure.

The storage space of PPCs cannot be shared as each demands storage of a specific size. Therefore, the storage areas should be the starting point for a rough building layout. If the information can be placed on a Computer Aided Drawing (CAD) figure, then so much the better. If not, the way forward is to make a large scale drawing of the site (the largest sensible size would be A0) and use paper cut-outs on the same scale for the following areas of each PPC:

- dispatch;
- receiving.
- storage;
- movement; and
- transport.

Mark each PPC with a separate colour. Mark each of the cut-outs according to its function.

Place the cut-outs for the receiving and dispatch transport areas (not the parking) on the site drawing. The transport areas should preferably be located near the entrance road, on the boundaries of the site. Depending on the shape of the land and the number and types of PPCs, the receiving and dispatch transport areas can be either on two sides

of the site boundary or both on one side of the site boundary. The flows of individual PPCs tend to show which of these choices is preferable, but the most attractive option is usually where the receiving and dispatch areas are on opposite sides of the building. This orientation provides the least overlap of flows in the warehouse and the least interaction of transport around the building. The result is the easy and effective movement of products into and from the warehouse. One can argue that the receiving and dispatch areas need to be on the same side for security reasons. While this is a valid argument, it is more important to concentrate on good flows, as the movement of the goods is generally a much larger cost factor. The size and orientation of these areas need to be determined first, and then it is possible to identify the area that remains for the warehouse.

Arrange the storage areas so that those with the most similarities are adjacent to each other. For example, the dry groceries and the haberdashery have different racks. There is a bigger difference between a grocery area and, for example, a cross-dock area where not only the storage but also the operation is different. Arrange the storage areas in a linear fashion between the transport areas. Between the storage and assembly areas, add the movement areas. Overlap the movement areas of one storage area with those of the next area. Determine the density of the combined traffic in these movement areas by indicating the traffic from each PPC on the drawing. Add the appropriate receiving and dispatch assembly areas between the storage area and the transport area.

Design tips

- When allocating space for temperature-controlled zones, place them against the outer walls of the building. The walls have to be erected anyway, and the cost of insulating them is significantly less than the cost of erecting new walls in the warehouse.
- If there are, say, three PPCs and the traffic density is categorised as low, medium, and high respectively, assign a number (1, 2, and 3) to the traffic density of each PPC. Then write the

numbers in the appropriate common movement areas. Add up the totals to determine the potential traffic density. Now you can make changes to create the desired traffic patterns, such as low (1 to 4), medium (5, 6, or 7), and high (8 or 9). If there is two-way traffic, the split should reflect each direction – for example, 3 to 8 for low density, 9 to 13 for medium density, and 14 to 18 for high density.

The size of the areas allocated for storage, assembly, and so on is calculated in terms of square metres. Their shape, however, needs to be altered until all the PPCs fit. This iterative process must take place when all areas are designed. Play around with different shapes to find the best combination. It is laborious doing it with paper cut-outs, but the process gives you a visual understanding of the warehouse, its operation and layout. It ensures that the best choices are made at the design stage. The time taken to design the desired warehouse is insignificant compared with the misery a poorly designed facility will impose on its operators in the future.

At the end of the processes discussed in the foregoing pages, you will have derived the best warehouse that operational experience and capability will allow. The unoccupied areas allow for growth and determine the direction the growth can take.

Fire

A storage facility must be prepared for fires. This requires that there is at least a sprinkler system in the roof of the building. Sprinkler systems are fitted with quartz iodide bulbs which break above a certain temperature.

Insurance companies often insist on sprinklers in the racks. These prevent fires from spreading to the point where they activate the roof sprinklers. The sprinkler pipes and iodide bulbs in the racks can easily be damaged in the course of storing and picking operations, resulting in water release that may damage goods. Make sure that this type of damage is covered by the insurance.

Both the local fire brigade and the insurance assessors need to approve the system. Not every-

thing these parties ask for is compulsory. Discuss it with them and make rational, economical choices.

Security

Security measures need to be taken to prevent break-ins and theft of primarily individual items (pilferage) from within the warehouse. Both forms of theft impact on the design of the warehouse.

Preventing theft from within the warehouse involves a thorough check of goods loaded into trucks. Additional staff and space may be needed for this purpose. Remote or hidden areas where theft can take place must also be identified. If such areas exist, the design should allow for cameras to be installed. In addition, the design must include an appropriate security system (to protect the warehouse against break-ins) and secure the perimeters of the property (to prevent theft of or from trucks).

We distinguish between *passive electronic security*, such as an alarm that gets triggered when a door or window is opened, and *physical presence security*, which refers to human labour. The best mix depends on the risks for and the access to each facility. It is unlikely that the security measures will need to consist entirely of either passive or physical security. All facilities should have some form of fencing, whether around the building or around the complex. Perimeter beams detect movement and can be used to protect the perimeter with or without physical security.

Below is a short summary of the various security options for the warehouse itself.

Guards

Guards offer physical security. A physical presence is required where a search of the personnel needs to be effected when they enter or exit a building. The verification of the handover of physical goods is also best done with a physical check by an independent person.

The disadvantage of security guards is that they work in the same environment as the operations staff, and eventually cannot be deemed independent unless they are rotated regularly and randomly.

Alarms

A local, audible alarm which indicates a forced entry may cause burglars to flee. The use of an alarm linked to an armed response unit may significantly reduce the time available for removing the goods. These alarms are triggered either when a door or window is opened or when the passive infra-red (PIR) beams record movement inside the warehouse.

A refinement of the infra-red beams used to measure movement is the use of infra-red to measure temperature. Besides detecting movement in the warehouse, this advanced beam system also rings an alarm when there is a fire.

Video cameras

Video recording cameras provide visual records of remote or obscure corners of the facility. The recordings can either be watched by security staff or checked only if a problem is detected. As searching these tapes is time-consuming, they are not very useful for determining whether a problem exists or not. It is more effective to use them to find the cause of a problem once the problem has been identified.

A useful development is to save the images to a computer. Software is available for identifying a specific item or place in the warehouse. It also allows one to search for periods when movement occurred in the area, making it easy and quick to track a problem.

Lighting

Generally, the lighting inside the building is left to the architect. This is a mistake. There are guidelines for lighting intensity in the building codes that the architect will utilise, but these do not take the operation into account. Operations may take place at night or at times when the external ambient light levels are low. The operations may involve storing a pallet up to 15 m from the floor or reading the bar code of the product on this pallet. Pallets may frequently need to be moved at high speed, inspected, and checked. While bar coding reduces the need to read information during the operation, it does not eliminate it.

Lighting is a science. Consult with a specialist when deciding on the intensity requirements. Identify all the areas where very good lighting is needed. The storage area may need to be free of shadows that might inhibit the safe and effective storage of a pallet. Lighting specialists will design the lighting to provide sufficient intensity in all the working areas, eliminate glare, and make the operation both safer and more efficient. A chart of the lighting intensity should be reviewed as part of the design.

The replacement of tubes or lamps must also be considered, as this can be very disruptive to operations. For example, the lifetime of an incandescent light is on average 2 000 hours, or 83 days. If the warehouse has one thousand lights and these burn on average for twelve hours per day, six bulbs need to be replaced every day. Alternative types of tube/lamp can reduce the maintenance load by up to ninety per cent. The various options are shown in Table 9.2.

Type	Lumens	Lamp life per hour
Incandescent	12-29	Up to 2 000
Fluorescent	40–83	Up to 12 000
Mercury vapour	50	Up to 16 000
Metal halide	100	Up to 10 000 to 20 000
High pressure sodium	120	Up to 24 000

Table 9.2 Lifetime and intensity for lighting [5]

Bad lighting cannot be corrected easily or cost-effectively once the facility is established.

> **Test yourself**
>
> 9.11 Good lighting involves sufficient _____ in all the working areas, eliminating _____ and no _____.

Conclusions

In this chapter, we discussed the methodology for designing a warehouse that is practical and sensible for operations. We also explored how to make decisions about segregating and combining different processes. The logistics manager who applies these principles will acquire a far more effective and efficient facility than what would have been the case without a design review.

Questions

1 Comment on the following statement: The design of a warehouse involves a large amount of calculations and repeated work. It seems to have little value for the logistics manager to get involved, as professionals such as architects design the building.
2 Placing aisles around storage racks is complicated. Block stacking is much simpler and easier to design. Could the design be simplified by using block stacking initially and then adding racking once the warehouse is operational? Motivate your answer.
3 It is determined that the loading doors need dock-levellers, additional movement aisles,

plus canopies. As these doors are expensive, either the very minimum number of doors must be supplied or the extra items must be omitted to leave only basic doors. Is this a sensible argument? Motivate your answer.
4 The plan for the growth of the facility should simply consist of building a new extension when additional space is required. Determining growth is so difficult that the problem is best left to the future, when the issues are better known. Comment on this statement.

Notes

1 See Chapter 10 for comments on the transport for the warehouse.
2 See Chapter 7 for storage methods.
3 See Chapter 7 for working space in aisles.
4 See Chapter 17 for financial aspects.
5 Morreale, R. and Prichard, D. 1995: 41.

Contents

Learning Outcomes

After you have studied this chapter, you should be able to:

- understand that the majority of facilities have the same basic operating principles;
- identify the processes that are a prerequisite for the smooth operation of a facility and be able to review and describe these processes;
- understand the importance of stock management and the methods of stock counting;
- describe the principles of efficient operation;
- set the principles for efficient transport operation;
- describe a cross-dock operation and how it differs from a storage facility;
- describe the advantages and disadvantages of bar coding and scanning in a facility;
- identify the focus that world class operations require; and
- understand the need for good housekeeping and the adherence to safety regulations.

Introduction

The operation of a warehouse is a complex series of processes. It makes little difference whether the facility handles steel coils on a berth in a port or whether it is a large distribution facility for groceries; the processes are essentially the same. The function of a warehouse is conceptually very simple: to receive goods into the facility, to store these goods and, when required, to dispatch the goods. This seemingly simple function hides a complex set of operations, all of which must be performed well for the facility to operate efficiently and effectively. There are usually also stringent time limits and little room for errors.

To manage a facility successfully, the personnel must be able to work under time pressure. Every stage of each operation needs to be recorded so that the progress can be monitored. The right person for this job is not someone who seeks a quiet life!

> **Test yourself**
>
> 10.1 The warehouse _____ goods, stores these goods, and _____ the goods when required.

Processes

We are now going to discuss the processes that support the simple concept of receiving, storing, and dispatching. In Figure 10.1, the processes are shown as flows. There are thirteen different flow processes in a warehouse. Each one of these must be provided for and performed precisely. Each flow needs to happen at the right time and must be recorded correctly. Failure to do so will result in faulty stock records, so that finding the stock will become problematic and time-consuming – leading to an exponential drop in efficiency.

One of the processes in the facility is the let-down of pallets. Full pallets are generally stored in the upper levels so that the easily accessible levels are left for pick faces. The process of removing the full pallets from these upper storage levels, either to the pick face or to the dispatch area, is known as let-down.

Other processes may be needed for specific operations. These may include bond storage for imported goods that have not been released by the customs department, or the combination of several existing items or components into a new item. For example, a compact disk may be added to a CD player for a promotion. The CD and CD player are taken from stock and a new item – a CD player with a CD – is added to the stock. The warehouse must be prepared for these special operations. However, the processes in Figure 10.2 are the essential ones that all warehouses must follow all the time.

> **Test yourself**
>
> 10.2 There are _____ processes in a facility. _____ of these must be performed correctly _____ time.

Errors in operation

The essential purpose of any warehouse is to be able to manage the stock in storage, the stock received, and the stock dispatched in such a way that the warehouse can supply the right stock at the right time and place. If the wrong item is delivered, it implies that there is an operational error. The same applies for late delivery, delivery of damaged items, or even failure to deliver. This discussion confirms the definition of logistics and its focus on supporting the marketing effort. The cost-effective delivery of goods is only possible if the correct goods are received into the warehouse, the stock is managed while in the warehouse, and the correct stock is picked in time to be delivered to the customers.

Any error needs to be detected and corrected first, and then the correct procedure must be followed. As information records need to be matched, this is a labour-intensive process. Errors effectively quadruple the work load: First, one incorrect process occurs; the second step is to identify the error; the third step is to rectify the error; and the last is to follow the correct process. Errors also place time constraints on operations.

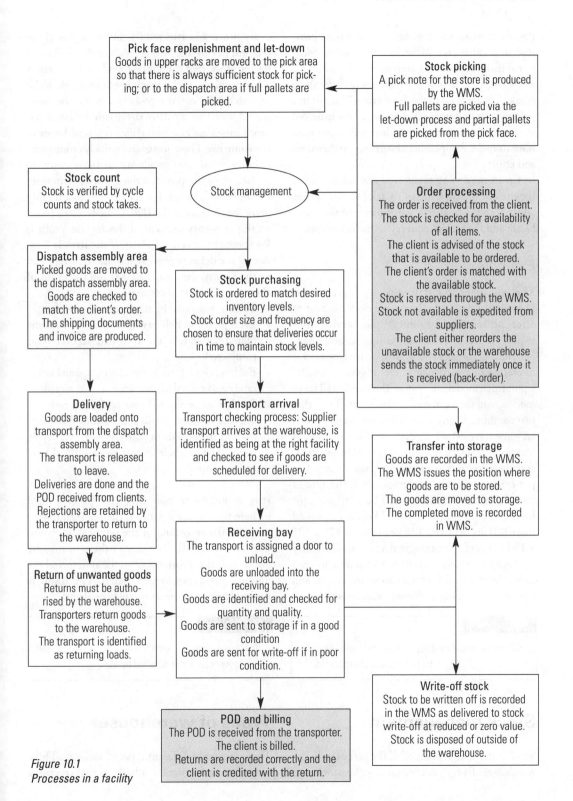

Pick face replenishment and let-down
Goods in upper racks are moved to the pick area so that there is always sufficient stock for picking; or to the dispatch area if full pallets are picked.

Stock picking
A pick note for the store is produced by the WMS.
Full pallets are picked via the let-down process and partial pallets are picked from the pick face.

Stock count
Stock is verified by cycle counts and stock takes.

Stock management

Order processing
The order is received from the client.
The stock is checked for availability of all items.
The client is advised of the stock that is available to be ordered.
The client's order is matched with the available stock.
Stock is reserved through the WMS.
Stock not available is expedited from suppliers.
The client either reorders the unavailable stock or the warehouse sends the stock immediately once it is received (back-order).

Dispatch assembly area
Picked goods are moved to the dispatch assembly area.
Goods are checked to match the client's order.
The shipping documents and invoice are produced.

Stock purchasing
Stock is ordered to match desired inventory levels.
Stock order size and frequency are chosen to ensure that deliveries occur in time to maintain stock levels.

Delivery
Goods are loaded onto transport from the dispatch assembly area.
The transport is released to leave.
Deliveries are done and the POD received from clients.
Rejections are retained by the transporter to return to the warehouse.

Transport arrival
Transport checking process: Supplier transport arrives at the warehouse, is identified as being at the right facility and checked to see if goods are scheduled for delivery.

Transfer into storage
Goods are recorded in the WMS.
The WMS issues the position where goods are to be stored.
The goods are moved to storage.
The completed move is recorded in WMS.

Return of unwanted goods
Returns must be authorised by the warehouse.
Transporters return goods to the warehouse.
The transport is identified as returning loads.

Receiving bay
The transport is assigned a door to unload.
Goods are unloaded into the receiving bay.
Goods are identified and checked for quantity and quality.
Goods are sent to storage if in a good condition
Goods are sent for write-off if in poor condition.

Write-off stock
Stock to be written off is recorded in the WMS as delivered to stock write-off at reduced or zero value.
Stock is disposed of outside of the warehouse.

POD and billing
The POD is received from the transporter.
The client is billed.
Returns are recorded correctly and the client is credited with the return.

Figure 10.1
Processes in a facility

Personnel make more mistakes under time pressure than otherwise. More mistakes means additional time pressure and even more mistakes. This is a vicious circle which is extremely difficult to break. Any increase in the error rate will result in a reduction in customer satisfaction, as the expected service level will deteriorate. Customers may then start to make complaints, absorbing further time and effort.

Errors need to be monitored and minimised as they result in stock losses or sales losses. These affect both the financial performance of the warehouse and the service delivery to the customers.

Example

The consumer industry seeks to maximise its December sales and salespeople do their best to offer prospective customers the service they require. In the store in our example, it often happens during the year that a prospective customer is interested in a particular range of goods, consisting of three models. The store then orders all three models, and the customer chooses one. The other two are immediately returned to the warehouse as an unwanted stock order. If this practice is increased in December by, say, twenty per cent, and the sales in that month increase twenty-five per cent over the year average, then the rate of returns to the warehouse will be fifty per cent higher than in other months. (This is calculated from 120 per cent and 125 per cent, or 120 x 125 = 150 per cent of the original 'error' rate). A fifty per cent increase in the returns to a warehouse can easily throw an efficient warehouse into chaos and turn it into a highly inefficient warehouse.

every process is affected by the stock. For these reasons, having the wrong stock in the facility, or having stock that cannot be found immediately, is a big problem. If the stock is not available to be sent to customers, the processes cannot be completed and the result is dissatisfied customers. Stock losses are also immediate financial losses to the company. These losses can quickly erode profitability, as the lost goods are far more costly to replace than the profit derived from performing the logistics function. For the delivery of a R1 000 item, the charge may be R20. If the facility's profit on this is twenty per cent of this fee, the profit is R4 (twenty per cent of R20). If the item is 'lost' during the delivery process and has to be replaced by the facility, the cost is R1000 and the profit of R4 is insignificant in comparison.

Stock is managed by three control processes:

- Each pick and delivery of stock must be completed accurately and recorded accurately as completed.
- Each receipt of stock must be completed accurately and recorded accurately as completed.
- Stock must be audited continually (i.e. counted, and the physical goods matched to the information recorded in the system) via cycle counts. These cycle counts are described later in this chapter.

It is important to note that each process must include two separate actions: the physical operation and the recording of the physical operation with the WMS. To do either of these incorrectly means that the information on the system and the physical goods no longer match. The result is further errors and the associated problems.

Stock management

Stock is the central point of all the processes in the warehouse. Every process affects the stock and

Types of warehouses

There are many different types of facilities. These range from a terminal in a harbour that receives a product from a production facility inland and loads it into a ship for export, to a large distribution centre where finished goods are accumulated and sent to the store or customer. In fact, some supply chains have a manufacturer's warehouse, a third party or a common user warehouse, and finally a store regional distribution centre (DC) delivering to the retail store. All these operations have a receive and dispatch function, all of them track stock and final deliveries. The only exeption is the cross-dock facility, where the storage function is absent, and the processes of storing and picking are combined into a sorting operation.[1] The operation of a cross-dock facility will be dealt with in detail after the generic processes have been described.

Efficiency in a warehouse

Three tenets underlie the efficient operation of any facility. These reflect the criteria against which all operations must be measured for efficiency. The facility controls the operation from its boundaries as goods are moved into the warehouse, handled and stored, and moved from the warehouse to the customers. The operation encompasses not only the operation within the building, but also the interaction with the transport. For the purposes of this chapter, transport refers to either the rail or the road vehicles used to move goods over land or onto ships.

Principle 1

Goods at rest within the boundaries of the facility but outside a designated storage area reflect an inefficient operation.

There are only two desired areas of storage in a facility. These are the long-term storage areas (including the pick faces) and the dispatch assembly area, where goods are accumulated to build a load. Any other areas, e.g. the receiving area, where goods are at rest are reflections of inefficiency.

Principle 2

The location of goods within the boundaries of the facility must be known for an efficient operation.

The processes of the warehouse require that the whereabouts of the goods must be known. If it is not known, the goods may not be available for efficient delivery or problems may arise with the receipt of additional goods.

Principle 3

People will perform the operation efficiently only if they are trained to do each job in the best way, and are given sufficient time to do the job without errors.

Time and effort are required to rectify errors. Proper, formal training is the best way of preventing errors.

The training must focus on the specific manner in which each job should be performed and the sequence in which it should be performed. This requires that every job be defined as a set of written procedures that specify the actions in the appropriate sequence. In this way, the personnel are trained to do the job right the first time and every time. Personnel become efficient if they understand and practice a job. This should not stifle innovation or improvement. Everyone should be encouraged to effect changes, but these changes cannot be made by individuals as and when they decide to try something new. A proposed change may improve the local operation, but have a detrimental effect on the overall performance. Changes must be carefully tested and measured. Improvements must be recorded in the procedures and communicated to all the employees.

Leaving training to chance or to the individual operators will result in fluctuating performances between different operators, and varying standards of operations for different teams. After some time of allowing this ad hoc training, inefficiencies in the way the work is done will be transferred to new employees and the operation will fall far short of its most efficient level.

Processes and operations

Overview

There is no one perfect model for operating all warehouses. The design, goods, and time pressures vary from facility to facility. We present here the principles that underlie all good operations. Any facility that fails to comply with these principles operates ineffectively or inefficiently.

The following processes are inherent in all facilities:

- receipt of transport and identification of loads;
- unloading of transport and confirmation of the quantity and quality of the goods delivered to the receiving bay;
- transfer of stock into storage;
- replenishment and let-down of stock to pick face;
- picking of ordered goods from storage;
- assembly of the goods to create a transport load;
- delivery of the goods and obtention of proof of delivery (POD);
- stock purchasing;
- stock write-off;
- POD and billing;
- order processing;
- return of unwanted goods; and
- stock counting.

The principles in the operations that form part of these processes will be described in some detail. Stock purchasing and the financial aspects are covered in other chapters and are omitted in this chapter.

Receipt of transport and identification of loads

Transport must be scheduled. This may sound difficult and restrictive, but it is essential to the successful operation of any facility. The arrival of transport must be planned so that the facility can provide the staff to handle the unloading, the equipment to move the goods, and the capacity to handle any discrepancies between the stock ordered and delivered. Without this planning, the workload in the facility will fluctuate excessively. Time delays will result in irate transporters. The pressure on the operations staff increases in these peak times and this reduces efficiencies and the accuracy of the receipt.

The recommended process is to handle transport as follows:

- The supplier books the transport load to be delivered to the facility.
- The load details are confirmed with the facility.
- Transport arrives at the facility within the scheduled arrival period and the check is merely a confirmation of the load.
- The order number is checked.
- With good planning, the door where the truck should be discharged can now be allocated.
- The truck waits for the door to become available, and is then discharged quickly and efficiently.

There are practical considerations in this process. Preparation and planning on the part of the facility is essential. On arrival, the transporter must present the documentation for the order to the transport management section. This section must have arranged the allocation of doors with the facility operations. This ensures that all loads are allocated to doors where the load can be received by the appropriate number of personnel and equipment. The transport management section often gives the transporter authorisation identification, such as a coloured disk, for a particular door. This indicates that the order has been confirmed against the WMS, the transporter is in the queue for a particular door, and the operations staff can receive the load without rechecking the time and the validity of the order.

Failure to follow these procedures may result in the delay of transport, and problems in receiving goods and matching them to orders. The efficiency of the facility suffers dramatically as the workload fluctuates and personnel and equipment must be moved from one area to another in random patterns. The example below illustrates this.

Example

A facility receives transport on a first come, first served basis. Trucks arrive early in the morning and begin to queue in front of the receiving area. The facility receives the documentation from each of the transporters as they join the queue, and begins to process the documentation. One by one, the loads are received. More trucks arrive than can be handled by the facility. The transport area becomes congested and trucks trying to leave have to manoeuvre their way out of the area. This delays the next truck trying to get to the receiving door. Some of the trucks still in the queue by mid-afternoon can see that they are unlikely to be discharged, as the queue is too long. However, their documentation is with the facility and has been entered into the facility's system, so they cannot leave. The warehouse closes the receiving function early to record the return of the documentation for loads it is unable to receive on that day. This documentation is then handed back to the transporters who can return the next day to try to deliver the goods.

Such delays may add over fifty per cent of the usual transport cost to the costs of the suppliers. Taking back full loads and then recommitting the loads the next day to the same warehouse cause a considerable increase in processes for the supplier. The most distressing part of this example is that the warehouse does not have the right goods at the right time – the receipt of goods is random, based on who arrives first.

Sounds fanciful? This actually describes the observed operation of many retail stores.

Test yourself

10.7 The planning for transport must include the appropriate _____ and _____, and the capacity to handle _____.

Receiving bay

Once the receipt of transport has been arranged, the orders can be unloaded. The facility must transfer the goods into storage. In so doing, they incur the financial responsibility for the purchase of the goods. The process therefore involves not just accepting goods, but also checking the quantity and the quality. The packaging must be in good condition and suitable for storage and sale. The unloading must be efficient and cost-effective for all parties, yet allow for checking the quality and quantity of the goods. The best method for achieving this is the following:

+ Allocate the receiving bay for the goods.
+ Load the goods from the truck and place them on the floor, starting as far from the truck as possible in the first of the demarcated rows.

This is illustrated in Figure 10.2.

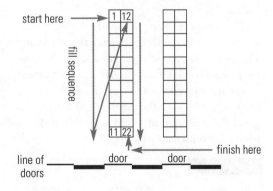

Figure 10.2 Fill sequence of the receiving area

This sequence is recommended for the following reasons:

The goods from the truck need to be moved the minimum distance in order to utilise the available demarcated areas – in this case twenty-two spaces. While this is being done, the warehouse staff can begin to identify the received goods and start the storage process. The warehouse staff will take the goods from slot 1 first and progress down the fill sequence, as the goods are unloaded from the transport. The transporter can begin to fill up the second row while the warehouse is processing the first row. As long as the warehouse completes the move from the first row before the transport has filled row two (or spaces twelve to twenty-two), there will be no delay to the unloading of the goods as the transporter can begin filling row one (spaces one to eleven) again. This reduces the space required, minimises delays in the unloading and makes the operation as efficient as possible. It does require that the operation is co-ordinated correctly so that there are enough personnel and equipment available to perform the WMS data entry and the storage.

Placing goods into more than two rows limits access and restricts the ability to move the goods efficiently. Goods cannot be identified if three or more rows are used. Two rows give the greatest amount of useful space at the greatest level of utilisation.

The rate of receiving stock into the warehouse is dependent on the ability to store stock. Closing a receiving bay because stock has clogged the storage process is as inefficient as having excess capacity and not enough stock to store. By matching the truck schedules with the capability to receive and store, the operation proceeds smoothly and at a reasonably consistent rate.

Test yourself

10.8 The _____ of receiving stock into a facility
is _____ on the ability to _____
the _____ in the facility.

Transfer of stock into storage

The goods must be moved into the designated storage space. Once there, the move must be confirmed with the WMS. This is very important. Until the confirmation is received, the WMS assumes the goods are in transit between the receiving bay and the stock location, and therefore not available for picking.

Clear marking of all storage locations, whether permanent or temporary, will eliminate a large portion of the errors. The most common error is the storage of goods into the location adjacent (above, below, or beside) the correct location. A code number can be used for each space to confirm that the process has been completed correctly.

Racks are often identified by designating three groups of alphanumeric characters to each space. Thus A05E may refer to a location in the row of racks marked 'A', the '05th' column of spaces in the row (two characters are used in this group as the number of columns may exceed ten), and the space marked 'E', which is the fifth space in this column. This location number is used on the storage instructions. At the storage location, the operator needs to read another, different code to confirm that the goods have been stored in the correct space. The WMS knows that the location code and this confirmation code refer to the same space. The use of these separate codes reduces errors significantly. The second code can be simply a two-digit one designated to each space, in sequence. In storage racks, the first space may be AA, the next AB, and so on. In the example above, the confirmation code for A05E would be BC if the racks were six spaces high (see Table 10.1).

Replenishment and let-down of stock to pick face

Pick face replenishment

The pick face[2] is the area where the pick occurs and is usually at floor or walkway level, where the goods can be easily accessed. As stock is picked from a full pick face, the pick face needs to be

F	AF	AL	AR	AX	BD
E	AE	AK	AQ	AW	BC
D	AD	AJ	AP	AV	BB
C	AC	AI	AO	AU	BA
B	AB	AH	AN	AT	AZ
Ground: level A	AA	AG	AM	AS	AY

	Column 01	Column 02	Column 03	Column 04	Column 05

Table 10.1 Rack location code and location identification by row, column and vertical space.

replenished. The correct way to do this depends partly on the design and partly on the operating process.

With racks, the biggest challenge is to fit a full pallet into the pick face while there is still stock in the pick face. In the general rack configuration, the rack height is only just higher than the pallet height to maximise the utilisation of the rack volume. This rack configuration should not be used for the pick face, as the remaining stock in the pick face will prevent the full pallet from being added. This problem cannot be solved by simply leaving the full pallet in the aisle. Instead, rack heights in the pick face should be higher than those in the standard storage racks. This allows operators to place the existing stock on top of a full pallet in the pick face. If the WMS automatically moves a pallet once fifty per cent of the stock has been removed from the pick face, then the pick face height should be up to fifty per cent more than the standard height.

Pick face replenishment must be done as the highest priority activity in the pick cycle. If the pick face is not replenished in time, the result may be a stock shortage at the pick face, delaying the pick process.

Let-down for full pallet stock pick

When an order is received for more goods than what are held on one pallet, the less sophisticated operation will pick what stock is available in the pick face. A full pallet will then be let down. The new pallet will be moved to the pick face. The stock will be confirmed to be available to the WMS. If still more goods are needed to fulfil this order, a further let-down will be required and further delays will occur.

The ability to take full pallets of stock as part of an order will prevent these problems. The best WMS logic is to always allocate full pallets first. Only the remaining part of the order is then picked from the pick face. In the above example, only one pallet will be moved to the pick face, while another full pallet will be moved directly to the dispatch area. This is far more efficient and less time-consuming. The replenishment of the pick face is time-critical, as a lack of stock in the pick face halts the picking process.

Example

A storage facility receives an order for a hundred units. Forty of these units are stored on each pallet. There are twenty-five units in the pick face when the order is issued for picking.

Action	Pick face stock	Let-down pallets added to pick face	Items picked from pick face	Let-down pallets to the dispatch assembly area
Start	25		25	
Delay for one pallet let-down		40	40	
Delay for one pallet let-down		40	35	
Finish	5		Total pick = 100	

Table 10.2 Products taken from the pick face only

If the stock is only moved via the pick face, the transactions will occur as shown in Table 10.2.

There are fewer delays when full pallets are moved directly to the assembly area. The impact on the picking is also less, as Table 10.3 shows.

Picking goods from storage

Most facilities will at some point get orders for less than a full pallet of goods or whatever the storage unit is. The storage unit must then be broken up into smaller parts so that these lesser amounts of goods can be picked for each customer.

The instruction to pick a certain quantity of a particular product comes from the WMS in the form of a pick note. The pick note contains information regarding the order and the location of the pick face where the product is stored (in a racked system a location such as A05E). It can also contain other information, such as the full description of the product, to assist the picker. The pick note can be done on a printed form or on a wireless terminal which the picker carries when picking.

It is difficult to detect errors in picks. Double checks of the picked goods are not effective, as one generally does the check to look for occasional errors. Boredom will ensure the check is of little value, unless there are major errors. Random

Action	Pick face stock	Let-down pallets added to pick face	Items picked from pick face	Let-down pallets to the dispatch assembly area
Start	25			
Pallet let-down				40
Pallet let-down				40
Pick face	25		20	
Finish	35		Total pick = 100	

Table 10.3 Products taken from both the pick face and storage.

checks are more useful, as boredom is not an intruding factor. The consequences of incorrect picks are physical stock and information records that do not match, and customers who receive wrong goods or even no goods. If errors occur frequently, the stock in the pick face may differ so much from what is recorded in the WMS that the WMS does not provide the replenishment via letdown and the pick is delayed. One then has to resort to manual methods of letting down stock, which is inefficient. The stock in the pick face must be reconciled with what has been picked to discover the extent of the errors. This is a mammoth task, especially when there are significant numbers of pick errors.

Many WMS systems add to the problems associated with the pick face. The WMS issues a pick note and allocates stock in the pick face to the pick note. This is done in order to calculate the amount of stock left and to determine when the pick face should be replenished. The removal of goods from the pick face is generally only confirmed when the system records them in another position. This confirmation often only takes place once the goods are ready for the transport, which may be hours later. The stock in the pick face can therefore not be reconciled while there is a pick note in the facility and while the goods are not confirmed to be in the dispatch assembly area. A scanning system may record the removal of the stock immediately. This alleviates the problem somewhat, but the goods are still in transit until they are recorded in a new location, so that stock reconciliation is still not simple or even practical.

A practical method to speed up the replenishment process if the WMS system is not sophisticated is to allocate a disk for each product pick face. The disk identifies the product in the pick face. The picker takes the disk from the pick face as soon as the bay is, say, fifty per cent empty. The picker places the disk on a hanger or board adjacent to the storage area. The disk may be colour coded to reflect the rate at which the item is ordered. One colour represents very fast (e.g. red), another fast (e.g. blue), and yet another moderately fast (e.g. yellow). The personnel moving stock from the storage to the pallet area see these disks and know from the colour which stock has to be moved first for the replenishment of the pick face. The disk is returned to the pick face with the replenishment stock. This method originates from the Japanese KanBan system.

As the negative consequences of wrong picks are substantial, the pickers must be the most competent personnel to ensure efficiency.

Assembly of the goods to create a transport load

In the assembly area, goods from all the sections or PPCs in the facility are accumulated into suitable loads for transport. This must be done very systematically, as the goods need to be loaded onto the transport in the shortest possible time and in the most efficient way to minimise the transport costs. The goods should be recorded as they are received in this area so that the outstanding goods are easy to identify.

The best way to accumulate loads is to allocate a lane for each customer. The lanes must be segregated from one another so that items on partially filled pallets can be manually consolidated onto pallets in the same lane. This increases the density of the goods loaded into the transport, making the delivery more effective.

Test yourself

10.9 What are the consequences of wrong picks?

Delivering and obtaining a POD

There must be a positive means of confirming the transfer of the goods to the customer. The ownership and the risk for the goods pass to the customer on handover, and there cannot be confusion over when this happens and how. Some firms require that a company stamp be added to the signature of a senior employee authorised to receive the goods. Some businesses allow receiving bay clerks with little or no supervision to sign for valuable goods, with no formal authorisation or procedures. The latter process reflects poor management of assets and leads to problems. A proof of delivery document (POD), signed in accordance with an agreed procedure, is a prerequisite for transferring goods to the customer. It records the completion of the task of the facility. Without it, the firm will not get paid and may be held liable for any loss regarding the goods.

Return of goods

Goods may be returned to the facility because stock was delivered in error, over-ordered or damaged.

- Stock delivered in error means the stock was not delivered to the correct customer. The process includes returning the stock to the facility and crediting the customer to whom the goods should have gone with not having received the goods.
- Stock damaged in transit must be returned to the facility and the customer credited with not having received the damaged goods.
- Stock which the facility agrees to accept back from the customer must be recorded as returned stock.

Goods that are returned to the facility must be credited to the appropriate customer at the price charged by the facility. The returned goods, whether damaged or not, must be received into the facility as an increase in the stock. This is important, as the value of the goods must be retained when returned to the facility and when crediting the customer for these goods (the double entry concept of accounting). If the returned goods are immediately suitable for stock, then the goods must be put into storage. Damaged goods need to be stored in a separate area and dealt with as described in the next section.

Write-off of stock

Damages may be incurred during operation, transport, and loading or unloading. Damaged stock has to be removed from the stockholding in the facility. In the WMS, the goods should be sent to a specific zone designated for goods that are sold at a reduced price (where the goods can still be sold) or have zero value (where the goods are scrapped). Once any value received is recorded, the stock must be removed from the facility.

POD and billing

The POD allows a facility to bill for the service it renders. Inevitably, customers will query some of the deliveries. It is difficult for a facility that delivers significant quantities of goods to keep accurate records and to find the record appropriate to a specific query. A computer record of the delivery date and time is insufficient in most cases, as customers will need the POD and the signature and/or company stamp as prove that delivery was effected.

There are a number of practical solutions to this. A very comprehensive and practical method is to have the POD imaged onto a computer system. The POD images are sorted according to the reference number on the POD. When a customer queries a delivery, the POD image can be found very quickly and faxed to the customer for confirmation of the delivery.

An even better solution is to bar code the goods. The customer should have the ability to read the bar code information into their system. The system will print a receipt and send the facility a copy of the information received from the scanned bar codes.

Test yourself

10.10   The POD records the _____ of goods to the _____.

Stock counting

All errors are ultimately reflected as stock problems because the WMS records and the physical stock do not match. Counting stock is imperative to eliminate stock errors. There are two prime methods for counting stock: a full stock count and a cycle count.

A full stock count is done by two independent teams verifying each other's results. This is often done to confirm the stock for the financial auditors. If the teams agree on the numbers, these are inserted into the WMS as the correct stock quantities. If there is a discrepancy between the results of the two teams, a third team is introduced to recount the stock. This process is repeated until two of the teams agree. The agreed figure is inserted into the WMS. The process relies on the controlled counting of the stock and the figures obtained from counting the physical goods override the WMS figures. Even though reconciliation needs to be done later on between the physical and the WMS stock figures, the initial figures recorded in the WMS reflect the physical counts.

Cycle counts reconcile small sections of the facility on a continual basis. The pick faces are counted every morning when all picks are completed and recorded in the WMS. (Remember: If a pick note is issued, one cannot know whether the stock has been removed from the pick face or not until it is confirmed to be in the dispatch assembly bay.) The stock count and the WMS are reconciled immediately. The storage areas are also checked continuously. Cycle counts do not interfere with the operations of the facility and they ensure that discrepancies between the WMS and the physical stock are minimised or eliminated. When effective cycle counting is performed, facilities often do away with the large and time-consuming full stock count, as it adds no value to their operations.

The stock is often categorised for the purposes of cycle counting. One system is to distinguish between high, medium, and low value stock. The high value stock is counted more frequently than the medium value stock; and the medium value stock is counted more often than the low value

stock. Another system is to distinguish between fast, medium, and slow moving stock. In this case, the fast moving stock is counted more frequently than the medium and slow moving stock. These categorisation systems are generally based on financial considerations and are an attempt to minimise the risk of storing stock. The above systems do not really address the problems related to the operation of the facility. The facility operators need to know where all stock is, irrespective of how the stock is categorised. An error in any category could delay an order, so that the category does not qualify to be counted. The categories can assist in identifying problems in the most cost-effective way.

Considering the above, stock takes for financial audits – whether done once a year or more frequently – are of value only to the auditors. The operation must do cycle counts every day to eliminate the build-up of errors in the stock.

Test yourself

10.11 _____ reconcile small areas of the facility on a _____ programme.

Transport operations

As transport usually accounts for the largest cost for a facility when capital charges plus receipt and dispatch movement costs are included, the transport must be used efficiently. This is achieved by packing full loads and utilising the transport for as long as possible each day.

The operation of the transport system must allow for trucks to be loaded to the maximum volume or mass, without compromising the standards of service required by the customers. The loads must be built up from goods picked from the various sections of the facility. Separate transport fleets for various sections of the facility constitute gross inefficiency. The transport should be regarded as one fleet serving all customers. Loads must be accumulated in a dispatch assembly area in the facility. The loads should be built to fill the truck. Where the load does not fill the truck, the orders of two or more customers must be loaded into the same truck. This truck then travels a route that services the customers in sequence.

Trucks can only do a limited number of deliveries as they must travel between the stops, discharge the goods and then complete the documentation before moving to the next stop. The number of stops that are feasible depends on the distances, the time taken to unload and the times when customers will accept goods. Many customers will agree to accept goods not only during office hours, but also very early in the morning and later in the evening. The utilisation of a truck that normally operates from 8:00 to 16:30, or for 8,5 hours, can be significantly improved if it is allowed to discharge goods between 07:00 and 08:00 while peak traffic occurs in cities. The same applies for the evening.

Planning transport is a complex exercise. Accumulating goods into loads in one area may be difficult, particularly as various customers may have different size orders on different days. This also means that the routes are constantly changing. It is very difficult to plan the truck utilisation manually. It is better to have an information system that can analyse the data to find the best combinations of loads and truck routes. These systems range from simple to very sophisticated and can improve the transport efficiency and effectiveness significantly.

Whether the transport is optimised by a system or not, extended hours and flexible delivery times significantly improve productivity. These are negotiated between the customers, suppliers, and the facilities within the logistics chain.

Example

Parts and accessories for the motor industry are regularly moved to service centres to replace items used in repairs. The service centre maintains a stock facility, but items only arrive one day after they were ordered. At first, the parts were delivered before 10:00 the next day using a courier service. This was expensive, and it was often midday by the time the parts were placed into the stock facility. This affected the centre's ability to repair vehicles and often left the customers

unhappy. A new system was devised. The parts and accessories were placed into a cage on wheels (called a rolltainer) and sealed. Each centre created a locked storage area large enough to store the rolltainer. The transporter could access the storage area after hours. The transporter then delivered a rolltainer at night, at a time that suited its transport capability. There were no delays for traffic congestion, nor for the handover of the goods. The customer had the opportunity to check the rolltainer into the store in the first hour of the morning when vehicles were still being accepted into the centre. Parts became available to the technicians by 08:00 and at a lower cost.

Cross-dock operation

The cross-dock operation is often spoken about as a different operation from that of a warehouse or distribution centre. The cross-dock[1] is the same as any facility, except that the goods are not put into storage. The storage is eliminated by combining the storage and pick operations into a receive, sort, and dispatch operation that excludes storage on the floor of the facility. This operation has a number of significant advantages, if done properly. The primary advantage is that the turnover time of the inventory drops to less than one day. This also has financial benefits. Furthermore, the goods are in the supply chain for a shorter time, so the operation is ideal for goods with limited life times, such as groceries and fresh foods.

The cross-dock operation may be ineffective for a number of reasons. The sorting must be done in a very limited period. The whole process, from the receipt to the dispatch of the goods, happens within one day of operation. If it is not completed in one operating cycle or twenty-four hours, the process will be inefficient as it will include a storage process. In such a case, the goods occupy a large floor area and are difficult to find.

The speed with which the operation must be performed can cause problems if large quantities are handled. Therefore, the operation needs to be carefully managed, the processes must be designed to be as simple as possible, and the staff must be well trained in the proper method of operation. The suppliers are critical to the success of a cross-dock facility. The supplier must deliver the correct quantity of goods. Any shortages will result in the customers not receiving the ordered amount, as additional supplies cannot be found in the time scale of a few hours. As there is no storage, surpluses are also not acceptable. Suppliers need to be committed to deliver every day to maintain the reliability of supply. This increases the transport costs of the supplier. To balance these costs, the supplier benefits from a steady supply and the commitment from the purchaser to place orders regularly.

As the process takes place in a limited space, one must adhere to the three principles of operation:

+ Goods must not be at rest.
+ The whereabouts of goods must be known.
+ The personnel must be trained in the proper operation.

The limitations of space and efficiency require that the process be seen as a pull system. The pull system means the goods are pulled into the sort process only as fast as they can be sorted to the dispatch assembly lanes. This keeps the flow of goods equal at all stages of the process and prevents a build-up of goods in any area. (A push system means goods are pushed into the process irrespective of whether the downstream processes can receive them or not. This decreases the space available for sorting and movement and significantly reduces efficiency.)

The sorting must be completed in time to allow for the goods to be checked and added to the loads so that the dispatch transport can leave on time. The period available for sorting determines the rate at which sorting must be done. The receiving rate should be the same as the sorting rate to create the pull system. Transport must be scheduled in order to ensure an even receipt of products, rather than trucks, throughout the receiving peri-od. The ideal operation uses at least two doors, so that one vehicle can unload while the next prepares to unload. This allows just sufficient goods on the receiving bay floor so that the goods can be drawn at a consistent rate for sorting. Any excess goods received will spill onto the sorting floor and reduce efficiency. The receiving bay contains buffer stock, which ensures that the sorting process operates at a constant and efficient rate.

An identification label should be attached to each item to permit simple sorting to the appropriate assembly lane or bay. The label may be designed for an automatic sorting capability or for manual sorting by personnel.

For the pull effect to work, there must be a buffer of stock that is ready for sorting between the sorting area and the receiving bay. The receiving bays must have clearly marked areas for the prepared items with the sort labels attached. This area must be kept as full as possible by unloading goods from the vehicles, but the unloaded goods must never exceed the available receiving floor space. Pressure from the transport to unload quicker must be ignored and only the goods needed to feed into the sorting area must be unloaded.

Example

A certain facility receives boxed goods. The facility builds loads in the dispatch assembly area between 18:00 and 20:00 every night. The goods arrive at random times between 08:00 and 19:00 each day. On an average day, some 12 000 boxes are received.

The sorting in this example is done manually. The process is as follows: The boxes are received from the trucks on pallets, with fifty boxes on each pallet. It takes two minutes to label the boxes on one pallet. Each pallet is moved from the receiving bay to the sorting area within three minutes and the sorting of the fifty boxes on the pallet takes ten minutes.

The total time to label, move, and sort the boxes on one pallet into the proper lanes is fifteen minutes (two minutes for labels, three minutes to move the pallet, and ten minutes to sort the boxes on the pallet). This means that twenty-four pallets per hour can be received and sorted in the ten hours currently set aside for unloading. The transport, whether road or rail trucks, must deliver and unload twelve pallets per hour, every hour, to each of the two receiving doors. One truck will need to arrive early so that boxes are ready for the sort operation at the start of the ten-hour period. At twenty-four pallets per hour, this example will need a ten-hour shift to get the operation completed at 18:00. Such a long shift is difficult to arrange, and it may be more sensible to operate at thirty pallets per hour in an eight hour shift.

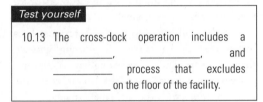

Test yourself

10.13 The cross-dock operation includes a _____, _____, and _____ process that excludes _____ on the floor of the facility.

Bar coding and scanning

The description and principles of the operation of a facility are the same whether the stock records are kept on bin cards (sheets of paper held in each pick face) or the most advanced WMS. The practical operation of a WMS requires a significant amount of data capturing. Every move of goods from one location to a next, every receipt, and every dispatch must be recorded. The operator performs the action, notes the action, and the information is captured into the WMS. This action is usually the factor that holds up the operation. For example, a pallet of goods is let down from storage and placed in the pick face. The move must first be recorded in the WMS as complete before the system will allow further picks to be issued from that pick face. The faster the recording process, the more efficient the operation.

Scanning and bar coding reduce the delays associated with data capturing, increases the accuracy of data capturing, and provides more detailed information of where goods are in the process than manual data capturing does. The scanning allows the operator to record the action into the terminal (the equivalent to noting the action in the manual

process). The terminal automatically updates the WMS. The scanning system speeds up data collection and reduces the need for written records. The communication between the scanner and the WMS can also be wireless. Wireless scanning eliminates the time taken for the scanner to update a terminal which then progressively updates the WMS. Wireless communication also allows instructions and information to be downloaded from the WMS and displayed on scanners or terminals in vehicles.

Bar codes can be introduced to identify products. The bar codes reflect a number that is specific to a product and a pack size. For example, a pack of six red lipsticks has a specific number. Different numbers are given for other colours in the same pack size. A single scan will identify the product and the pack size.

Once the product is recorded as received, the movement to storage can be much more efficient if wireless communication is available. The driver of the movement vehicle scans a received pallet, and the WMS sends a message to the driver's terminal with instructions about the storage location of the pallet. Once the pallet is put into the correct rack, the rack code is scanned, and the WMS checks the scanned slot number to ensure it is the correct slot before recording the movement as complete. This requires significant time if done with a paperwork record system and manual data capturing. The advantages of bar coding and scanning are similar for the majority of processes in the system.

Because scanning yields such a speedy response, it allows for the receipt of cases, boxes, or pallets rather than the entire load. This reduces the area required for receiving. Similarly, the pick and dispatch process can be made much more efficient. The product and quantity to be picked can be displayed on a terminal. The completion of the pick of each product can be confirmed to the WMS. The WMS can instruct a vehicle to move picked goods to the appropriate assembly area bay and confirm the arrival of goods at the bay, all without operators having to record the information, capture the information into the WMS, or wait until instructions for picking are printed.

Bar code scanning in conjunction with wireless communication introduces additional checks in the system. The processes, and the management of the processes, benefit from these. It also speeds up the processes, which can complicate operations if they lack the capacity and training to control this. Unlike with a manual system, operators now perform the physical tasks and the data capturing simultaneously. This places pressure on the operators, who must be carefully selected and trained. Supervisors must also be able to rectify errors quickly and effectively, as these will cause the process to grind to a halt fairly quickly in this type of operation. For example, a pallet (called X) is stored in the wrong space in the rack. The storage vehicle arrives to store a pallet in the slot which pallet X is wrongly occupying. The let-down truck arrives to take pallet X to a pick face, but the pallet slot is empty. Two drivers and two vehicles are now idle, while picking and storage slow down. A supervisor must be able to rectify the problem under great pressure.

More sophisticated labels can be used to assist in cross-dock operations. The supplier receives an order and confirms the exact quantity with the facility. The facility then issues the labels to the supplier who attaches them to the goods for delivery. The label contains the supplier information, product information, and the delivery point. This allows for the goods to be received and sorted using the same label. This label can also serve for delivering the goods to the customer.

The use of bar coding and scanning is of value to any operation, and even more so when the same bar code information can be retained throughout the supply chain. This extends the benefits to all the supply chain processes. This integration of the chain with regard to information is a major area for improvement in the local market as very few manufacturers, distributors, or retailers have managed to achieve this.

Test yourself

10.14 Scanning and bar coding _____ the _____ associated with the capture of data, _____ the _____ of the data capturing, and provides more _____ of where goods are in the process than manual data capturing allows.

The challenge of managing continuous change

The research into firms that are setting the standards in the world and the reasons why they have achieved this status isolates a number of issues that directly reflect on how facilities should be operated. Whether the facility is the most modern or not, and whether it has the best WMS or a less sophisticated one, research records that:

'World class competency is a managed result.'[3]

To be world class, the research shows, there are four areas of competency:
- strategy;
- measurement;
- integration; and
- agility.

The strategy has no bearing on the operation of a facility, but the remaining three areas do. Operations can only aspire to improve towards world class standards if they adopt the issues surrounding measurement, integration, and agility. These directly influence the operation and its ability to grow.

The secret to a world class operation is that the fundamental principles of the operation, sometimes called the 'drivers' of the operation, are sought and measured. Measurement allows for improvements to be prioritised, justified, and implemented.

Integration has a number of factors:
- supply chain unification;
- information technology;
- information sharing – key information is given to all parties;
- connectivity – the capability to exchange data in a timely, responsive, and compatible format;
- standardisation – common operations designed to be the most efficient and effective;
- simplification; and
- discipline – to do the right action at the right time in the right way each time.

Agility is the ability to be flexible in areas that add value to all parties.

One of the cornerstones of world class logistics is that continual improvement is necessary. More efficient and effective processes need to be pursued at all times. In all cases, the improvements must benefit the entire chain and not individual segments only.

Example

A large range of grocery items are manufactured and packed into small bottles. The manufacturer wraps six bottles of each product with plastic. Twelve of these packs are placed in a box. The box is the minimum unit for delivery. The distribution centre has to purchase the boxes from the supplier. After receipt, it has to open the boxes and store the goods as packs of six. The receipt, the opening of the box, and the storage of the packs of six into stock, require physical movement and data capturing for each step to be correctly recorded in the WMS. The box is disposed of, so it adds unnecessary cost to the process. Using returnable containers instead of boxes is one alternative that will save costs and simplify the processes in both the manufacturing and the distribution centre.

Operations that continually improve are those that offer added value to their customers, suppliers, and shareholders.

> **Test yourself**
>
> 10.15 An operation requires competency in the four areas of _____, _____, _____, and _____ to be world class.

Safety in operation

The statutory requirements for safety in facilities in South Africa are spelt out in the Occupational Health and Safety Act.[4] This Act prescribes the actions that must be taken to provide a safe working environment. It also prescribes that accidents must be reported to inspectors who have the power to investigate the accident and fine the firm or even recommend prosecution.

The cost of an accident is significant when adding up the lost time for the personnel involved in the accident, as well as for the personnel who are involved in investigating the cause of the accident. It is cheaper to ensure a safe working environment.

No facility can be operated efficiently or effectively and be dirty, cluttered with goods, or badly maintained. A clean and orderly facility, with all areas clearly demarcated, has the potential to be efficient and effective. Housekeeping renders far more value than the effort taken to achieve it. It offers a good impression to prospective customers, and it sets a professional standard for the people who work there.

> **Test yourself**
>
> 10.16 Housekeeping renders far more _____ than the _____ to achieve it.

Conclusions

Three themes recur when discussing the operation of facilities:
- The facility must be organised.
- All the operations must be co-ordinated.
- All the processes must be performed correctly the first time and at the proper time.

To achieve this, staff must be well trained and operations must be continually improved. This requires that information (which suggests measurement) and feedback be given to operators. The location and movement of stock must be managed and stock must be reconciled to the WMS continually. While technology in the form of WMS and scanning systems offer improvements, the thirteen fundamental processes must be managed at all times. Errors in all processes must be carefully controlled.

Questions

1 There are a number of principles that underpin efficient operation in facilities.

a) Describe the principles in your own words and explain why a facility benefits from adhering to these.

b) During a short visit, how would you determine whether the facility has recognised these principles and is applying them?

2 The training in a certain company consists of an experienced operator showing new employees how the processes have been performed for the last ten years. Is this the best way to train new operators? If not, which is the best way? Give a specific example of how you would train someone in a process of your choice.

3 Stock counting in a facility should be done only once a year, as intermediate stock counts are a waste of time and effort. Do you agree with this statement? What operational and financial value can intermediate stock counts add to the business?

4 A cross-dock operation is simpler to introduce and to run than a warehouse. Comment on this statement, and discuss the importance of ensuring that the work load of the operation is maintained at a constant level throughout the period of operation.

5 All facilities must move with the times and introduce bar coding and scanning in order to be effective. Comment on this assertion and motivate your arguments.

6 Economies in transition should not look at world class standards, as these standards are not applicable to operations in such countries. Is this statement valid? Motivate your answer.

7 Give one example each of a successful and an unsuccessful operation that you have encountered as a consumer. Try to think of reasons for the success or lack of success. Could you trace it to superior or inferior facility operation, or to the purchasing aspect of the stockholding?

Notes

1 See Chapter 9 for the definition of a cross-dock facility.

2 See Chapter 7 for the definition of a pick face.

3 The global logistics research team at Michigan State University 1995: 31.

4 Occupational Health and Safety Act of 1993.

Contents

Learning Outcomes

After studying this chapter, you should be able to:

- explain the role of transport in the business logistics process;
- discuss the service characteristics of the basic modes of transport;
- identify the various components of the transport system and discuss the role(s) of each component;
- discuss the characteristics of goods, and explain the way in which each characteristic influences the transport cost of the goods;
- identify the four types of service providers and discuss the function of each service provider;
- discuss the ways in which freight forwarders and freight transport brokers can add value in the logistics channel; and
- discuss the various reasons why governments involve themselves in transport.

Introduction

The carriage of goods between origins and destinations, known as freight transport, is a key activity and usually the largest cost component within the business logistics process. Freight transport adds value to this process by creating place and time utility.

+ Place utility is the value added to goods by transporting them from a place where they occur in a useless form or where they are plentiful (i.e. in over-supply) to a place where they are processed into a useful form or where they are relatively scarce in relation to needs (i.e. effective demand exists). Place utility can be seen as the value of the availability of goods at a place where they are wanted to satisfy customers' needs.
+ Time utility is the value added by making a product available at the time it is required for consumption or use.

Goods may be grouped according to the stage they have reached in the series of processes within the supply chain, extending from primary production to consumption or final use. The groups are raw materials, semi-finished goods, and finished goods. This grouping allows one to match the physical characteristics of the goods with the appropriate transport technology; and to judge the ability of the goods to bear transport costs in relation to their value.

+ Raw materials represent the primary products of agriculture (e.g. crops and livestock), forestry (e.g. timber), fishing, and mining (e.g. ore, coal, and crude oil).
+ Semi-finished goods are in the process of being converted from raw materials to finished goods, but are not yet in suitable form for consumption or final use.
+ Finished goods are those goods that have been processed (e.g. manufactured and assembled) into the form required for consumption or final use.

Raw materials are generally moved from their primary production source (i.e. the point of origin) to a place of intermediate processing. Semi-finished goods are moved from a place of intermediate processing to a place of final processing. Finished goods are moved from a place of final processing via the warehouses and marketing facilities of distribution intermediaries to consumers (i.e. the place of consumption or final use). Waste materials are carried from places of processing and consumption to places of disposal. Returned goods – for example, empty containers, reusable packaging, and defective goods – are transported from users back to suppliers.

In this chapter, the physical components and constituent members of the transport system are identified and discussed. The main physical components of the transport system are the various modes of transport, terminals, and the goods carried (i.e. the freight). The main stakeholders of the freight transport system are service providers, transport users, and the authorities.

Operational characteristics of the various modes of freight transport

Classification

There are three basic forms of transport: air, land, and water transport.

The two forms of surface transport, i.e. land and water transport, can be further divided into sub-forms or modes of transport, distinguishable by the physical right of way (or the fixed route the mode must travel) and the technology on which they rely.

- Land modes are represented by road, rail, and pipeline transport.
- Water carriage can be grouped into sea transport and inland water transport. The latter includes navigable rivers, lakes, and human-made waterways or canals. Due to the fact that inland water transport is only common in some countries in North America, Europe, and Asia, this mode of transport is not discussed in detail in the text.

The following five modes of freight transport are discussed below: air transport, road transport, rail transport, pipeline transport, and sea transport.

Test yourself

11.3 The three basic forms of transport are _____, _____, and _____ transport.

Air transport

Operational overview

In most countries, air carriers convey less than one percent of ton-kilometre traffic. (Long distance transport is often measured according to the mass of the load and the distance the mass is moved, hence the use of ton-kilometres as a measurement.) Although increasing numbers of users are using air freight, it is mostly viewed as an emergency service because of the higher costs. In instances where an item must be urgently delivered to a distant location, or in the case of highly perishable goods, air freight offers the shortest time-in-transit of any transport mode. However, these time-sensitive shipments are generally relatively few in number or frequency.

Aircraft have cruising speeds of up to a thousand kilometres per hour and they travel internationally. With respect to intercontinental shipments, the major competitor for air freight is water carriage. Domestic air freight carriers compete directly with road freight carriers over long regional distances, and to a lesser degree with rail freight carriers.

Air carriers generally handle valuable items. The high price of air freight would represent too great a proportion of the total cost for less valuable products to be viable. Customer service considerations may influence the choice of transport mode in the case of lower-valued items, but only if service considerations are more important than cost considerations.

Although air transport provides short transit times, delivery delays and congestion at terminals may substantially reduce some of this advantage over short distances. The total origin-to-destination transit time is more important to the shipper than the transit time from terminal to terminal. In a domestic market, road transport often matches or outperforms the total transit time of air freight.

The frequency and reliability of air freight service is generally very good, but services are usually limited to movements between big cities over relatively long distances.

Air transport cost structure

Air transport, as is the case with sea transport, does not need a supplied right of way. Besides the high initial cost of acquiring aircraft, the vast majority of other cost commitments are of a variable or semi-variable nature. The limited carrying capacity and high capital and operating costs of aircraft lead to high unit costs of mostly small consignments.

Typical strengths of air transport

- Aircraft attain high speeds over long distances, which leads to high utilisation and increased revenue to the user. This feature of air transport has expanded the geographical range of markets for high-valued perishable goods such as cut flowers.
- The mode does not encounter physical en-route obstacles as other modes do.
- Air freight is not exposed to unfavourable in-vehicle conditions for long periods.

- Standardised packing units and containers are used, which reduces packaging costs. Relatively little protective packaging is required, with the understanding that products are handled with care at terminals.
- Air transport has a good security record which can be ascribed to stringent self-regulation, government safety and technical control, and the employment of well-trained and specialised staff.

Typical limitations of air transport

- Feeder and distribution services are needed.
- Carrying capacity (weight and volume) is limited.
- Congestion at airports can increase total transport time.
- Frequent flights are not always available, although the high speed may compensate for this.
- Air transport is directly influenced by inclement weather conditions such as thunderstorms, gusting wind, fog, and snow at airports; and turbulence and head winds during flights.
- Low accessibility: Airports are often situated far away from industrial and commercial areas.
- The unit cost per consignment is high.

Freight characteristics

Air transport is the favoured mode of transport for the conveyance over long distances of perishable items of high value, exotic products and fashion wear, collectors' items, pets, items for which a short lead time is vital, and courier parcel/mail consignments – theoretically all items of which the air cargo tariff is less than the additional value added by receiving the goods sooner than with the next fastest mode of transport.

Conveying items by air is the most desirable form of transport under the following conditions:[1]

When the commodity is:
- perishable
- subject to quick obsolescence

- required on short notice
- valuable relative to weight
- expensive to handle or store

When the demand is:
- unpredictable
- infrequent
- in excess of local supply
- seasonal

When the distribution problems include:
- risk of pilferage, breakage, or deterioration
- high insurance or interest costs for long in-transit periods
- heavy or expensive packaging required for surface transportation
- special handling or care needed
- warehousing or stock in excess of what would be needed if air freight were used

Test yourself

11.4 Domestic air freight carriers compete directly with _____ freight carriers over long regional distances, and to a lesser degree with _____ freight carriers.

Road transport

Operational overview

Road transport has replaced rail carriage as the dominant form of long-distance freight transport. On long hauls (also called through-traffic), road freight carriers are able to transport certain primary products of an organic nature such as timber, fish, and agricultural products (for example, livestock, fresh and frozen meats, fruit, vegetables and dairy products); some semi-finished goods; and most finished goods.

Road freight transport is more flexible and versatile than other modes because of vast networks of roads. It can therefore offer point-to-point service between almost any origin and destination. Road freight carriers can transport goods of varying size and mass over long distances. It is this flexibility and versatility that has enabled road freight transport to become dominant in most countries.

Road freight carriage offers the client reliable service with little damage or loss in transit. It generally provides much faster service than rail transport and compares favourably with air carriers on short hauls. Many road freight carriers, particularly those involved in just-in-time services, operate according to a scheduled timetable. This results in reliable transit times. Road freight carriers are, therefore, able to compete with air transport for small shipments – i.e. partial loads or less-than-truckload (LTL) consignments – and with rail transport for larger shipments.

Road transport cost structure

Of all forms of transport, road transport has the highest proportion of variable costs to total costs. Among the factors leading to this are the following:

- The road infrastructure is publicly owned. Governments typically recover road-user cost responsibility through levies included in the price of fuel, thereby converting a fixed cost into a variable transport expenditure.
- Terminal facilities are less capital intensive than the terminal facilities of other forms of transport.
- The fuel consumption of road transport vehicles is relatively high, making fuel cost a proportionally large variable cost component.

Typical strengths of road transport

- Door-to-door service: Road transport is not limited to a fixed route or to fixed terminals. Consignments can be conveyed directly from a shipper (or consignor) to a receiver (or consignee) without the need for specially built terminals.
- Accessibility: Road carriers can deliver in every country or economically active region in the world. Deliveries are therefore usually prompt.
- Freight protection: As a result of the ability to supply a door-to-door service, little handling and few transhipments take place between origins and destinations. Separate feeding/collection and line-hauling are often not necessary, and neither are delivery or distribution activities.
- Speed: This mode maintains short door-to-door transit times, especially over short distances. When delays occur as a result of traffic congestion or other incidents, it is often possible to follow alternative routes.
- Capacity: The carrying capacity, although relatively small compared with other modes of transport, is adaptable and can be readily increased.
- High frequency: A high service frequency can be maintained as a result of the small carrying capacity and high speed of road vehicles.

Typical limitations of road transport

- Limited carrying capacity: The dimensions and gross mass of road vehicles are limited through legislation.
- High environmental impact: Road vehicles create considerable noise and air pollution.
- Vulnerability to external factors: Inclement weather conditions and traffic congestion can impact on the reliability and punctuality of road transport operations – especially in countries with severe climatic conditions such as heavy fog and snowfalls.
- High energy consumption: To convey one unit of freight, road vehicles consume more energy/fuel than other forms of surface transport.
- Shared right of way: On public roads, the right of way is shared with other traffic, which increases safety and security risks and the occurrence of unexpected delays. An accident involving a truck with hazardous goods on board may result in a road closure lasting several hours. In addition to high accident risk, road vehicles are vulnerable to theft and hijacking.

Freight characteristics

Road transport is the most accessible and comprehensive mode of transport. It is exceptionally suitable for conveying high-value finished products over relatively short distances. It is therefore also suitable for collection and distribution in inter-modal operations (i.e. operations where more than one mode of transport is used). Owing to the relatively limited carrying capacity of road vehicles, they are well suited for transporting small consignments.

Test yourself

11.5 Road freight carriers are able to compete with _____ transport for small shipments and with _____ transport for larger shipments.

Rail transport

Operational overview

In some countries, and especially in Eastern Europe and Asia, rail is the dominant form of transport. In most countries, rail freight services are available between almost every metropolitan area. However, the rail network is never as extensive as the road network. Because rail transport is limited to fixed routes, it lacks the flexibility and accessibility of road freight carriers. Rail transport provides terminal-to-terminal service rather than point-to-point service for clients, unless they have a rail siding at their facility. If a facility is not connected to a rail link, another transport mode has to be used to gain access to the rail service.

Another disadvantage is the long transit time. Load consolidation in marshalling yards adds to the slow transport speed. Rail transport also cannot offer such frequent service as road transport. However, since the deregulation of land freight transport, rail transport has improved significantly in these areas. Transport deregulation increases competitive pressure to lower rail rates, resulting in the increasing use of contract rates by rail carriers.

Rail carriers, in an effort to increase freight traffic volumes, are entering new markets and are participating increasingly in intermodal transport. Freight trains do travel on timetable schedules, but departures are less frequent than those of road

freight transport. If a client has strict arrival and departure requirements, road transport has the competitive advantage over rail transport. Some of these disadvantages of rail transport may be overcome through the use of intermodal transport, which offers the advantages of rail transport combined with the strengths of other forms of transport.

Rail transport cost structure

Due to the high capital investment in infrastructure (e.g. railway lines and terminal facilities such as large administrative buildings, stations, marshalling and classification yards, sheds, goods depots, and workshops) and the longevity of rolling stock such as freight wagons, the ratio of fixed costs to total costs is very high.

Because the unit cost decreases when output increases, rail transport can gain the benefits of economies of scale when utilisation increases – and even more so in the case of a double-track operation with long trains. As a result, rail transport possesses a cost advantage over road transport with respect to bulk loads that are conveyed over long distances.

Typical strengths of rail transport

♦ Almost any type of commodity can be conveyed by rail in special train compositions.
♦ Large volumes of bulk loads can be carried in single trains over long distances, which can reduce air pollution and ease the traffic burden on roads.
♦ Rail transport generally costs less (relative to weight) than air and road freight transport, especially over long hauls.
♦ The mode is not as vulnerable to traffic congestion as road transport is. Theoretically, trains can be scheduled more reliably than road and sea transport.
♦ The mode is less affected by inclement weather conditions than other modes.
♦ Rail wagons cannot be stolen or hijacked as easily as road vehicles.

- High average trip speeds can be achieved by trains over long hauls when shunting and the special composition of train sets are not necessary (e.g. unit trains).
- Private sidings can connect the facilities of clients to the rail network to allow for loading and unloading.
- Rail transport is cost- and energy-efficient over long distances and when the carrying capacity is well utilised.
- The accident safety record of rail transport, especially with the transport of hazardous goods, is good.

Typical limitations of rail transport

- Owing to the limitations of a fixed track and specific terminals, rail services often need to be supplemented with additional feeder and distribution services.
- Rail transport has a high damage record. Because strong packaging is required to safeguard the goods, the packaging costs are high.
- Users often still perceive rail services to be of lower quality because of damage to freight and inconsistent service, despite the efforts of rail transport carriers to become more competitive since the economic deregulation of land freight transport.
- Rail transport requires enormous capital investment.
- Rail transport is vulnerable to pilferage when rail wagons remain stationary in marshalling yards for long periods.
- Directional traffic volume imbalances cause a high degree of empty running, so that return freight revenue often does not cover the costs of the return journey.

Freight characteristics

Rail transport can carry large and high-density commodities and bulk consignments over long distances and at low cost. Rail transport is therefore well suited to carry raw materials and semi-finished goods, such as mining and agricultural products. The introduction of containers has promoted the conveyance of high-value finished products.

In the bulk, long-distance transport market, throughput and price are more important to the client than transit time. For example, as long as stockpiles of iron ore or coal at a port are sufficient, the arrival times of individual trains are not important. However, in many transport segments, such as containers and parcels, rail transport is losing ground because road freight carriers offer regular, shorter, and more consistent transit times.

> **Test yourself**
>
> 11.6 Rail transport is primarily a _____-distance, _____-volume mover of low-value _____-density goods.

Pipeline transport

Operational overview

Pipeline transport has unique characteristics:
- The infrastructure is also the carrying unit.
- It does not necessarily require a return journey or return pumping process. This eliminates joint costs.
- Product intake, haulage, and discharge are combined in one process.

Pipelines are suitable for long hauls of fluids, like crude oil, petroleum products, liquid chemicals, water, and gas. The greatest utilisation can often be accomplished by using the same pipeline for different products at different times. Excessive mixing of these products is limited by the use of physical separators.

Pipeline transport offers superior reliability at a relatively low cost. Pipelines are able to deliver commodities punctually for the following reasons:
- Pipelines are not labour intensive; they are largely automated and only a few employees are needed to control pumps and valves, or to undertake maintenance.
- Worker strikes and absence have relatively little effect on their operations.

- Commodity flows through pipelines are electronically monitored and controlled.
- Weather conditions do not disrupt service.
- Losses due to pipeline leaks or damage are extremely rare.

Pipeline transport cost structure

As with rail transport, pipelines provide their own right of way. Since the pipe component, the pumps, and the tank and plant facilities are highly specialised and durable, fixed cost constitutes a high portion of the total cost – the highest of all modes. Common costs make petroleum pipelines more cost-effective, since a variety of petroleum products can be pumped consecutively. Because a return journey or return pumping process is not necessary, joint costs are eliminated and high economies of scale can be achieved if demand requires continuous pumping. Pipeline transport is highly efficient when utilisation of capacity consistently remains high. Transport cost per unit handled rises rapidly if actual usage falls below capacity, because of the high ratio of fixed cost to total operating cost.

Typical strengths of pipeline transport

- Pipelines are environmentally sound as they can be buried and run over difficult terrain (also under water). They do not generate fumes or noise, and can be disguised to prevent visual intrusion. Pollution or spillage only occurs if they are damaged. The monitoring of pipelines is advanced and effective, which enables early detection of any defects that might cause pollution.
- Pipelines are able to move bulk loads of fluids and gas very reliably over long distances at a low unit cost and low risk. Pipeline transport is highly reliable because it is both secure and punctual.
- Once the investment is made, the variable costs are low. There is also no joint cost, resulting in the highest level of economies of scale of all modes of transport.

- Although the transit speed is low – between 10 and 15 km/h – the product is immediately discharged into storage tanks upon arrival. This, coupled with the fact that the pumping process can take place continuously, without the need for a return journey, reduces the total transit time. For example, at a pump speed of 15 km/h through a pipe with a 40 cm diameter, the effective delivery rate can exceed 1,8 million litres per hour, which cannot be matched by any other mode of transport.

Typical limitations of pipeline transport

- Pipelines are able to transport only a limited range of products commercially, mainly fluids and gas.
- Pipelines are geographically inflexible as they are designed to serve fixed locations. Access to pipelines is limited due to their fixed right of way. Clients whose facilities are not connected to a pipeline must use another accessible mode of transport.
- There is a finite capacity that cannot be altered to accommodate sudden surges in demand.
- Pipelines require a high investment cost. This cost is fixed (i.e. unavoidable) and it rises rapidly per unit when throughput falls. Pipeline transport is therefore not suited for businesses that need small product volumes on an irregular basis.

Freight characteristics

Pipelines are able to transport only a limited number of products for commercial purposes, such as natural gas, fluids (which include crude oil, petroleum products, water and liquid chemicals) and slurry products. Slurry is a solid product that is suspended in a liquid (often water), so that it can be transported more easily. Pipeline conveyance of slurry coal is at present taking place as a commercial experiment in the United States of America, while commercial water pipelines serve irrigation purposes in agricultural activities and cooling purposes in power-generation plants. In South

Africa, petroleum products account for the majority of commercial pipeline traffic, followed by crude oil and gas. Considering the world's dependence on energy products, pipelines will probably become more important in the future.

Sea transport

Operational overview

Ocean carriage is the most cost-effective way of transporting high-bulk commodities over long distances and is therefore the most widely-used international shipment method. It is used for both inbound and outbound shipments, although there is usually an unbalanced flow of freight. The development of large bulk carriers has enabled sea transport to assume a vital role in the transportation of bulk materials such as ores and minerals, grains, and timber products; and especially coal, crude oil, and petroleum products between energy-producing and energy-importing countries. Because there is such a big demand for energy resources in industrialised countries, sea transport will continue to play a significant role in the transportation of these products.

Water transport is often limited to international deep sea transport and coastal shipping between local ports. Inland water carriers are dependent on the availability of navigable lakes, rivers, and canals. In North America, Europe, and Asia, for example, a significant portion of the total intercity freight tonnage is transported on inland waterways by river barges and small vessels.

Shipping has become highly specialised since the 1960s, each type of specialist ship being designed to be more productive than the ship it replaces.[1] Specialisation has resulted in ships becoming complementary to other modes of transport in the logistics chain. They are therefore often designed for a specific trade route and commodity type, with little prospect of employment on other trade routes.

- Bulk carriers carry cargoes with low value-to-weight ratios, such as ores, grain, coal, and scrap metal.
- Tankers (mostly crude oil vessels) carry the largest amount of cargo by tonnage.
- Roll-on/roll-off (Ro-Ro) ships carry cargo that is driven directly onto the ship, and allow for standard road vehicle trailers to load and unload cargo.
- Oil-bulk-ore (OBO) vessels are multi-purpose bulk carriers able to carry both liquid and dry bulk products.
- Container ships have greatly expanded the use of sea transport for many commodities. Most international shipments involve the use of internationally standardised containers suitable for intermodal carriage.

Sea transport cost structure

The cost structure of sea transport is similar to that of air transport. It is characterised by a high proportion of variable costs due to the fact that the way (the sea) does not require investment and seaports are not owned or supplied by shipping firms. Expenses in ports can be as high as forty per cent of sea transport costs. However, these obligations only arise when a port is visited.

Typical strengths of sea transport

- A low-cost service can be supplied. Large volumes of high-density freight can be conveyed over long distances.
- Standard intermodal containers can be utilised to facilitate freight handling and transhipment.
- Traffic congestion is virtually non-existent on the open sea.
- Sea transport offers a very safe and secure service.

Typical limitations of sea transport

- Service can only be rendered to and from seaports that have the facilities to receive the ship and conduct the required transhipment. A door-to-door service is therefore not possible.

♦ Because transhipment is unavoidable at both ends of a voyage, more freight handling takes place than with other surface transport modes.

♦ Ships are vulnerable to inclement weather and stormy sea conditions. This can delay delivery and in some cases prevent it altogether.

♦ Sea transport offers a slow and low-frequency service.

Freight characteristics

Almost any kind of freight can be conveyed by ship at a relatively low cost. Short delivery times are not of critical importance as far as the vast majority of commodities that are transported by ship are concerned. Clients make a trade-off between long transport times and the relatively low tariffs offered by sea transport.

Test yourself

11.8 Ocean carriage is the most cost-effective way of shipping _____ commodities over _____ distances.

Terminals

A terminal is a special area – situated at the end of a route or where different routes meet, branch out, or cross – including structures and equipment, where in-transit goods are transferred between different carriers, modes of transport, or vehicles of the same mode.

We have seen that the technologies that provide movement or mobility within the transport system are classified as modes of transport (for example, air, road, rail, pipeline, and sea transport). Terminals are classified as a specific class of node.

A node is a fixed point or place in the logistics chain where goods come to rest.

Other examples of nodes are the points of origin of raw materials, places of processing, warehouses, marketing facilities, and points of consumption or use. However, out of all nodes in the supply chain, only terminals serve primarily a transport function. Examples of terminals are airports, seaports, and stations. Terminals for land transport (i.e. rail, pipeline, and road transport) are referred to as stations, but in colloquial language the term 'station' refers to a train station or a pipeline pump station. Road transport terminals are widely referred to simply as terminals.

The following meanings should be attached to the various terminal facilities referred to in this book:

♦ Airport: a facility where the transfer of freight (air cargo) takes place between aircraft and modes of land transport.

♦ Seaport: a facility where the transfer of freight (sea cargo) takes place between different ships and/or modes of land transport.

♦ Pipeline terminal: a facility where pipelines link, or transfer takes place between, a pipeline and another mode of transport or a storage facility.

♦ Rail terminal: a facility where transfer of freight between rail wagons and road vehicles takes place.

♦ Road terminal: a road transport terminal.

Functions of terminals

In addition to accommodating the temporary storage or direct transhipment of freight, terminals also provide for the maintenance, repair, parking, and garaging of vehicles.

Terminals perform various value-adding activities to facilitate the transport of freight:

♦ Terminals provide a freight consolidation function by receiving small consignments and combining them into larger loads. Consolidation can maximise the utilisation of vehicle payload capacity. A fully consolidated vehicle may also be able to provide improved service because its freight does not need to be handled before the final destination.

♦ Terminals provide a bulk breaking (i.e. dispersion) service. This is the opposite of consolidation and involves separating larger units of freight into smaller units, usually for delivery to a final destination. Consolidation and dispersion are often performed simultaneously at terminals.

♦ Terminals perform a warehouse and transfer service. This involves the storage and protection of those consignments that are awaiting transhipment onto vehicles which are dispatched to destinations different from those of the vehicles on which the consignments arrived at the facility.

♦ Terminals often provide vehicle services. These may include the refuelling, garaging, and maintenance of vehicles and equipment, and sometimes also repairs. Examples of repair facilities at terminals are dry docks at some seaports and workshops at airports and at road terminals.

Test yourself

11.9 The technologies that provide movement or mobility within the transport system are classified as _____ of transport. Terminals are classified as a specific class of _____.

The goods carried in the transport system

The characteristics of goods

Goods can be grouped into raw materials, semi-finished goods, and finished goods. From the characteristics of goods, five factors can be isolated that determine the type of storage, handling, stowage, and carriage they require.[2,3] These five factors therefore influence the transport cost. They are:

♦ in-transit care, necessitated by the intrinsic properties of goods;

♦ density of goods, represented by the mass-to-volume ratio of the goods;

♦ size and divisibility, determined by the physical dimensions of a consignment;

♦ stowage ability and ease of handling, determined by the form of goods; and

♦ potential liability of goods, determined by their value-to-mass ratio, their fragility, their susceptibility to theft or pilferage, and their potentially hazardous characteristics.

In-transit care

In-transit care refers to special arrangements required to secure goods while stowed on board a vehicle. Special vehicle features and other in-transit precautions to keep goods secure are significant determinants of transport costs.

The intrinsic properties which determine the special care and treatment that goods require while in transit are:

Form: The distinct differences between solids, liquids, and gases have a significant influence on the required methods of packaging, handling, and carriage.

Animation: Live animals require confinement, handling, and carriage different from that suitable for inanimate materials to protect them from hunger, thirst, injury, and undue stress.

Destructibility: During transportation, goods may be exposed to fire, the elements, vibration, jerking, jolting, chafing, and violent impact. Goods that can withstand these hazards without damage can be regarded as indestructible. Examples of such goods are stone, ore, minerals, sand, and soil.

Fragility: Not all destructible goods are fragile. Fragility implies that goods are delicate and can easily be damaged, broken, destroyed, or become dysfunctional. Glassware, electronic items, mechanical instruments, and lightwood products are examples of fragile goods.

Wetness: Some goods are moist, or their physical characteristics result in the exteriors of their packaging being wet. Such goods are often classified as 'wet goods'. The significance of the classification is that proximity of wet goods to dry goods is usually undesirable.

Potential danger: Some goods have inherent characteristics that can potentially threaten health and safety. This necessitates precautions when storing, handling, stowing, and moving the goods. The packaging sometimes creates a potential hazard, for example when gases are compressed into liquid form. The various broad commodity classes, their potential hazards, and examples of specific dangerous products are summarised in Table 11.1 below.

Perishability: Goods may perish because of natural physical deterioration and obsolescence.

- Natural physical deterioration, such as the over-ripening and decay of fruits, vegetables, and flowers, and the maturation and decay of wine, cheese, and certain yoghurts may be accelerated in the transport process. Natural chemical actions within the goods may be accelerated by exposure to external bacteria, shaking, humidity, and heat. Edible goods may be rendered unfit for consumption through contamination or vermin. Grains, for example, may be rendered inedible through premature germination.
- News (e.g. as presented in newspapers) is highly obsolescent because it becomes stale after any

lapse of time. There is a similar time limit for the transportation of goods for special occasions, fashion items designed for a particular season, and medication required urgently to meet an emergency (e.g. vaccines).

Density of goods

The density of goods refers to their mass-to-volume ratio, expressed in kilograms per cubic metre. Density is an important factor when classifying goods, because both the payload space and the payload mass limit the carrying capacity of vehicles. Low-density goods, i.e. those with a small mass-to-volume ratio, are usually per kilogram more expensive to transport than high-density goods. Low-density goods absorb the space capacity without attaining maximum load mass, while high-density goods attain the maximum permissible load mass before the space is filled. By transporting goods with a density equal to the mass-volume ratio of the carrying capacity, one can make maximum use of a vehicle's payload capacity.

If the payload mass capacity is 20 000 kg and the volume of the payload space is 40 m^3, the mass-

Commodity group	Type of hazard	Example
Combustibles	fire, heat, and smoke damage; suffocation	crude oil, cotton, wood products
Contaminators	pollution or tainting of other goods due to direct contact and vapours	petrochemical products
Corrosives	vapour and chemical actions causing damage to persons and other goods through direct contact	sulphuric acid
Explosives	devastating explosions and fire	blasting material, compressed gases
Inflammables	ignition by spontaneous combustion or external heat	petroleum products
Malodorous materials	disagreeable odours	manure
Oxidisers	rapid oxidisation and combustion	nitrates, chlorates
Poisons	noxious to life and health of living beings	arsenic
Radioactives	emission of harmful rays, causing injury and damage	radium
Water-reactors	harmful reaction with water	calcium carbide

Table 11.1 Broad classes of dangerous goods

space relationship is 500 kg per cubic metre. Should the load have a density of 500 kg per cubic metre, both the loading space and the payload mass capacity can be fully utilised. The payload is not fully utilised if the density of the goods is greater or smaller than 500 kg per cubic metre.

The example above implies that the form, size, and shape of goods permit full utilisation of any available load space. However, space between packages and between small partial load lots might be inevitable – or indeed required – to avoid contact, for ventilation, temperature control, or easy access. Even when transporting liquids, one must allow space for changes in volume due to temperature changes. With loose or bulk commodities (for example, grain) the loss of payload space is limited to the voids caused by the irregular shape of the particles. The loss of payload space increases when transporting goods with bigger and more irregular shapes (for example, iron ore and coal). Indivisible articles that are not rectangular or cubic (for example, cylinders and casks) and odd-shaped items (for example, unpacked machinery and animals) occupy a relatively large proportion of unused space.

The practical density of goods, expressed as a ratio, is the stowage factor. It is calculated by dividing the consignment mass of the goods by the vehicle payload space required for transporting the goods. The stowage factor is representative of the vehicle utilisation or payload space required for the goods. Where additional space is required to stow the goods appropriately, the additional allowance is added to the payload space for the calculation.

Size and divisibility

The size of individual items may be measured in the cubic dimensions (length, width, and height), volume (for liquids, e.g. litres), or mass (e.g. kilograms). Cubic size is important for matching handling and carrying capacities with the size of the articles. The permissible size of articles may be limited by handling equipment and cubic (i.e. space) carrying capacity available. It is often more

economical to assemble articles such as power generators and electrical transformers at the place where they are manufactured, rather than at the destination where the ability and facilities for proper assembly might be lacking.

Stowage ability and ease of handling

Stowage ability and ease of handling are reflected in the cost of securing (from shifting) and handling a consignment. Items that are difficult to handle cost more to transport, and even more so when a consignment is subject to transhipment. The form and shape of goods, as well as the method used to pack them, affect their stowage ability and ease of handling. In this respect, goods can be divided into two broad classes: loose or bulk commodities and packed commodities.

Loose or bulk commodities

The natural properties of some goods permit them to be transported in bulk (i.e. without any wrapping or packaging). These commodities may be resistant to damage and may be transported in sufficiently large quantities to permit handling equipment and vehicles to be specially constructed for their conveyance. Examples are crude oil, petroleum products, timber, grain, ores, minerals, and coal.

Packed commodities

The features of many commodities necessitate wrapping and packaging. The packaging should allow for ease of handling and safe and secure carriage. Packaging consolidates materials into bigger lots that can be marketed and handled conveniently. It also protects the goods from damage. In the case of dangerous goods, it protects people and animals from injury; and equipment, other goods, and property from damage. When making decisions about packaging, the cost of packaging should be compared with savings in transport costs resulting from the packaging.

Liability

Four factors are important when considering the impact of liability on the choice of transport:

- The value of the goods determines how high the transport costs can be. The transport costs should be compared with the value of the particular commodities.
- The packaging of fragile items needs to be robust enough to withstand vibration or impact with other goods. Special packaging arrangements may assume importance when it becomes necessary to determine liability for loss or damage in transit. For example, carriers sometimes require packaging to be of a specific standard due to known vehicle vibration during travel and jerking during marshalling (shunting) in a rail marshalling yard.
- Robust and non-transparent protection may be necessary to secure valuable items against loss through theft and pilferage, adding to their transport costs.
- Liability may stem from the risk-bearing characteristics of dangerous goods. This necessitates additional insurance coverage against liability due to fatalities, injuries, illness, damage, etc. caused by dangerous goods.

Test yourself

11.10 The density of goods refers to their _____ ratio.

Freight transport service providers

Any transport system fulfils two principal functions: to provide accessibility and to provide mobility.

Accessibility refers to the availability of a suitable transport system close to users and potential users, and it reflects the ease with which destinations can be reached. Accessibility is dependent on the supply or availability of transport infrastructure and services. Infrastructure includes fixed facilities, for example, railway lines, pipelines, roads, airports, seaports, and road transport terminals. With the exception of road transport terminals, virtually all other types of transport infrastructure have traditionally either been provided by authorities or supplied by the private sector through government mediation, or through government concession.

Mobility refers to the frequency of transport activities, or the intensity with which users make use of a transport system or service. Mobility is measured through actual transport demand, i.e. the volume of passengers and freight transported between places on the infrastructure network (roads, railways, rivers etc.).

An important part of the business logistics process is identifying the providers of transport, and to be aware of their role in the supply chain. Two groups of transport service providers can be distinguished. They are transport operators and non-operating transport service providers.

- Transport operators can be classified as private transport operators (firms with an in-house transport function) and professional carriers (operators whose core business is to provide transport services to clients).
- Non-operating transport service providers can be classified as freight forwarders (also known as freight consolidators) and freight brokers (so-called freight agents).

Test yourself

11.11 Accessibility is the _____ of a suitable transport system _____ to users and potential users.

11.12 Mobility refers to the frequency of _____, or the intensity with which users make use of a _____ or service.

Private transport operators

Private transport refers to a firm operating its own leased or hired vehicles for ancillary purposes as a secondary business function in support of its primary (i.e. core) business, rather than making use of a professional carrier. Private or ancillary operators are 'first party' operators who provide carriage to their customers (the buyers of their products), the latter being the 'second party'. Ancillary operators not only conduct inbound movements of goods supplied by their vendors, but also intra-firm movements, i.e. conveyance between subsidiaries or facilities belonging to the same owner.

Private transport costs may be less than the cost of hiring professional carriers. The service advantages of control and flexibility may also be greater. The choice between private and professional carriers is not a straightforward or standard decision. It is complicated and requires careful evaluation.

Test yourself

11.13 Private transport takes place when a firm operates its _____ vehicles for _____ purposes as a _____ business function in support of its _____ business, rather than making use of a _____ carrier.

Professional carriers

Professional carriers offer transport services for financial reward. They are known as professional hauliers in road transport, but they operate within all modes of transport. Professional carriers serve clients on a contractual basis. The contracts may be long-term when they form part of a standing business logistics arrangement, or they may be single transactions (i.e. one-off and infrequent consignments) bound to agreed conditions. Professional carriers thereby act as 'third party' operators who enter into a specific carriage agreement with a consignor (the 'first party') who sends consignments of goods to a receiver (the 'second party').

Since the advent of economic deregulation of freight transport, an increasing number of users are turning to professional road transport carriers to fulfil their transport requirements under long-term agreements or contracts. Within the framework of these agreements, carriers often customise their services to fit the needs of their clients.

Contract carriers are also extending their services into a broader field of contract logistics, or so-called third party logistics. This means that a package of integrated and co-ordinated logistics services is negotiated and offered to clients. This package serves to complement and enrich traditional professional transport activities, which were mostly limited to carrying goods between points of origin and points of destination.

Test yourself

11.14 Professional carriers offer transport services for _____. They serve _____ on a _____ basis.

Freight forwarders

Freight forwarders undertake to have consignors' freight shipments transported. They are not carriers – they act as 'fourth party' service providers or transport wholesalers. Freight forwarders are often a worthwhile service alternative for shippers in the supply chain. They acquire carriage from professional operators within any of the modes. They then collect small shipments (consignments) from shippers, and consolidate them into larger rail wagon, road truck or container loads for long-distance, inter-terminal movements. At the destination terminal, i.e. the bulk breaking point, the separate consignments are dispersed to their destinations with delivery transport arranged by the freight forwarder.

Freight forwarders assume full responsibility for the freight entrusted to them, from the points of origin to the points of destination. They have agreements with consignors to have the service performed; and they enter into contracts with carriers to supply the required transport. Freight forwarding offers consignors comprehensive transport services: The consignor needs a single contract and single insurance for the consignment despite the fact that the movement may require the use of the facilities of several operators.

Freight forwarding only requires consolidation and bulk breaking terminals. They may, however, also own and control a limited number of vehicles for the purpose of collecting and delivering consignments from clients in close proximity to the consolidation and bulk breaking terminals. By carrying out their own collections and deliveries, freight forwarders do not purport to be professional transport operators. They merely provide these services for ancillary purposes as a secondary function in support of their core business of freight forwarding.

> *Test yourself*
>
> 11.15 Freight forwarders act as _____, or _____.

Freight brokers

Freight brokers are intermediaries who bring shippers and carriers together. As is the case with freight forwarders, brokers act as 'fourth party' service providers in transport transactions. Brokers find carriers for shippers' consignments, or recruit clients for carriers. They charge a proportionate fee (percentage commission) for their services. Receivers or consignees can also use the services of brokers for inbound goods. In this respect, brokers fulfil a vital role in activating and enhancing the ability of the transport system to supply quick-response service, emergency services, and ad hoc services during peak demand periods or during sudden upsurges in the demand for specific products.

Since the deregulation of freight transport, the scope for transport brokerage has also broadened. For example, private operators (ancillary operators) increasingly make use of brokers to obtain loads for return trips (back hauls) that would otherwise have been made with empty vehicles. Professional carriers also use freight brokers in an attempt to maximise vehicle utilisation when their contractual obligations leave them with spare capacity on certain hauls.

The development of electronic communication and information technology, such as the emergence of the Internet, has greatly improved the opportunity for consignors, carriers, and consignees to meet one another in the 'market place' through the mediation of freight brokers.

> *Test yourself*
>
> 11.16 Freight brokers are _____ who bring _____ and _____ together.

The freight transport user

In the market for transport, the user is the client. The user is the 'first party' in transport transactions. Depending on the context, the transport user is also known as the sender, shipper, or consignor. Transport users are dependent on adequate access to their resources and to their markets. In order to maximise their revenue, transport users strive towards having their products delivered to their clients (the 'second party') as effectively as can be afforded. The desired level of transport effectiveness, within the constraints set by efficiency, dictates whether users should conduct their own (ancillary or private) transport or seek the services of a professional (i.e. a 'third party') transport operator.

Government as stakeholder in the transport system

Throughout history, governments have involved themselves in transport. Governments apply various mechanisms, deemed to be in the public interest, to intervene in transport. This is done because transport is indispensable for sustaining the welfare and economic development of societies. Transport therefore has significant economic, social, political, and strategic functions. Governments are to a lesser or greater extent involved in transport both as producers or providers of infrastructure, facilities, and services and as regulators. A diverse range of arguments have been advanced for this involvement in transport, including the following:[4]

Control of excessive competition

Unregulated competition may limit the quality of service offered to users, giving rise to instability in the transport market.

Co-ordination of transport

Owing to the general inability of vehicle operators to accurately perceive their true transport costs, oversupply of transport capacity may occur, leading to a waste of resources. Under-supply could unduly inhibit transport-dependent economic activities if the transport market is not co-ordinated through government intervention.

Integration of transport with economic policy

The interaction between land use and transport needs to be co-ordinated. For example, industrial settlement should be close to where sufficient labour is available and manufacturing should occur close to the point of origin of resources. This type of co-ordination may form part of the authority's wider macro-economic strategies.

Maintenance of safety, security, and order

Technical regulation and safety measures are needed for safe, secure, and orderly use of transport infrastructure and operation of services. The need to drive on a certain side of the road, not to overload freight vehicles, not to drive too fast, and to secure dangerous freight are examples of such regulation.

Provision of costly infrastructure

Certain infrastructure developments involve high investment costs, long periods for recouping capital costs, and high levels of risk. The result is that these developments, which are usually a prerequisite for effective logistics service (for example, seaports and airports), are provided by government.

Provision of public goods

Certain types of infrastructure cannot be supplied at an acceptable profit; or an effective manner to collect income from users is not readily available to private investors. Examples are the road network and lighthouses that benefit coastal shipping and sea traffic at ports. These cannot be adequately supplied by the private sector in the absence of government intervention.

Recovery of the true resource cost of transport inputs

The market mechanism may fail to reflect the scarcity value of exhaustible resources such as petroleum. Governments may therefore steer transport decision-makers away from over-utilisation of such resources through pricing tactics. One example of such tactics is indirect taxes built into the price of certain fuels.

Regulation of externalities

Transport activities may impose costs on others not party to the transport activity, for example, pollution by freight vehicles, traffic congestion, and third party and public liability caused by accidents. These costs are often excluded in private sector decision making.

Restraint of monopoly power

Measures to prevent transport monopolies were previously particularly related to rail transport and they were applied to reduce the potential for exploitation. In industrialised countries, technical advances within other modes of transport have reduced the potential for monopolistic exploitation. More pertinent, nowadays, is the potential for cartel formation, where a small number of operators (i.e. an oligopoly) dominate a market segment.

Social support

Social criteria may be needed to guide transport resource allocation in order to afford all spheres of society mobility and access to economic activities.

Conclusion

Freight transport adds value in the business logistics process by creating place and time utility. The goods carried in freight transport can be classified as raw materials, semi-finished goods, or finished goods.

There are five modes of transport. These are

air, road, rail, pipeline, and water transport.

Any transport system fulfils two principal functions: to provide accessibility and to provide mobility. Accessibility refers to the ease with which users can participate in the transport process between chosen locations. Mobility refers to the measure of transport activity taking place.

Transport operators and non-operating transport service providers provide for the mobility of goods. Transport operators can be classified as private operators or professional carriers. Non-operating transport service providers act as freight forwarders or freight brokers. The user, also known as the shipper or consignor, seeks access to resources and to the market, and requires optimal mobility to serve customers. Governments are involved in transport as providers of infrastructure and services and as regulators.

Questions

1 Why is transport imperative in the business logistics process?
2 Discuss your understanding of accessibility, mobility, place utility, time utility, transport modes, transport nodes, and a logistics channel.
3 Discuss the five modes of transport by comparing each of the following: operational overview, cost structure, typical strengths and limitations, and freight characteristics.
4 What are terminals and what functions do they fulfil?
5 Discuss the stages of processing and the characteristics of goods, and explain how the characteristics of goods influence their transport costs.
6 Why will a firm make use of a freight forwarder and a freight transport broker?
7 There may be four parties involved in a transport transaction. Who are they and what is the role of each one?
8 Identify and briefly describe the two types of transport operators and the two types of non-operating service providers.
9 Discuss the various reasons why governments involve themselves in transport.
10 Briefly describe the reasons why governments also act as producers or providers of aspects of the transport system.

Notes

1 Wells, A.T. 1999: 375.
2 Schumer, L.A. 1974: Chapter 3.
3 Bowersox, D.J. and Closs, D.J. 1996: 365–367.
4 Button, K.J. 1993: 244–245.

Contents

Learning Outcomes

After studying this chapter, you should be able to:

- explain what efficiency and effectiveness in transport management mean;
- discuss how economy can be achieved in transport;
- outline the cost structure of each mode of transport;
- discuss traffic consolidation;
- supply guidelines for the efficient routing and scheduling of long-distance trips and of collection and delivery trips;
- discuss the considerations of efficiency and effectiveness when choosing ancillary transport and professional carriers;
- discuss the features of transport service effectiveness and the ways of selecting a professional carrier;
- explain how incoming traffic can be co-ordinated in order to enhance effectiveness;
- outline why profit planning and control are crucial at operational, tactical, and strategic management levels; and
- discuss how the financial integrity of a professional transport carrier can be supported by making use of total cost, marginal cost, and value-of-service pricing tactics.

Introduction

We have seen that the emphasis in business logistics is not simply on the cheapest or the fastest transport or on reducing inventories, but rather on an integrated and co-ordinated systems approach to the logistics process. The acceptance of the total cost logistics concept has led to logistics cost trade-offs between the various transport services provided; and to the operations at facilities assuming greater importance.

This chapter is devoted to:

- aspects of efficiency in the supply of the transport function within business logistics practice;
- service effectiveness as demanded by transport users; and
- transport pricing tactics which link the aspects of service efficiency and effectiveness of transport supply and demand.

Efficiency in transport

Transport is not demanded in its own right, it is a means to an end: that of moving goods. At the basis of any analysis of the demand for transport is the fact that this demand is a function of other activities. Freight transport forms an inescapable cost in the supply function of consignors and consignees and they seek to minimise it whenever possible.

The efficiency with which one uses and organises inputs to achieve set goals has a direct effect on the competitiveness of a business. The lower the cost per unit of output (without sacrifice of service quality) in relation to the value or price of the delivered product, the greater the efficiency of the logistics process. Technically, efficiency refers to the combination of the best and most modern production, marketing, and logistics techniques; prudent management; a highly skilled work force; and organisation of the business (including its logistics function) to operate at that scale or size where maximum economy is enjoyed.

Economy is the optimum use of resources so that the maximum benefit is gained from any given input of resources.

Economies of scale

Economies of scale exist when an expanded level of output results in reductions in the total unit cost of transport (per ton-kilometre). Therefore, with increasing output, the fixed cost per unit of output declines faster than the variable cost increases per additional unit of output. The following three transport management strategies can contribute to the attainment of economies of scale in transport:

- *Increase vehicle sizes and maximise utilisation of their capacity.*

The capacity utilised in a vehicle is proportional to the volume of the load; while the costs are proportional to the area the load occupies. Thus, the capacity can increase at a greater rate than the costs of transporting the increased capacity. This relationship accounts for the trend toward very large bulk-cargo vessels, wide-body aircraft, and long-haul road vehicles of which the length, width, and height are the maximum that road traffic legislation allows.

- *Increase fleet size and maximise utilisation of its capacity.*

Overhead charges generally increase at a much slower rate than the revenue generated by an increased fleet size. Larger fleets can also obtain larger discounts with bulk purchasing, for example, rebates on fuel, finance costs with vehicle acquisition, spare parts, and group short-term insurance. The business also benefits from the improved utilisation of its own workshop and consolidation facility, while standardisation results in lower spare part inventories.

- *Intensify the use of indivisible facilities and infrastructure whenever these are owned.*

When indivisible facilities and infrastructure are used to their maximum capacity, the result is a lower fixed unit cost for these facilities. The unit cost decreases as long as there is no congestion. For example, when increasing the utilisation of a rail network, the fixed unit cost decreases until the level of traffic starts to cause delays due to congestion.

Whenever congestion becomes lasting and forecasting indicates that demand will grow even further, one should contemplate capacity expansion. Whenever demand growth can be sustained, incremental expansion of infrastructure may result in substantial returns of scale.

With rail transport, the move from a single-track to a double-track system may quadruple line capacity by eliminating directional conflict, and a quadruple track should increase capacity even more as it permits segregation by speed.[1]

Engineers involved with petroleum refining and pipeline transport capacity extension use a so-called two-thirds rule: The capacity of any facility can be doubled at only a two-thirds increase in cost.

With terminal buildings, the reduced cost associated with size increase can be explained by simple arithmetic. A single-truck square-shaped garage with an area of 36 m^2 requires an enclosing wall of twenty-four linear metres. A square-shaped garage that is one hundred times bigger, i.e. 3 600 m^2, requires an enclosing wall of only ten times the length, i.e. 240 linear metres.

Sub-groups of economies

Economies of scale in transport depend on the attainment of one or more of three sub-groups of economies: economies of density, economies of scope, and long-haul economies.

Economies of density

A quantity of goods can often be transported at a lower unit cost when moved together in one consignment or load, or in one uninterrupted flow, rather than in different consignments or loads. The economy stems from the fact that one can serve the largest possible portion of a market with the same technology. The same volume of throughput occurs, but the movement is concentrated into one process, permitting more intensive use of the capital involved.

To achieve economies of density, one usually needs specialised technology to handle large volumes of a specific or homogeneous type of goods. The inherent danger of this is the empty return

trip. To reap the optimum rewards of specialisation, handling equipment at terminals should allow for rapid loading and unloading of freight in order to maximise the number of full vehicle load kilometres per unit of time. Economies of density imply maximum utilisation of durable assets over as long a period as is possible.

Economies of scope

Economies of scope exist when the cost of producing two or more products together, in either a joint or a common process, is less than the cost of producing them separately.

Joint products (also called by-products) are the inevitable and inseparable consequence of a single production process. For example, an outbound journey automatically gives rise to an inbound journey. This implies that if a full vehicle load is hauled from A to B, a backhaul from B to A would be cheaper than carriage in any other way as the vehicle must return to the original depot.

Common production (also called shared production) occurs when different products are deliberately produced together in a common process. In this case, the similarities of the production processes permit the use of the same technology. For example, the same vehicle can be used for passengers and freight transport; and when fleet capacity exceeds the demands set by seasonally fluctuating contractual agreements, the spare capacity can be filled with spot market shipments solicited through reduced tariffs.

The achievement of economies of scope usually requires standardised, or at least compatible, technology that can accommodate product diversification. This implies that one must be able to share the technology between two or more users, and spare capacity must be available to accommodate product diversification.

Long-haul economies

Long-haul economies exist when the transport costs rise proportionally less as the trip distance increases. In other words, the total transport cost per ton-kilometre decreases with increasing trip distance.

Long-haul economies arise when there are trip-specific fixed costs that are not affected by the distance of the journey. Examples are terminal costs such as aircraft landing fees and seaport charges; trip documentation; and loading, stowing, and unloading costs. As one has to pay these costs regardless of the distance, doubling the length of a haul will not result in doubling the costs.

Note that long-haul economies are not synonymous with increasing the number of full vehicle load kilometres – this refers to economies of density. For example, ten trips of twelve kilometres each will be more costly than one trip of 120 kilometres. The lower cost of the latter case reflects long-haul economies. However, economies of density can be achieved in both cases if all the work is done with existing fleet capacity.

Test yourself

12.1 One can achieve economies of scale in transport by attaining any or all of three sub-groups of economies. These are economies of _____, economies of _____, and _____ economies.

12.2 To achieve economies of scope, one usually needs standardised, or at least _____, technology that can accommodate product _____.

Competition within modes of transport

Competition within modes of transport is largely related to cost structure, distance of haul, and the diversity and physical characteristics of the goods carried. The various modes are therefore characterised in terms of forms of competition and cost economies.

Air transport

Since the economic deregulation of air transport markets, there has been a trend towards an oligopolistic market structure.

In air transport, there is a technical limit to the economies of scale that one can achieve with increasing the fleet size. The optimal use of number and size of aircraft will require large operations, but this is feasible only if there is a high demand for the number of aircraft, and if economies of scale with respect to the size of aircraft are present.

Although increasing fleet size does not result in significant economies of density, larger but mixed operations may be justified by economies of scope. It may be more economical for one carrier to undertake both scheduled and charter flights than for separate carriers to specialise in one of the two types of service. In seasonal markets, having aircraft with flexible cargo–passenger combinations may result in increased loads.

Road transport

Road freight transport competition ranges from open to oligopolistic. Fleet sizes in this market vary between one and more than a thousand vehicles. The fixed costs of single-vehicle hauliers who do not own any terminal facilities are extremely low, and this market sector is very competitive.

Specialised carriers and carriers of partial loads and parcels generally require terminal facilities, which increases their fixed costs. Their unit costs decrease with increased traffic volume (economies of density) and distance of haulage (long-haul economies).

Increased vehicle size and, generally, fleet size result in increased economies of scale. Infrastructure such as terminals, particularly for specialised carriers, provides further economies of scale. Other potential sources of economies of scale are specialised vehicles, an own workshop for vehicle maintenance and repairs, specialisation in terminals, and management efficiency. However, none of these potential advantages preclude competition from smaller operators.

Road transport carriers can achieve considerable economies of scope by consolidating consignments effectively.

Owing to the high ratio of variable (i.e. running)

costs to total costs of individual vehicles, and the relatively small terminal facilities, road transport does not enjoy significant long-haul economies.

Rail transport

In Europe and Australia, ownership of rail infrastructure and of train operations have in recent years been organisationally divorced. With this arrangement, any prospective rail transport operator may gain open access to existing rail infrastructure and tracks under certain prescribed conditions. The advocates of this new rail transport agreement argue that it limits monopolies, making the rail transport market more competitive, thus functioning more efficiently and effectively.

When analysing rail transport, one should distinguish between unit costs decreasing due to economies of density and due to long-haul economies. A rail transport operation may, through economies of density, enjoy a natural monopoly on a particular route. If one expands capacity by linking different routes where natural monopolies exist without increasing economies of scale over the whole route, no long-haul economies can be achieved.

Generally, however, the opposite is the case. The combination of long-distance haulage, double-track operation with increased frequency of trains, and capacity loads (also on back hauls) on long trains may lead to significant unit cost advantages, all related to long-haul economies and economies of density.

Pipeline transport

Because the fixed costs of pipeline transport are proportionately much greater than variable costs, and continuous pumping may take place with no need for any return flow, economies of scale do prevail in pipeline transport. On the principle of economies of density, an increase in pipe diameter can result in a lower unit cost. An uninterrupted and prolonged throughput of a large volume of homogeneous product increases economies of density.

Longer pipelines do not give rise to significant long-haul economies, as additional pump stations are required for longer haulage distances.

Because of the high capital costs of a pipeline, the barrier to entering the market is high. Owing to the inflexible capacity limits of a pipeline once installed, a new method of moving the product (such as road or rail) needs to be found once the pipeline reaches capacity.

Sea transport

Ocean shipping competition ranges from open competition, as in the case of tramp shipping (individual ships seeking cargo), to oligopolistic cartels, as in the case of liner shipping conferences. A liner shipping conference is a number of ships from various shipping lines working on a route in conference, or sharing the loads on the route.

As is the case with air transport, economies of scale are possible with large individual vessels and not necessarily with large fleet operations. Single-ship operators, for example owners of tramp ships, are therefore able to compete with larger scheduled conference liners.

Test yourself

12.3 On the principle of economies of _____, an increase in pipe diameter can result in a lower unit cost.

Cost structure of different transport modes

A cost structure refers to the relationship between the fixed and variable components of total cost.

Total transport cost is traditionally divided into vehicle operating and overhead costs. Vehicle operating cost is subdivided into standing costs and variable costs. Overhead and standing costs jointly represent the fixed cost of transport supply.

Overhead costs are not directly related to vehicle operation, but represent the costs involved in general management, administration, overall support services, land, buildings, and other facilities. Overhead costs are therefore common to all vehicles.

Standing costs are period-bound costs inherently associated with vehicles. These costs include depreciation because of the lapse of time, vehicle leasing, fixed crew cost, licences, and vehicle insurance.

Standing costs usually occur on an annual basis. Many individual journeys may take place within a financial period under different conditions. The standing cost responsibility for each journey is therefore not directly traceable. The common standing costs are proportionately allocated for each journey.

Variable costs fluctuate proportionately to variations in transport output. Whether a trip takes place or not, fixed costs cannot be avoided. Variable costs are avoided if a trip is not undertaken. This cost is readily determinable, even in the case of very short trips. It is therefore a direct cost at any level of vehicle performance. Figure 12.1 illustrates the proportional increase in variable, fixed, and total transport costs when one increases the trip distance.

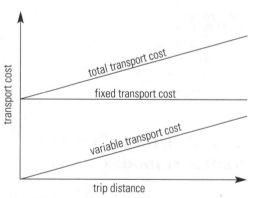

Figure 12.1 Proportionate increase in costs

The marginal cost of carrying one additional ton of freight usually includes the additional storage, handling, and stowage costs; minor additional fuel costs; and sometimes also additional terminal charges.

In the case of a full consignment on a return trip, i.e. where the trip must take place whether a consignment is available or not, an operator will seek to recover the following:

♦ all variable costs;
♦ an appropriate time apportionment with respect to fixed costs for including the consignment; plus
♦ a mark-up for profit.

Air transport cost

Fixed cost

Fixed costs are those costs that are not affected by fluctuating levels of air transport activities. These costs include:

Overhead costs

♦ acquisition and maintenance of buildings, equipment, and facilities;
♦ insurance of assets other than aircraft;
♦ management, administration, and supervision; and
♦ training costs.

Standing costs

♦ depreciation, interest, and aircraft insurance;
♦ aircraft operating permits and licences;
♦ salaries; and
♦ routine maintenance.

Variable cost

The following variable cost items relate to air transport:

♦ fuel costs;
♦ engine and component overhaul and replacement costs; and
♦ flight crew expenditures.

A few operating cost items vary according to the number of flights. These items include:

- airframe maintenance necessitated by number of landings (e.g. wheel fittings and tyres);
- charges for traffic control and navigation;
- landing charges;
- terminal services (such as cleaning, power connection, and charges for cargo handling, loading and unloading, and parking); and
- insurance against individual flight risks, for example, crew, cargo, and other property.

Road transport cost

Fixed cost

Overhead costs

- land and buildings (premises, offices, and warehouses);
- terminal facilities (vehicle depots, parking areas, garages, fixed loading facilities, and equipment); and
- managerial and administrative expenditure and other support functions.

Standing costs

The various standing cost items can be defined as follows:
A business has to invest capital when purchasing a vehicle or make a commitment when leasing or renting a vehicle. The standing cost can be either the cost of the lease or rental, or the depreciation plus the interest burden of the investment.

Depreciation
The depreciation of a vehicle amounts to the difference between the purchase price of the vehicle, excluding tyres (since tyre wear is a separate running cost item), and its resale price.

Interest on capital (opportunity cost)
Interest is not an autonomous cost item, but rather an inseparable and unavoidable part of the cost of capital employed. The interest cost arises from the opportunity cost associated at all times with money or capital invested in the purchase of the vehicles.

Licences
This item represents a compulsory levy for the right to use public roads. It is a fixed cost since it involves the annual payment of a given amount.

Insurance
There are various types of insurance relating to transport operations. These range from comprehensive fleet insurance to separate insurance for individual vehicles against a variety of risks. Insurance is generally taken out against the damage and loss of:

- a firm's own vehicles and damage to the vehicles of other parties;
- pay-load and crew;
- damage caused to other property; and
- public and private liability.

Comprehensive insurance packages also provide cover against theft, fire, and other damage to vehicles and property occurring when the vehicle is off the road. If one insures each vehicle separately, the annual premium is merely allocated to each vehicle. If the fleet is insured as a whole, apportionment of the annual premium becomes more intricate. It can either be divided equally among the total number of vehicles, or it can be allocated according to the type, size, capacity, accident record, operating area, and distance covered by each vehicle.

Crew costs
If vehicle crews (drivers, drivers' assistants) are appointed permanently, they are paid even when a vehicle is not in service. Their basic remuneration package is a standing cost item. Costs incurred for overtime and sundry allowances are part of the trip cost and therefore vary. If the overtime assumes a fixed pattern (for example, shifts), it becomes a standing cost.

Variable cost

Running cost items of road transport are fuel consumption, tyre wear, engine oil consumption, and maintenance cost.

Fuel consumption

Fuel consumption constitutes the largest single running cost item and, in the case of the majority of road transport modes, the biggest component of total transport cost. It amounts to between twenty-five and thirty-five per cent of the total transport cost of the various road transport vehicles.

Tyre usage

The cost of tyre usage can be ascribed to three factors: tread wear, punctures, and casing damage. Tyre cost is expressed in terms of cents per kilometre, and it is calculated by dividing the purchase price of the tyres by the expected amount of kilometres they should cover.

Engine oil consumption

Consumption of engine oil is aggravated through impurities – which necessitate oil replacement – and through loss from leakage, combustion, and evaporation – which necessitate oil replenishment. Engine oil consumption constitutes the smallest running cost item and, although its cost is expressed in c/km, physical consumption is usually expressed as litres (or fractions of a litre) per thousand kilometres.

Maintenance cost

Maintenance cost refers to the cost involved in keeping a vehicle:

- in good mechanical and electrical working order;
- roadworthy in terms of legal regulations; and
- in an appropriate condition for the purpose for which it is intended.

It includes the cost of servicing and lubrication (excepting engine oil, which is a separate running cost item), examination and adjustments of parts, and the overhaul, repair, and/or replacement of defective parts. Maintenance cost is generally the second largest running cost item.

A few trip-specific operating cost items occur on certain journeys. These are:

- toll fees, whenever road sections are tolled;
- permit fees, in the case of trips into neighbouring countries;
- escort fees, when certain abnormal loads are carried;
- accommodation allowances for vehicle crews when they need to overnight; and
- handling costs at trip ends when consignors and consignees are unable to provide handling equipment.

> **Test yourself**
>
> 12.5 Total road transport cost can be divided into vehicle operating cost and _____ cost. Vehicle operating cost can further be classified into _____ cost and _____ cost.

Rail transport cost

Total rail transport costs can be classified in a continuum of fixed to variable costs:

- depreciation;
- administration and management overheads;
- maintenance of facilities, rail tracks, and rolling stock;
- traffic expenditure;
- running costs; and
- general costs.

The first two items above are fixed costs, while the rest are predominantly variable costs.

Depreciation and overheads are not affected by traffic fluctuations. Maintenance of railway tracks, and especially of rolling stock, varies according to the volume of traffic. Maintenance of facilities, to an extent, keeps pace with traffic fluctuations. Traffic expenditure, running costs, and general costs are directly dependent on the volume of traffic.

The allocation of cost to transport units is very difficult, because direct and indirect costs are almost indiscernible, and because joint and common costs occur. These problems have prompted rail carriers to find other criteria for identifying and allocating costs. The following five main cost groups, where the allocation of the costs is based on performance criteria, are indicative of one method of recording rail transport costs:

- terminal costs (expressed in cost per ton freight);

- track costs (expressed in train kilometres);
- traction power cost (expressed in locomotive kilometres);
- train operating costs (expressed in train kilometres); and
- marshalling costs (expressed in shunting hours).

The ratio of fixed cost to total cost of rail transport is substantially higher than that of road transport. For this reason, it is usually cheaper to use road transport rather than rail transport for short distances, and to use rail transport for long hauls. Point A in Figure 12.2 represents the distance where road and rail transport costs per ton of freight are equal. For distances shorter than A, road is the cheaper mode; for distances longer than A, rail is the cheaper mode. (The equal cost distance for the carriage of standard intermodal containers by road and rail is approximately 520 kilometres, with minor variances for different economies).

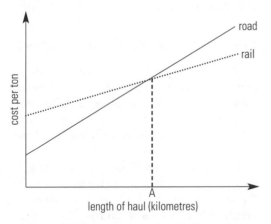

Figure 12.2 Comparative road and rail cost per ton freight over different distances

Pipeline transport cost

Virtually all cost components of pipeline transport are fixed. The costs of infrastructure (right-of-way acquisition, pipes, pumps, and storage facilities) are regarded as permanent (non-wearing) assets.

The only discernible variable costs in pipeline transport is the electricity consumed during pumping, overtime wages paid to maintenance staff to repair faulty pumps and valves, and the actual repair costs.

Sea transport cost

Fixed costs

Overhead costs:

- general overheads (management, administration, and office commitments)
- marketing costs (advertising, sales costs, and agents' commission)
- marine costs (land administration directly involved in shipping activities)

Standing costs:

- maintenance and repairs
- vessel inspection and check-ups (usually every four years)
- insurance
- depreciation
- fixed crew costs (unless contracted for individual voyages)
- radio and communication dues
- auxiliary stores aboard

Variable costs

Variable costs of shipping are voyage-specific and include:
- fuel;
- crew costs (when contracted for individual voyages);
- port and other terminal costs;
- insurance to cover risks on the water;
- maintenance relating to motion;

- freight (all costs associated with freight storage, loading, stowing, and unloading); and
- miscellaneous sailing costs.

Consolidation of traffic

Consignments

A consignment consists of a specific lot of goods tendered together by a consignor at a point of origin, for conveyance to a consignee at a single point of destination. Consignments are also known as shipments, even if they are carried in vehicles other than ships.

Consignments may vary in size (mass, volume, and number of items) and may consist of bulk or packed goods stowed together.

- The mass of individual consignments or shipments varies from less than a kilogram to many thousands of tons. The upper limit is constrained by the carrying capacity of vehicles, which varies according to the mode of transport. The range extends from as small as a one-ton truck (in the case of a road transport parcel service) to a long heavy-haul train or a bulk ocean carrier carrying over a quarter of a million tons of iron ore.
- The state in which goods are best carried and the maximum quantity that can be carried in a single trip affect the volume of consignments. The 'state of carriage' refers to the bulk or packed condition of the goods. The optimum size of the package depends on the handling requirements between origin and destination, and on the protection required against the standard hazards associated with carriage.
- The quantity of goods that constitute a consignment is affected by the methods applied for marketing the particular commodity, convenience in transport, and trip frequency.

The best way to achieve efficiency is to carry large mass, volumes, and quantities. When the size of individual consignments is less than the carrying capacity of vehicles, the shipments should be consolidated so that every vehicle trip may constitute a full load, or as close to one as is possible. When there is a mixture of small and large consignments as a result of marketing efforts, freight carriers consolidate them into single vehicle loads whenever it is economically viable.

Methods of consolidation

There are three broad methods for consolidating traffic:[2]

- Transfer goods from small to large vehicles for the part of a journey that is common to all vehicles. For example, one can make use of consolidated line-haul or through-movements between consolidation and bulk breaking terminals.
- Pool, and redistribute traffic to reduce the total distance travelled.
- Reduce trip frequency.

Consolidated through-movements

To illustrate this method, let us assume that a number of consignments originate at separate points and are intended either for a common destination or for various destinations. A part of the route, however, is common to all the consignments.

If there is a single destination, the consignments are consolidated at a terminal, from where through-movement takes place on a common vehicle or combination of vehicles. The consignments are unloaded at the common destination.

Should the consignments have different destinations, the common vehicle takes them to a conveniently located bulk breaking facility. There they are dispersed into other vehicles that carry them to their various destinations.

These situations are illustrated in Figure 12.3.

Traffic pooling and distribution

In addition to changing the size of the load or the number of vehicles, as illustrated in Figure 12.3,

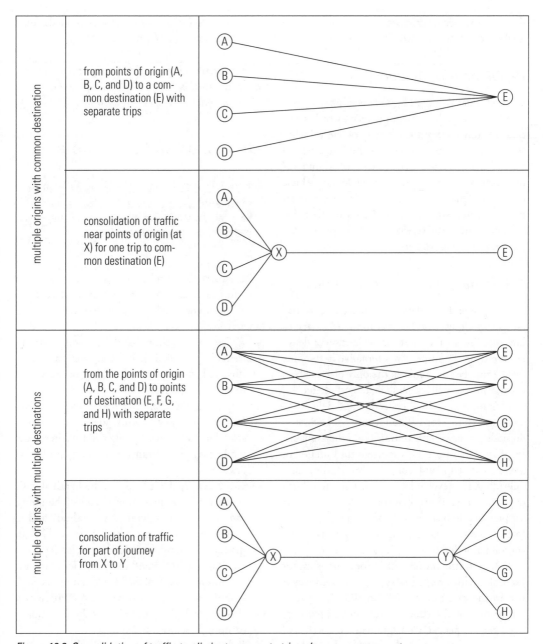

Figure 12.3 Consolidation of traffic to eliminate separate trips along a common route

consolidation may be directed toward preventing any overlap of movement.

Traffic from each point of origin may carry a full vehicle load comprising a number of consignments for separate destinations. Each vehicle may travel directly to all the various facilities of the consignees.

Alternatively, all consignments may be moved to a concentration point located close to all points of origin. At the concentration point, all the consignments are unloaded, sorted according to destination and transferred to other vehicles, so that one vehicle carries all consignments for a particular consignee or destination. This reduces the total overall distance travelled.

Reducing trip frequency

If a particular volume of goods needs to be conveyed every day, the consignments may be insufficient to fully engage the capacity of the vehicles. In such a case, one can reduce the frequency of trips. If the frequency is so reduced, consignments must be stored until the time scheduled for vehicle departure. This implies a trade-off between transport costs and storage costs. Take care that this does not reduce the service level to below what is required by the customers.

Other methods of consolidation

The origins and destinations of consignments may be spread along a route, making it necessary to interrupt line-haul trips at each collection or delivery point on the route. An alternative is to nominate a number of points as the only places where consignments will be collected and delivered, necessitating some local collection and delivery to and from these stops. The location of each stop depends on the volume of traffic and the availability of local transport. This shortens the duration of a line-haul trip and consolidates loading and unloading. However, it has no effect on the volume of goods carried in any one trip. Unless consignors are prepared to bear the cost of operating partially loaded vehicles, carriers should always consider consolidation to increase vehicle utilisation.

Where traffic movement is continuous as, for example, with a pipeline system (or a conveyor belt in the case of materials handling), capacity can be measured as the quantity throughput during a certain period. Consignments or batches of such commodities can be handled by the facilities in succession. Where compatible products are transported successively through the pipeline, the segregation between the batches can be reduced. Where the products are identical, no segregation is necessary.

With rail transport, traffic can be managed by consolidating:

- partial wagon loads into full wagon loads; and
- wagon loads into train sets.

Where carriage is provided by single road vehicles, consolidation is limited to loading two or more consignments into rigid vehicle units.

Unit loads and containers

A unit load is a collection of items grouped together by being bound as a package, stacked securely on a portable platform (for example, a pallet), or packed into a container.

The greater the number of items transported in the unit load, the smaller the transport cost per item. Grouping goods into units has the following advantages:

- *Efficiency:* Storing, handling, and carrying items in unit loads is more efficient as repetitive and costly manual handling of individual items is eliminated.
- *Goods identification and consignment tracing:* Goods are more readily identifiable when stored in unit loads. Tracing and tracking items while they are in transit is also less problematic.
- *Goods security:* Unit loads can be handled with mechanical equipment. Mechanised handling requires orderly operational methods and is therefore more secure (and safe for staff) than manual handling. Unit loads are also less susceptible to damage and theft than loose items.
- *Space utilisation:* Unitised loads can be stacked, stored, handled, and stowed more efficiently than individual items, reducing the investment in storage facilities and vehicles.
- *Transit time:* Unit loads can be handled and stowed in less time, thereby providing better vehicle utilisation.

Containers are rectangular, box-like devices used to consolidate, store, protect, and handle a number of items as a freight unit.[3] Once in the container, the goods are not handled again until unpacked from the container at the final destination. The container can be transferred from carrier to carrier – whether road, rail, sea, or even aircraft – when transhipped from mode to mode.

Shipments of less than a vehicle load vary substantially in size. There is therefore a need for a preliminary consolidation into standard containers capable of enclosing a number of small shipments. A vehicle load can consist of one or more such containers, as Figure 12.4 illustrates.

The use of containers may enhance efficiency, as it reduces:[4]

- goods handling cost at trip ends and transfer points, by eliminating the handling of individual packages;
- the turnaround time of vehicles, as loading and unloading speed is increased;
- theft and damage while in transit, by providing protection and security; and
- labour requirements, as containers are too large and heavy to be handled manually.

Containers have disadvantages:

- They cannot be handled in every port, which limits the number of shipping routes available.
- The difficulty in finding freight for return trips leads to the transportation of empty containers.

The size (external dimensions and gross mass) of containers that can be used effectively in each mode is constrained by:

- the linear and cubic dimensions of the payload space of vehicles and the mass-carrying capacity;
- the capacity of handling facilities at transfer points; and
- lateral and overhead obstructions on the routes.

These three factors vary between modes. With intermodal movement, the handling facilities at some transfer points may be inferior to others, or obstructions on the routes may vary in degree. The size of the containers is then governed by the most unfavourable conditions. Alternatively, the freight can be reloaded from one container to another at a transfer point, or the use of containers can be limited to a part of the trip only.

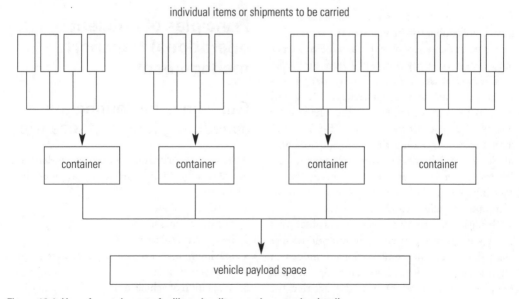

individual items or shipments to be carried

Figure 12.4 Use of containers to facilitate loading, carriage, and unloading.

Intermodal transport

> Intermodal transport is a logistically linked movement using two or more modes of transport on the line-haul part of the route.[5]

Intermodal transport typically (but not always) involves the interchange of freight between containers or loaded road trailers among different transport modes. The containers and road trailers are of standard sizes and have common handling characteristics. This allows for efficient transhipment of containers between modes.

A logistically linked origin-to-destination movement (sometimes referred to as seamless transport) is one where the consignor contracts a single service provider to co-ordinate or organise the entire movement. The service provider may be

- a non-operating (or fourth party) service provider who facilitates the service;
- a multimodal operator who physically conducts the entire movement; or
- a unimodal carrier who subcontracts carriers within other modes in order to complete the movement.

Because it is a single transaction, all the risks and service obligations associated with the transaction are vested in the service provider; and the consignor only needs to make payments to the service provider.

The basic reason for using intermodal services is the differing operational characteristics and costs of the various modes. By complementing modes in a co-ordinated fashion, the logistics manager can overcome the disadvantages of a mode while benefiting from its advantages. Intermodal services maximise the primary advantages inherent in the combined modes and avoid their operationally weak characteristics.

Because road transport is so accessible, road carriers frequently participate in intermodal services. However, the combination of modes in intermodal service depends on the co-operation of the carriers concerned. Despite the fact that the economic deregulation of freight transportation

has made intermodal freight operation possible, the reluctance of carriers to participate in intermodal combinations has inhibited the introduction of such services.

It is important to note that a line-haul movement refers to the part of a trip that takes place between:

- a point of origin and a bulk breaking terminal;
- a consolidation terminal and a point of destination; or
- an origin and a destination (i.e. a direct, consolidated movement).

Therefore, if the line-haul part of a movement and the local collection and delivery movements are conducted by different modes, such a service is not regarded as being intermodal. In practice, a line-haul trip usually includes an intercity or port movement.

Test yourself

12.8 Intermodal transport is a logistically linked movement using two or more modes of transport on the _____ part of the route.

12.9 Because road transport is so _____, road carriers frequently participate in intermodal services.

Principles of efficient operational transport management

Guidelines for routing and scheduling long-distance trips

A set of nine principles can act as guidelines to promote efficient freight transport operations. These are:[6]

1 continuous flow
2 maximum unit size
3 maximum vehicle size
4 maximum mass carrying capacity in relation to total vehicle mass
5 adaptation of vehicle unit to volume and nature of traffic

6 standardisation
7 compatible unit load equipment
8 long-haul freight consolidation
9 maximum utilisation of inputs

Carriers should endeavour to implement as many of these principles as is practically feasible. Although some of them may appear to contradict each other, they can be carefully traded off to complement one another in an efficiently integrated transport function. When professional carriers and third party logistics providers provide line-haul transport services, the efficiency preferences of the carriers must be carefully balanced with the effectiveness requirements of their clients. The principles are discussed below.

1 Continuous flow

The objectives of minimum transport cost and in-transit time require that:
- reverse, out-of-line, and unduly delayed or slow movement is avoided; and
- handling and transfer of goods is minimised.

This principle links with principle 9 in this section.

2 Maximum unit size

The optimum size unit of freight is the largest size that all vehicles can carry and the equipment can handle securely. Within the capabilities of standard vehicles and freight-handling equipment, the cost per ton-kilometre of handling freight tends to vary inversely with the size of the unit of shipment. The reason is that, as the size of units increases, a less than proportional increase in time and effort is needed to handle, transfer, load, and stow them. For example, the costs of handling or stowing a quarter-size, half-size, and full-size container are almost the same.

3 Maximum vehicle size

As the carrying capacity of vehicles increases, vehicle-specific costs increase less than pro-portionally. Vehicle-specific costs are running costs such as fuel consumption, maintenance, and tyre wear. The costs of handling, dispatching, drivers, and load documentation tend to remain the same regardless of load or shipment size.

4 Maximum mass carrying capacity in relation to total vehicle mass

The vehicle running costs are related to the total (i.e. gross) mass of the vehicle, whereas revenue is only related to the payload. The larger the vehicle, the higher the ratio of payload mass capacity to gross vehicle mass. Lightweight materials and design can help to minimise the tare (i.e. empty) mass of containers and vehicles.

5 Adaptation of vehicle to traffic

The traffic volume handled by a carrier may vary from hour to hour, day to day, week to week, and season to season. The size of the vehicle, or combination of vehicles, should be adapted to match the traffic volume.

For example, a small vehicle can be assigned to carry a small load when time constraints prohibit consolidation of loads. Multiple units of rail wagons or road trailers can be combined so that the capacity of the train or combination exactly matches the volume of traffic.

Specialised vehicles can also be introduced to maximise the potential for economies of density. Examples are rack trailers for the delivery of new passenger cars, and double- and triple-deck trailers for conveying livestock.

6 Standardisation

Standardise vehicles, equipment, and facilities whenever feasible in order to maximise the potential for economies of scope. Specialised vehicles and equipment are often necessary to carry certain goods efficiently. However, general-purpose vehicles can be used to:
- transport a broad scope or variety of goods;

◆ top up vehicle loads with one-off shipments when fleet capacity exceeds standing contractual obligations; and

◆ obtain back hauls to avoid empty return runs.

Examples of such vehicles are standard rail wagons, road trailers, cargo ships, and intermodal containers.

The use of standardised containers also increases the opportunity for intermodal freight movements and minimises handling of freight during transfer between collection, line-haul, and delivery movements. Standardised manufacturing of vehicles and other mechanical equipment may reduce both maintenance costs and the required levels of spare part stock.

7 Compatible unit load equipment

This principle is an extension of the principle of standardisation. Freight handling equipment fitted onto vehicles should not occupy any space that could have accommodated payload. Unitised packages, pallets, and containers should be of dimensions that readily fit into the payload space to maximise volume utilisation. In addition, equipment and packages/containers should be positioned to minimise damage to freight and reduce load shift during carriage.

8 Long-haul freight consolidation

Identify the areas within the entire region of operation where traffic generation and attraction are concentrated. Consolidate traffic into line-haul freight movements to and from the locus or hub of each area of concentration.

9 Maximum utilisation of inputs

Utilisation of inputs is related to the periods when a vehicle moves with a load compared to when it remains idle or runs without a load. The effective utilisation of resources can be inhibited by seasonal variations in business activity. In addition, the imbalance of traffic between destinations induces empty vehicle movement. To reduce this imbalance, carriers may:

◆ solicit casual or spot consignments through low tariffs based on marginal costs during times when fleet capacity exceeds standing contractual obligations,

◆ offer lower back haul rates;

◆ invest in rigorous promotion to gain further consignments; or

◆ merge or form alliances.

Guidelines for routing and scheduling collection and delivery trips

A set of ten principles can be used as guidelines for the efficient routing and scheduling of local collection and delivery trips[7,8]. As is the case with line-haul trip planning, these principles are not always perfectly compatible. However, should distribution management succeed in employing all of them in a well-balanced and complementary fashion, a high level of efficiency will be achieved. The principles are:

1 Cluster service points as densely as possible.
2 Cluster service points according to daily trips.
3 Determine routes starting with the furthest service point.
4 The sections of a route must not cross.
5 Two routes must not overlap.
6 Use the largest available vehicles.
7 Collect and deliver in the same trip.
8 Minimise the distance the heaviest loads will travel.
9 Avoid single service points located far from a cluster.
10 Avoid narrow time windows at service points.

Collection and delivery trips are predominantly undertaken using ancillary transport, not line-haul transport. An important reason for this is that customer service and consumer demands play a prominent role in the marketing of the final product toward the end of a product's supply chain. As a result, end-of-chain marketers often use private transport for service effectiveness, sometimes at the cost of efficiency.

When planning collection and delivery trips, it

is important not to lose sight of the above-mentioned ten principles. They are discussed below.

1 Cluster the service points

Cluster delivery and collection points so that the distances between the stops on each trip are as short as possible. This will minimise total route distance and trip time. Figure 12.5 shows examples of inefficient and efficient clustering. In (a), the total distance of the two routes is longer than that in (b).

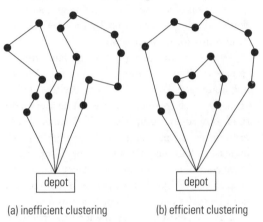

(a) inefficient clustering   (b) efficient clustering

Figure 12.5 Clustering service points

2 Cluster service points according to daily trips

Whenever delivery and collection points need to be served on different days, they must be tightly clustered according to the day of visit. The clusters should not overlap geographically. (Any overlap will violate guideline 5 below.) Clustering points according to daily trips will minimise the number of vehicles needed, total distance travelled, and total trip time.

3 Start with the furthest service point when determining routes

When clustering the service points on a trip, commence with the service point furthest from the terminal. Once the furthest point from the terminal has been identified, assign the largest available vehicle and select the densest concentration and greatest number of service points that will fully occupy the vehicle carrying capacity. Select the furthest point from among the remaining service points, and repeat the sequence until each service point is covered by a trip.

4 Sections of a route must not cross

The service points must be sequenced so that the path of the route is raindrop-shaped (see Figure 12.6). The introduction of time window constraints and the collection of large volumes only after completion of all the deliveries can result in sections of the route crossing.

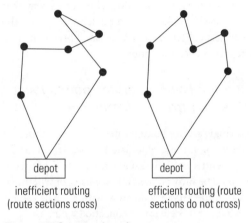

inefficient routing   efficient routing (route
(route sections cross)   sections do not cross)

Figure 12.6 Construction of routes

5 Two routes must not overlap

Cluster service points in such a way that the paths of two separate routes do not cross. Each route should therefore lie within distinct contiguous service areas. When routes overlap, unnecessary distance is covered.

6 Use the largest vehicles

This principle links closely with principle 3. Using the largest available vehicle will minimise the total distance travelled, the total trip time, and the number of vehicles required. A potential disadvantage is that service frequency will be reduced. Take care that this does not reduce service levels to below those required by customers.

7 Collect and deliver in the same trip

The results of collecting only after completion of all the deliveries are that route sections cross and that some service points are visited twice. Conformation to this guideline depends on the type and size of vehicle, the load volume, and the extent to which new collections will obstruct the delivery of consignments that are still on board.

8 Minimise the travelling distance of the heaviest loads

Choose the direction of travel in such a way that the heaviest deliveries are made first, or that the heaviest collections are made last. This will help to reduce fuel consumption.

9 Avoid single service points locat ed far from a cluster

A single service point located far from a cluster of service points is a candidate for a separate visit. Its size and extent of isolation dictate whether it should be incorporated into a cluster or whether it should be served separately with a small vehicle matching its delivery or collection volume.

10 Avoid narrow time windows at service points

Narrow time windows can disrupt the desired sequence of visits to service points. When narrow time windows unduly distort the efficiency of delivery and collection, one should negotiate the widening of the time windows. This will allow more latitude in the routing and scheduling of trips.

Test yourself

12.10 _____ and _____ trips are predominantly undertaken using ancillary transport, not line-haul transport.

Selecting transport service

A business may decide to invest exclusively in private (i.e. ancillary) transport, to outsource the transport function comprehensively to professional carriers, or to make use of a combination of the two types of operations.

Productivity can be improved through cost savings and increased returns. Cost savings are achieved by conducting the transport function more efficiently. Increases in return may stem from the selection of a transport operating arrangement that leads to greater output by more effectively conforming to customer service requirements.

The economic deregulation of land freight transport allows more opportunity for users to negotiate rates and services with carriers. There are now more road and air freight carriers, and thus more open competition. This makes customers more important to the carrier and so increases their negotiating power. Users exert more control and pressure on carriers than in the past, so that freight tariffs have been reduced and tariff increases have been kept to a minimum.

The transport services ownership spectrum ranges from exclusively private to exclusively outsourced. The position of the transport function of a business on this spectrum depends on considerations of efficiency and effectiveness.

Efficiency considerations

Firstly, the volume of traffic, especially on line-haul movements, might be insufficient for private (i.e. ancillary) transport to achieve the economies enjoyed by professional carriers. The latter generally operate at an output level more conducive to economies of scale.

Secondly, it may be difficult for ancillary operators to obtain back hauls. This contributes to wastage and therefore to lower levels of vehicle utilisation than those achievable by professional carriers.

Thirdly, professional carriers often have greater opportunity for labour specialisation. They are geared towards training, occupying, monitoring, administering, and utilising staff employed as drivers, loaders, packers, and mechanical and other technical staff.

Fourthly, the adoption of an ancillary transport function entails new and additional issues that need to be dealt with within the management and administration of the firm. Examples include additional trade unions, separate traffic and trade legislation, and fleet vehicle management matters that are not in line with the core management focus of the firm.

Fifthly, private transport involves large capital investment. The capital that the firm invests in the transport fleet has alternative uses (forgone opportunities). This capital must therefore provide a return that at least equals the return yielded by the firm's primary investment opportunities. However, the current deregulated environment has produced substantially lower professional carrier rates, occasionally making ancillary transport more costly.

Regardless of the five considerations discussed above, one can sometimes manage to conduct private transport just as efficiently as professional operators do. If the same levels of efficiency and fleet utilisation are possible, private transport theoretically should cost less, since the business does not pay for the profit of the professional carrier.

Effectiveness considerations

If the transport decision-makers are frustrated with inconsistent service performance, it might be necessary to move away from professional transport to private transport. Private transport gives a business greater control and flexibility in responding to buyer and facility requirements. This increased control and flexibility may result in lower inventory levels, better client service and satisfaction, and greater efficiency at the loading and unloading docks. The business can also use private vehicles as an advertising medium. This can be especially effective when the vehicles are attractively designed and have courteous drivers, leaving a positive impression with potential customers.

The most pertinent service performance determinants are suitability, accessibility, goods security, transit time, reliability, and flexibility. Suitability and accessibility determine whether a carrier is capable of physically performing the desired services. Goods security, shorter and more reliable transit time, and greater service flexibility are sources of competitive advantage.

Suitability

Suitability refers to the technical ability of a carrier to provide the equipment and facilities required for transporting a particular commodity. Appropriate technology is needed for a mode of transport (or vehicle types within a mode) and handling equipment to accommodate the conveyance of goods according to:

- their physical characteristics and stage of processing;
- their size (in terms of both mass and volume);
- the distance of conveyance; and
- the natural element on or in which they have to be moved.

These four factors are usually interrelated so that they determine, in combination, the suitability of a mode or intermodal combination to conduct the required service.

For example, a small consignment of finished goods destined for another continent will most likely be transported by air. A full container load of semi-finished goods destined for another continent will probably be moved by ship. A bulk load of raw material that has to be moved over a long distance within a country will most likely be transported by rail. A small shipment of finished goods that has to be conveyed between two neighbouring cities will probably be transported by road.

The ability to provide controlled temperatures or humidity and special handling facilities are examples of suitability factors.

Accessibility

Accessibility is the ability of a carrier to provide service across a particular link and to physically gain access to facilities. More specifically, it is the ability to move goods from a designated point of origin to a desired point of use or consumption.

Accessibility lies at the heart of the attainment of place utility. Within the supply chain of a product, the linkage of nodes where form utility is created (i.e. where raw materials and semi-finished goods are processed) constitutes the inbound or supply part of the chain. The distribution of finished goods (i.e. tangible products) to places where they are relatively scarce constitutes the outbound or distribution part of the supply chain. The method and tempo of processing and the marketing requirements during distribution greatly influence how close to the actual point of processing or storage the goods need to be delivered or collected.

Air and sea transport provides terminal-to-terminal service only.

Rail transport can at best provide a yard-to-yard service if both the origin and destination have a private siding at their disposal. Other origin-destination combinations for rail transport are yard to terminal, terminal to yard, and terminal to terminal.

Pipeline transport (in the case of petroleum commodities) can provide a tank farm to tank farm service only. Tank farms are situated at oil wells, refineries, seaports, pipeline terminals, and wholesale depots. In theory, therefore, pipeline transport can provide a fully accessible service upstream between wholesale depots and a petroleum refinery. Downstream from depots, pipelines supply zero accessibility. Consequently, the distribution of petroleum products from the depot to the customer is conducted almost without exception by road transport.

Road transport provides the greatest accessibility of all modes of transport. Although constrained in its ability to provide a high-volume service over long distances, its unparalleled accessibility to facilities makes road transport the best mode of transport for the collection and delivery of almost all types of goods.

Goods security

Goods should arrive in the same physical condition and quantity as when tendered to the carrier. Insecure links in the service result in opportunity costs of forgone profits or productivity because the goods are not available for sale or use, or have to be sold at a lower price than intended.

Transit time

Transit time is the total time that elapses between collection and delivery. Of specific importance from a time management perspective is the total time lapse between a consignment's prearranged collection time and the moment of its delivery. It is often assumed that the higher the speed, the higher the transport cost. In logistical terms, speed means short replenishment and delivery cycles and consequently less stock within the system.

The following high-value goods tend to be transported more effectively with the faster modes:
+ goods in which a relatively large amount of capital is tied up;
+ goods that can realise high profits and must therefore reach the market quickly; and
+ goods that are susceptible to theft and therefore bear high insurance costs while in transit.

This is usually called the supply time sensitivity of freight.

Other types of freight that tend towards the faster modes are those with their own product-specific time sensitivity. Their intrinsic properties necessitate special in-transit care. Examples are highly perishable commodities, highly obsolescent items, fragile products, and live animals.

Some goods need to be transported in the shortest possible time due to demand time sensitivity. This occurs when the demand is unpredictable, infrequent, seasonal, or when goods are needed urgently or at short notice.

In summary, faster modes should be used whenever the premium paid for utilising them is less than the value added by transporting the goods faster than is possible with the next fastest mode of transport.

Reliability

Generally, the most important service criterion is reliability.[9] Reliability refers to the consistency of the transit time provided by a carrier. It reflects the record or reputation for consistently maintaining punctual performance in terms of prearranged collection and delivery times.

Certain modes, such as pipeline transport, are associated with reliability by virtue of their physical characteristics. However, operators of all modes have to demonstrate ability, readiness, and willingness – and need to build a sound track record – before the customer will regard them and their mode of transport as reliable.

Reliability lies at the heart of the attainment of time utility. Business logistics developments have led to large inventory reductions, so that the consequences of uncertain collections and deliveries have become serious. For example, with short production runs and within a system where there is only enough stock for a day's production, delayed supply delivery may stop the entire production process due to lack of stock.

Reliable transit time impacts on inventory and stock-out cost and customer service. Consistency of service is generally more important than transit time. It is the cornerstone on which customers base their scheduling and planning. Therefore, if a carrier provides a shorter transit time, but is inconsistent in delivering that level of service all of the time, customers will more likely choose a carrier with a longer transit time, but with greater consistency of service.

Many benefits may result from providing a consistently punctual service. These include improved customer goodwill, marketing and sales advantages, ability to plan more precisely, fewer stock-outs, inventory cost savings, and improved efficiency resulting from increased opportunity to adhere to production schedules.

Flexibility

Flexibility is the proven ability, readiness, and willingness to effectively handle variations in load volumes, load mass, and collection and delivery times and locations without any significant loss in overall efficiency. Flexibility supports reliability when the transport operator is able to accommodate supply disruptions, schedule deviations, expedite the progress of a consignment, and alter collections and deliveries.

In order to be able to respond effectively to customer requests for flexibility, carriers need to have effective, user-friendly information services in place. Successful information and communication services presuppose the ability to:

+ promptly transfer complete and accurate information about the movement specific consignments at different points along the logistics channel; and
+ notice quickly as soon as anything goes wrong.

Transit time, reliability, and flexibility affect the nodal costs of inventory and stock-outs. Shorter transit times, higher reliability, and greater flexibility lead to lower inventory levels and stock-out costs.

Carrier selection criteria

The potential carriers are limited to those who have the technical capability to perform the desired service. Technical capability refers to the suitability and accessibility of the carrier.

From the available technically capable carriers, a business selects those who offer services that promise to provide the greatest operational capability at an acceptable price. Operational capability refers to a carrier's ability, willingness, and readiness to provide a secure service at desired transit times in a reliable and flexible fashion. The measure of success that the carrier achieves in providing a technically and operationally effective service determines the willingness (or not) of the business to pay for the carrier's efforts. When the carrier and the business agree on the price, the service, and the standards, the selection process has been completed.

Co-ordinating incoming traffic

Inbound traffic supports the supply effort of a business by providing goods from vendors or materials suppliers at the desired time and place. Inbound goods can be classified into inputs used to manufacture products (e.g. raw materials and the components needed to assemble vehicles) and finished goods purchased for resale (e.g. products purchased by a wholesaler or a retailer).

The smooth flow of materials to the firm is necessary to ensure uninterrupted operations. Serious operational bottlenecks can result from poor materials flow into receiving and storage. Some causes of bottlenecks are inadequate layout (size and location) of the receiving area, inadequate materials handling design, poor labour utilisation, inferior information systems, and poor delivery scheduling.

The physical delivery of goods can be the responsibility of the business buying the goods, the supplier, or a third-party service provider. Suppliers are generally responsible for the control of their outbound transport. If a business receives daily deliveries from many suppliers, incoming traffic should be carefully managed to avoid congestion at the receiving point. Effective communication between the business and its suppliers is required to plan the daily delivery schedules efficiently. Logistics channel partners should share information to improve scheduling of deliveries. If the incoming transport activity is under the con-

trol of the business, it is easier to co-ordinate daily collections with other activities.

Professional carriers provide certain complementary terminal and line-haul services that enhance the flexibility of their service. Logistics managers can use these services to co-ordinate the flow of incoming materials effectively. These additional services may include tracking and tracing, expediting, diversion, in-transit privileges, and demurrage and detention. [10]

Tracking and tracing

Tracking and tracing is often necessary to trace lost or late consignments during the course of a move. Tracing is critical in situations where on-time delivery is necessary to ensure continuous manufacturing operations. The use of information technology, such as on-line freight information systems, satellite communications, and bar coding, assists in tracing a consignment after its departure and in recording its movement. Bar coding enables one to transfer information quickly and error-free at intermediate points. On-line freight information systems allow consignors and consignees to link directly with the carrier's computer system in order to determine the status of a particular consignment.

Expediting

When it is crucial that a consignee receive a specific consignment by a particular date or at a certain time, the consignor or the carrier can be requested to expedite or accelerate movement of the consignment through the carrier's system. Ideally, the arrangements should be made before dispatching the consignment in order to afford the consignor or the carrier the greatest opportunity to speed up the movement. However, the request for expediting a consignment may be lodged at any stage before its arrival at a junction or transfer point, from where faster movement may be arranged.

Diversion

Diversion privileges permit a consignor (often on behalf of a consignee) to notify a carrier that a shipment needs to be diverted to a new destination. This must happen before the shipment's arrival at junctions or transfer points from where diversion can be arranged. Diversion is a convenient option when unexpected changes in market conditions or production requirements necessitate a change in the destination of a consignment.

In-transit privileges

In-transit privileges permit the consignor (on behalf of a consignee) to unload a consignment en route, perform some processing function on the goods, and reload the consignment into the waiting vehicle(s) for its final destination. In-transit privileges are based on the principle of long-haul economies. For example, a trip of 120 kilometres is less costly than two trips of sixty kilometres each.

Demurrage and detention

Demurrage is incurred when ships or rail wagons are not moved in time. When consignees receive a rail wagon, the rail carrier allows them a specified amount of free time to unload the wagon. When the rail wagon is retained beyond the allowed time, the rail carrier assesses a demurrage charge. The argument to justify demurrage charges is that rail equipment produces no revenue for the rail carrier, and therefore bears an opportunity cost, when it stands idle at a customer's siding.

Demurrage charges fluctuate according to supply and demand. They may vary according to the type of rail wagon and according to the specific contract between the rail carrier and the customer.

When a road truck, trailer, or container is retained beyond the specified free loading or unloading time, road freight carriers use the term detention charges for the same concept. In the road freight industry, the allowed time (the time window) is specified in the tariff and is generally limited to a few hours. There are no fixed or standard detention charges in the road freight industry and shippers must negotiate the free time and detention charges with each carrier.

Demurrage and detention can be regarded as the charges payable when consignees use transport equipment for storage beyond the periods acceptable for in-transit storage.

Good co-ordination between the various departments can ensure the orderly flow of consignments to a business. Efficient planning and control of the inbound traffic not only minimise congestion but also reduce demurrage and detention charges. By capitalising on a carrier's flexibility, the business does not suffer delays or interruptions in its operations.

Test yourself

12.14 Logistics managers can use complementary services to co-ordinate the flow of incoming materials effectively. These additional services may include _____, _____, _____, _____, and _____.

Profit planning and control

Profit planning and control are crucial to carriers at operational, tactical, and strategic management levels.

Tactical and operational aspects

Since profit results are sometimes available as late as eighteen months after the beginning of a financial year, these results have little value for tactical and operational transport management. A faster method of controlling transport cost is needed to monitor daily activities.

When rendering a transport service, one apportions inputs such as labour, vehicles, and fuel in a certain ratio. Each cost item comprises a quantity component and a price component which, when multiplied, represents the cost per item. Costs for fuel, lubricants, maintenance, direct labour, and so on are therefore easy to determine.

It is more difficult to calculate the item cost of overheads such as managerial and administrative costs, since one must first determine realistic criteria for apportioning each of the respective services to specific journeys.

Other cost items that are difficult to calculate and therefore often erroneously omitted, are durable means of production such as vehicles and handling equipment; and non-durable but slow-wearing inputs such as tyres and vehicle parts. The result is often that the cost is not apportioned to certain transport outputs or services, simply because actual cost and perceived trip cost do not correlate.

The difference between actual trip cost and perceived trip expenses can be illustrated as follows: A certain vehicle is capable of doing 40 000 km with the same set of tyres. If the vehicle covers on average 2 000 km per week, then the weekly cost of tyres will amount to one-twentieth of their purchase price. The same problem arises with the costs of interest and of depreciation.

Only by continuously monitoring the accrual of all the costs during the transport process can the approximate profit generated by each journey be calculated and can the carrier institute remedial measures when necessary.

Strategic aspects

To show an acceptable rate of return at the end of a financial period, a carrier must have a sound profit policy. The ideal is to add a sufficient profit margin to transport costs, subject to market constraints, to meet or exceed the desired return on capital invested.

The rate of return required by a carrier can be expressed through two values.

The first value is the cost of capital for the business. This value includes the opportunity cost of the capital needed to fund investments, as well as factors such as the risk of the market and the sector in which the business operates and the competitive position of the business.

The second value is the current return earned by the firm. This return needs to be above the former for the company to sustain its current profitability in the long run.

Any investment should exceed the cost of capital. If it does not, the firm loses value as the capital could be utilised more profitably elsewhere. One wants to preserve or enhance the current return to maintain current profitability.

The profit margins of the various segments of the business are not identical. Carriers need to divide the activities into categories and calculate specific returns for each category. Take care not to make substantial investments in lower return categories without realising that this will reduce the overall returns.

Tariff quoting

To attain business logistics objectives such as maximum long-term profit, it is essential to cover total costs plus a sufficient surplus. The nature of transport activities, however, precludes total cost coverage on all individual link services at all times. Consequently, market factors relating to demand as well as supply will have a decisive impact on tariff policy. In some cases, say where fleet capacity is not fully utilised, marginal cost pricing may be justified. Services operating at a loss have to be subsidised in the short term by services that generate surplus revenue. Carriers must therefore keep track continuously – in other words, with each trip – of the full extent of the costs involved in their services.

Broadly speaking, transport services may be priced using any of three tactics:
- The price (tariff) covers transport cost and makes provision for a profit. This is also known as total cost coverage or individual cost coverage.
- The carrier may, because of tactical business considerations, decide to accept consignments at a tariff that does not fully cover the total costs, but covers all the direct costs associated with undertaking the service. This is known as marginal cost coverage.
- The carrier may charge higher tariffs that yield

supernormal profits when an unparalleled and superior customer service is supplied. This method of maximum-limit or premium tariff quoting is based on the value-of-service principle.

Total cost coverage and marginal cost coverage are supply-side pricing tactics. The minimum price, using these tactics, depends on how efficiently the transport function is being conducted. Value-of-service pricing is demand-oriented. The maximum price, using this tactic, depends on how effectively customers are being served.

Total cost pricing

Overhead costs are usually associated with the strategic aspects of transport supply, standing costs usually relate to the tactical aspects, while variable costs result from operational activities.

Overhead costs

Overheads can only be apportioned, and not allocated according to determinable cost criteria, to transport activities. One should select a method of apportionment that adequately reflects overheads for each trip. The most common bases for apportioning overhead costs are:
- number of vehicles;
- payload carried by vehicles;
- distance travelled by vehicles;
- a combination of the previous two, expressed as ton-kilometres; and
- a surcharge on operating cost.

A one-ton truck may bear the same amount of overhead costs as a combination vehicle with a carrying capacity of thirty tons, thereby imposing an intolerable tariff load on parcels or the small consignments carried with the one-ton truck. Therefore, ton-kilometres travelled per period (in other words, the fourth option above) is commonly regarded as an equitable method of apportioning costs, although it may place an excessive tariff load on heavy commodities with a low value, such as raw materials. In these circumstances, the carrier may decide to apportion overhead costs in proportion to the value of the commodities transported.

The apportioning method depends on the type of business and loads carried. Carriers must find the most appropriate method to ensure that each sector of their operations bears the overall costs and hence delivers the desired profits.

Standing costs

Standing costs are period-bound obligations that are inherently coupled with a vehicle. They include depreciation, interest, licences, insurance, and drivers' wages. Because standing cost has a direct bearing on a particular vehicle and does not relate to other vehicles, it is apportioned to individual trips for the period of use.

The apportionment of standing costs is generally effected as follows: The total time the vehicle is used for each trip is expressed as a fraction of the time it can realistically be utilised over a certain period. This fraction is then multiplied with the total standing cost per period.

Running costs

Running costs vary with vehicle output and are assigned according to the distance travelled.

In order to realise a return on each service, the tariff quoted should cover all of the above-mentioned costs plus a margin for profit. Transport services that are characterised by effective competition and few opportunities for cross-subsidisation are typically priced at levels that cover full costs including a profit that equals the opportunity cost of capital.

Marginal cost pricing

The variable cost items of transport represent marginal trip costs. Overhead costs represent indirect fixed cost inputs that are common to all carrier activities and vehicles. There is not a causal relationship between individual trips or services taking place and overhead costs.

A direct causal relationship exists between standing cost and the use of vehicles during given financial periods. However, it is not possible to link standing costs directly to particular trips. Consequently, these costs are divided among the total number of trips simply on a proportional basis – often in relation to time consumed. This implies that the shorter the accounting period, the more fixed the costs tend to be. Conversely, the longer the accounting period, the greater the tendency of the fixed costs towards variability. Wages, which are a fixed item in the short term, will be the first to display signs of variability. The more intensively a vehicle is used, the more variable are the items that are fixed for the short term. When a vehicle is put to such intensive use that its lifespan is reduced so that the length of the accounting period exceeds the actual life of the vehicle, even depreciation assumes a purely variable character.

Direct cost responsibility can therefore readily be allocated to a service or particular performance. In effect, it may be regarded as the incremental cost associated with actual performance. The direct cost of using a vehicle includes the variable vehicle cost and the specific fixed (i.e. standing) costs that are automatically coupled with the vehicle.

When applying the marginal cost principle in tariff decision making, it is essential to ensure that the minimum cost recovered is equal to the costs that might be avoided by cancelling a service (the direct cost). The avoidable costs form the 'floor' in marginal cost pricing.

Carriers will undertake to carry loads at marginal cost for tactical reasons, provided they are able to cross-subsidise their total deficit – either from other remunerative services during the same period or from the same service during a period of surplus recovery. The latter method of recovering deficits attributable to marginal cost pricing may also be applied in extremely competitive conditions. If a tariff war develops or a market intruder makes its appearance, the carrier could lower its tariffs to the marginal cost level until the market stabilises. At this stage, it can increase its tariffs to generate a surplus from which it can recover the earlier loss.

Value-of-service pricing

Whereas the minimum or floor tariff that can be charged for a transport service is determined by marginal cost, the maximum tariff is determined by the value users attach to it. Value-of-service is therefore also known as effectiveness pricing.

The value that a customer attaches to a transport service is determined by:

- the place and time utility obtained in getting a certain commodity to a specified destination at a certain time; and
- the reliability of the service, i.e. the consistency with which this level of service is achieved.

The level of utility is determined by the extent to which a carrier satisfies the needs of the user by supplying the desired level of service quality through offering acceptable goods security, transit time, reliability, and flexibility of service.

It is only feasible to charge this type of tariff where a superior service, that cannot be matched by a competitor, is offered. If the use of this tariff is taken to extremes, a competitor will emulate the service or the user will resort to private transport.

Conclusion

The efficiency and economy with which inputs are organised to achieve set goals have a direct effect on the competitiveness of the firm. Economy refers to the optimum use of resources so that the maximum benefit is gained from any given output. Economies of scale in transport are dependent on the attainment of any or all of three subgroups of economies. These are economies of density, economies of scale, and long-haul economies.

Goods are transported in consignments. Efficiency may be best achieved by carrying goods in large mass, volumes, and quantities. In order to lower the cost of carrying and handling small consignments, carriers consolidate consignments and create unit loads whenever feasible.

A set of nine principles can act as guidelines to promote efficiency when conducting long-distance trips. These are:

1 continuous flow
2 maximum unit size
3 maximum vehicle size
4 maximum mass carrying capacity in relation to total vehicle mass
5 adaptation of vehicle unit to volume and nature of traffic
6 standardisation
7 compatible unit load equipment
8 long-haul freight consolidation
9 maximum utilisation of inputs

The following set of ten principles can be used as guidelines for routing and scheduling local collection and delivery trips:

1 Cluster service points as densely as possible.
2 Cluster service points according to daily trips.
3 Determine routes starting with the furthest service point.
4 The sections of a route must not cross.
5 Two routes must not overlap.
6 Use the largest available vehicles.
7 Collect and deliver in the same trip.
8 Minimise the distance the heaviest loads will travel.
9 Avoid single service points located far from a cluster.
10 Avoid narrow time windows at service points.

Effective transport helps ensure that customers receive the right goods at the right place and time in the right condition and quantity. The most pertinent service performance determinants are suitability, accessibility, goods security, transit time, reliability, and flexibility.

Purchasers and suppliers can make use of private transport or professional carriers. In addition to the primary transport service, professional carriers also provide certain complementary terminal and line-haul services that enhance the flexibility of their service. Logistics managers can use these services to co-ordinate the flow of incoming materials to the firm effectively. These additional services may include tracking and tracing, expediting, diversion, in-transit privileges, and demurrage and detention.

Profit planning and control are crucial to the carrier at operational, tactical, and strategic management levels. Broadly speaking, transport services may be priced using any of three tactics: total cost coverage, marginal cost coverage, or premium (or value-of-service) tariff.

Questions

1 Explain what efficiency and effectiveness in transport mean and discuss whether it is possible to operate efficiently when customers need to be served effectively.

2 Define economies of scale and mention three aspects (with supporting examples) that can help to attain economies of scale in transport.

3 Outline the cost structure of each mode of transport and identify the cost items that appear on the strategic, tactical, and operational levels.

4 Indicate the marginal cost and avoidable costs of:

♦ adding or withdrawing a single consignment, consisting of a small parcel, to or from a large vehicle load,

♦ scheduling one additional trip or cancelling a trip; and

♦ adding or withdrawing a specific haulage service, involving four vehicles, to or from an existing transport operation engaging forty vehicles.

5 Supply guidelines for the efficient routing and scheduling of long-distance trips and collection and delivery trips.

6 Discuss the efficiency and effectiveness considerations involved in the decision between making use of ancillary and professional transport.

7 Explain in detail what you understand by

technical capability and operational capability of a professional carrier.

9 Is transport price a separate service performance criterion, or is it determined through other service performance criteria? Motivate your answer.

10 Discuss how incoming traffic can be co-ordinated in order to enhance effectiveness.

11 Outline why profit planning and control are crucial at operational, tactical, and strategic transport management levels.

15 Discuss how the financial integrity of a professional transport carrier can be supported by making use of total cost, marginal cost, and value-of-service pricing tactics.

Notes

1 Button, K.J. 1993: 72.
2 Schumer, L.A. 1974: 38–43.
3 Muller, G. 1995: 256.
4 Schumer, L.A. 1974: 43–44.
5 Muller, G. 1995: 262.
6 Principles 1 to 7 and 9 are based on:
    Fair, M.L. and Williams, E.W. 1981: Chapter 6.
    Principle 8 is proposed by the author.
7 Ballou, R.H. 1999: 199–201.
8 Visagie, S.E. 2001: 65–75.
9 Coyle, J.J., Bardi, E.J. and Langley, C.J. 1996: 318–322.
10 Heyns, G.J. 2001: 3–6.

Contents

Learning Outcomes

After studying this chapter, you should be able to:

♦ name the factors that distinguish international logistics from domestic logistics;

♦ describe why it is important for logistics managers involved in international distribution to acquaint themselves with marketing channels;

♦ identify the intermediaries who may become involved in international marketing and describe their respective functions;

♦ identify the operating and non-operating service providers in international transport and describe their respective functions;

♦ explain for what Incoterms stands and for what these terms are used;

♦ indicate the seller's and buyer's obligations within each of the thirteen Incoterms;

♦ identify the various categories of international trade documents; and

♦ discuss the function of the most important transport documents.

Introduction

International economic developments have a serious impact on the domestic economic activities of countries. A business cannot ignore competitive situations and technological innovations in other countries. Modern economies are highly interdependent and the successful ones are those that compete effectively on international markets. In a rapidly integrating and globalising world market, therefore, efficient and effective international logistic support structures relating to international goods transactions are of particular importance. International logistics practice must accommodate all domestic logistics demands. In addition, logistics managers have to deal with more channel partners or intermediaries, longer distances, greater diversity, and more statutory requirements and documentation.

This chapter focuses on those aspects that distinguish international logistics practice from domestic logistics activities:

- aspects pertinent to the choice of an appropriate international distribution channel;
- international goods transport;
- uniform rules for the interpretation of commercial terms in international goods transactions; and
- the most important documents used in international goods transactions and movements.

Distribution channels

Distribution channels are the marketing routes that a product follows to flow from the seller to the importer. A seller can choose an appropriate distribution channel for its product(s) once it has identified a target market. An appropriate distribution channel enhances the efficiency of the international marketing effort. Sellers and logistics managers involved in international marketing and distribution must acquaint themselves with distribution channels because they need to understand how products flow to foreign consumers.

Choice of a distribution channel

Successful international marketing often results from partnering with a key intermediary who has access to distribution channels in the foreign market. Sellers need to appreciate the importance of the role of intermediaries in getting products to their target markets and in ensuring that they receive them at a reasonable price. Forming a business alliance with a reputable partner who can channel export products to appropriate distribution points is called the 'push strategy'.

The longer the distributions channel, the greater the number of intermediaries – resulting in less profit accruing to the seller. Sellers can use the following criteria to determine the length of their distribution channels:[1]

- the price of the product;
- the lifespan of the product;
- service requirements;
- complexity of technical requirements; and
- turnover.

Whenever profit taking within a channel is not related to the amount of risk accepted and the cost of distribution functions performed, conflict may arise among the channel members. As for channel performance, the objective is to bring about co-operation and co-ordination within the channel and not disharmony or conflict.

Channel leaders usually earn a larger share of profits because of their initiative and their innovative roles in organising and promoting the channel and providing services and credit. The seller should assume the role of channel leader. Being a larger shareholder within the channel, the seller (i.e. exporter) will most likely be motivated to conduct more market research and to add value to its export products.

If sellers were to market their products to end-users by means of their own sales force, they would be the only profit-earning party. However, direct marketing in foreign countries may be very difficult and extremely expensive, eroding all profits. Exporters therefore have to trade off the costs and benefits of employing intermediaries instead of conducting their own sales, and of continuously monitoring the situation. Choosing to deliver products directly to end-users, as is often the case with manufactured products, is called the 'pull strategy'. As this is often a costly strategy, it is generally only feasible for large exporting firms.

Producers and manufacturers who enter the international market may be tempted to entrust the entire export process to an established international distributor. In doing so, sellers may not become aware of the way consumers react to their products. Furthermore, all the initiative for increasing market share rests with the distributor. This strategy of risk avoidance may cost exporters dearly in lost marketing opportunities.

Distribution channels may include sole distributors, trading houses, government departments, industrial buyers, wholesales, retail stores, chain stores, or export agents. These intermediaries are discussed in turn in the following sections.

Distributors

Distributors purchase and carry large product inventories. In return, they are granted an exclusive right to sell the product(s) in a specific area or to a specific type of customer, usually wholesalers. Distributors usually import large consignments but do not pay for them immediately. The seller has to wait for payment until the distributor has resold the consignment or a part thereof. The seller may have to invoice the distributor separately for each part of the consignment that is sold and file a separate exchange-control application for each invoice in order to receive payment.

The biggest advantage of making use of a distributor is the saving in the cost, time, and trouble as a result of dealing in large consignments. Another advantage is a better profit margin, because the distributor pays the seller a higher price for delaying payment until products are sold. It can also be useful to have large product inventories readily available in the foreign market.

Distributors operating on a consignment basis must be chosen very carefully. Most of them sell the products as quickly as possible because of the opportunity costs of keeping the products in stock. However, they may be less eager to sell products that they have yet to pay for.

Trading houses

A trading house may deal in import and export, i.e. two-way trade. It may buy directly from the seller, acting as an agent for the exporting seller. It may also act as an agent for an importing buyer.

Sales to trading houses are mostly single and complete transactions. Trading houses usually do not enter into a contract for exclusive rights over a period as distributors do. Trading houses conduct their own marketing, carry the credit risk, administer all documentation, and oversee the physical distribution of products to their final destination.

Government departments

Government departments in some countries occasionally import commodities, often on a long-term basis. For example, they may want a certain quantity of grain to be delivered at regular intervals over a number of years. They could enter into import agreements with sellers to do this.

Industrial buyers

Large industrial firms often purchase directly from manufacturers. For example, a ship builder may purchase steel sheeting or furnishing material directly from foreign sellers if importation constitutes the cheapest way of building ships. An aircraft manufacturer may source certain highly advanced aircraft components directly from foreign specialist component manufacturers. Multinational sourcing of specialised components may be the most affordable way for a group of nations, or even the entire international community, to obtain certain types of aircraft. The aircraft manufacturer does not need to develop the capability to also manufacture the components in question at a high cost. In this way, an additional market is being generated for the component manufacturer. The country in which the manufacturer resides may now be in a position to import completely manufactured aircraft from the buyer of the components, without having to develop and manufacture the aircraft at a higher cost.

Wholesalers

Some wholesalers may be direct importing purchasers, or they may obtain their supplies through an importing distributor. Wholesalers usually do not have exclusive selling rights for the products they buy. However, they may have a commanding market position with little competition.

Retailers

Large chain stores and franchise retail groups may also buy directly from exporters. They often negotiate exclusive selling rights. Occasionally, a number of independent stores establish a joint buying group and employ a single buyer for the group. Chain stores and supermarkets are often multiples with a central buying organisation. Multiples are becoming increasingly important as direct importing clients. They may be particularly interested in the way products are packaged and presented to be attractive on store shelves and in showrooms. They often purchase in bulk and demand that the products be packed in their own consumer packs.

Export agents

An agent is an individual or legal entity authorised to transact business for and in the name of another, known as the principal. An agent's authorised actions bind the principal. In export practice, the export agent is a party who acts for the exporter, the latter being the principal. Agents work on a commission basis and do not assume risks.

When examining the role of the export agent, it is also important to consider distributors, as their role in the international market has become increasingly significant. Exporters may market their products in certain countries through agents for a commission, but in other countries through distributors, who buy the goods for their own account and earn a profit. Table 13.1 lists the salient points of difference between distributors and export agents.[2]

Whenever a seller decides to market products directly in a specific country, it has to consider whether to make use of an agent or appoint its own marketing staff in that country. If the seller is new to a country or region, market penetration can often most effectively be achieved through appointing an export sales agent. The potential value of an agent in such circumstances can stem from the following:

◆ Remuneration is based on sales volume. There are no sales expenses unless sales are achieved.
◆ The agent has local knowledge.
◆ An agent's experience with other products may help when introducing a new product.
◆ Agents are usually highly motivated because they are only paid if they succeed in selling.

International goods transport

All modes of transport, including pipelines, can offer international services. However, the majority of goods transport between continents is conducted by sea and by air. Approximately eighty per cent of all international trade is carried by sea transport and ten per cent by air transport. The remaining ten per cent of international trade is carried over land by road, rail, and pipeline transport. Because transport between neighbouring countries is so similar to domestic transport, we focus here on sea and air transport. We also give attention to the transport intermediaries who are critical components of international transport.[3]

Ocean transport

The ocean carriers involved in international transport are liner operators, tramp ship operators, and private ship operators.[4] Each type provides specific service features to the international transport user.

Liner ship operations

Liner ships provide service on fixed routes according to published schedules. They usually charge according to published tariffs that are either unique to the independent liner operator or fixed by several lines forming a group conference operation on a particular trade route. A shipping conference is a legal cartel or oligopoly.

Liner services offered are either container, break-bulk, or bulk. The shipper must transport the freight to the liner's terminal at the port after making the reservation. The freight is loaded onto the ship with a machine if it is bulk; or by crane if it is container-ised. It is then stowed in accordance with ship mass, balance, safety rules, and the shipper's requirements.

Container ship operations

Container shipping is rapidly gaining market share over the traditional break-bulk method of ocean carriage. Containers provide much of the protection needed for goods that have to be heavily crated and packaged for break-bulk movement. It may take days to unload a break-bulk ship and load its new cargo with a small crane and human labour. An entire container ship can enter, unload, load, and clear a port in less than twelve hours. Such speed brings about labour savings to both the users and the ship operators. It also increases ship utilisation and, because a ship only earns revenue at sea, capital utilisation.

Export agent	Distributor
no financial involvement, works for commission	buys for own account and sells to earn profit
leaves importation to the buyers and passes their orders to the principal	imports the products
paid a commission at an agreed percentage on orders secured	marks up the supply price to cover own profit
any service necessary is rendered by the buyer	where necessary, undertakes responsibility for the service
carries no stock except for showroom purposes	usually carries stock
unlikely to be involved in publicity except where required to give advice or report on impact	likely to be involved in local publicity
may be authorised to engage subagents	appoints sub-distributors
no control over resale prices	controls selling prices in countries where retail price maintenance is possible
leaves distribution to the buyers	conducts distribution in the market

Table 13.1 Differences between distributors and export agents

Container service has introduced various operating and management concerns for ship operators. For one, this service requires a large investment in containers. While some containers are on board, many more are being distributed, delivered, or loaded; or are awaiting collection. For every hundred containers that a ship can carry, an investment of 150 to 250 containers is typically required to support its operation. Two sets of containers are needed – one on board and the other on land. A further concern is control over the containers. Previously, liner operators were port-to-port orientated. With inland movement of containers, control over the land movement becomes a necessity, especially with logistically linked intermodal transport. Computerised container-tracking systems make this possible.

Lighter-aboard ship operations

The lighter-aboard ship (LASH) carries barges from an inland river or waterway point to the sea port by water tow. A specially designed ocean ship carries the payload and barge intact to a foreign port to be dropped off in the harbour. This system minimises port handling and enables short ship turnaround times and high utilisation. The disadvantages of the LASH ship are similar to those of the container ship in that the ocean ship also requires a high capital investment, while the presence of barges or containers reduces the stowage factor. These two factors are generally traded off against the short port turnaround time provided by these systems. LASH ships operate mostly in North America and to some extent in Europe.

Roll-on/roll-off ship operations

The roll-on/roll-off ship is commonly known as a Ro-Ro ship. This type of vessel has ramps upon which vehicles can be driven directly into its cargo hold. Ro-Ro ships are often used to transport road vehicles, trailers, construction machinery on wheels, and other wheeled consignments. A Ro-Ro vessel can be more flexible than a container ship, because it can call at ports that do not have extensive container handling equipment. How-

ever, Ro-Ro vessels often carry conventional containers on their top deck.

Tramp ship operations

Tramp ships are bulk or tank ships that are hired for a voyage or a specific period.

If an exporter wants to hire a tramp ship for a voyage, it seeks a ship that will be emptied at the local port. It then hires (or charters) the ship for a one-way voyage to a foreign port. Port fees, a daily operating rate, and demurrage are part of the charter contract.

Time charters are period-based agreements that allow for more than one voyage. The exporter can decide whether the ship owner must provide a crew or not. A time charter of a ship without a crew is known as a bare-boat charter. By the nature of their business, tramp ships do not operate on fixed routes or on fixed schedules. Tramp ships, and especially bare-boat charters, lend themselves to be used almost as a form of private transport.

Private ship operations

Private ships are owned or leased long-term by firms for whom transporting the goods is an ancillary function. Many oil tankers and bulk ore ships fit into this category. The advantages of this form of operation are similar to those of ancillary road truck operations. In the short term, e.g. during peak trade periods, private ship operations may be supplemented with tramp ships.

An interesting aspect of international shipping is ship registry. For example, a ship may be owned by a South African citizen and ply a route between Australia and Japan; but it may be registered in and fly the flag of Liberia or Panama. These countries allow so-called flag of convenience arrangements. Ship owners derive certain benefits with respect to taxes, staffing, and relaxed safety requirements by being registered in those countries rather than in, say, South Africa or Australia.

Air carriers

As in the case of domestic carriage, air transport offers the international transport user short airport-to-airport transit time. Four types of air carriers are available for international users: air parcel post, express or courier, passenger, and freight aircraft.

Air parcel postal services

Air parcel postal services are provided by the public mail service of a country and are designed for carrying small packages. Mail service providers contract air transport providers to carry the parcels from one country to another. The operator's obligations are limited to carriage between airports only. There are restrictions on the size and mass of the items handled by air parcel post. The maximum mass of airmail parcels is often restricted to thirty kilograms, but this limit varies from country to country.

Express or courier services

Express or courier services are generally restricted to small consignments weighing less than thirty kilograms. Short transit time is the outstanding characteristic of this service, and next-day or second-day delivery is a standard service level. Examples of major carriers providing this service include Federal Express, United Parcel Service (UPS), and DHL. Courier service includes collection and delivery by road, and the service is offered on a door-to-door basis.

Passenger carriers

Regularly scheduled international passenger flights carry freight in the cargo hold of the aircraft. These carriers focus on transporting passengers, but the excess capacity in the freight compartment permits the carriage of freight along with passengers. (So-called combi aircraft are used, where passengers and freight form a payload combination.) Freight capacity and freight size are limited by the size of each aircraft, but high-frequency flight schedules usually afford consignors the choice of many international flights between large cities.

Freight carriers

Freight (or all-cargo) aircraft have larger hatch openings, freight compartments, and higher floor-bearing ratings than passenger aircraft. Many freight aircraft have mechanised materials-handling devices on board to permit the movement of heavy cargo inside the aircraft. Some of the larger aircraft are capable of transporting twelve-metre container and road vehicles. These operators accept consignments weighing considerably more than thirty kilograms.

Non-operating service providers

In addition to the basic modes, the international goods transport user can make use of non-operating service providers. These non-operating service providers offer several functions that afford the user lower costs, improved service, and technical expertise.

Airfreight forwarders

International airfreight forwarders reserve space on an operator's aircraft and solicit freight from several consignors to fill the reserved space. The airfreight forwarder can offer the sender of small consignments a rate saving as a result of advance booking. In addition, the airfreight forwarder offers convenience to the user when more than one airline is involved or when ground transport is necessary at one or both ends of the flight. They may also assist in completing all documentation and taking care of statutory requirements.

International freight forwarders

These service providers arrange transport for the consignor of international shipments. They do not necessarily act as consolidators. International freight forwarders act as agents for users, applying their experience and expertise to facilitate through-movement. They represent the consignor in arranging activities like inland transport, packaging, documentation, booking, and legal and government formalities. They charge a percentage of the tariffs levied for these services. They fulfil an indispensable function for consignors who are not familiar with the intricacies of international ocean transport or who do not have the scale or volume to warrant the employment of such expertise.

Non-vessel operating common carriers

Non-vessel operating common carriers (NVOCC) provide scheduled ocean shipping services without owning, operating, or chartering ships. NVOCC are a modified form of freight forwarder: they assemble and disperse partial container shipments so that these are transported as full container consignments. Instead of a consignor moving a small item by break-bulk ocean carrier or airfreight, an NVOCC consolidates it with others and gains the advantages of full-container transport. Some NVOCC operate from inland cities, especially in landlocked countries, where they unload inbound containers and distribute the

goods to consignees. They then solicit outbound freight, consolidate shipments, and send them back to a seaport for outbound movement. Through the NVOCC solicitations, the shipping line benefits from broadened territorial traffic and additional services, and gains control over containers. Consignors and consignees gain from the shipping expertise and business practices of the NVOCC, as well as from expanded and simplified import and export operations. Foreign freight forwarders may select an NVOCC instead of an ocean liner for the ocean segment of the freight movement.

Shipbrokers

Shipbrokers act as intermediaries between tramp ship operators and chartering consignors or consignees. The brokers' extensive exposure to, contacts within, and knowledge of the tramp ship market make them valuable parties in shipping arrangements. They charge a percentage of the chartering fees.

Ship agents

Ship agents act on behalf of a liner operator or tramp ship operator in facilitating ship arrival, clearance, loading, unloading, provision of supplies, and fee payment at the port. Liner operators appoint agents when the frequency of voyages is so irregular that it is not economical for them to invest in their own terminals or to employ staff at a specific port.

> **Test yourself**
>
> 13.8 Shipbrokers act as intermediaries between _____ and _____.

Incoterms

Introduction to Incoterms

Incoterms (International Commercial Terms) are the worldwide standard for the interpretation of trade terms. The International Chamber of Commerce (ICC) developed these terms to serve as a set of uniform rules for the interpretation of commercial terms defining the costs, risks, and obligations of sellers and buyers in international goods transactions. First published in 1936, Incoterms have been periodically revised to account for technological developments and changing modes of transport and document delivery. The current version is called Incoterms 2000.[5]

Use of Incoterms

Incoterms are a set of contractual instruments facilitating the sale and transport of goods in international transactions. However, Incoterms are not implied by default in an international sales contract. If a contractor wants to use them, they must specifically be included in the contract. The contract should expressly refer to the rules of interpretation as defined in the latest revision of Incoterms, for example, Incoterms 2000. Additional contract provisions should ensure proper application of the terms. Incoterms are not laws, but precise definitions of the costs, risks, and obligations of both parties in a contract. In the case of a dispute, courts and arbitrators will look at:

- the sales contract;
- who has possession of the goods; and
- what payment, if any, has been made.

Incoterms 2000 may be included in a contract of sale if the parties want to:

1 complete a sale of goods;
2 indicate each contracting party's costs, risks, and obligations with regard to delivery of the goods; and
3 establish basic terms of transport and delivery in a short format.

The costs, risks, and obligations in 2 above may be specified with respect to the following:

- the conditions that constitute completion of delivery;
- how a party ensures that the other party has met the required conditions;
- which party must comply with requisite licence requirements and/or government-imposed formalities;
- the mode(s) and terms of carriage;
- the delivery terms and requirements for proof of delivery;
- the stage when the risk of loss will transfer from the seller to the buyer;
- how transport costs will be divided between the parties; and
- the notices that the parties are required to give to one another regarding the transport and transfer of the goods.

Incoterms can be very useful, but if they are used incorrectly, contracts may be ambiguous, if not impossible to execute. It is therefore important to understand the scope and purpose of Incoterms – when and why they might be used – before relying on them to define such important terms as transport mode of delivery, customs clearance, passage of title, and transfer of risk.

Organisation of Incoterms 2000

Incoterms 2000 are grouped into four categories:[6]

The E term (EXW)

This is the only instance where the seller makes the goods available to the buyer at the seller's own premises. (See Figure 13.1 on page 217.) Note: In this chapter, 'seller' means seller, manufacturer, or exporter; and 'buyer' means buyer or importer.

The F terms (FCA, FAS, and FOB)

These terms indicate that the seller is responsible to deliver the goods to a carrier named by the buyer. (See Figure 13.2 on page 219.)

The C terms (CFR, CIF, CPT, and CIP)

According to these terms, the seller is responsible for contracting and paying for carriage, but not for additional costs or for risk of loss or damage once the goods have been shipped. C terms are appropriate for departure or shipment (as opposed to arrival) contracts. (See Figure 13.3 on page 221).

The D terms (DAF, DES, DEQ, DDU, and DDP)

These terms indicate that the seller is responsible for all costs and risks associated with transporting the goods to the destination. D terms are appropriate for arrival contracts. (See Figure 13.4 on page 223.)

Table 13.2 sets out the four categories. Not all Incoterms are appropriate for all modes of transport. Some terms are applicable to carriage by ship, while others are applicable to any mode of transport. Table 13.3 sets out which terms are appropriate for each mode of transport.

Description of Incoterms 2000

EXW – Ex Works (named place)

'Ex works' means that the seller has completed delivery when it places the goods at the disposal of the buyer. This must be done at the seller's premises or another named place (for example, point of production, factory, or warehouse) before the goods are cleared for export and loaded onto a collection vehicle.

This trade term places the greatest responsibility on the buyer and minimum obligations on the seller. The seller does not clear the goods for export and does not load the goods onto a means of transport at the named place of departure. The parties to the transaction may, however, decide that the seller should be responsible for the costs and risks of loading the goods onto a vehicle. Such a stipulation must be made in the contract of sale. If the buyer cannot handle export formalities, the EXW term should not be used. In such a case Free Carrier (FCA) is recommended.

The EXW term is often used when making an initial quotation for the sale of goods. It represents the cost of the goods without any other costs included. Payment terms for EXW transactions are generally cash in advance and open account. An open account is a credit and invoicing arrangement whereby the seller invoices the buyer periodically and payments are made over a specific period.

Group	Code	Name of term
Group E Departure	EXW	Ex Works (named place)
Group F Main carriage unpaid	FCA	Free Carrier (named place)
	FAS	Free Alongside Ship (named port of shipment)
	FOB	Free On Board (named port of shipment)
Group C Main carriage paid	CFR	Cost and Freight (named port of destination)
	CIF	Cost, Insurance, and Freight (named port of destination)
	CPT	Carriage Paid To (named place of destination)
	CIP	Carriage and Insurance Paid To (named place of destination)
Group D Arrival	DAF	Delivered at Frontier (named place)
	DES	Delivered Ex Ship (named port of destination)
	DEQ	Delivered Ex Quay (named port of destination)
	DDU	Delivered Duty Unpaid (named place of destination)
	DDP	Delivered Duty Paid (named place of destination)

Table 13.2 Incoterm categories

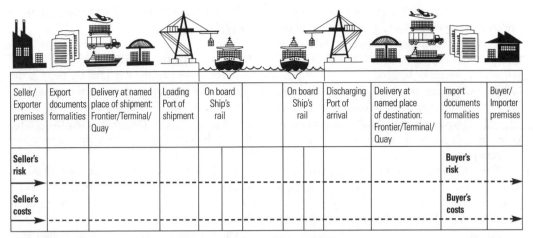

Seller/ Exporter premises	Export documents formalities	Delivery at named place of shipment: Frontier/Terminal/ Quay	Loading Port of shipment	On board Ship's rail		On board Ship's rail	Discharging Port of arrival	Delivery at named place of destination: Frontier/Terminal/ Quay	Import documents formalities	Buyer/ Importer premises
Seller's risk →									**Buyer's risk** →	
Seller's costs →									**Buyer's costs** →	

Figure 13.1 Division of risk and costs between seller and buyer: EXW

Examples:
- EXW KWV Winery, Paarl, South Africa
- EXW XYZ Printing Plant, Heidelberg, Germany

FCA – Free Carrier (named place)

'Free Carrier' means that the seller delivers the goods at the named place, cleared for export, to the carrier nominated by the buyer. The 'named place' in FCA and all other F terms is domestic to the seller. If the named place is the seller's place of business, the seller is responsible for loading the goods onto the vehicle. lf the named place is any other location, such as the loading dock of the carrier, the seller is not responsible for loading the goods onto the vehicle.

The FCA term may be used for any mode of transport, including multimodal transport. 'Carrier' has a somewhat expanded meaning. A carrier can be a shipping line, airline, road freight operator, or a rail transport operator. The carrier

Mode of transport	Geographical point designation	Code	Term
Any mode of transport, including multimodal	Named place	EXW FCA DAF	Ex Works Free Carrier Delivered at Frontier
	Named place of destination	CPT CIP DDU DDP	Carriage Paid To Carriage and Insurance Paid To Delivered Duty Unpaid Delivered Duty Paid
Sea and inland waterway transport only (ship)	Named port of shipment	FAS FOB	Free Alongside Ship Free On Board
	Named port of destination	CFR CIF DES DEQ	Cost and Freight Cost, Insurance, and Freight Delivered Ex Ship Delivered Ex Quay

Table 13.3 Mode of transport and appropriate Incoterm 2000

can also be a non-operating service provider who undertakes to procure carriage within any of the above modes of transport, including multimodal transport. In such a case, the buyer names the carrier who is to receive the goods.

The FCA term, like the EXW term, is often used when making an initial quotation for the sale of goods. Payment terms for FCA transactions are generally cash in advance and open account.

Examples:
- FCA ABC Shipping Lines, Athens, Greece
- FCA South African Airways, Johannesburg International Airport, South Africa
- FCA AZ Freight Forwarders, Sydney, Australia

FAS – Free Alongside Ship (named port of shipment)

'Free Alongside Ship' means that the seller has completed delivery when the goods are placed alongside the vessel at the named port of shipment. The buyer has to bear all costs and risks of loss of or damage to the goods from that moment. The FAS term requires the seller to clear the goods for export. (This requirement is a new provision to Incoterms 2000.) The parties to the transaction may, however, stipulate in their contract of sale that the buyer will clear the goods for export. The 'named port' in FAS and all F terms is domestic to the seller.

The FAS term is used only for ocean or inland waterway transport. The term is commonly used in the sale of bulk goods such as oil, grains, and ore.

Payment terms for FAS transactions are generally cash in advance and open account, but letters of credit are also used. A letter of credit is a document issued by a bank stating its commitment to pay the seller a stated amount of money on behalf of the buyer, providing the seller meets very specific terms and conditions.

Examples:
- FAS Buenos Aires, Argentina
- FAS Le Havre, France

FOB – Free On Board (named port of shipment)

This means that the seller has completed delivery when the goods pass the ship's rail (or ramp in the case of a Ro-Ro ship) at the named port of shipment. The buyer has to bear all costs and risks of loss of or damage to the goods from that point. The FOB term requires the seller to clear the goods for export.

The FOB term is used only for ocean or inland waterway transport. Payment terms for FOB transactions include cash in advance, open account, and letters of credit.

The FOB term is commonly used in the sale of bulk goods such as oil, grains, and ore, where it is important to deliver the goods on board the ship. It is also used for shipping container loads.

The key document in FOB transactions is the 'On Board Bill of Lading'.

Examples:
- FOB 'Vessel ABC' Dar es Salaam, Tanzania
- FOB 'Vessel XYZ' Auckland, New Zealand

CFR – Cost and Freight (named port of destination)

'Cost and Freight' means that the seller clears the goods for export and has completed delivery when the goods pass the ship's rail (or ramp in the case of a Ro-Ro ship) at the port of departure (not destination). The 'named port of destination' in CFR and all C terms is domestic to the buyer.

The seller clears the goods for export and is also responsible for paying for the costs associated with transporting the goods to the named port of destination. Once the goods pass the ship's rail or ramp at the port of departure, the buyer assumes responsibility for risk of loss or damage as well as any additional transport costs. The seller may, however, have 'insurable interest' during the voyage. Prudence may dictate procurement of additional insurance coverage.

The CFR term is used only for ocean or inland waterway transport. It is commonly used in the sale of indivisible large or heavy items that do not fit into a container or that exceed the mass limita-

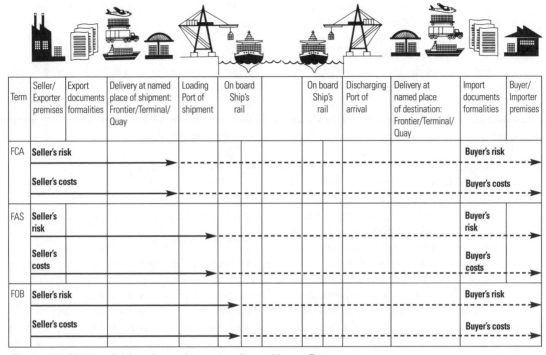

Term	Seller/ Exporter premises	Export documents formalities	Delivery at named place of shipment: Frontier/Terminal/ Quay	Loading Port of shipment	On board Ship's rail		On board Ship's rail	Discharging Port of arrival	Delivery at named place of destination: Frontier/Terminal/ Quay	Import documents formalities	Buyer/ Importer premises
FCA	Seller's risk									Buyer's risk	
	Seller's costs									Buyer's costs	
FAS	Seller's risk									Buyer's risk	
	Seller's costs									Buyer's costs	
FOB	Seller's risk									Buyer's risk	
	Seller's costs									Buyer's costs	

Figure 13.2 Division of risk and costs between seller and buyer: F terms

tions of containers. The term is also used for LCL (less than container load) consignments. Payment terms for CFR transactions include cash in advance, open account, and letters of credit.

Examples:
- CFR Casablanca, Morocco
- CFR Antwerp, Belgium

CIF – Cost, Insurance, and Freight (named port of destination)

This means that the seller has completed delivery when the goods pass the ship's rail (or ramp in the case of a Ro-Ro ship) in the port of departure (not destination). The 'named port of destination' in CIF and all C terms is domestic to the buyer.

The seller clears the goods for export and is responsible for paying for the costs associated with transporting the goods to the named port of destination. The seller is also responsible for procuring and paying for marine insurance in the buyer's name. Once the goods pass the ship's rail or ramp at the port of departure, the buyer assumes

responsibility for risk of loss or damage as well as any additional transport costs. The buyer may exercise prudence and acquire additional insurance coverage.

The CIF term is used only for ocean or inland waterway transport.

Payment terms for CIF transactions include cash in advance, open account, and letters of credit.

Examples:
- CIF Walvis Bay, Namibia
- CIF Seward, Alaska, USA

CPT – Carriage Paid To (named place of destination)

'Carriage Paid To' means that the seller nominates a carrier and delivers the goods to the nominated carrier. The 'named place of destination' in CPT and all C terms is domestic to the buyer, but does not necessarily refer to the final delivery point.

The seller clears the goods for export and pays the cost of carriage to the named destination. The seller is also responsible for the costs of unloading, customs clearance, duties, and other costs of carriage. Once the seller delivers the goods to the carrier, the buyer becomes responsible for all additional costs. If subsequent carriers are used for carriage to the agreed destination, the risk is passed on when the goods are delivered to the first carrier. While neither the carrier nor the buyer is obligated to provide insurance during the main voyage, both may have an 'insurable interest'. Prudence may indicate the acquisition of insurance coverage.

The CPT term is valid for any mode of transport, including multimodal transport.

A 'carrier' can be a shipping line, airline, road freight operator, rail transport operator, or a non-operating service provider who undertakes to procure carriage from a transport operator.

The CPT term is often used in sales where the carriage is by airfreight or containerised ocean freight as well as for courier consignments of small parcels and Ro-Ro shipments of road vehicles.

CIP – Carriage and Insurance Paid To (named place of destination)

'Carriage and Insurance paid to' means that the seller nominates a carrier and delivers the goods to the nominated carrier.

The seller must pay the cost of carriage to the named destination. The buyer bears all risks and any additional costs occurring after the goods have been delivered at this destination. However, in CIP the seller has to procure and pay for insurance against the buyer's risk of loss or damage during carriage. If subsequent carriers are used for the carriage to the agreed destination, the risk is passed on when the goods are delivered to the first carrier. Although the seller has to provide insurance coverage during the main voyage, the buyer may have additional 'insurable interest'. Prudence may dictate the acquisition of additional insurance coverage.

The seller is also responsible for the costs of unloading, customs clearance, duties, and other costs included in the cost of carriage.

The CIP term is valid for any mode of transport, including multimodal transport.

The CIP term is often used in sales where the carriage is by airfreight, containerised ocean freight, or courier; or where road vehicles are transported with Ro-Ro ships. A 'carrier' can be a shipping line, airline, road freight operator, rail transport operator, or a non-operating provider who undertakes to procure carriage within any of the above modes of transport, including multimodal transport.

Examples:
- CIP Frankfurt, Germany
- CIP Cairo, Egypt

DAF – Delivered At Frontier (named place)

'Delivered at Frontier' means that the seller has completed delivery when the goods are placed at the disposal of the buyer on the arriving vehicle, not unloaded. The seller has to clear the goods for export at the named point and place at the frontier, but not for import. However, goods have to be cleared for import before the customs border of the adjoining country. The term 'frontier' may relate to the country of export or import.

When using the DAF term, it is very important to name the precise place and time of delivery at the frontier, as the buyer must arrange to unload and secure the goods in time. The seller is not responsible for procuring and paying for insurance.

The DAF term is valid for any mode of transport – providing the final carriage, to the named place at the frontier, is by land.

Examples:

- DAF Beit Bridge, Northern Province, South Africa.

The consignment is transported by road truck from the premises of the seller in South Africa to the frontier at Beit Bridge. Here, the buyer takes possession and carries the goods by road truck to its premises in Zimbabwe. (See Figure 13.4.)

- DAF Basel, Switzerland.

The seller arranges for the consignment to be transported from Manchester in England via truck and ferry to the Netherlands; and then by

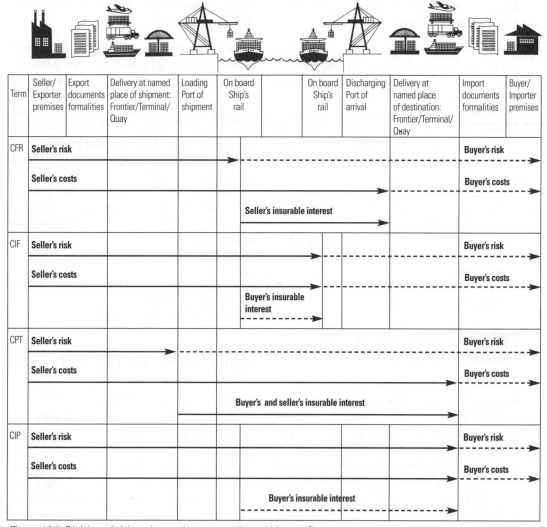

Term	Seller/ Exporter premises	Export documents formalities	Delivery at named place of shipment: Frontier/Terminal/ Quay	Loading Port of shipment	On board Ship's rail		On board Ship's rail	Discharging Port of arrival	Delivery at named place of destination: Frontier/Terminal/ Quay	Import documents formalities	Buyer/ Importer premises
CFR	Seller's risk									Buyer's risk	
	Seller's costs									Buyer's costs	
					Seller's insurable interest						
CIF	Seller's risk									Buyer's risk	
	Seller's costs									Buyer's costs	
					Buyer's insurable interest						
CPT	Seller's risk									Buyer's risk	
	Seller's costs									Buyer's costs	
				Buyer's and seller's insurable interest							
CIP	Seller's risk									Buyer's risk	
	Seller's costs									Buyer's costs	
					Buyer's insurable interest						

Figure 13.3 Division of risk and costs between seller and buyer: C terms

truck to the border of Switzerland. The buyer takes possession of and arranges carriage for the consignment from this point onwards to the final destination in Bern.

DES – Delivered Ex Ship (named port of destination)

'Delivered Ex Ship' means that the seller has achieved delivery when the goods are placed at the disposal of the buyer on board the ship, but not cleared for import at the named port of destina-

tion. The seller is responsible for all costs related to transporting the goods to the named port of destination prior to unloading.

The DES term is used only for shipment by ocean or inland waterway, or by multimodal transport where the final delivery is made on a vessel at the named port of destination.

All forms of payment are used in DES transactions.

Examples:
- DES Port of Marseilles, France
- DES Port of Genoa, Italy

DEQ – Delivered Ex Quay (named port of destination)

'Delivered Ex Quay' means that the seller has completed delivery when the goods are placed at the disposal of the buyer on the wharf at the named port of destination. The seller clears the goods for export but not for import. The buyer assumes all responsibilities for import clearance, duties, and other costs related to import; as well as for transport to the final destination. (This is a new provision for Incoterms 2000.)

The DEQ term is used only when shipments arrive at the port of destination by ocean or by inland waterway transport.

All forms of payment are used in DEQ transactions.

Examples:
♦ DEQ Alexandria, Egypt
♦ DEQ Dublin, Ireland

DDU – Delivered Duty Unpaid (named destination)

'Delivered Duty Unpaid' means that the seller is responsible for making the goods available to the buyer at the named destination; but not for unloading the goods from the arriving means of transport. The seller clears the goods only for export. The seller assumes all responsibilities for delivering the goods to the named destination. The buyer assumes all responsibility for import clearance, duties, administrative costs, and any other costs related to import. The buyer is also responsible for transport to the final destination.

The DDU term can be used for any mode of transport. However, if the seller and buyer prefer the goods to be delivered on board a sea vessel or on a wharf, the DES or DEQ terms are recommended. The DDU term is used when the named destination is beyond the seaport or airport of entry.

All forms of payment are used in DDU transactions.

Examples:
♦ DDU Rome, Italy
♦ DDU Nairobi, Kenya

DDP – Delivered Duty Paid (named destination)

'Delivered Duty Paid' means that the seller is responsible for making the goods available to the buyer at the named destination, but not for unloading the goods from the arriving vehicle. The seller clears the goods for export and import and, therefore, assumes all responsibilities for delivering the goods to the named destination – including import clearance, duties, and other costs payable upon import.

The DDP term can be used for any mode of transport. It is often used when the named destination (point of delivery) is beyond the seaport or airport of entry.

All forms of payment are used in DDP transactions.

Examples:
♦ DDP Xi'an, China
♦ DDP VAT Unpaid, Paris, France

Notes on Incoterms 2000

Appropriate contract

Incoterms were designed to be used within the context of a written contract for the cross-border (international) sale of goods. Incoterms therefore refer to the contract of sale, rather than the contract of carriage. Buyers and sellers should specify that their contract is governed by Incoterms 2000.

Added wording

It is possible, and in many cases desirable, for the seller and buyer to add additional wording to an Incoterm. For example, if the seller agrees to DDP terms and is willing to pay for customs formalities and import duties but not for VAT (Value Added Tax), the term 'DDP VAT Unpaid' may be used.

Customs of the port or trade

Incoterms are an attempt to standardise trade terms for all nations and all trades. However, different ports and different trades have their own

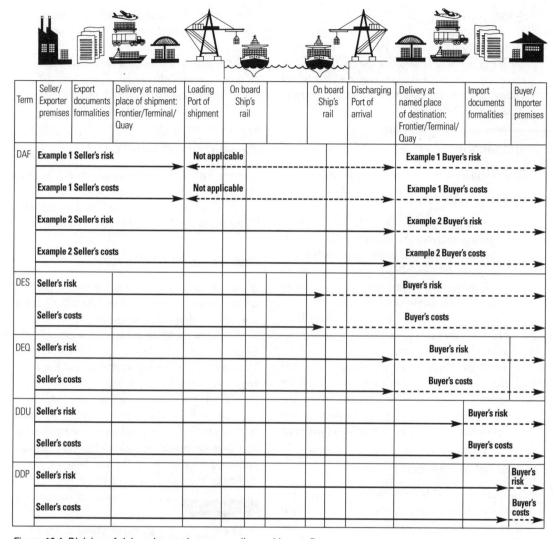

Figure 13.4 Division of risk and costs between seller and buyer: D terms

customs and practices. It is best to specify customs and practices in the sales contract.

EDI: Electronic Data Interchange

It is increasingly common for sellers to prepare and transmit documents electronically. Incoterms provide for EDI, provided that buyers and sellers agree on its use in the sales contract.

Export and import customs clearance

It is usually desirable that the seller handles export customs formalities and the buyer handles import customs formalities. However, some trade terms require that the buyer handles export formalities and others require that the seller handles import formalities. In each case, both the buyer and seller have to assume risk stemming from export and import restrictions and prohibitions. In some cases, foreign exporters may not be able to obtain import licences in the country of import. This should be researched before accepting the final terms.

EXW and FCA

When goods are bought Ex Works or Free Carrier, the buyer needs to arrange for the contract of carriage. Since the shipper does not receive a bill of lading, it is not possible to use a letter of credit requiring a bill of lading.

Inspection

The original contract should include the terms of inspection. The following conventions often apply:
- The seller is responsible for the costs of inspecting whether the quantity and quality of the shipment conform to the sales contract.
- The party responsible for export formalities needs to take care of pre-shipment inspections as required by the export authority.
- The party responsible for import formalities needs to take care of pre-shipment inspections as required by the import authority.
- Third-party inspections for independent verification of quality and quantity (if required) are generally the responsibility of the buyer. The buyer may require such an inspection and inspection document as a condition of payment.

Insurable interest

In many cases, either the buyer or the seller is obligated to provide insurance. Sometimes neither party is obligated to provide insurance. Prudence often dictates purchasing insurance coverage. However, in some cases neither the buyer nor the seller may have provided insurance coverage and are at risk for the portion of the trip specified in the Incoterms in the contract.

Packaging

It is the responsibility of the seller to provide packaging, unless the goods are customarily shipped in bulk (e.g. ore, oil, or grain). The buyer and seller should preferably agree in the sales contract on the type and extent of packaging required. If the type or duration of transport is not known beforehand, the seller is only responsible for providing safe and appropriate packaging to withstand the circumstances that the buyer has made known beforehand.

If the seller is responsible for sending goods in an ocean or airfreight container, it is also the seller's responsibility to see that the container is packed to withstand shipment.

Passing of risks and costs

The general rule is that risks and costs pass from the seller to the buyer once the seller has delivered the goods to the point named in the trade terms. These points are illustrated in Figures 13.1 to 13.4.

Precise point of delivery

If the buyer is unable to name the precise point of delivery in the contract in time, the seller has the option to deliver at a range of points that fall within the terms of the contract. For example, the original terms of sale may state CFR Port of Rotterdam. The Port of Rotterdam is huge and the buyer may favour a particular point within the port. The buyer should state this point in the sales contract and in the trade terms. The buyer becomes liable for the goods once they arrive and may be responsible for unloading costs, storage, and other charges once the goods arrive at the named point.

Test yourself

13.9 _____ are the worldwide standard for the interpretation of trade terms.

13.10 'Ex works' means that the seller has completed delivery when the goods are placed at the disposal of the buyer at the _____ or another _____.

13.11 Payment terms for FCA transactions are generally cash in advance and _____.

13.12 'Free Alongside Ship' means that the seller has completed delivery when the goods are placed alongside the vessel at the _____.

13.13 The FOB term requires the _____ to clear the goods for export.

13.14 'Cost and Freight' means that the seller has completed delivery when the goods pass the

---

_____ (or ramp in the case of a _____) in the port of _____.

13.15 The CIF term is used only for _____ or _____ transport.

13.16 'Carriage paid to' means that the _____ clears the goods for export and delivers the goods to the nominated carrier.

13.17 The CIP term is valid for _____ of transport, including _____.

13.18 The DAF term is valid for any mode of transport, providing the final carriage of the consignment to the named place at the frontier is by _____.

13.19 'Delivered Ex Ship' means that the seller has completed delivery when the goods are placed at the disposal of the buyer _____ the ship, but not cleared for import at the named port of _____.

13.20 'Delivered Ex Quay' means that the seller has completed delivery when the goods are placed at the disposal of the buyer on the wharf at the named port of _____.

13.21 The DDP term is used when the named destination is beyond the _____ or _____ of entry.

International trade documents

Documentation forms an integral part of all international goods transactions. Sellers and buyers need documents for bookkeeping, invoicing, cost accounting, taxation, export and import formalities, and payment.

This section provides examples of the most common documents used in international goods transactions and transportation.[7] These documents can be divided into several overlapping categories:

Transaction documents

The key transaction document is the commercial invoice. All parties to the transaction use this document for invoicing, cost accounting, and bookkeeping purposes. It is also required for export and import formalities and for most banking and payment procedures.

Export documents

These are documents required by the customs or export authority of the country of export. Export documents include licences, permits, export declarations, inspection certificates, the commercial invoice, and sometimes transport documents.

Inspection documents

These documents are usually issued by (third party) inspection firms acting on behalf of the buyer to certify the physical condition and quantities of the content of a consignment. Inspection documents are also issued to meet export and import requirements and health and safety regulations. In certain countries and for certain commodities, the health and safety inspection certificate must be issued by an appropriate government entity or by a government-accredited inspection body.

Insurance documents

These documents describe the exact insurance coverage of a consignment and can be in the form of an insurance policy contract or certificate.

Financial documents

These include banking and payment documents such as letters of credit, amendments to letters of credit, and financial advice pertaining to a transaction. To conclude the financial aspects of an international goods transaction, virtually all the other documents used in international trade (e.g. bill of lading, commercial invoice, insurance documents, and inspection certificate) must be available.

Import documents

These are documents required by the customs authority of the country of import. The minimum requirement is an entry form and a commercial invoice. Additional documents may be required if:

- the imported merchandise is sensitive (e.g. live animals, dangerous goods, drugs, foodstuff);

- the importer is requesting special tariff treatment under an import programme; or
- the goods are imported from certain countries.

Transport documents

These documents – issued by the transport operator or non-operating service provider – detail the terms of transport. The key transport document is the bill of lading. A packing list often supplements the bill of lading.

> The bill of lading is a document issued by a carrier to a consignor and signed by the carrier or agent in charge of the means of transport. It furnishes written evidence of the receipt of the freight, the contractual conditions, and the engagement to deliver a consignment at a prescribed destination to the legitimate holder of the bill of lading.

A completed bill of lading contains at least the following elements:
- the name of the carrier or multimodal transport operator, together with the signature of one of the following persons: the carrier, multimodal transport operator, ship's master, person in charge of the transport if not a ship, or agent
- an indication that the consignment has been 'dispatched', 'taken in charge', 'loaded on board', or 'loaded on deck'; along with the date
- an indication of the place of departure, which may be different from the place of loading
- an indication of the place of delivery, which may be different from the place of discharge
- an original copy or, if multiple originals are issued, the full set of originals
- the terms and conditions of carriage or a reference to the terms and conditions of carriage in another source or document.

A bill of lading is both a receipt for merchandise and a contract to deliver a consignment. There are various types of bills of lading:

Non-negotiable bill of lading

A non-negotiable bill of lading indicates that the consignor will deliver a consignment to the consignee only. Possession of the document itself does not entitle anyone to the goods – thus 'non-negotiable' – so the consignee needs some form of identification to claim the goods. A non-negotiable bill of lading is often used when the buyer has paid in advance or when goods are shipped on open account. A non-negotiable bill of lading cannot be transferred by endorsement. It is also known as a straight bill of lading.

Negotiable bill of lading

A negotiable bill of lading is a title document to the goods. It is issued 'to the order of' a party, usually the consignor, whose endorsement is required to effect its negotiation. Because it is negotiable, it can be bought, sold, or traded while goods are in transit. The buyer needs an original as proof of ownership in order to take possession of the goods.

Air waybill

An air waybill is a bill of lading used for air transport. It is not negotiable.

Ocean bill of lading

An ocean bill of lading – also known as a marine or port-to-port bill of lading – is a document covering port-to-port consignments carried solely by sea transport. An ocean bill of lading must contain a notation that the goods were loaded 'on board' or 'on deck'.

An 'on board' notation means that the goods were loaded on board or carried onto a ship. The carrier, the carrier's agent, the master of the ship, or the ship's agent may make this notation. The transport document issued by the carrier must reflect that the consignment is 'on board' in order for the seller to obtain payment under a documentary credit.

An 'on deck' notation means that the goods were secured on the deck of a ship, rather than in its hold, and are therefore subject to the elements. Such a notation is generally not acceptable in documentary credit transactions unless specifically authorised. If the transport document shows that the goods are loaded on deck, the enclosed insurance documents must show cover against 'on deck' risks. Live animals, dangerous goods (including certain chemicals), and odd-sized items are often carried on deck.

Clean bill of lading

A clean bill of lading is one on which the carrier notes that the merchandise has been received in apparent secure and good condition. Most transaction contracts require a clean bill of lading in order for the seller to obtain payment.

Claused bill of lading

A claused bill of lading – also called an unclean bill of lading – is the opposite of a clean bill of lading. It serves to confirm that a consignment was not delivered securely. It contains notations that specify a shortfall in quantity or deficient condition of the goods or packaging.

Packing list

This document, prepared by the consignor, lists the types and quantities of merchandise in a particular consignment. A copy of the packing list is often attached to the consignment and another copy is sent directly to the consignee to assist in checking the shipment when it is delivered. The packing list includes the following elements:

◆ name and address of seller
◆ name and address of buyer
◆ date of issuance
◆ invoice number
◆ order or contract number
◆ quantity and description of the goods
◆ shipping details, including mass of the goods, number of packages, and shipping marks and numbers
◆ quantity and description of the contents of each package, carton, crate, or container
◆ any other information as required in the sales contract or documentary credit (e.g. country of origin).

Test yourself

13.22 The key transaction document is the _____ invoice.

13.23 The key transport document is the _____.

13.24 A bill of lading is both a receipt for _____ and a contract to _____.

13.25 A packing list is prepared by the _____. It lists the _____ and _____ of merchandise in a consignment.

Conclusion

In a rapidly integrating and globalising world market, efficient and effective logistics support structures relating to international goods transactions are indispensable. Logistics managers involved in international distribution must acquaint themselves with distribution channels because they need to understand how products flow to foreign consumers. The longer the channel, the greater the number of intermediaries. International goods transport is provided by all modes. However, the vast majority of goods are moved by sea and air transport.

Incoterms are the worldwide standard for the interpretation of international trade terms. Incoterms are a set of contractual instruments facilitating the sale and transport of goods in international transactions. Documentation forms an integral part of all international goods transactions. Sellers and buyers need transaction documents for bookkeeping, invoicing, cost accounting, taxation, export and import formalities, as well as for making payment.

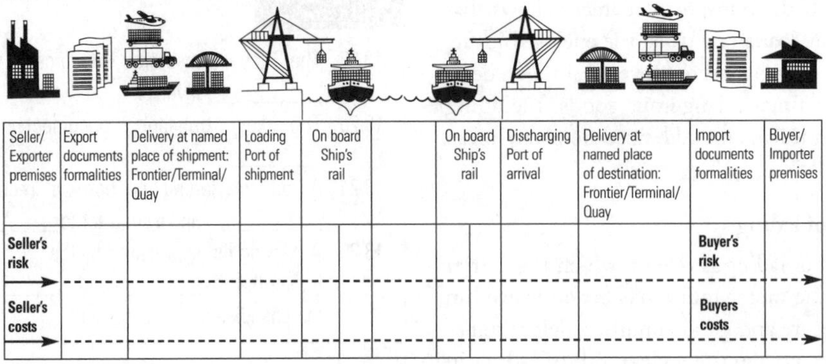

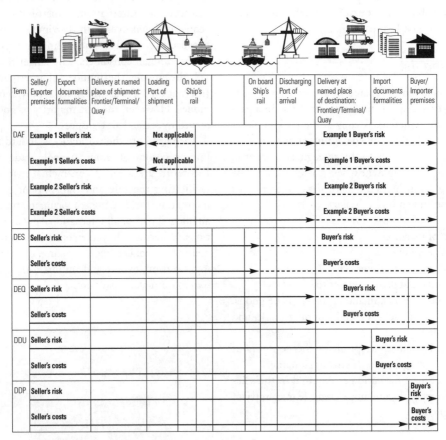

Figure 13.1 Division of risk and costs between seller and buyer: EXW

Figure 13.4 Division of risk and costs between seller and buyer: D terms

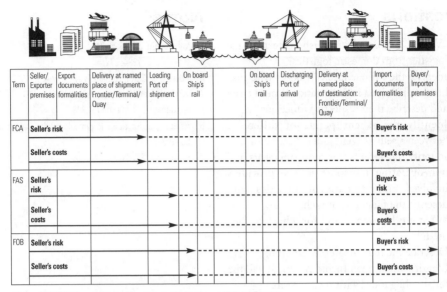

Term	Seller/ Exporter premises	Export documents formalities	Delivery at named place of shipment: Frontier/Terminal/ Quay	Loading Port of shipment	On board Ship's rail		On board Ship's rail	Discharging Port of arrival	Delivery at named place of destination: Frontier/Terminal/ Quay	Import documents formalities	Buyer/ Importer premises
FCA	Seller's risk									Buyer's risk	
	Seller's costs									Buyer's costs	
FAS	Seller's risk									Buyer's risk	
	Seller's costs									Buyer's costs	
FOB	Seller's risk									Buyer's risk	
	Seller's costs									Buyer's costs	

Figure 13.2 Division of risk and costs between seller and buyer: F terms

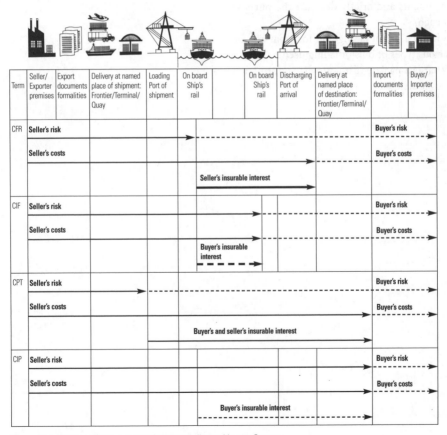

Term	Seller/ Exporter premises	Export documents formalities	Delivery at named place of shipment: Frontier/Terminal/ Quay	Loading Port of shipment	On board Ship's rail		On board Ship's rail	Discharging Port of arrival	Delivery at named place of destination: Frontier/Terminal/ Quay	Import documents formalities	Buyer/ Importer premises
CFR	Seller's risk									Buyer's risk	
	Seller's costs									Buyer's costs	
					Seller's insurable interest						
CIF	Seller's risk									Buyer's risk	
	Seller's costs									Buyer's costs	
					Buyer's insurable interest						
CPT	Seller's risk									Buyer's risk	
	Seller's costs									Buyer's costs	
					Buyer's and seller's insurable interest						
CIP	Seller's risk									Buyer's risk	
	Seller's costs									Buyer's costs	
					Buyer's insurable interest						

Figure 13.3 Division of risk and costs between seller and buyer: C terms

Questions

1 Which factors distinguish international logistics from domestic logistics?
2 Identify the various intermediaries who may become involved in international marketing and describe their respective functions.
3 Identify the salient points of difference between a selling agent and a distributor.
4 Identify the various transport operators and non-operating transport service providers involved in international logistics and describe the functions of each.
5 What are Incoterms and for what are they used?
6 Describe the four Incoterms groupings.
7 Identify the thirteen Incoterms and detail the seller's obligations within each term.
8 Identify the categories of international trade documents and briefly describe the purpose of each.
9 What is a bill of lading and for what are the various types of bills of lading used?
10 What is a packing list and what information does it include?

Notes

1 Van Vuuren, J.P. 1996: 74.
2 Branch, A.E. 1994: 372.
3 Coyle, J.J., Bardi, E.J. and Novack, R.A. 2000: 241–244.
4 Wood, D.F. and Johnson, J.C. 1996: 356–551.
5 Hinkelman, E.G. 2000: 275–303.
6 Ramberg, J., Rapatout, P., Reynolds, F. and Debattista, C. 2000: 96–103.
7 Hinkelman, E.G. 2000: 395–416.

14 Reverse logistics

Contents

Learning Outcomes

After you have studied this chapter, you should be able to:
- define reverse logistics;
- interpret a flow diagram that indicates the primary flow of goods, information, and money;
- draw a flow diagram, indicating the typical primary and reverse flows of goods, information, and money;
- explain the financial impact of the return of unsold goods;
- discuss the impact of the return of unsold goods on the logistics system;
- discuss the impact of product recalls on the logistics system;
- discuss the importance of waste management;
- discuss the implications of waste management on business logistics; and
- identify the main components of waste management.

Introduction

Only in recent years has the business world awoken to the high cost involved in reverse distribution, as it was called at first. Activity Based Costing, or ABC analysis, contributed significantly to this increased focus as it emphasised the costs associated with the reverse distribution. Reverse distribution has now become reverse logistics to encompass a wider scope.

This field of study has evolved dramatically over the past few years as more effort was put into researching the economic impact of reverse logistics. Impetus was added when businesses realised that 'Green Management' could become an alternative source of competitive advantage. It is also important to have a good understanding of the potential financial impact of reverse logistics on the business enterprise.

Reverse logistics today is a wide field that encompasses a diverse range of activities including:

* the reverse distribution of products;
* the return of unsold goods,
* product returns;
* product recalls; and
* waste management.

Definitions of reverse logistics

There are many emerging definitions of reverse logistics. The reason for these varying definitions is that this is one of the fastest developing fields of business logistics, with the result that it continuously changes in scope and significance. We prefer the broad definition below:

Reverse logistics is the management of all the activities involved in goods, demand information, and money flowing in the opposite direction of the primary logistics flow. It involves reducing the generation of waste, as well as managing the collection, transport, disposal, and recycling of both hazardous and non-hazardous waste in a way that maximises the long-term profitability of the business.

Reverse logistics therefore involves a significant number of aspects of logistics.

Test yourself

14.1 Reverse logistics is the management of all the activities involved in goods, demand information, and money flowing in the _____ of the _____.

Reverse distribution of products

Product, information, and money flows

Primary distribution occurs when goods flow from the point-of-origin (input or raw materials) to the point-of-consumption (end user). The financial or money stream flow is in the opposite direction of the goods flow in primary distribution. For example, the end user pays the upstream member of the supply chain, who in turn pays the next member directly upstream.

However, not all goods flow through the entire supply chain (from the raw material stage to the consumer). These secondary channels are often part of reverse logistics and comprise such diverse issues as product returns, recalls, and waste management.

Value carriers

Some goods flow in the opposite direction of the primary flow. Examples are empty containers and packaging, empty gas cylinders; and pallets returned for reuse.

As they are reusable, these items are also known as value carriers. They have a value of their own. Some of these items may even be worth more than the products they carry. Containers are continually reused and must therefore be designed to last and to fulfil the functions of packaging and of unitising the goods they carry.

The value carriers are part of the inventory of the business. Fluctuations in demand can result in a surplus or a shortage of these items if they are not carefully managed. The financial implications could be significant if a soft drink manufacturer, for example, does not have enough empty bottles at the bottling plant or enough crates to pack and distribute the filled bottles. These shortages can bring production to a halt. Breakage, age, theft, or items accumulating in inappropriate locations in the logistics chain cause reductions in the inventory of value carriers. One needs to be aware of the level of shrinkage in order to maintain the inventory level of the value carriers. As with any inventory item, the cost to a business is significant if there is too great a stockholding, while the consequences of shortages severely affect operations.

Costing of value carriers

The cost of the initial purchase and the subsequent management and replacement of value carriers is significant and cannot be ignored where these are extensively used in a business. There are two categories of value carriers: carriers that are distributed to the consumer and carriers that are used in a closed loop, effectively forming a closed supply chain for the value carrier.

Value carriers distributed to the consumer

Value carriers distributed to the consumer can be used repeatedly. A number of mechanisms are used to encourage consumers to return these carriers. For example, a deposit is redeemable when the carrier is returned in good condition. Carriers can also be created to be specific to the duty they perform so that they have little value outside the particular chain. The method applied depends largely on the initial cost of the carrier.

An example of a returnable carrier is a plastic crate made for soft drinks, while the plastic bottle in which the soft drink is packaged is a non-returnable container. Gas cylinders are long lasting carriers made for a specific purpose in industry. These cylinders can only be used for specific industrial gases. The owner of the cylinder charges a monthly fee for hire, rather than a deposit. This fee covers the cost of the cylinder, as well as the high costs of maintenance and safety inspections.

Value carriers are filled within the limits of either mass or volume. This capacity represents the restriction on the quantity of goods that the container can carry. By allocating the cost of the container to the total amount of goods that the container will carry during its lifespan, one can determine the cost that needs to be allocated to each item.

For example, fifty items fit into a container that costs R2 000. The container has an estimated lifespan of twenty journeys. The calculation is done as follows:

50 items x 20 journeys = 1 000 item-journeys
R2 000 ÷ 1 000 = R2 per item-journey

Value carriers in a closed loop

Value carriers in a closed loop are not sold but are used in sections of the logistics chain to facilitate movement and/or storage. These can be items such as pallets, containers, and roll-tainers. Often the name of the owner is stencilled on them. The carriers are moved with the primary flow and at an appropriate point are sent in the reverse direction to be reused by the owner.

Empty rail wagons can also be regarded as empty or unused value carriers. It is very difficult to predict where these empty wagons will be needed next and where they must therefore be kept. Empty wagons distribution is one of the most challenging and costly reverse logistics operations for rail companies. This can also apply to other modes of transport, especially when an immediate return load is not forthcoming.

Value carriers such as pallets and containers can alternatively be hired from third parties. While hiring value carriers may be costlier than purchasing them, the advantage is that the carrier can be obtained from a depot nearest to where the goods are collected. They can also be returned to an alternative depot nearest to where the goods are delivered. This eliminates the cost of returning the carrier and reduces the time and effort involved in managing this process.

Reusable containers are often gathered in depots to consolidate loads and minimise the transport costs. Empty rail wagons can also be stored at depots or hubs until they are returned by coupling them to block trains. Road vehicles cannot be returned to the next point in this manner. Costly empty back hauls are therefore inherent to road transport.

The cost of these value carriers is often deemed an overhead and is allocated to the total cost of the operation over the lifetime of the carrier, as it is generally not feasible to allocate it to specific goods.

Other examples of reverse distribution

Recycling of paper, used motor oil, used batteries, and glass are other examples of reverse distribution.

> **Test yourself**
>
> 14.2 Reusable containers are also known as _____.

Return of unsold goods

In certain industries, goods are distributed to downstream members in the supply chain with the understanding that the goods may be returned for credit if they are not sold. Newspapers and magazines serve as examples. This acts as an incentive for downstream members to carry more stock, because the risk of obsolescence is borne by the upstream supply chain members. However, there is also a distinct risk attached to this logistics concept. The downstream member in the supply chain might exploit the situation by ordering more stock than is required and returning large volumes. In this way, the downstream partner is able to offer a high level of service without carrying the risks associated with large inventories. The supplier effectively finances the inventory for the downstream member. It is therefore important to analyse customers' accounts for hidden costs.

A different example of the return of unsold goods can be found in the bread industry. Old bread is often returned to bakeries, where it is reprocessed into croutons. Collecting the old bread does not add any significant cost, because the delivery vehicle is already committed to calling at each point. The raw material (old bread) also does not add to the cost, because the alternative is to let the old bread go to waste. Bakeries that employ this concept can gain a competitive advantage by offering another product without having to carry added input costs.

Returned goods that can be resold must again be packed and labelled. When the goods need a different form of packaging or when bar coding on the initial packaging is not appropriate, the initial packaging must be disposed of as waste.

> **Test yourself**
>
> 14.3 Logistics policies that accommodate the return of unsold goods act as an incentive for the downstream member to _____.

Product returns and exchanges

Product returns and exchanges stem from damaged goods, incorrectly ordered goods, incorrectly supplied goods, warranty claims, product support service, or after sales service. All these causes of returns and exchanges must be managed and controlled. Product returns must be monitored to ensure that patterns of returns are identified and broken. This will enable management to proactively manage the demand for reverse logistics capacity.

Damaged goods

Goods can be damaged during transport or storage. The sooner damage is detected, the cheaper it is to rectify the problem. As goods flow through the logistics process, they gain in value. (If this is not the case, there should not be intermediate steps.) This benefit is wasted if it is added to damaged goods which will be returned at a later stage.

Incorrectly ordered goods

Communicating an order by telephone or fax allows for inaccuracies in the capturing of order details into the order management system. The method with the least potential for errors is one whereby the customer captures the order, and whereby the order is transmitted and received in an electronic format. This can be achieved by means of direct linkage through Electronic Data Interchange (EDT), or via the Internet.

Incorrectly supplied goods

The only difference between a wrong customer order specification, incorrect data capturing, and an incorrect pick is the party responsible for paying for the mishap. All parties loose out when goods are supplied incorrectly: The supplier must take the goods back and the customer has to wait for the appropriate order to be delivered.

Warranties and repairs

The cost of warranties and repairs apply when customers reject products due to quality problems. It is in the best interest of a business to detect defective goods as soon as possible, with the view to reduce the unnecessary cost of return. The business also needs to decide whether returned goods should be recycled, repaired, or disposed of.

Test yourself

14.4 It is important to identify emerging patterns of product returns in order to manage the demand for _____.

Product recalls

If a range of goods that has already been delivered to customers is defective, the manufacturer may decide to recall the products or even replace them. This is especially important if the products may cause injury or damage – for example, defective components in automotive vehicles or dangerous toys or equipment. There was a recall in the United States of America during the second half of 2000 of a brand of motor vehicle tyre that had been found to have contributed to accidents. Further examples are the recall of tainted cold drinks in Europe in 1999 and the recall of a brand of rooibos tea in the mid-1990s in South Africa.

What differentiates product recalls from the return of damaged goods? Damage to the goods is often caused by one of the logistics functions and is restricted to a small quantity of the goods. A product recall is usually the result of a design or manufacturing defect affecting the performance and the safety of every item. The essential difference is that different parties are financially responsible for the cause of the defect.

The reverse flow of goods can be substantially more expensive than the primary flow. It is therefore important to determine the causes of the reverse flow in order to determine who should pay for the additional expenditure. The potential cost of product recalls must be considered when a business determines the cost of quality.

Test yourself

14.5 Product recalls occur when a range of products that has already been delivered to customers is discovered to be _____.

Waste management

It is important to manage waste by reducing the generation of waste, sorting it as close to the source as possible, transporting it as cost-efficiently as possible, and disposing of and recycling it on a commercially viable basis.

Hazardous and non-hazardous waste

Non-hazardous or general waste (G category) has no effect on the environment and human health if managed properly. General waste includes domestic waste, garden refuse, and light industrial and commercial products.

Hazardous (H category) waste refers to those materials that may have a negative effect on the environment and on human health. Hazardous waste can be divided into extremely to highly hazardous (H), moderately to slightly hazardous (h category), and de-listed waste. Many of these products are not biodegradable. There are specified ways of disposing of products such as radioactive waste, toxic waste, and tyres. In some instances, waste must undergo treatment to avoid hazards during disposal or to reduce pollution of the environment.

Reducing waste generation

The reduction of waste generation is arguably one of modern society's greatest challenges. Being more 'green sensitive' throughout the value chain not only brings about economical benefits but also environmental benefits.

Waste is an expense for any enterprise. The processes of waste management must be designed, and the operations carried out, with an eye on minimising the costs. Goods and materials that leave the enterprise must be measured and altered so that the waste component is reduced. Reusable containers are a viable alternative to traditional packaging methods.

Collecting waste

Various methods are used for collecting general and hazardous waste. The most important way of reducing the cost of the waste management programme is to sort the waste as close to the source as possible.

Specialist waste removal firms collect hazardous waste with special containers or tanker vehicles.

Local authorities collect general and domestic waste. Collection vehicles can be rear-end loaders (REL), tractor-trailers and, in some areas, side loaders. Bulk containers or skips are used for businesses and industry. These containers come in various sizes and designs: The size of open bulk containers varies from 4,5 m³ to 11 m³. Special vehicles (sometimes called 'load luggers') that are able to pick up these containers are used to remove them. Smaller mobile containers (between 1 m³ and 1,2 m³), used at smaller businesses, are emptied by front-end loaders (FEL).

Roll-on/roll-off containers are either open or closed. The open version varies in size between 15 m³ and 30 m³ and the closed version between 11 m³ and 35 m³. The closed containers are used at large shopping centres and transfer stations and can be connected to a compacting unit. The open containers are used at garden refuse sites and transfer stations. Special roll-on/roll-off vehicles remove and transport these containers.

Transporting waste

Waste is usually transported by road because the shorter distances and frequent stops make it the most economical method. The waste can either be transported to the disposal site with the vehicle collecting it, or it can be transferred to long-haul vehicles. In some countries with inland waterways, boats or barges are used as these are very economical. Where waste disposal sites are situated some distance from the collection area and the site is adjacent to a rail siding, the waste is transported by rail. The waste is baled or compacted and loaded onto specially adapted rail wagons.

In small towns with small quantities of waste, the most economical transport is often a tractor with an open trailer.

Larger town councils may use tractor-trailers to transport waste to a central waste site. If there is no waste site, the waste can be transferred to a larger vehicle at a transfer station. Larger long-haul vehicles transport waste from the transfer station to the waste disposal site.

In the larger cities and metropolitan areas, a combination of collection vehicles deliver waste to transfer stations. Long-haul vehicles transport the waste from the transfer station to the waste disposal site.

Special permits and pre-determined routes for transport vehicles ensure the safe transportation of hazardous waste.

Disposing of waste

Waste disposal has become a science. The old dumpsite is outdated. Waste disposal sites are scientifically located, designed, operated, and eventually closed.

Waste sites are classified according to the type of waste, volume of waste per day, and climatic water balance or potential for leachate (liquid run-off from the site).

Waste disposal sites are classified according to landfill size. The classification systems vary between countries and local authorities, but the following is a good example:

Size of site	Tons per day (t)
Commercial (C)	$0 < t \leq 25$
Small (S)	$25 < t \leq 50$
Medium (M)	$50 < t \leq 150$
Large (L)	$t > 150$

Table 14.1 Landfill size classification

Where the potential for leachate is significant, the site is classed as a B+ site. Sites where leachate is expected to be sporadic are classified as B- sites. Where co-disposal occurs (when liquid waste is introduced to a solid waste site), the site is also classified as a B+ site.

Sites are classified according to a combination of the type of waste, such as general waste (G); the size, as per Table 14.1; and the potential for leachate. General (G) waste sites can therefore be classified as a GCB-, GCB+, GSB-, GSB+, GMB-, GMB+, GLB-, or GLB+.

There are two classes of hazardous waste disposal sites:

- H site: This site can receive all types of hazardous waste.
- h site: This site can only receive moderately and slightly hazardous material, de-listed waste and general waste.

Some of the more toxic or dangerous waste at hazardous waste disposal sites is encapsulated in drums or in blocks of concrete. Owing to the toxic nature of medical waste, it is generally incinerated (the waste, including the container, is burned at a very high temperature).

Recycling waste

Many countries have imposed legislation enforcing recycling to protect the environment. The most common materials recovered from waste for recycling are glass, plastic, tin, aluminium, and paper.

The benefits of recycling can be summarised as follows:

- The volume of waste is reduced. Fifty per cent of all waste disposed at waste disposal sites can be recycled. Recycling reduces the space utilised for waste, so sites have less impact on the environment.
- Recycling reduces the overall amount of energy utilised, reducing pollution.
- Natural resources are conserved, as fewer raw materials are needed if waste is recycled.

The following are the most common ways of recycling waste:

- Separation at source: This is the most effective method. It usually takes place at home or in industry where all the different kinds of waste are sorted into separate bins.
- Scavenging: Separation of material at the drop-off point of the waste disposal site should be precluded from the landfill operation for health reasons.
- Street collection: Paper and boxes are left on the sidewalk and collected by contractors.

Creating compost from garden refuse also reduces

the volumes of waste disposed at the waste site. Grass cuttings, tree branches, and leaves are separated from the main stream of waste and delivered to a garden waste disposal site.

A very effective material recovery facility (MRF) is used extensively in the USA. This is a facility with a drop-off point, a conveyor system, storage containers for recyclable materials, balers, and a rejection point for non-recyclable material. Workers are stationed at the conveyor belt and sort recyclable materials into containers allocated to each type of material. The materials suitable for recycling are baled and transported to the recycling business. The non-recyclable material is taken to the waste disposal site. In some MRFs, up to seventy-five per cent of all the material received is sent for recycling.

Test yourself

14.6 Recycling leads to a reduction in the _____.

Environmental Management: ISO 14000

ISO 14000 is a series of standards for environmental management issued by the International Standards Organisation (ISO). The standards record an enterprise's environmental policy, objectives, measurements for and commitment to the management of the environment. Senior management commitment is recorded and communicated. All this information is used internally to monitor progress towards and compliance with the standards set by the enterprise. External audits by professional auditors are also required.

The use of ISO 14000 is not mandatory. It is a comprehensive means of raising awareness in an enterprise of the importance of environmental management.

ISO 14000 sets in place the formal structure of the process of managing the environment. It encompasses the following issues:

- an environmental policy that records the commitment of the enterprise – and in particular of senior management – to a specified level of environmental performance;
- the development of a strategy to meet these commitments, including objectives and plans to deal with current environmental issues and potential environmental issues the enterprise may face;
- the structures that will undertake the compliance with the strategy;
- setting the enterprise's required objectives and measurement targets;
- plans to give effect to the overall policy and to maintain the standards, including training, communication, and the response to situations;
- measurements to monitor compliance; and
- review and auditing processes (external and internal).

It requires considerable time and effort to establish this comprehensive process. Once established, it becomes a formal system for monitoring the environmental management of the enterprise and, because it is subject to an external audit, it reflects an international standard. Compliance with ISO 14000 assists in marketing the company's products. As the enterprise is not at risk from environmental problems, insurance premiums may be reduced.

ISO 14000 is often monitored and audited with ISO 9000, the quality management system from the ISO. This integrates the quality and environmental systems of an enterprise and ensures that the enterprise complies with international standards for both quality and environmental management.

Financial implications of reverse logistics

Studies done by the Council for Logistics Management (CLM) in the United States of America have indicated that reverse logistics costs account for approximately four per cent of the total logistics costs in that country. After the advent of Business to Consumer (B2C) Internet trading, an increasing percentage of on-line purchases are being returned. The primary reason for this is that customers are disappointed when the real goods do not match the catalogue impressions from which they were chosen.

The cost of reverse logistics adds no value to the logistics function of providing the right goods at the right time and place. Reverse logistics does add unwanted costs. The total costs for reverse logistics therefore needs to be managed to control the costs of the products delivered to the consumers. It is critical to measure and report on the cost component of reverse logistics in absolute terms as well as in relative terms as a percentage of total logistics costs, cost of sales, or gross profit.

The costs that are not an integral part of the product delivered to the consumer need to be minimised. The costs associated with waste are part of any business but add no direct value to the product from the consumer's perspective. The responsible and economical disposal of this waste needs to be measured and monitored.

The costs for value carriers must be carefully monitored. These items can represent significant investments. The initial lifetime forecast may not match the actual lifetime, so that the cost allocated to the goods may be either too high or too low. The price competitiveness of the product can be adversely affected if the charges for value carriers are too high, while too low charges can result in an unrecovered cost.

The costs for the total management of reverse logistics need to be considered. These include the cost of purchase, the cost of disposal, and the cost of monitoring and managing the overall process.

Test yourself

14.7 The cost of reverse logistics can be expressed as a percentage of _____, _____, or _____.

Conclusion

Reverse logistics deals with the logistics activities or flows that occur outside the primary flow of goods and products to customers. It encompasses the waste generated in the logistics process, the re-use of certain value carriers such as containers and pallets, and the return of goods for various reasons. Reverse logistics must be managed. The ability to deal with reverse logistics in a cost-effective manner can be a source of competitive advantage.

Waste is an automatic by-product of any society. The disposal of the waste is a challenge. The essential logistics processes involved in waste management are:

- reduction of waste generation;
- sorting;
- collection;
- transport;
- disposal; and
- recycling.

Where the potential impact on the environment is high, formal systems to monitor and manage the disposal of waste may add significant value to the enterprise.

The processes to control reverse logistics must be in place. The returns policy and procedures need to be recorded and known. The disposal of waste needs to be done in an environmentally safe manner. Reusable items reduce the waste, but constitute a capital cost. Managing the return of these items for reuse requires effort.

The ISO 14000 system is of particular value in establishing the overall objectives and monitoring standards.

Reverse logistics is rising in prominence. The environmental lobby will put increasing pressure on enterprises to comply with the legal requirements for waste disposal. Successful companies will tackle the reverse logistics aspects to reduce unavoidable costs, eliminate unnecessary costs, and to gain a competitive advantage.

Questions

1. Define reverse logistics.
2. Discuss the financial impact of the return of unsold goods.
3. Discuss the importance of waste management.
4. List the main components of waste management.

Contents

Learning Outcomes

After you have studied this chapter, you should be able to:
- describe the key role of information in logistics;
- distinguish between the information flow and the goods flow;
- discuss how logistics information can be used to co-ordinate logistics functions;
- recognise what logistics information is required at the various levels;
- discuss how the customer order management process can positively or negatively affect customer service; and
- list the steps in the customer order management cycle.

Introduction

Logistics systems can serve to integrate the functional activities, make the functional activities more efficient, and make the logistics chain more effective.

> Logistics management systems are the management tasks that integrate procedures, equipment, and resources in order to support and enable the processing of inputs into actions that provide the desired customer service level at the least total logistics costs.

Logistics information systems

> Logistics information systems (LIS) are vehicles for utilising signals or data from the environment to manage logistics activities, and to feed back information to the environment through management actions and changes. This process constitutes an open system.

It is important to differentiate between data and information. Data is a collection of 'raw' facts. Data is not necessarily organised in any sequence. Information is refined, processed, organised, and integrated data. For example, when counting stock, a list of bin locations and part numbers in random sequence constitutes data and does not help the stock controller. Transforming the same data into information by listing the bin locations in sequence, grouping A, B, and C inventory classifications, and sorting the list in descending order of value, will help the stock controller to render an informed support service. A weekly schedule can now be determined: A category stock items may be cycle counted, high value items can be counted on a daily basis, and B and C stock keeping units (SKUs) may be relocated to distant bin locations.

Almost all LIS can integrate demand information, rough capacity plans, master plans, master production schedules, material requirement plans, and distribution requirement plans. In fact, an order management system cannot function properly without accurate and reliable information at appropriate points in the logistics system.

> **Test yourself**
>
> 15.1 Information is _____, processed, _____, and _____ data.

Functionality of logistics information

Functionality of logistics information can be classified into three categories: effectiveness, availability, and accuracy of information.

Effectiveness

Effective (or timely and relevant) information satisfies the needs of the recipient and the purpose for which the information is required. It is important to differentiate between the functional area of the information and the purpose of the information (or level of decision making for which the information is needed). If a marketing manager requires sales information, the functional area is marketing. The information may be needed for any aspect of marketing, from strategic scenario planning to order processing. For the strategic planning process, the manager needs sales trends, sales forecasts, economic growth scenarios, and so on. For order processing purposes, the information required may be the number of orders, the status of back orders, and possibly the current customer service levels.

Similarly, if a manager requires warehousing information, the functional area has been determined, but the purpose must be established. For strategic or capacity planning purposes, the manager needs to know the number and location of warehouses, whether they are owned or leased, and their size and capacity. For the operational level, the manager needs information such as inventory locations, forklift utilisation, picking sequences, throughput times, and vehicle turn-around times.

Availability

The appropriate information for each purpose needs to be distilled and this information must be provided in time. Screeds of data are of little use. Equally, late reports have little value for managing a process, as the situation may have altered.

Accuracy

Accuracy is arguably the biggest challenge. If a logistics information system – and especially data capturing – is not accurate, the information is worthless. Computerised systems assist greatly with faster processing of larger quantities of trans-actions, but they cannot enhance the accuracy of the data input. The old saying of 'garbage in equals garbage out' is still true.

Test yourself

15.2 Functionality of logistics information can be classified into three categories: _____, _____, and _____.

Applications of logistics information systems

LIS, like all management information systems, are used to manage processes. In a management process focused on objectives, LIS can be used to acquire data, measure actual results, and analyse the variances. The system can repeat this process as required. We briefly discuss each of the steps.

Acquiring data

The data necessary for the strategic to the opera-tional levels is gathered into the LIS. Data is acquired from sources external to the enterprise or from within the enterprise. The external data may originate from:

- political climate and international trade condi-tions;
- 'green' management policies and regulations;
- institutional information;
- social policies;
- economical conditions;
- technological developments and trends;
- threats of new entrants to the market;
- current rivalry amongst competitors;
- barriers to entering a market; and
- the availability of substitute products and services.

The most immediate need is for information about the capacity and the operational issues. One can obtain this information as work progresses and as equipment is utilised to record the activities of the enterprise. It can include such diverse data as the ordering of raw materials and the storage and delivery of finished goods.

Setting objectives

For this step, LIS is mainly used as a planning instrument. All objectives must be SMART. SMART is an acronym that stands for:

S – Simple
M – Measurable
A – Achievable
R – Realistic
T – Time based

Obtaining agreement

It is fundamentally important that people must be empowered to measure themselves. With the modern LIS, this is totally feasible. Information is available easily and quickly.

Measuring results

The LIS can measure performance and report where the measurements transgress the acceptable norms for the process. It can identify trends and determine cycles such as seasonal cycles. One can manipulate the data to illustrate a pattern, using smoothed curves.

Analysing the variances

The analysis of information gleaned from the data can identify deviations from set parameters. The deviations that exceed the measurement standards by a specific quantum can be presented. This helps to keep the focus on the important variances.

Logistics information technologies

The European Certification Board for Logistics (ECBL) developed the so-called 'PCIS' model, illustrated in Table 15.1.

- process
- control
- information
- software

Table 15.1 The PCIS model

Process

First record the processes for the entire logistics chain, including those of the suppliers and customers. This allows the business to analyse the logistics chain as a whole. Thereafter, record the logistics processes within the business, including the interfaces with the suppliers and the customers.

Control

Analyse the recorded processes to see whether they comply with the objectives of the overall logistics chain. Then make the detailed processes as efficient as possible by removing unnecessary stages. Highlight the points where control needs to be exercised.

Information

Two types of information are required for each stage of the process. The first is information for managing the phase, and the second is information that must be fed into other systems or phases.

This information must be identified for every stage and system, and it should preferably be acquired only once in the overall LIS. This requires management participation and control. The presence of operations and management personnel maximises the opportunity to make the processes more efficient, and ensures that only the relevant data is captured and the appropriate information is supplied. It is unreasonable to expect Information System (IS) or technologist personnel to understand the business processes as well as the operational and management personnel of the processes do.

Software

Businesses often acquire the software first and then try to re-engineer the business process to suit the software. This undesirable approach, where software drives the processes, is the predominant reason why many LIS fail in practice. The ideal is to first identify the processes, the control points, and the data input required for yielding the desired information output. In this way, the full functional specifications can be developed to accurately reflect the desired process and information requirements. The available software can then be compared to the required processes until a suitable match is found.

It is increasingly cheaper to implement software technology. The following technologies are currently available to the logistics practitioner:

- artificial intelligence systems;
- bar coding and scanning technology;
- satellite communication in vehicle management systems;
- radio frequency communication in warehouse management systems;
- business to business (B2B) e-commerce, including the Internet and electronic data interchange (EDI); and
- business to consumer (B2C) e-commerce via the Internet.

The logistics information hierarchy

There are four levels of the logistics information hierarchy illustrated in Figure 15.1. These levels are consistent with the four levels in the planning hierarchy. Figure 15.1 presents a summary of the hierarchy of decision making needed in the logistics information systems. It is not intended as a comprehensive listing of all the systems but rather as a guide for the major systems, focusing on the information systems. The logistics information hierarchy is a component of the logistics strategy and takes its direction from the logistics strategy – which in turn takes its direction from the enterprise strategy, as discussed in Chapter 3.

The various levels of the logistics systems are discussed here sequentially from the strategic to the operational levels.

Level 1: Strategic LIS

The business logistics strategy sets the objectives for the logistics systems. A range of choices are available for the systems: from manual to fully computerised, and from individual to integrated systems. The choice, which needs to be made at the strategic level, depends on the broad strategy of the business, and the cost-effectiveness of each option. Many businesses have a combination of manual and computerised systems in place. For computerised systems, one needs to choose the type of database and the operating system or platform on which the database will run.

A business may choose to acquire a combination of individual systems to perform its critical processes. To make these effective and efficient, data capturing may need to be minimised, and data and information may need to be transferred to the other systems to minimise manual intervention. Larger enterprises may be able to justify a centralised database, with one overarching system

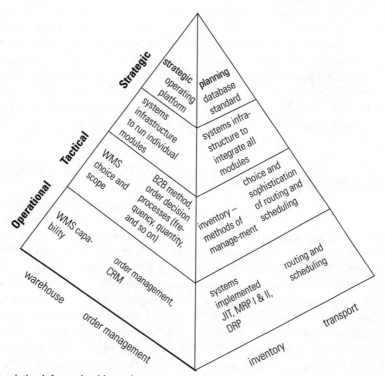

Figure 15.1 Logistics information hierarchy

taking care of the data transfer. The strategic principle for achieving these objectives should be chosen at this level.

Level 2: The capacity creation level

On the first level, the business decided on the database, the systems, and the principles for the transfer of data. On this level, it must specify for each of the systems the size and location of the database or databases, the method of networking, and the computing power required. The personnel and training needed for manual systems are also specified at this level. The business must decide how to backup the systems and data, and how to protect them from external threats.

Level 3: The functional level

The functional capability of the systems must be established on this level. The business acquires and installs the functional modules. Where data needs to be transferred between individual systems, the business provides the capability needed to perform this transfer. Physical equipment is acquired in accordance with the capacity plan in the previous level. The individual systems are made to perform, and are integrated, as decided on the strategic level.

Level 4: The implementation level

This is also known as the transactional level or the order processing level. On this level, logistics information facilitates the management of the detailed actions in the order management cycle. The data and information needed to manage the operation is produced by installed logistics systems such as warehouse management systems, material requirement planning systems, distribution requirement planning systems, and vehicle scheduling systems.

Test yourself

15.3 Name two of the issues pertaining to computerised systems that a business should address at the second (or capacity) level.

Logistics systems

The logistics processes are complex and interrelated. To highlight the systems underlying these processes, as well as the interrelationship between these systems, we follow the stages of an order from generation to completion. Figure 15.2 illustrates the overall process.

The availability and quality of information has a significant and direct effect on the efficiency of the customer order processing cycle. To satisfy the needs of customer, the communication and information flow must be fast and accurate.

We describe the systems here in summary. Techniques such as Just-in-time are described in detail in other chapters. We place the systems in Figure 15.2 under the common headings of inventory management, order management, warehouse management operations, warehouse management stock control, and transport management. These headings were chosen to highlight the various categories of the overall system. The categories may vary as different functional systems are used with different functionality.

Customer order management

The warehouse must understand and measure the size and frequency of orders from customers. Customers can utilise point of sale information to record the stock sold. The purchasing and inventory policy of the warehouse then determines how the sales are agglomerated into an order. The various categories of products are often treated in different ways. The warehouse may need to more often replenish goods that are sold frequently, or hold a larger stock. The supplier may set minimum order quantities, particularly if the order involves a production run and it is uneconomical to manufacture a smaller quantity.

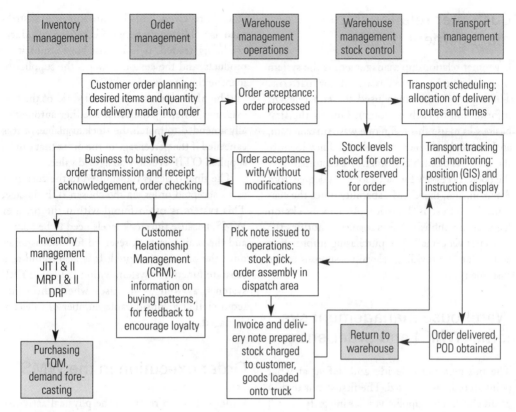

Figure 15.2 Logistics systems for processing an order

It is more economical for the supplier to deliver a number of orders at a time than to do repeated deliveries. Suppliers therefore prefer to combine various orders in order to reduce the cost of delivery. The result is that the customer needs to order a larger quantity, as there are longer periods between the stock replenishing deliveries. This increases the inventory carrying cost. Discounts for bulk purchasing may mitigate this additional cost. Increasing the order size and combining orders may also result in the order being too big to deliver in one trip. This affects the stockholding of the customer and reduces the value of the service offered by the supplier.

The supplier and the customer continuously need to collaborate to balance their needs.

Business to business (B2B) communication

Transmitting the order from the customer to the supplier is effectively a B2B communication. This can be done by telephone, fax, or via electronic data interchange (EDI) or the Internet. The last two choices are discussed in detail in Chapter 16. Electronic transfer is becoming more prevalent as it allows data to be transferred without the need to recapture data with the attendant problems of accuracy and time.

Inherent in the transfer of information to the receiving business is that the receiving business must perform a number of steps and checks to ensure that the process is complete and that the receiver's system has received valid information. The receipt of the order always needs to be confirmed with the customer.

Customer relationship management (CRM)

Customer relationship management is the system whereby purchases are analysed for patterns. These patterns are then used to send relevant information to each customer. One of the first businesses to use this technique was Amazon.com, an Internet bookseller in the USA. They identify the interests of each customer. If a customer buys the books necessary for, say, a logistics degree from Amazon.com, the CRM capability notes the customer's interest in logistics. As new books on logistics are published, Amazon.com notifies the customer via e-mail. The purchasing information adds value by providing relevant responses to the customer.

Warehouse management systems (WMS) and order entry

The business must decide and define at what point an order is accepted. The first step is to do a credit check. The supplier verifies integrity, as well as the accuracy of the data with respect to part numbers, prices, discounts, and availability of inventories.

The last step is to confirm with the customer that the order has been accepted and to state the conditions under which the order was accepted. Ideally, the supplier accepts and agrees to supply the order in full. However, the supplier and customer should have a service level agreement (SLA) in place that stipulates how deviations from the 'on-time-in-full' (OTIF) customer service level will be handled. The SLA may include an adjustment to the customer's order, binding the supplier only to supplying whatever it can in the agreed time scale. The advantage of this is that customers can update their purchasing system immediately and order substitute products from elsewhere. This is common in commodity industries, such as office stationery, where customers may have both preferred and alternative suppliers. Alternatively, the supplier can schedule backorders and supply the customer as soon as the

stock is received. This is common in industries such as publishing where differentiated products are being traded, it is impossible to substitute products, and the customer wants the supplier to manage the situation.

The SLA may also specify a hybrid of the two extremes, whereby the order is either automatically amended to match the stock available, or it is cancelled if the percentage of the order that can be supplied OTIF is below an agreed value.

The final order is transmitted to the customer as an accepted order via the chosen B2B linkage. This system is often found within the broader WMS, because the stock levels need to be known and the available stock reserved for the customer once the order is accepted. It is also found as a separate functional system within the larger ERP systems, as well as in cases where the order requires that a considerable number of rules are managed.

Order execution in the WMS

Order execution refers to the physical activities related to ordering. In this phase, the sales department recognises the order for sales commission calculations. Information is sent to the transport load scheduling system. The WMS generates picking notes, and the items are picked, packed, and assembled in the dispatch area, ready for the transport function to effect delivery.[2] Delivery notes and invoices are produced. The customer is charged for the goods as soon as the invoice is printed.

Transport routing and scheduling

The information pertaining to the value and mass of each consignment is known once an order is finally accepted. This information, together with the customer's details obtained from the WMS, allows the business to determine the best or optimal routing and the size of the vehicles required. The system then assists with consolidating the loads,[2] planning the size and number of vehicles, routing, and sequencing stops for each vehicle to optimise the transport efficiency.[3]

Transport tracking and monitoring

Geographical information systems (GIS) can monitor the position of vehicles. Information that can be fed back to a control point includes the speed of the vehicle, whether it is stationery, and whether the doors are open. One can also send information to the vehicle to alter a route or delivery schedule. Proof of delivery (POD) information can also be communicated from the vehicle – although the technology for the latter is more expensive.

Order delivery

The driver is often the only person who has direct, face-to-face contact with the customer. The driver is also responsible for returning the POD to the warehouse. The warehouse captures the completion of the delivery and keeps the POD in case of queries. The POD may be scanned and retained in electronic format for fast reference.

Purchasing and inventory management

A warehouse can only be effective if it has the required stock. This stock is provided via inventory management systems and the purchasing function. The inventory management system[4] determines when stock must be ordered and in what quantities. Purchasing or procurement management[5] chooses the supplier of the stock and determines the terms and conditions of the purchase. Various systems support these processes: examples are JIT[6], MRP I, MRP II, and DRP. These systems can function separately or be integrated with the inventory management and operating systems.

Conclusion

Information needs to be effective, available, and accurate to be of value to the logistics manager. The use of information to measure and control is fundamental to logistics. A functional specification can be produced through the methodology of determining the processes, introducing the control points, and defining the data and information requirements. The software systems available can be compared to this specification to identify the most suitable software package.

The hierarchy of the logistics information systems was presented in this chapter.

- On the strategic level, the business chooses between manual and computerised systems. This choice includes the type of database and operating system in computer based systems.
- On the capacity level, the business plans for the capacity to implement these systems and makes provision for system to system communication within the business and externally.
- On the third level, the business sets up the operation of these systems and establishes the systems as working capabilities.
- On the fourth and final level, the business establishes the input of data and the use of the information in the systems.

Numerous logistics process systems are required to ensure an order is correctly managed. These systems can be very complex and interrelated. The various systems in a logistics chain were shown and discussed in terms of a customer order management process. The relationship between the various systems was discussed. If a business utilises these systems appropriately, minimises data capturing, and uses the information to effect management of the logistics chain, the overall logistics chain will be more effective and efficient.

Questions

1 What is meant by 'open' management systems?

2 Describe how an effective logistics informa-

tion system can contribute to co-ordination between the logistics functions.

3 Differentiate between data and information.

4 Discuss in detail the information required to manage the customer order processing system.

5 What approach may be used to specify the type of computer software needed?

6 List the six steps in the customer order management cycle and discuss each step in detail.

Notes

1 See Chapter 10.
2 See Chapter 12.
3 See Chapter 12.
4 See Chapter 5.
5 See Chapter 6.
6 See Chapter 6.

16 E-business in logistics

Contents

Learning Outcomes

After studying this chapter, you should be able to:

- differentiate between the terms e-business and e-commerce;
- understand the concepts of EDI and ERP, and know what functions they perform;
- identify the benefits that can be gained from electronic information tools;
- classify B2B market places as either vertical or horizontal;
- discuss the role of e-business in recent trends in supply chain management;
- understand the developmental impact of e-business on business logistics;
- describe how e-business has changed the materials management and physical distribution sides of business logistics; and
- recognise the importance of the role of logistics in e-business.

Introduction

Electronic business (e-business) has changed the way information flows between members of a supply chain and it is increasingly improving the performance of the supply chain. At the same time, e-business has also posed many challenges and provided opportunities for the logistics manager. It is important to understand the challenges, opportunities, benefits, and disadvantages of e-business.

In this chapter, we focus on various issues that are important to businesses already involved in e-business or considering the introduction of e-business into their operations.[1] We discuss the new terminology of e-business and the technology that is used used when implementing the various aspects of e-business. Following a discussion of ways in which e-business has influenced various activities in the supply chain, we conclude the chapter with a discussion of the important role that logistics plays in the successful functioning of e-business.

Definition and scope of electronic business and electronic commerce

The perception among many people is that the concept of e-business and e-commerce only came about with the development of the World Wide Web (www) in late 1994. In reality, electronic business and electronic commerce (e-commerce) are not completely new in the business world. The roots of e-commerce extend back to the 1970s, when organisations started experimenting with electronic data interchange (EDI). This form of e-commerce was originally limited to non-financial transactions. In recent years, firms have increasingly undertaken to combine their financial and non-financial business transactions into fully electronic relationships with their business partners. Frequently, these include the use of electronic mail (e-mail) for unstructured communications,

EDI for structured transactions, and electronic funds transfer (EFT) for payments.

The growth of e-commerce has given rise to a variety of new terms. Figure 16.1 illustrates how some of these new concepts are related.[2]

Electronic business refers to the application of information and communication technologies (ICT) to conduct business. Numerous forms of business-related ICT-based interactions can occur between businesses, or between a business and a consumer. These do not necessarily directly concern buying and selling.

Only those forms of interaction that have to do with commerce (buying and selling) are part of electronic commerce (e-commerce). These include advertising of products or services, electronic shopping, and direct after-sales support. E-commerce does not include inter-organisational collaboration or the use of ICT-based collaboration systems to develop a new product.

The Association for Standards and Practices in Electronic Trade (UK) defines e-commerce as follows:

> Electronic commerce (e-commerce) covers any form of business or administrative transaction or information exchange that is executed using any information and communications technology (ICT).[3]

This is a very wide definition, which covers a variety of media, including the mobile phone and the personal computer (PC) with a modem to the Internet. The definition also includes various stages of a transaction – from its initiation, to the negotiation of a contract or the bidding for a tender, to the conclusion and execution of the terms of the transaction.

E-commerce is not restricted to the Internet. In fact, a great deal of B2B e-commerce is still conducted via private networks, using traditional electronic data interchange (EDI) channels and value-added network (VAN) service providers.

Within Internet commerce, the dominant medium is web commerce – a component of e-commerce conducted strictly via the World Wide Web.

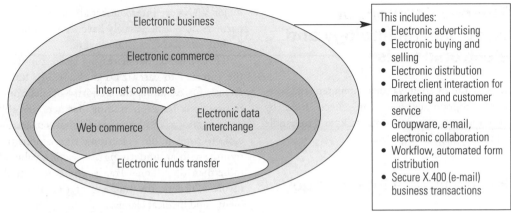

Figure 16.1 New terminology of electronic business

E-commerce embraces four main areas of activity:

- business-to-business (B2B);
- business-to-consumer (B2C);
- consumer-to-consumer (C2C); and
- government-to-nation (which includes both business and the citizen).

Users of e-commerce can make transactions in three capacities: as consumers, as manufacturers, or as citizens.[4]

As consumers

E-commerce can be used to purchase goods and services from local or international sources. Almost all of these transactions take place via the Internet, where sites offer anything from home banking, insurance purchasing, and home shopping to share dealing. This could be of great benefit in rural areas, where these goods and services would otherwise not be available. However, most B2C transactions currently require credit cards to make purchases. These are not always widely available in the poorer rural communities of many economies in transition.

As manufacturers

E-commerce can be used to increase the market for locally manufactured goods by making them available for foreign purchases by consumers (B2C), or by marketing them to potential foreign importers (B2B). The tourism industry can benefit greatly from this relatively cheap method of advertising their products and services to international travellers. Small businesses can use e-commerce to build networks of collaborative producers who can, amongst other things, tender jointly for larger contracts. E-commerce provides a level playing field on which small new entrants to a market can present 'shop fronts' that can compete with those of larger, established businesses.

As citizens

There is great potential for the use of electronic links to increase the two-way flow of information between citizens and various governmental institutions. For example, it is possible to submit an income tax return via the Internet, saving time and paperwork for both parties. In Germany, various municipal authorities already have interactive websites through which citizens can receive and submit official forms.

> **Test yourself**
>
> 16.1 E-commerce embraces four main areas of activity: _____, _____, _____, and _____.

The development of electronic technology and electronic tools

Besides the Internet, various computers and software programmes have long been used by businesses to perform specific tasks and to handle structured data in large databases.

Electronic data interchange

Electronic commerce started to take root in the 1970s with what was called electronic data interchange, or EDI. EDI was primarily driven by the recognition that firms in transactional economic relationships were wasting time and money by printing, transferring, and then having to re-key inter-business transaction data. To avoid this cumbersome process, a group of firms collaborated and agreed on common formats and structures for exchanging computer-based data.

The term EDI describes all computer-to-computer exchanges of structured data objects – irrespective of whether these are within a single firm or between firms – in a format that allows for automatic processing without manual intervention. These data objects are formatted into a commonly recognised standard, which is published and maintained by various standard bodies, such as:

- EDIFACT (Electronic Data Interchange for Administration, Commerce, and Transport), which is a United Nations effort; and
- ANSI (American National Standards Institute), used in North America.

Large companies created the earliest EDI applications. They designed their own private formats for data interchange since no standards existed at the time.

EDI messages have conventionally been transferred via value-added network providers (VANs). VANs serve as EDI buffers: A company sends its EDI transactions to its VAN, which forwards them to the intended trading partners. Most major VANs are interconnected, so that trading partners do not necessarily have to be connected to the same VAN for EDI to work.

There has been an increasing interest in using the Internet to carry EDI messages. In South Africa, for example, the majority of electronic transactions between trading partners are still exchanged via VAN providers. FirstNet carries close to three million electronic transactions per month, with an underlying transaction value of more than R5 billion.[5] Transaction types include invoices, orders, the tracking of freight movements, and medical claims.

Originally, EDI was limited to non-financial transactions, for example, order placements and acknowledgements. Payments were still made by printing and mailing paper cheques. Over time it became clear that if financial transactions were excluded from the EDI process, a business would only reap a portion of the potential benefit of EDI. The earliest examples of e-business were various EDI initiatives. These initiatives generally took place within vertical industries, for example, the retail industry and its associated product supply chains, as well as the transport and logistics industries.

EDI was one of the first forms of technology that enabled computer-to-computer communication. This development meant that the sales information from point-of-sales (POS) terminals could now be linked to the inventory management system, enabling the latter to keep up-to-the-minute track of the status of inventory. It also enabled companies to access the information systems of their partners in the supply chain. Standardised trade and transport documentation such as Bills of Lading, purchase orders, and invoices could now be generated.

The EDI system has, however, a number of shortcomings. As with most forms of specialised computer technology, this system is expensive to implement, thus barring smaller companies from using it. EDI data sets were also designed for structured information only, as contained in purchase orders, invoices, and receipts. Over the years, various EDI standards were developed by several industries in different parts of the world.

Therefore, even though partners in a supply chain may each have an EDI system in place, automated communication may still be impossible because of differing EDI standards and incompatible technology.

Enterprise resource planning

Enterprise resource planning (ERP) systems are operational IT systems that gather information from across all of the functional areas of a firm. ERP systems monitor materials, orders, schedules, and finished goods inventory. They also track orders through the entire logistics channel, from procurement to delivery. The ability to keep track of orders and have broad visibility in general has become more important as product supply chains and the logistics channels of individual firms become more global and complex.

ERP systems typically have many modules, each covering a seperate function within a firm. These modules are linked together so that users in each function can observe and monitor other functional areas. The following key modules of an ERP system can be installed individually or in combination with other modules of a firm:[6]

- *Finance module*
  This tracks financial information such as revenue and cost data through various areas.

- *Logistics module*
  This is often broken into several sub-modules covering separate logistics functions such as transport, inventory, and warehouse management.

- *Manufacturing module*
  This tracks the flow of goods through the manufacturing process, and co-ordinates the performance times of the required processes as well as the parts that are involved in the processes.

- *Order fulfilment module*
  This monitors the entire order fulfilment cycle, keeping track of the progress the company has made in meeting demand.

- *Human resources module*
  This handles all kinds of human resources tasks, for example, scheduling workers for the manufacturing process.

- *Supplier management module*
  This monitors supplier performance and tracks the delivery of suppliers' products.

ERP systems were specifically designed to integrate the processes within a firm into one networked computer system. All the information that was previously only accessible from individual servers and personal computers (PCs) were now put into one – sometimes global – system, where it could be accessed from various locations. ERP aimed to reduce the price of goods by making delivery or service provision more efficient.

Although ERP systems are powerful tools for optimising business processes within an organisation, there are a number of reasons why these systems have not been widely implemented in some countries:[7]

- The information displays on ERP workstations are not user-friendly. Information required for analysis at a decision-making level is often not available in an easily accessible form. This negates somewhat the value of having all the information in one database.

- A great deal of training is initially necessary for personnel to utilise these systems effectively.

- The hardware, software licensing, installation, and maintenance of an ERP system are all very expensive. For example, suppliers such as SAP and Baan quote the prices of their products in US Dollars. Some ERP packages were developed in South Africa to offer a local, often cheaper, solution to this problem.[8]

- ERP systems tend to be designed in a top-down fashion. This imposes set procedures, which means that the firm implementing the system has to alter its own procedures to match those of the system. This is generally expensive and requires substantial effort.

- ERP databases are designed to handle structured information, whereas it is often more important to make unstructured information and knowledge available.

- Although ERP brings together the internal transactional processes into a more useful format, no ERP system contains all the external systems available. The firm needs to integrate external systems in the new electronic business environment.

Despite these problems, ERP systems still play an important role in large firms. These firms, once they have realised the benefits of ERP applications, are usually more eager to move into the external phases of business optimisation through e-commerce.

Test yourself

16.2 ERP systems monitor materials, _____, _____, and _____. They also _____ through the entire logistics channel, from procurement to delivery.

The Internet

The rise of the Internet as a medium for conducting business transactions has changed the meaning of e-commerce. Today, the concept of e-commerce is often equated with 'doing business over the Internet'. The Internet itself is also not as new as many people think, since it has existed in one form or another since 1969 and has been used as a business medium for decades. Initially, the scale of business was very small and there were few participants. The creation of the World Wide Web, often referred to only as the Web, dramatically changed the face of Internet commerce.

There is sometimes confusion about the difference between the Internet and the Web. The distinction can be illustrated by comparing the Internet to a highway network – the information highway – as an infrastructure on which numerous services operate. The World Wide Web is a service (an 'information vehicle') that operates on the highway network.[9] Numerous other services also operate on the Internet, for example, e-mail and file transfer protocol (FTP). The service termed World Wide Web is, however, becoming so dominant that many people nowadays equate the Internet with the World Wide Web.

The Internet can be used to facilitate the co-ordination of work in various ways:

E-mail

This is by far the most common use of the Internet. The most powerful benefit of e-mail is that it makes instantaneous communication possible. Messages with attached information files can be copied to any number of collaborating partners. Answering machines and written or verbal messages are avoided, so that efficiency of communication is greatly improved. By copying messages to a group, all interested parties can be kept involved in the development of a project, enabling fewer managers to handle multiple reporting lines.

Work flow messaging systems

E-mail work flow systems can be programmed so that the work flow rules that govern paper forms can be used to govern the messaging system. Such systems are used for materials management, manufacturing, and distribution processes. The entire work flow, from the manufacturer to the production floor and back to the client, can be tracked with the e-mail messaging system.

Groupware

This is a virtual workshop for distant collaborators. It allows a team of individuals to work on ideas by sharing and exchanging information in common documents and databases. Groupware is an attempt to transfer and present unstructured information between members of a group. It can be a powerful tool for research and development teams, or for the scheduling of tasks.

Test yourself

16.3 _____ is by far the most common use of the Internet.

Benefits to be gained from electronic information tools

A range of possible benefits can be gained from the above-mentioned electronic information tools. These benefits include greater efficiency and effectiveness and the evolution of market places.[10] We discuss some of the major benefits here.

Information systems can help to eliminate errors and to reduce dependence on clerical efforts. A business should first analyse where most of the time and resources are consumed. Then it can examine whether these areas can benefit from automation with electronic information tools. Applying e-commerce to existing activities can reduce transaction-level costs, improve time-scales, and reduce errors.

Technology can help redesign the interface between business partners. Business flow models can be used to analyse the movement of goods, funds, and information through a supply chain. Sources of delay, redundancy, and unnecessary costs in the overall process can then be identified and improved through business process redesign. For example, self-billing and automatic replenishment can improve effectiveness.

New markets are evolving in e-commerce and existing markets are redefining themselves. Supply chains are being restructured, redefining the role of key players. In some cases, the retailer's role can be reduced to that of a 'shelf renter', allowing manufacturers to maintain ownership and control of their products right through to the point of consumption. (This is called Vendor Managed Inventory – VMI.)

Other benefits include financial savings, reduction in inventory, the elimination of inventory holding points, simplification of procedures, improved information from the point of sale, improved response, and improved market intelligence regarding the changing demands of consumers.

Business-to-business market places

Business-to-business market places (also referred to as B2B exchanges) are electronic market places on the Internet where suppliers and buyers interact to conduct business transactions. These market places provide an opportunity for huge value creation through the reduction in transaction costs, improved supply chain visibility, and the more efficient allocation of supply and demand. Three kinds of B2B market places are formed based on industries, products, or functions.[11] These are vertical, horizontal, and functional market places.

Vertical market places

A vertical B2B market place is based on an industry and revolves around a specific industry sector (see Figure 16.2). Such a market place comprises a wide range of industry-specific upstream and downstream segments.

For example, in the automotive industry, DaimlerChrysler, Ford, General Motors, Nissan, Renault, Commerce One, and Oracle are developing Covisint, an e-business exchange that will provide the industry with an Internet-based procurement tool.[12] The aim of this B2B market place is to reduce costs and to add efficiencies to the respective businesses. The vision for Covisint is to build an on-line environment that enables individual enterprises and the automotive industry to achieve, amongst other things, vehicle development cycles ranging between twelve and eighteen months, compressed order-to-delivery cycles, greater asset efficiency and utilisation, more integrated supply chain planning, and reduced business process variability.

Horizontal market places

A horizontal B2B market place is based on products and is formed around a supply market segment that cuts across several industries. A need in any service or product segment across industries is

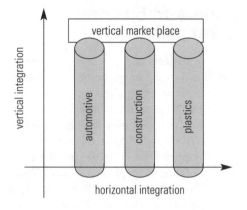

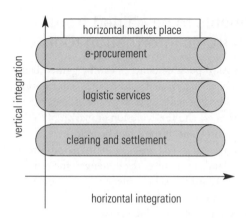

Figure 16.2 Vertical and horizontal market places

addressed through horizontal B2B solutions. These market places are usually set up to buy and sell products that are used on the plant floor or in the company offices, but do not become part of the final product. An example of such a market place is Econia, where anything from office furniture and printing paper to hardware, software, and analogue and digital peripheral devices can be bought at on-line auctions.[13]

Functional market places

Market places that focus on functions emerge when value can be gained from concentrating functional skills. The functional skills may include from maintenance firms to firms that supply truck tractors for moving trailers. Such market places create value in the form of less paperwork and easier ways for suppliers to find firms that procure or offer such services. TradeOut is an example of a market place which concentrates on the sale of excess inventory that could otherwise end up as dead stock.

Types of transactions

The B2B market places have fostered many types of transactions. The most basic are the spot purchases or sales of goods. These can be done

through a variety of transactional means such as auctions (one seller and multiple buyers), reverse auctions (one buyer and multiple sellers), fixed price transactions (one buyer and one seller), and bid/ask auctions (in which multiple buyers and sellers bid). These transactions are often conducive to for short-term relationships, but market places can also provide value for long-term relationships, where tight integration is beneficial.

> **Test yourself**
>
> 16.3 Three kinds of B2B market places are formed, based on _____, _____, or _____. These are _____, _____ and, _____ market places.

The influence of e-business on logistics activities

The role of e-business in recent trends in supply chain management

E-business has played an important role in many of the recent trends and developments in supply chain management:[14]

Customer service

The increasing importance of customer service as a way to gain a competitive advantage has meant that firms have to respond much faster to the needs of their customers. The speed and accuracy of e-business supports this trend. Customer service requirements are met via call centres, information feedback, and similar customer-related functions.

Efficient Consumer Response (ECR)

ECR is a strategy whereby distributors and suppliers work closely together to bring better value to the customer by jointly focusing on the efficiency of the total supply chain. This trend is found primarily in the grocery distribution market. E-business plays an important role in transferring and sharing information.

Customer relationship management (CRM)

Technology enables firms to learn more about their customers, helping them to build an effective database that allows them to respond to customer needs in the context of a long-term relationship. Through this electronic CRM, large enterprises are trying to recapture the quality of relationship with individual customers that often exists in small traditional businesses.

Supply chain partnerships

Partnerships that can be formed by members of a supply chain include joint ventures and relationships based on shared technologies, shared warehousing, or shared transport equipment. These partnerships are often critically dependent on information sharing, which is made easy through linking their information systems.

Core competencies

Manufacturers, and even retailers, are increasingly focusing on their core competencies. This means that transport, packaging, and other supply chain services are often outsourced to third-party providers. The outsourcing process can take place via a B2B market place.

Focused manufacturing

Many global manufacturers are using a strategy of focused production, whereby a given plant manufactures one or two items of the firm's total product line. These plants are typically located in different countries, but within a global logistics system that links the plant with the customer. Fast communication lines between the plant, customer, and third party logistics providers are important. E-business is an essential tool for managing this flow of information.

> **Test yourself**
>
> 16.4 ECR is a strategy whereby _____ and _____ work closely together to bring better value to the customer by jointly focusing on the efficiency of the total supply chain.

The developmental impact of e-business on business logistics

E-business is changing the face of business logistics, speeding up the way firms communicate with suppliers and customers. The following example illustrates how e-business is overhauling the way Nutcrackers Inc. (who sells cashew nuts) does business with its customers – in this example a retailer, Pick 'n Pay.[15]

Transport

Old way: When the cashews arrive at the port, a freight forwarder does the necessary paperwork to clear the shipment through customs and has the nuts delivered to the Nutcrackers plant. The truck sometimes travels only half full and has no freight on the return trip, making the trip costly for the manufacturer or its distributors.

New way: Shippers and freight carriers have up-to-date information via an on-line exchange. The collaborative logistics network connects multiple manufacturers, distributors, and carriers. The exchange serves to match orders and ensure full truckloads.

Ordering

Old way: Nutcrackers informs its Brazil office by fax or phone to place an order with local cashew growers. Employees deliver orders in person to the cashew growers. Farmers load the raw cashews onto trucks which carry them to the port. The shipping company notifies Nutcrackers when the cashews set sail.

New way: Nutcrackers contacts its Brazil office via e-mail, enabling them to contact the local farmers much faster.

Forecasting

Old way: Nutcrackers guesses the volume of cashews that Pick 'n Pay might sell in a quarter, without consulting them.

New way: Nutcrackers and Pick 'n Pay exchange sales forecasts via the Internet and agree on the volume to be supplied to Pick 'n Pay. Calculations are based largely on current sales data from the checkout counter, past sales patterns, and forthcoming promotions.

Third-party consolidation

Old way: Trucks carry the cashews to Nutcrackers's production plants. After the nuts are roasted and packed, trucks carry them to Nutcrackers's warehouses.

New way: After arriving at the production plants, the cashews are roasted and packed. Nutcrackers sends Pick 'n Pay's cashews to the warehouse of a consolidator which replaces the Nutcrackers distribution centre.

Regional demand

Old way: The nuts are in a warehouse and ready for shipment, but they may not be close to the store where Pick 'n Pay needs them because regional demand was not discussed. If Nutcrackers orders too many cashews, they become soft in its warehouses. If it does not order enough, Pick 'n Pay buys cashews elsewhere and Nutcrackers loses potential revenue and profit.

New way: Because Nutcrackers knows Pick 'n Pay's needs, there is no shortage or oversupply of cashews. From the consolidator, the nuts are transported to Pick 'n Pay along with products from other suppliers. Transport, unloading, warehousing, and inventory costs drop.

Electronic procurement

The materials management function of business logistics has benefited from the efficient procurement of goods and services effected through e-business (especially the Internet). Procurement is not just about the actual buying activity, but also about finding reliable suppliers who offer the optimal price.

The Internet supports the purchasing process through electronic catalogues, electronic auctions, electronic market places, and on-line Requests for Quotes (RFQs). Firms can also use the Internet to develop collaboration relationships.[16]

The benefits of electronic procurement (e-procurement) are not simply a result of 'turning on the software'. Some benefits emanate from the fact the entire procurement process becomes more effective, as Table 16.1 shows.[17] E-procurement reduces manual interfaces (and consequently the paper and time used), and automates and speeds up the process of finding suppliers.

Electronic procurement of materials for the manufacturing process is still in its development phase. Various large corporations have already formed joint ventures to create industry-specific business-to-business (B2B) market places where they can source both MRO (maintenance, repairs, and operating) supplies and raw materials by tying all their suppliers into one market place.

Currently, most of the opportunities for cost saving with the Internet exist in the area of MRO items. Desktop Purchasing (DP), which is a term for purchasing software applications, is used for the procurement of goods with low strategic importance and a high potential for automation. It is estimated that one can save up to fifteen per cent of the MRO procurement costs through e-procurement. Considering the fact that these

Benefit source	Purchased unit cost reduction	Process improvement	Intangibles
Software-related benefits	• increased use of price agreements	• reduction in transaction costs, procurement, and accounts • lead time reduction	• availability of procurement data • simplification of user interface • harmonisation of systems
Process change benefits	• strategic sourcing leverage • compliance enforcement • better demand management	• logistics/inventory cost reduction • simplification of the control system	• automated controls and audit trails • end-user efficiency • increased customer satisfaction

Table 16.1 Benefits of e-procurement

items can make up as much as forty per cent of the total operating expenses, even a small saving in procurement costs can have a significant impact on earnings.[18]

The example of P&O Nedlloyd

Perhaps the most enthusiastic e-procurement client in the shipping industry so far has been P&O Nedlloyd. This company bought two years' worth of paint supplies through an Internet auction at the end of 2000.[19] At the time, the paint contract was, in terms of value, the largest single shipping purchase ever made via the Internet. Some believe that P&O Nedlloyd saved fifteen per cent by buying this way.

The paint auction was structured so that many factors were resolved off-line first. Coverage rates, payment terms, and delivery ports were negotiated during an off-line process that lasted six weeks. Only then did the on-line auction take place. The winning bidder was awarded sixty per cent of P&O Nedlloyd's paint business, while two other suppliers shared the rest.

P&O Nedlloyd has also bought a number of chassis and is now starting to recruit crew and arrange corporate travel in the same way. It uses GetThere.com to handle travel bookings and has installed a booking platform in co-operation with KLM. P&O Nedlloyd saves by buying directly from the airline, which prints the tickets and makes them available for collection at the airports.

Transport and courier services

A number of key functions in the transport and courier industry are subject to change as a result of e-business developments. These include document management or tracking, express courier services, maritime container services, co-ordinated haulage, and international freight movement.

Document management

Both paper and electronic systems can be used to manage the flow of information and documentation in the transport and courier business. Traditionally, the details of each transaction are physically entered on multi-part forms. A waybill number is then assigned for reference purposes. A part of the form accompanies the parcel for receipt acknowledgement, and is then returned for filing or saved on microfilm. The information is often also captured electronically at the origin and updated once delivery has been confirmed.

This kind of system is functional, but not conducive to good customer service, as customer enquiries concerning the whereabouts of a parcel cannot be answered immediately. The efficiency of the process can be greatly improved by setting up an on-line tracking system that allows customers access by way of the Internet or EDI. Transport personnel would need to carry wireless devices linking them to the tracking system. At each handover point in the delivery process, a code attached to the package can be scanned to record the status and time. Customers are now able to dial into the system and check on the status of their shipments, which saves the courier company the effort of responding to customer queries.

Benefits of such a system include reduced transaction fees, fewer errors, and improved management information systems. The four main international courier operators, Federal Express (FedEx), DHL, TNT, and UPS are already reaping the benefits of on-line tracking. Smaller courier firms will, however, struggle to match this functionality, as initial set-up costs are substantial.

Express courier services

E-business is expected to have a dual impact on the express courier industry. On the one hand, the increasing use of e-mail and networked systems that connect firms has already reduced the movement of physical documents – although the need for original documents still exists. On the other hand, growth trends in global communications and a shift towards an information-based economy should benefit the courier business.

The B2C market of e-commerce should provide a great amount of business to express courier services. One of the key drivers of B2C growth is the convenience of having goods personally delivered to the customer's door. Electronic retailers need to offer a fast delivery service to compete with traditional retailers, and courier companies are ideally placed to provide this service on behalf of the retailer.

Courier firms have advantages over the in-house delivery function of retailers. These include a global distribution service, warehousing, economies of scale, or an industry focus that may offer additional value. They are, however, expensive compared to traditional parcel distribution and are not generally geared to handle larger parcels.

The industry is therefore negating some of the savings e-commerce allows in order to reduce the delivery time.

Maritime container services

The ocean transport industry is also increasingly using e-business. INTTRA is an independent Internet platform that provides interaction with ocean carriers, amongst others Hapag-Lloyd, MSC (Mediterranean Shipping Company), Safmarine Container Lines N.V., Maersk Sealand, and P&O Nedlloyd.[20] INTTRA's goal is to provide a simple and standard access point to a number of carriers. Their mission is to eliminate inefficiencies from the current interaction between ocean carriers and consignees so that it is easier for clients to do business with ocean carriers and service providers, and to develop common information exchange standards for the ocean carrier industry.

When fully functional, INTTRA will provide services such as track-and-trace, container booking, exception reporting, and the provision of Bill of Lading documentation. Clients and carriers will be able to communicate efficiently with each other. The motivation for using INTTRA is not only to save money, but also to save time and gain access to information about all INTTRA's partners through one Internet portal. (It is possible to obtain the same information by accessing each line's website, but this is a time-consuming process.)

We discuss below how various parties stand to benefit from the services offered by INTTRA.

Logistics service providers

The visibility and transparency of information along the supply chain and between partners will improve, allowing logistics service providers to serve clients more efficiently. INTTRA's various modules will save time by eliminating repetitive phone calls and messages to various clients and carriers. The reduction of administrative time spent on data entry and re-entry, as well as on paperwork, may reduce costs.

Clients

Various information services are offered to the clients at the click of a mouse. These include instant tracking of containers and bookings, shipping details of participating carriers, client-controlled information flow between internal and external parties, sailing schedules, container booking requests, Bill of Lading information, event notifications, and reports and statistics summaries. All partners – including shippers, consignees, suppliers, customs brokers, forwarders, and ocean carriers – will be able to share information with clients. The tracing function will reduce the number of phone calls and follow-up faxes to various shipping lines, in the process saving time and money.

Container shipping lines

INTTRA allows carriers to reach a wider market, thereby extending and enhancing their existing customer base. Carriers can also reduce their costs by allowing a larger portion of business to be conducted electronically. This helps to provide economies of scale and reduces the administrative time spent on data entry, data re-entry, and paperwork, while increasing accuracy.

Co-ordinated haulage

Profitability of road, rail, sea, and air freight carriers is usually associated with full loads. Carriers often have set schedules to which they have to adhere, making it difficult for them to obtain return loads and to maximise the utilisation of their carrying capacity. Traditionally, a company wishing to transport freight contracts a freight broker, who in turn contacts various carriers to find available space at the best price. These arrangements are made by way of phone, fax, or e-mail.

For a carrier to consistently obtain return loads, a network between shippers and freight carriers is needed. A real-time system where orders are booked allows for the optimum use of available space. INTTRA is an example of such a system, where the Internet is used to integrate certain transport market segments.

International freight movement

Business entities throughout the world are increasing their efforts to capitalise on globalisation trends, entering international markets for the first time and expanding their cross-border trade. These businesses face several challenges in their efforts, including foreign trade regulations and tariffs, locating products, international financing, and global communication.

Tradeworld was developed in an attempt to address many of the challenges facing sellers who want to enter the export market.[21] It is an on-line, interactive community where businesses can arrange all areas of global trade, including procurement, logistics, finance, insurance, and product certification.

Members of the Tradeworld portal are able to:

- buy or sell products through on-line facilities;
- send immediate requests for quotes;
- arrange for financing and payment;
- secure freight insurance;
- co-ordinate logistics;
- generate the international paperwork required to carry out a transaction;
- produce inter-business communication;
- determine trade requirements and rules; and
- view trade-related news and educational broadcasts over the Internet.

Both the initiated and newcomers to the world trade market can use Tradenet to increase revenues and take advantage of tools and resources that enhance operating efficiencies.

Test yourself

16.5 One of the key drivers of B2C growth is the convenience of having goods personally delivered to the _____.

16.6 Tradeworld was developed in an attempt to address many of the hurdles facing sellers who want to enter the _____ market.

The importance of logistics in e-business

The business-to-consumer (or B2C) stream of e-commerce has had a profound impact on the logistics industry, especially on third-party logistics service providers. Electronic retailers (often referred to as dot-coms) have started to realise that what happens after the customer clicks on the 'buy' button is just as critical as a user-friendly website and competitive prices.

For a website to be successful, it is absolutely essential to deliver the ordered product accurately and on time. Therefore, retailers have to know what is in stock at any given moment and how fast they can deliver the product. Even though many of the 'Old Economy' firms have well-established warehousing and shipping systems in place, they are also looking for ways to get their products delivered to customers faster and cheaper.

It is important to understand the complexity of logistics in the global and e-commerce economy. According to Forrester Research Inc., it takes on average twenty-seven parties to complete a single global shipment.[22] Many things can happen along the way to delay delivery. A customs broker may fail to submit the right documents or a truck can get a flat tyre on its way to collect a consignment. The customer – and often also the seller – does not know why the delivery is late.

A recent Forrester survey showed that seventy-six per cent of logistics managers at major firms could neither trace their products en route nor get updates. Such a data gap can delay deliveries and potentially cost retailers and manufacturers dearly in lost sales or wasted resources. This happened to a leading United States toy supply company during the 1999 Christmas season. They were fined $350 000 by the Federal Trade Commission because of a breakdown in their order and delivery systems. The website mistakenly informed customers that their products were on their way, while they were actually experiencing a stockout situation and could not deliver until after Christmas. This kind of delivery disaster has persuaded many electronic retailers to turn to outside experts to help deliver products to their customers.

Fulfilment firms such as SubmitOrder.com are often used by dot-coms who do not want to handle the warehousing, order picking, and shipment functions. When a customer clicks on a website to order a product, that order is sent directly to SubmitOrder (or another fulfilment company). Within an hour, they transmit the order to a picker, who pulls the product from a shelf and sends it to the truck of a delivery firm. Every hour, SubmitOrder's computers send an update to the dot-com firm, so that it knows what is available in the warehouse and can replenish stock or remove a product from the website whenever a stockout situation occurs.

Collaborative logistics uses the Web to link manufacturers, retailers, and transport operators, helping them to pass along the information they need in order to share transport capacity and warehouse space with others. Many traditional and dot-com companies choose collaborative logistics to achieve higher levels of customer service, while reducing their total logistics costs. The Web allows all parties in the supply chain to share information and co-ordinate their movements in an almost real-time fashion. This makes possible quick adjustments in the product and information flow.

Conclusion

No matter how large or how small a business is, e-business will in future have an impact on its logistics channel. In order to benefit from this, logistics managers should be aware of the aspects of e-business that are of importance to them. The 'older' tools of e-business, EDI and ERP, are widely implemented or at least understood, but there is still ignorance about the 'newer' tools of e-business, such as the Internet and B2B market places. E-business provides many new opportunities, especially in the provision of third-party logistics services to electronic retailers. E-business is enabling technology, which makes information access and dissemination more efficient and effective. Successful e-business stands or falls by efficient and effective logistics support – indeed a formidable challenge.

Questions

1 What is the difference between electronic business (e-business) and electronic commerce (e-commerce)?
2 Identify and describe the main areas of e-commerce activity.
3 What is meant by the term EDI? What are the shortcomings of this system?
4 What modules can be installed in an ERP system?
5 Why have ERP systems not been widely implemented in many economies in transition?
6 In what ways can the Internet be used to facilitate co-ordination within the supply chain?
7 Discuss the benefits that can be gained from the use of electronic information tools.
8 Identify an example of either a vertical or a horizontal B2B market place. Identify the services that this market place offers, the benefits that can be gained from using it, and the ways in which the use of this market place may impact on a supply chain.
9 Explain the role of e-business in recent trends in supply chain management.
10 How does e-procurement improve the procurement of goods and services?
11 How has document management and tracking through the Internet helped to improve customer service?
12 Explain the following statement: e-business has had both a positive and a negative effect on the express courier industry.
13 How does e-business help carriers to optimise the use of their carrying capacity?

Notes

1 Substantial parts of this chapter are directly based on work performed by Ulrike Kussing as part of a Masters programme in Logistics Management at the Department of Logistics at the University of Stellenbosch. The title of her research project is: 'Electronic Procurement: A management tool for the logistics manager in the supply chain'.
2 Huff, S.L., et al. 2000: 5.
3 E-centre UK. http://www.e-centre.org.uk
4 Stavrou, A., May, J. & Benjamin, P. 2000.
5 Van den Berg, M. 2000: 21.
6 Chopra, S. and Meindl, P. 2001: 343.
7 *The e-commerce handbook 2000,* pages 23–24.
8 The Compact software package developed by Datasoft.
9 Huff, S.L., et al. 2000: 3–4.
10 Bytheway, A. & Goussard, Y. 2000.
11 Ramsdell, G. 2000: 174–184.
12 Covisint. http://www.covisint.com
13 Econia. http://www.econia.com
14 Bytheway, A. & Goussard, Y. 2000: 9–10.
15 Adapted from: Keenan, F. 2000.
16 *The e-commerce handbook 2000,* page 41.
17 Hadamitzky, M.C. 2000.
18 Peck, B. 2000: 41.
19 *Fairplay*, March 1, 2001: 28–29.
20 INTTRA. http://www.inttra.com
21 Tradeworld http://www.tradeworld.net
22 Keenan, F. 2000.

Contents

Learning Objectives

After you have studied this chapter, you should be able to:

- discuss fixed and variable costs;
- discuss the fixed and variable storage costs;
- discuss the fixed and variable transport costs;
- discuss trunking costs;
- discuss distribution costs;
- discuss time costs and explain how they affect logistics activities;
- explain the importance of the break-even analysis; and
- discuss the cost of capital concept.

Introduction

There are certain costs involved in all logistics activities which affect the net profit of a business enterprise. (Net profit = total income − total costs.) The higher the costs, the lower the net profits. Management must therefore keep the costs as low as possible at all times while maintaining, or increasing, the total income.

In this chapter, we discuss the financial aspects of logistics. All the various costs are examined: storage costs, handling costs, transport costs, distribution costs, cost of time, the break-even analysis, and the cost of capital. In addition, break-even analysis and the cost of capital will be explored.

Storage costs

Storage costs, also known as warehousing costs, are the various costs associated with the storage of raw materials, production materials, components, semi-finished products, and finished products. The storage costs can be divided into fixed and variable costs. Fixed and variable costs have been defined in previous chapters and we only give a short summary here:

- When an increase or decrease in the production volume of a certain product has no influence on certain costs, these costs are fixed costs. The fixed cost per unit is reduced when the volume of goods manufactured increases and vice versa.
- When an increase in the production volume of a product results in an increase of certain costs, and a decrease in the production volume reduces the costs, these costs are regarded as variable costs.

It is important to remember that one must consider the influence of an increase or a decrease in production volume on the costs. Do not consider the influence of the costs on the production volume.

We now examine the fixed and variable storage costs.

Fixed storage costs

The fixed storage costs include:
- depreciation of the warehouse building and handling equipment;
- insurance;
- electricity for the lighting and air conditioning that stay on permanently;
- municipal rates and taxes;
- telephone rent;
- rental of storage space; and
- the salaries of the warehouse staff.

If the stock levels rise above the current production capacity, additional space and machinery must be acquired. This results in increased fixed costs. The total fixed costs also increase if the business enterprise decides to use machines instead of manual labour, as the depreciation on the fixed assets in use increases. It is important to know that higher fixed costs can create problems for a business when the demand for the final products decreases. It is very difficult to change an automatic warehouse into a labour intensive one in order to decrease the fixed costs.

Other factors may affect the total fixed costs negatively. Refrigeration equipment may be required. Employing a security firm or security guards also increases the total fixed costs. The business makes provision for the total fixed costs in the annual budget. Management must decide beforehand, on the basis of the capital budget, whether additional fixed assets must be used instead of labour.

Variable storage costs

The variable storage costs include repairs and maintenance, telephone calls, electricity used by the handling machinery, and casual wages. Management must take care that no excess stock is kept, as this leads to an increase in the variable costs.

Transport costs

The nature of the various transport costs is the same for a transport company and for the transport department of a business. Although businesses use a variety of transport vehicles, we choose trucks and delivery vans as examples in this chapter.

Like storage costs, transport costs can be divided into fixed and variable costs. In addition, we discuss trunking costs as a part of delivery costs.[1]

Fixed costs

Fixed transport costs include depreciation of the transport vehicles, licenses, insurance, drivers' salaries, and administration costs.

Each specific delivery vehicle can be regarded as a cost centre. The direct costs in such a case comprise the licences, insurance, depreciation, and the salary of the driver of that specific vehicle. The indirect costs are the administration costs and the other warehouse overheads related to that specific vehicle.

Variable costs

The variable costs are also known as the running costs. These are only incurred when the vehicle is in operation. Examples of variable costs are repairs and maintenance, tyre replacements, fuel, oil, and toll fees. The variable costs can be expressed as cost per litre or per kilometre.

Trunking costs

> If one large truck delivers a full load to a wholesaler, retailer, depot, or customer, the trunking costs are the total transport costs of this delivery.

If a manufacturer delivers a full load of shoes to a wholesaler with the manufacturer's own truck, it is easy to calculate the transport costs per pair of shoes: One simply divides the total transport costs by the total number of pairs of shoes. The transport costs include all the variable and fixed costs that can be apportioned to this delivery. These transport costs form part of the cost price of each pair of shoes to the wholesaler and must be added when calculating the selling price of every pair of shoes.

If the manufacturer of the shoes uses a transport contractor to deliver the shoes, the contractor issues an invoice for the transport costs. The amount on the invoice is used as the transport cost and is included in the cost price of the shoes to the wholesaler. The wholesaler then adds the invoiced amount when calculating the selling price of the shoes.

It is more difficult to calculate the trunking costs when a truck delivers the load of shoes to a number of wholesalers or other customers. The calculation must then be done on the basis of the volume of each consignment (where volume and not mass is the limiting factor in loading the truck).

Distribution costs

If one large consignment is transported from one enterprise to another, the trunking costs of this single load also comprise the total distribution costs to be included in the cost of the product. If further deliveries need to be made from a depot where a load was unloaded, these delivery costs must be added to the trunking costs to calculate the distribution costs.

Test yourself

17.7 Distribution costs are made up of _____ plus delivery costs.

Time costs

Time costs have two dimensions. These are the impact of inflation on the valuation of stocks and the competitive edge that saving time can provide.

The influence of inflation on the valuation of stock

Inflation means that demand surpasses supply, so that the prices for goods and services increase. This is why the prices of the goods ordered are higher every time a new batch is received. Inflation causes two kinds of problems for logistics: the valuation of raw materials and components issued to the factory, and the valuation of the closing stock at the end of the financial year.

Valuation of raw materials and components issued to the factory

The raw materials and components stored in the warehouses are received in separate consignments at separate times. Some of the raw materials move faster than others. This means that separate consignments are issued to the factory at different prices. Management has to value stock at the prices paid for the stock, as these values affect the production costs and the cost and selling prices of the finished products. The selling prices have a direct impact on the net profit

Management must decide whether to issue stock to the factory at the earlier prices, the latest prices, or at an average price. The most popular methods for valuing stock are LIFO, FIFO, and AVCO.[2]

Test yourself

17.8 Time costs have two dimensions. Name them.

LIFO (Last In First Out)

The latest raw materials and goods received are issued first. This method works well for non-perishable raw materials, as the business can hold old inventories in stock without risk. The stock is issued at the price of the most recent stock received.

Example of LIFO:

TV Experts Limited manufactures television sets for the local market. The company buys a certain electronic component in bulk and issues these components as the production of television sets proceeds. The company uses the LIFO system when issuing these components to the factory.

The transactions in Table 17.1 were recorded for a stock item.

The table shows how the stock is issued at the prices of the last stocks received.

Date received	Quantity	Price (cents)	Date issued	Quantity	Price (cents)
2001/03/07	60 000	75	2001/03/10	30 000	75
			2001/03/12	20 000	75
2001/03/15	40 000	80	2001/03/17	20 000	80
			2001/03/31	30 000	
				(20 000)	80
				(10 000)	75

Table 17.1 Example of LIFO

FIFO (First In First Out)

All perishable goods, such as fruit and vegetables, must be issued according to the FIFO method. Foodstuffs with expiry dates, such as canned foods and yoghurt, also fall into this category.

Example of FIFO:

BBS Meat Canneries Limited is a big company that cans a variety of meat products for the local and the foreign markets. The transactions on pork in Table 17.2 below were recorded. They issue stock at the prices of the first stock received. In this case, the company would have saved on production costs had it used the LIFO method.

AVCO (Average Cost)

Two types of average cost methods can be applied: the simple and the weighted methods.

Simple average cost method

The simple average cost method is very straightforward. One adds together all the prices of the various products received and then divides this sum by the total number of deliveries made.

Example of AVCO:

BEMCO Limited is a South African company that manufactures steel drilling machines for the mining industry. It has received a certain component – at the various prices stated below – for the drilling machines during the month of May 2001.

2001/05/04	R25,00
2001/05/06	R28,00
2001/05/10	R32,00
2001/05/12	R35,00

The part will be issued at R30,00 per unit. This price is calculated as follows: (R25,00 + R28,00 + R32,00 + R35,00) ÷ 4. This method does not take the volumes of items at different prices into consideration and cannot be recommended.

Weighted average cost method

The weighted average cost method is especially suitable for liquid products, such as petrol and diesel. It works the same as the average cost method but the volume of stock is also taken into account. For example, if five litres of fuel is purchased at R2,00 per litre, and twenty litres is purchased at R3,00 per litre, the weighted average cost of the fuel can be calculated as follows:

weighted average cost = [(volume 1 × price 1) + (volume 2 x price 2)] ÷ (volume 1 + volume 2)
= [(5 x 2,00) + (20 x 3,00)] ÷ 25
= (10 + 60) ÷ 25
= R2,80 per litre

Date received	Quantity in kilograms	Price (c/kg)	Date issued	Quantity in kilograms	Price (c/kg)
2001/06/08	2 000	557	2001/06/10	500	557
			2001/06/13	500	557
2001/06/15	3 000	520	2001/06/18	400	557
			2001/06/24	3 600	
				(600)	557
				(3 000)	520

Table 17.2 Example of FIFO

Valuation of closing stock at the end of the financial year

The accurate valuation of the closing stock at the end of the financial year is of critical importance. It affects the net profit in the income statement as well as the value of assets in the balance sheet of a business.

Example:

The following is an example of the effect of different values of closing stock on the net profit of a business enterprise.

Sales	1 000 000	1 000 000
Less: cost of sales	500 000	500 000
Opening stock	250 000	250 000
Plus: purchases	450 000	450 000
	700 000	700 000
Less: closing stock	200 000	300 000
Gross profit	500 000	600 000
Less: operating expenses	300 000	300 000
Net profit	R200 000	R300 000

The net profit varies while all the other income and expense items remain the same. The higher valuation of closing stock inflates the net profit. It also inflates the current assets in the balance sheet.

The South African Income Tax Act[3] provides the legal requirements for the valuation of closing stock. The Act states that all closing stock items must be valued at the lowest cost or selling price of each stock item. The LIFO method of valuing stock is prohibited.[4] The South African Revenue Services realises that a business enterprise will pay much less income tax should it value its closing stock at lower prices. It is important to take note of the fact that the closing stock figure of one year is the opening stock figure of the next. This means that the tax advantages of undervaluing stock in the first year will become disadvantages during the next.

Test yourself

17.12 An overvaluation of the stock figures at the end of a financial year _____ the net profit.

Competitive edge of time savings

During the last century, companies succeeded in increasing productivity in functions related to materials, labour, and capital. This led to enormous cost savings. Only recently have companies started realising that saving time increases profits substantially.

This realisation surfaced when product design and production improved. The motor vehicle manufacturing industry started to design motor vehicles with computer technology. This has reduced the new vehicle design lead time by more than fifty per cent.[5] A great deal of the resurgence of the motor vehicle industry of the USA was a result of reduced design times and more flexible manufacturing.[6] The introduction of 'Just-In-Time', materials requirements planning (MRP I), and manufacturing resource planning (MRP II) also led to reduced inventory levels.

Reducing the lead-time with the 'quick-response' technique in turn reduces the customer's inventory and storage costs and adds value to the entire supply chain. Carriers can reduce delivery times. Companies that order small quantities at a time may even decide to make use of airline companies to ensure quick deliveries. The result of this is smaller inventories on customers' premises.

The days of manufacturing final products for long-term warehousing are numbered. Companies are increasingly starting to manufacture according to demand. This is the so-called 'pull system', whereby the demand for a product determines its production volume. For this pull system to perform well, business enterprises are forced to reduce lead-times.

Break-even analysis

The break-even point is where the total income from the production and sales volume of a product exactly equals the total cost of that product. At this point no profit or loss is made, since the income exactly equals the costs.

The break-even analysis is an excellent technique for determining how fluctuations in the sales and production volumes affect the costs and net profit of a business enterprise. Management can use this technique to determine how many products should be manufactured, what the selling price of the products should be, and how much should be spent on fixed and variable costs respectively.

The challenge in many countries is to provide jobs for ever-increasing populations. However, for the countries to be competitive internationally, costs must be reduced and one of the most effective ways to do this is to cut the wage bill. By replacing expensive labour with more efficient machinery, businesses incur more fixed costs but reduce the overall costs of the business. Should the turnover rise, the net profit will increase faster than with low fixed cost structures. This is because the fixed costs (now higher due to the employment of more machinery) remain constant and, as the turnover increases, the fixed costs are proportionally reduced. The variable costs will rise at a slower rate due to the reduced wages. This may sound more favourable than the employment of expensive labour. The disadvantage of this is that the net profit will drop significantly when the turnover falls. It is difficult to sell some of the machines or close part of the factory when this happens. Labour is often more flexible. More overtime can be worked to meet higher demand and shorter or fewer shifts can be implemented should the demand for a certain product drop.

The break-even analysis in the supplement to this chapter shows how to determine the point in various cost structures where no profit is made.

> **Test yourself**
>
> 17.13 The employment of more machinery and equipment instead of labour _____ the fixed costs.

Cost of capital

The cost of capital reflects the average future cost of funds over a long period.[7] Management determines what the future need for capital will be in order to calculate the cost of the capital needed. They may decide to use external capital obtained from long-term loans, issuing of shares, creditors, or bank overdrafts. It may also use internal sources, such as the accumulated undistributed profit of the business.

The policy one should apply when making this decision is that the business enterprise can borrow money while the internal rate of return (IRR) remains higher than the cost of borrowing additional capital. The IRR is the return the business generates from its activities. If a business makes fourteen per cent on the current capital it invests internally and it costs twelve per cent to borrow money for a new project, it is better to borrow the money because the return on the capital internally is higher than the cost of the new loan.

Cost of keeping inventory

The cost of keeping inventory (inventory carrying costs) has been discussed in Chapter 6. To procure inventory, the business enterprise uses money that could be used for other investments.[8] Management must calculate what rate of return the business can realise from other investments it can make with this money. They then compare this with the rate of return on the investment in inventories. The option that yields the highest rate of return is the best. This cost is called the business's opportunity cost of capital.

Businesses are increasingly searching for new ways to reduce inventory holdings. Many new techniques, such as Just-in-Time and Materials Requirements Planning, are already available to keep the inventory levels low. The money thus saved can then be used to invest in other projects.

Certain businesses, such as agricultural co-operatives that cater for seasonal products, are forced to carry large amounts of inventory at certain times. Maize co-operatives buy all the maize harvested by farmers during harvest time and store it in their silos. The maize is sold out of the silos for the rest of the year. They need to make sufficient provision for the cost of buying the maize and for the cost of storing it for long periods.

Test yourself

17.14 Management's choice for investing capital is called the _____ cost of the business enterprise.

Cost of new projects

Should a business wish to open a new depot or start a new venture, it needs to calculate the cost of this operation. It also needs to calculate the discounted cash flow over the next few years to determine if the income generated out of the new project will be more than the running costs, and that an adequate return is generated on the capital invested in the business. Once the business has made the decision to make the investment, it can decide where to get the capital

A business may decide to borrow money from a bank, issue debentures, or issue shares. Issuing of shares may seem to be the best option, but it will take some of the control of the company out of the hands of the present shareholders. If the business decides to borrow money, the control remains in the hands of the present shareholders once the loans are repaid.

Conclusion

In this chapter, we identified the costs related to the various logistics activities. We discussed storage costs, handling costs, transport costs, distribution costs, the cost of time, and the cost of capital. The break-even analysis was discussed briefly and receives more attention in the supplement to this chapter.

Questions

1 Define fixed costs in your own words.
2 Define variable costs in your own words.
3 Discuss fixed transport costs and distinguish between the direct and indirect transport costs.
4 Discuss the variable transport costs.
5 Define trunking costs using your own words.
6 Explain how trunking costs influence the distribution costs of a product.
7 Discuss two ways in which inflation affects the valuation of stocks.
8 Discuss the LIFO and FIFO methods of calculating the issuing prices of raw materials and other products.
9 Discuss the two AVCO methods of calculating the issuing prices of raw materials and other products.
10 Explain the effect of an overvaluation of the closing stock on the net profit and the balance sheet values of the assets of the business.
11 Explain how the break-even analysis can assist a business enterprise in the calculation of the future selling price of its products.
12 Discuss the two dimensions of capital in logistics management.

Notes

1 Fawcett, P. McLeish, R.E. and Ogden, I.D. 1992b: 243–245.
2 Fawcett, P. et al. 1992b: 235–236.
3 South African Income Tax Act No. 58 of 1962 (as amended), Section 22.
4 South African Income Tax Act No. 58 of 1962 (as amended), Section 22(5).
5 Bentley, J. 1995: 100–103.
6 Coyle, J.J., Bardi, E.J. and Langley C.J. (Jr) 1996: 19.
7 Gitman, L.J. 2000: 451–459.
8 Lambert, D.M., Stock, J.R. and Ellram, L.M. 1998: 153–154.

Supplement: Break-even analysis

There are two methods for determining the break-even point: the numerical and the graphic method.

The numerical method

The break-even point is calculated by means of the numerical method using the following formulae:

$$BEP(U) = \frac{TFC}{SPU - VCU}$$

$$BEP(C) = \frac{TFC}{1 - \dfrac{TVC}{S}}$$

Abbreviations:

U = Units
TFC = Total Fixed Costs
SPU = Selling Price per Unit
VCU = Variable Costs per Unit
S = Total Sales
TVC = Total Variable Costs

BEP(C) = Break-even point (Currency)
BEP(U) = Break-even point (Units)

The graphic method

The break-even point is calculated by means of the graphic method as shown in Figure B17.1.

Note: The costs and volumes may vary. This figure is only an example.

Assumptions in calculating the break-even point

The following assumptions are made when determining the break-even point:

+ The total costs can be divided into fixed and variable costs. The total fixed costs remain constant when the production volumes fluctuate, while the total variable costs respond to a fluctuation in production volumes.
+ The difference in inventory levels at the beginning and at the end of each period (year, quarter, or month) is not taken into account as the break-even analysis compares the total costs with the total income for the quantity of products manufactured.

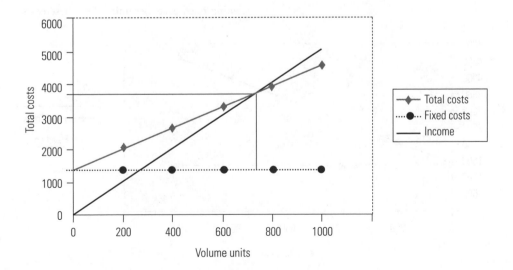

Figure B17.1 Determining the break-even point by means of the graphic method

- The efficiency and productivity of the business enterprise must remain constant. A fluctuation in efficiency and productivity levels for separate quantities will distort the break-even figures.
- The cost and revenue behaviour can be determined accurately and is related to the production capacity levels. Should a motor vehicle manufacturing company have a set production capacity of between 30 000 and 50 000 units per year, the total fixed costs will remain constant within those capacity levels and the total revenue and variable costs will fluctuate in proportion to the production volumes.
- The sales mix must remain constant. The sales mix is the combination of products which forms the total sales of the business. If a restaurant sells mixed grills consisting of portions of eggs, fillet steak, sausages, and bacon, the portion size of each type of food must remain the same. If one of the sausages is replaced with an additional portion of steak, which is generally more expensive than sausage, the break-even point will rise because of an increase in the variable cost per mixed grill.

Concepts of break-even analysis

We briefly discuss the concepts relevant to the break-even analysis.

Fixed costs

These costs remain constant within a certain period and within certain predetermined capacity parameters.

Variable costs

These costs increase or decrease in proportion to an increase or decrease in production volumes.

Total costs

These are the sum of the total fixed costs and the total variable costs. The graph in Figure B17.2 below shows that the variable costs amount to the difference between the total costs line and the fixed costs line.

The total cost per unit is calculated by dividing the total costs by the number of units manufactured. As production increases, the total costs per unit decrease to a certain level, due to the diminishing fixed costs per unit. Then these costs start

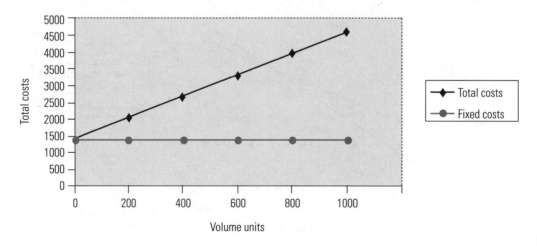

Figure B17.2 The trend of the total costs

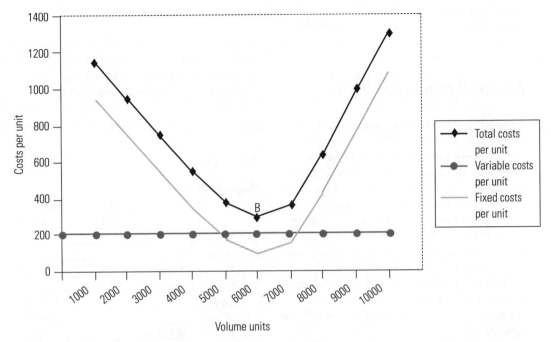

Figure B17.3 The trend of the total costs per unit

increasing again because an increase in the production capacity is required (see Figure B17.3).

The point where the total cost per unit (point B on the graph) is at its lowest is called the optimum point of production. This is the point where every business enterprise should endeavour to pitch its production volume.

Total income

The total income is calculated by multiplying the total number of units sold with the selling price per unit. It is important to note that all income from rent, interest, and dividends received must be excluded from the total income when determining the break-even point. The income per unit is then the total income divided by the total number of units sold.

Net profit

The net profit is the difference between total income and total costs.

Marginal income

Table B17.1 shows how to calculate the marginal income. It illustrates that the marginal income is the difference between income and variable costs. The marginal income covers the fixed costs and the surplus represents the net profit.

	Total	Per unit
Projected number of units manufactured	100 000	
Income (price x quantity)	100 000	1,00
Minus variable costs	70 000	0,70
Marginal income	30 000	0,30
Minus fixed costs	15 000	0,15
Net profit	15 000	0,15

Table B17.1

Marginal income ratio

The marginal income ratio is the marginal income divided by the total income. In Table B17.1, the marginal income is 0,30 (30 000 ÷ 100 000). The marginal income ratio will also be 0,30 (0,30 ÷ 1,00).

Practical example

Superbeer Limited manufactures beer for the local as well as the foreign markets. The company is very profitable and has embarked on a substantial expansion programme. At its annual general meeting last month, the directors were instructed to investigate the possibility of opening a new brewery in a distant harbour city. This brewery will produce a special lager beer exclusively for the export markets. The beer can be exported by ship, directly from the city's harbour.

The annual budget for the 20xx financial year is presented in Table B17.2. The year 20xx will be the first year of operation for the planned new brewery.

Selling price per 375 ml unit	5,00
Projected turnover for the year (375 ml units)	1 000 000
Advertising costs	500 000
Bank charges	5 000
Commission – sales people	750 000
Depreciation – fixed assets	75 000
Direct labour	1 200 000
Direct materials	1 000 000
Electricity and water (units)	45 000
Insurance	15 000
Rail transport	75 000
Rent – buildings	125 000
Rates and taxes	12 000
Salaries – supervisors	650 000
Telephone rental	35 000
Telephone calls	R85 000
TOTAL COSTS	4 572 000

Table B17.2 Budget for the financial year ending February 28, 20xx.

Requirements

1 Sort the costs into two columns representing fixed and variable costs respectively.
2 Determine the break-even point for units and for currency using the graphic method.
3 Calculate the break-even point for units and for currency using the numerical method.

Solution

Requirement 1

	Fixed costs	Variable costs
Advertising costs	500 000	
Bank charges		5 000
Commission – sales people		750 000
Depreciation – fixed assets	75 000	
Direct labour		1 200 000
Direct materials		1 000 000
Electricity and water (units)		45 000
Insurance	15 000	
Rail transport		75 000
Rent – buildings	125 000	
Rates and taxes	12 000	
Salaries – supervisors		650 000
Telephone rental	35 000	
Telephone calls		85 000
	1 412 000	3 160 000

Table B17.3 Sorting the costs into fixed and variable costs

Requirement 2

Figure B17.1 shows how to determine the break-even point by means of the graphic method.

Requirement 3

We have seen on page 279 that the break-even point is calculated by means of the numerical method using the following formulae:

$$BEP(U) = \frac{TFC}{SPU - VCU}$$

$$BEP(C) = \frac{TFC}{1 - \frac{TVC}{S}}$$

Abbreviations:

U	= Units
TFC	= Total Fixed Costs
SPU	= Selling Price per Unit
VCU	= Variable Costs per Unit
S	= Total Sales
TVC	= Total Variable Costs
BEP(C)	= Break-even point (Currency)
BEP(U)	= Break-even point (Units)

Determine the break-even point following these steps:
- Calculate the marginal income and the marginal income ratio.

Marginal income = Total Sales (S) – Total Variable Costs (TVC)
= 5 000 000 – 3 160 000
= 1 840 000

Marginal income (U) = marginal income ÷ total units
= 1 840 000 ÷ 1 000 000
= 1,84

Marginal income ratio = marginal income (U) ÷ selling price (U)
= 1,84 ÷ 5,00
= 0,368

- Calculate the break-even point

$$BEP(U) = \frac{TFC}{SPU - VCU}$$

= 1 412 000 ÷ [5,00 – (3 160 000 ÷ 1 000 000)]
= 1 412 000 ÷ (5,00 – 3,16)
= 1 412 000 ÷ 1,84
= 767 391 units

$$BEP(C) = \frac{TFC}{1 - \frac{TVC}{S}}$$

= 1 412 000 ÷ 1 – [(3 160 000 ÷ 5 000 000)]
= 1 412 000 ÷ (1 – 0,632)
= 1 412 000 ÷ 0,368
= R3 836 955

Test the answer by multiplying the break-even point in units with the selling price per unit. The answer must be the same as the break-even point in currency.

BEP(C) = 767 391 × 5,00
= 3 836 955

Problems

Steelammo Limited

Steelammo Limited manufactures steel point bullets. The company is currently investigating the possibility of opening a new factory. This factory will make a special kind of bullet that is going to be exported to several countries.

The following budget for the first year is presented to the directors:

Projected sales (bullets)	1 000 000
Projected selling price per bullet	0,90
Advertising	24 000
Depreciation – machinery	20 000
Direct labour	230 000
Direct materials	76 000
Rail transport	6 000
Rent – factory	84 000
Salaries – administrative	180 000
Salaries – supervisors	89 600
Telephone rental	2 400
Telephone calls	10 000
Wages – casual	16 000
Water and electricity (units)	12 000
TOTAL COSTS	R750 000

Requirements

1 Sort the costs into two columns representing fixed and variable costs respectively.
2 Calculate the break-even point in units and in currency using the numerical method.
3 What would the effect on the break-even point be if the turnover was increased by 50 000 per year due to an increase in sales?

TV Screens Limited

TV Screens Limited manufactures television

screens. The company is rapidly expanding as the demand for television screens is increasing by the day. The present factory is becoming too small and the directors are envisaging the extension of the current factory.

The following budget for the first year of the planned extended factory is submitted to you:

Budgeted turnover (tubes)	100 000
Selling price per tube	250
Advertising	80 000
Consumables	38 000
Depreciation – machinery	48 000
Direct labour	1 020 000
Direct materials	950 000
Insurance	30 000
Research	52 000
Salaries – directors	750 000
Salary – factory supervisors	40 000
Shipping	166 000
Telephone calls	18 000
Water and electricity (units)	58 000
TOTAL COSTS	3 250 000

Requirements

1 Sort the costs into fixed and variable costs respectively.
2 Calculate the break-even point in units and in currency using the numerical method.
3 What will the effect on the break-even point be if production and sales increase by 30 000 television screens per year?

Notes

1 Adendorff, S.A. and de Wit, P.W.C. 1997: 111–115.
2 Marx, S., Radermeyer, W.F. and Reynders, H.J.J. 1993: 168.

Contents

Learning Objectives

After you have studied this chapter, you should be able to:

- understand how each aspect of logistics might develop in the next few years;
- have an idea of the impact that advances in logistics might have on business; and
- have an understanding of the potential for logistics in the next few years.

Introduction

There are tremendous changes in the logistics arena around the world. These changes are taking place rapidly. The advances in some aspects outstrip those in other aspects of logistics. The integrated nature of logistics prescribes that advances in one area necessitate changes in the way logistics is performed. The nature of logistics always constitutes a combination of physical goods and information. These two issues are inseparable and any shift in or change to logistics needs to recognise this. Firms often see changes in specific areas of logistics or technology and believe that these will result in quantum changes that will revolutionise logistics. This is unfortunately not generally true. If a portion of the chain undergoes a quantum improvement, the total chain will improve, but not by the same measure or anywhere near the quantum of improvement achieved within that specific component of the logistics chain.

In this chapter, we discuss the current changes that affect the logistics industry and the potential impact of these on the industry for the next few years. These are merely pointers to what may happen, as there is only one issue of which we can be certain: change will happen and at a fast pace.

Computers and computing power

The past twenty years have seen a tremendous increase in the availability of computers and in the abilities of these computers. As a rule of thumb, computing capacity doubles approximately every eighteen months. Where the computer was once a luxury, it is now a ubiquitous commodity in businesses.

Most businesses have not, however, achieved the paper-free operations predicted in the early nineties. Many businesses have systems that are not integrated. Only the larger ones have managed to purchase and utilise larger integrated systems. These systems often provide integration within the firm while little integration occurs between the firm and its customers and suppliers. These interfaces remain to a large extent outside the integration process for many businesses. This, in part, has led to the large-scale belief that the Internet will be the means to achieve integration in future.

The computing power allows small and large businesses to run sophisticated models. These are no longer approximation models, but are in many cases mathematically based models that offer solutions to complex problems. The value of these models in each of the areas of logistics is increasing. The impact of the models and techniques is limited by the data accuracy and the acquisition of the data.

The accuracy of data remains suspect in the logistics field. Most businesses still track all the financial costs in accordance with the generally accepted accounting practice. This often results in delays and costs that have to be manipulated to represent value for logistics decision making and monitoring. The acquisition of data for logistics is often associated with a manual process, delaying the availability of the information. It is rare for all the data necessary for the logistics management to be available in what is called 'real time' and for such data to reflect the processes correctly without exceptions.

Where the processes fluctuate significantly due to external circumstances, the data is no longer representative of the standard processes. Decisions made without recognition of the fluctuations in the day-to-day activities may lead to inaccurate conclusions. This is simple to illustrate. At a certain warehouse, grocery distribution is different for each day of the week. Large orders are received on Monday after the weekend sales, so the Tuesday deliveries are larger than average. The Friday deliveries – and in some cases the Saturday deliveries – are also larger, as these deliveries must last for the weekend. The size of the deliveries also varies according to seasons and geographical area. During the holiday season, orders are bigger than the average during the rest of the year. This peak is even higher at stores in coastal holiday resorts.

All these changes need to be understood and they need to be incorporated into the model before its mathematical accuracy can be used to the full. This takes time and effort, and implies that changes in the business must be continuously added to the model for it to remain precise.

Computers have without doubt made the processing of information simple and fast. Models that assist with decision making have become more sophisticated and will become more common. The limited time for acquiring data and the resulting inaccuracies may restrict the effectiveness of these models. The interpretation of the information produced by the models will require new skills.

Strategy and planning

Changes in logistics strategy will probably be slow. The Internet will force some changes, but two factors will prove why these changes will not be as radical as was previously believed.

Firstly, logistics is not just about information. It is about offering a product at the right time and place together with accurate information. If any portion of the logistics chain alters by a quantum leap, the constraints are shifted from this area to other areas of the chain. The product still needs to be delivered, stored, and supplied to the distribution centre. These aspects now become the constraints within the chain and will severely restrict the impact that large improvements such as immediate information transfer will have on the total chain.

The second factor is the actual strategy of the business. For a business to successfully use the Internet to its advantage, it needs a strategy that creates a long-term competitive advantage – either by providing unique value for the customer, or by having a product or way of delivering the product that is unique or difficult to copy.[1] The Internet is available to all businesses and is enabling technology. It is not generally a competitive advantage of long duration.

One area where the Internet has shown to be the facilitator of major change that adds value to the logistics chain is the trading exchanges (TX). These 'shop on-line' exchanges, and the ability to manage purchases and procurement without the retail store, allow for radical disaggregation where steps of the traditional supply chain are removed from the process. It is most likely that the greatest strategic value of the Internet will lie in this area in the near future. It allows intermediaries to be eliminated and opens up business opportunities on-line for anyone who has the capabilities to utilise the technology.

Procurement and inventory

In the light of the above discussion, it is appropriate to explore the future of procurement and inventory operations. Trading exchanges are blossoming around the world. They are also folding rapidly in the search for the best format and model. Independent trading exchanges (ITX) were the first to be created and these are rapidly being supplanted by consortium trading exchanges (CTX). These are industries or sectors of an industry that create and manage the exchange. They are characterised by new exchanges. For example, the three largest motor manufacturers in the USA created their own e-market place called Covisint.[2] This (and others like it) very soon made the ITX concept unnecessary, forcing ITX companies to change their business model rapidly. Physical distribution is experiencing a similar dilemma. Large retailers or manufacturers can dominate and hence dictate the terms and methods of distribution for suppliers, who must adapt their systems and delivery processes to match those of the purchaser. To do business in future, suppliers now not only have to be able to deliver the goods; they also have to utilise the CTX of various industry sectors where their products are sold.

Inventory management always involves the difficult act of balancing the financial cost of carrying the inventory with the opportunity cost of not having goods available. New inventory management models will in future assist in managing both suppliers and inventory. These will yield significant financial benefits, provided that the process is a collaborative effort with clear responsibility and conformance criteria. Early delivery is as bad as late delivery. Suppliers who can deliver consistent performance and fulfil orders will be preferred to others. Very few suppliers have realised this, and there is potential for businesses to achieve a competitive advantage.

Some stores have adopted a different strategy whereby the supplier is required to manage the inventory on the display shelves. This is called Vendor Managed Inventory (VMI). A result of this strategy is that sales are highly dependent on the attractiveness of the display and the availability of the goods. However, as more shelf space is given to VMI, the necessity of supplier staff in the aisles and continuous replenishment may inconvenience customers.

Packaging

Packaging is perhaps one of the more mundane areas of the logistics capability. It is an area where change will be driven by external factors. As environmental issues become increasingly prominent, returnable containers and boxes become more attractive when compared to the traditional disposable packaging. The cost of certain such applications already shows that they have cost advantages over traditional packaging. Motor manufacturers use collapsible containers. These containers can be densely stacked into the standard sea container. The collapsible containers are reused and returned in the collapsed configuration, so that a large number of containers occupy a small space. Similar applications for boxes or crates – particularly those made from durable plastic – will increase in extent and cost-effectiveness. These are particularly useful where goods are supplied to regular customers, when the control and return of these crates or boxes is simplified.

Warehouses and facilities

Warehouses will change only moderately in the next few years. Firms increasingly approach warehouses in a professional manner and with the aim of ensuring the best possible logistics capability. The location and size of the facilities will be improved from ad hoc to custom-built facilities. The geography and delivery time-scale will be considered. For example, a company will first build a facility in the most densely populated area to service the majority of the purchasers. If the delivery time scale is reasonably restrictive or demanding, facilities may be built in other areas. It may be feasible to utilise cross-dock facilities in these smaller areas, as purchasing power in the region may require goods to be moved to customers,[3] but may not warrant holding stock in the region.

The warehouses in the major centres will require more utilisation of vertical space as land in the areas adjacent to the main roads becomes scarcer. This will increase the use of high racking and narrow aisle equipment in the warehouses.

Warehouse systems that integrate the order process and the warehouse operation will become commonplace. The purchasing function and the transport function will remain separate entities, with the exception of the few businesses that regard these as true logistics capabilities and try to purchase systems that integrate these in a seamless fashion.

All in all, the location and design of the warehouse will alter moderately and for the better. The one area that will need improvement is the choice of operating staff. Management will continue to be increasingly demanding and fast paced. Training of staff will become even more important as new systems allow for faster operation, allowing less time to uncover and rectify errors. A new breed of professional warehouse personnel has to emerge. They will understand continuous measurement and high quality operation. Without the quality staff, the improvements in technology, equipment, and warehouse design will not be used to its full potential.

Transport
Long-haul transport

The transport function will remain highly affected by political issues. A common argument is that long-distance transport should be dominated by rail transport, as this is the cheaper transport method. Before this can happen, the effectiveness of rail transport operators needs to be improved to offer more flexible services to and from the rail terminals. The argument has raged for many years now. Added to the issue of privatising rail transport, is the issue of whether or not rail is to be given the impetus to be the primary long-distance transport method. Rail transport will need to align itself internationally in order to conform to the logistics requirements of industry and business.

If no impetus is given, the current practice of long-distance transport will continue without major changes. The cost of transport in economies in transition will rise at a faster rate than inflation, as the majority of road transport vehicles need to be imported to these countries, and weakening exchange rates will make these units increasingly expensive.

If road transport remains the premier means of freight movement, the cost of the capital investment will encourage the recent trend of transport being owned by a limited number of firms, and there will be a shift towards oligopolies. The same will happen with the general parcel service. This service is difficult to sustain without significant volumes of parcels. As more businesses begin to amalgamate the line-haul and distribution functions to increase volumes of parcels, the parcel service operation will also tend to an oligopoly. These services also have to start offering track and trace capabilities on the web, which will require a fundamental change in the way they perform their business. Currently, the parcels in a consignment are transported together with the paperwork. The parcels need to be sorted into the consignment at every depot, and the paperwork needs to be matched to the consignment before it can be dispatched. This is not efficient. These businesses need to find a way of transporting multiple packages in a consignment without paperwork. Although this will require investment in systems, it will improve efficiency and margins, ensuring that the business is effective in the long run.

Many courier firms already provide this service, but it is orientated towards single-parcel rather than multiple-parcel consignments.

Short-haul road transport

Short-haul road transport will continue to be an important part of the distribution of products. Transporters will become increasingly specialised as customer demands become more onerous. Transport operations will probably be characterised by regional excellence, where local operators own trucks and can offer a superior service within a region. The service will include longer utilisation of the trucks, better routing, and drivers who are more sensitive to customer service. The professional carrier is becoming the external representative of the firm. Outsourcing will probably not make further inroads into the current mix between ancillary transport and third-party carriers.

Technological advance will improve inner city transport. As deliveries to smaller retail outlets, shops and homes are increasing, digital maps and systems that guide drivers from one location to another will become invaluable. These systems calculate the shortest time or the shortest distance and guide the driver to the location. In Europe, Japan, and parts of the USA, the more advanced systems (so-called intelligent transport systems) include traffic updates and offer alternative routes based on the traffic situation.

International and local

The growth of economies in transition is inextricably linked to their ability to import and export goods. Mining and industrial operations require specialised equipment and durable means of production. The output of local industry needs to be exported to assist in paying for these means of production. Goods for export will in future predominantly be carried in international standard containers. The ability to move containers efficiently and effectively between continents is important. Therefore, the ability to compare logistics supply chains and to match the chains with the required service is essential. The effectiveness of these chains will also determine the amount of inventory that has to be committed to the process. The speed and the frequency of sailing will need to be considered. To achieve the greatest economies of scale, as few ports as possible must be utilised for containers, and container terminals – as well as the processes associated with the transhipment of containers to and from terminals – need to be as efficient as possible. All these issues need to be addressed to create efficient and effective supply chains. This has not been done in many countries. For example, most container shipping lines have to call at three or more ports in South Africa, usually once to discharge and once to load containers. It would be better if they called at one or two hub ports only, to load and discharge concurrently; and if the containers were moved to these hub ports. At present, customs and port administration requirements are highly manual and segregated, making the process even less efficient.

In southern Africa, it is unlikely that this will change in future. There is still talk of creating a new port at Coega. The port of Richards Bay is trying to obtain a container terminal and the ports of Maputo and Walvis Bay are being rehabilitated and their respective road links with South Africa are being upgraded. There is little scope for economies of scale possible where this type of multi-port development continues. The privatisation of the port terminals is under discussion, but this is unlikely to provide the economies of scale necessary to achieve a significant improvement in this logistics area.

In the global economy, super hubs are developing. These take larger ships, more frequently, than South African ports. These super hubs provide a gateway that is efficient and effective for a large economic region. Singapore, for example, handles over ten times more containers than the port of Durban. The economies of scale for Singapore are much greater than for ports the size of Durban, enhancing the competitiveness of the products handled.

Systems and their impact for the future

New systems are being implemented that will assist the overall chain significantly in one particular area: that of co-ordinating the purchasing, manufacturing, and delivery processes. These are not ERP (Enterprise Resource Planning) systems where the functional entities are tied together in a common database, but systems specifically designed to integrate the processes and co-ordinate them. This has resulted in faster overall process times. As these systems improve a significant portion of the logistics chain, there will be great improvements to the overall supply chain.

Systems can also disaggregate services so that one or more steps are removed from the traditional sequence of performing a process. The transport function can be improved with systems that find the load most suited to a truck in a particular area. The home base, truck capacity, its reliability in delivering on time, and other factors are used to allocate loads to a truck that conforms to service and cost parameters. The trucks are advised by satellite communication about the next load and location.

Big volumes are required to sustain this capability. These are present in the USA and Europe, but not in economies in transition.

The future of southern African logistics

With all the technological developments impacting on logistics in the near future, the field will be exciting. However, the area with the most potential for fundamental changes in southern Africa is not technology. The logistics chain needs to operate for twenty-four hours per day, 365 days a year.

At present, it is unusual for transport to be utilised for more than eight or nine hours per day. To extend this period does require a second driver. However, the largest portion of capital in the logistics chain is invested in the assets of the warehouse and the transport. If these assets can be made to work constructively for not just eight hours, but the full twenty-four hours, efficiency can be improved up to three times. Transporting goods at peak traffic times is, at best, highly inefficient. Warehouses are rarely used effectively for the full twenty-four hour period. The benefits are not limited to the utilisation of assets. Goods delivered outside of store hours can be on the shelves before customers enter the store, improving the shopping experience.

It is accepted that the improvement in efficiency is not simply expressed as the ratio of current usage time to the full twenty-four hours. There are additional costs to having staff work at unusual hours. Safety is one such consideration. However, businesses can use technology to tackle this problem and achieve further incremental savings. By looking at the total logistics costs, a business will come to the logical conclusion that this type of operation is beneficial; but it has to be agile and flexible to successfully implement it.

Exports in particular should be more efficient and effective. Goods moved internationally face delays and additional costs. These negative factors need to be mitigated. The movement of goods to the port, onto the ship, and to the final destination needs to be as close to seamless as possible. Currently, the collection, assembly into loads, transport, port handling, and port and customs administration all have significant delays in the interfaces and execution. To be competitive in the manufacturing area, this issue is of critical importance. It is in effect a logistics problem and a logistics solution is required.

Conclusion

Technology will continue to effect major changes in the world and in the logistics business. The Internet will facilitate information transfer and will speed up portions of the logistics chain. The physical constraints of delivering the goods will be the limiting factor in the overall supply chain. Because economies in transition cannot produce and utilise the economies of scale, they will employ technological advances to a smaller extent. International logistics will not see major changes, but rather smaller incremental improvements in operational efficiency.

The greatest potential for improvement still lies in the ability of a business to be agile and flexible to improve the operation of warehouses and transport. This requires performing the logistics activities at the most appropriate times to make the overall chain more efficient and effective and – by operating for twenty-four hours per day – to make goods available in a shorter period.

Notes

1   *Fortune.* March 5, 2001.
2   *APICS.* February 2001 (a).
3   Christensen, D.E. 2001: 131–132.

Contents

Learning Objectives

After you have studied this chapter, you should be able to:
- understand the aspects that make up logistics and how they may interact with each other;
- better understand how to approach real-life logistics problems; and
- develop the ability be critical of information presented and conclusions drawn.

January

'Life has changed considerably over the last few months,' is Bulelwa's thought as she leaves the long discussions at the head office of the business where she has been appointed as Logistics Director. Just two months ago, there was a merger of two South African businesses, Active Wear and Sports Professionals. Before that, the businesses had been friendly rivals. Now, all this has changed. New shareholders own the businesses and a new business, called Active Sports International, was formed.

Before the merger, both businesses operated in the sports goods market. Active Wear concentrated on clothes and shoes for active people. Their range covered all sports, from aerobics to hiking. The majority of the clothing was made in Cape Town and the business had warehouses in Cape Town, Durban, and Johannesburg. Their own transport department did all deliveries.

Sports Professionals supplied sports equipment. The sales people were able to give customers advice on any item, from a tennis racquet to a home gym. Virtually no clothing was sold, with the exception of some imported footwear. Most of the goods were manufactured in Gauteng, near Johannesburg. The distribution was done from their own warehouse, located in Johannesburg, and from warehouses in Cape Town and Durban.

Bulelwa was recruited specifically to integrate the two logistics functions. At the discussions, the new board instructed Bulelwa that she, as the new Logistics Director, was now to add value to the new group by creating a single distribution capability. The method to achieve this was left to Bulelwa. As one board member commented, the board wanted to give Bulelwa the opportunity to think creatively and she was the logistics expert, not the board.

Bulelwa has decided that the core of her team will consist of a financial person, an IS person, and the heads of the logistics operations of the Active Wear and Sports Professionals businesses. She calls a meeting with Saaid and Peter, the Logistics Managers of the former Active Wear and Sports Professionals respectively, Anne (who is the IT manager), and Tenda (the financial manager) to discuss the board's instructions.

The stated intention of the marketing department is to retain the individual stores of each of the former businesses. These are well located in major shopping malls in the major cities. The marketing department also wants to introduce megastores where the full range of goods from both companies are available. These megastores will be located in shopping areas where land is cheaper than in shopping malls. All the stores will be branded as Active Sports International stores.

With the future needs of the new business clearer, Peter and Saaid begin to demonstrate why their respective logistics operations should supply the new group.

After a while, Bulelwa stops the discussion. 'We need to have a clear understanding of where we are going,' she states. 'The only way we can supply a superior logistics capability is to explore all the options before deciding which one to adopt. We need to know what each option will cost us and what services we will be able to offer. We should also know where to add value. With new stores opening, and the new marketing concept of the megastore, we need to know what we are trying to achieve. Is it minimum cost? Is it the greatest availability of the goods in the stores so the sales staff can achieve the highest possible sales? Is it a combination of the two? Is it something completely different, like minimum or even maximum inventory levels?'

After some heated debate, the meeting agrees that the needs are not clear to them and further input from other corporate executives will be necessary. Bulelwa realises that the answers will have to be determined outside the meeting. She asks members of the team to gather information.

- Tenda agrees to determine the levels of availability required for the business, and to find out what customers want from the stores and the logistics operations.
- Anne is tasked to investigate the systems in the two businesses and advise which suits the future operations best, as well as whether it will satisfy the future needs of the business.

Bulelwa says that, if necessary, the team members may co-opt additional personnel onto the task teams to find the answers, adding: 'Only with these questions clarified will we be able to see where we should be going and what we need to do.'

February

Tenda has requested a meeting with the team to report on the questions of the needs of the customers and the availability required by the store operations staff.

He starts his presentation with the preamble that what follows is information gathered from the stores, marketing department, and the members of his team. 'The most interesting issue is that this is not documented anywhere.' As the presentation progresses, it becomes evident that the business has no performance information for the logistics function. The strategic plan includes the product types to be sold, while the financial information projects sales of categories of products, as well as the associated expenses, into a detailed budget. The logistics charges constitute three lines in the budget, even though the costs of the warehouses, transport, and staff in logistics account for up to twenty-three per cent of the total costs incurred in the business.

Tenda summarises his findings as follows: 'The business has no idea of the value that logistics should add. Finance wants the costs reduced. Marketing wants the goods available instantaneously. Purchasing wants us to provide enormous warehouses so they can organise the largest discounts possible for bulk purchases. The sales staff in the store want the goods ready for the displays on the floor to make their job easier. Everyone wants something different!'

After a short silence, Bulelwa reluctantly begins the discussion. 'I see that everyone wants different things from logistics. I can even understand the requests from their perspectives. However, we cannot provide all these services. We can't be all things to all parties.'

Bulelwa asks Tenda whether all of the stakeholders were consulted. After some discussion,

they realise that no one has asked what the customers wanted. Some members of the team think the customers are not relevant for logistics, as marketing will reflect their needs. Others argue that the business is in existence because the customers buy the products, and their needs regarding the delivery and the presentation of the products are important to logistics.

Just as Bulelwa decides to give direction to the meeting, someone comments that they seem to be more confused now than before. Bulelwa takes this in her stride and thanks Tenda for the presentation.

'We now know that every stakeholder has a different view of what is needed. They can't all be right because we can't provide for all of these needs,' she says. 'What we can do, is understand why each functional group has these requirements and then use these motivations to choose our logistics channels. Before we start to look at change, we need to know what each of the businesses achieved before the merger. Tenda, may I ask you to find answers to the following questions from each of the former businesses and from each warehouse that the businesses had before the new business was created.'

Bulelwa passes a note to Tenda on which she has written the following questions.

- From which geographic region does each product come?
- What are the delivery times for products for each warehouse?
- How often do late deliveries occur?
- What is the level of stockholding in each warehouse in relation to the total sales?
- What are the operational costs – broken down into the facility cost, staff salaries, equipment, and services – of each warehouse?

Bulelwa concludes: 'I think you will need help to achieve this, so please ask a staff member from a store, Finance, and Operations from each of Saaid and Peter's areas to assist you. In the meantime, Peter, Saaid and I will try to define the way to balance the demands from each of the functions. This balance is something new to me and I need to think about it very carefully.'

March

After a large amount of research, discussion and thought, Bulelwa, Peter, and Saaid decide they need to update the team. Bulelwa asks Saaid to present their thoughts on the way to balance the demands from the functional departments. The process he presents is complex, but he makes it simple in the presentation.

'In essence, what we are saying is this: In the physical process, various parties must join to form a chain wherein one party passes the goods on to the next. The interface from one party to the next must be defined. If it is not defined, we will have arguments. The duties of each member of the chain must be written down and agreed to as well, so there is no ambiguity about who needs to do what.'

The first question comes from Anne, who points out that Saaid's presentation did not provide any guidelines for deciding which of the demands from the functional departments were the most important. Saaid's answer is somewhat surprising: 'All these parties are customers of logistics. However, the customers at the end of the logistics chain, who purchase goods in the store, are the primary ones and their needs have to be satisfied. We must do everything possible to make the right goods available at the right time and at the right place – that is the store – to ensure these customers buy as much as possible. All the other issues are aspects that determine how we perform logistics and they act as constraints. Our aim is to

assist the sales people and the marketing department with selling goods within these constraints. For example, we will try to keep the logistics costs to a minimum while ensuring the customer's service requirements are met. To balance the requirements of the internal departments, we will have to measure more than previously. We must be able to tell the purchasing department how much it costs to store large quantities of stock. This will enable them to decide whether the purchase of a larger quantity will be cost-effective. At present, they only look at the discount, but we need to give them the total costs of the entire chain so they can make the best decision. It is important to consider the impact of every action on the whole chain. If we concentrate on just a small portion of the logistics chain, we will not choose the best solution for the business but just for that small portion. It may sound obvious that this is wrong, but we all do it because of our background of looking at functional areas and not at the overall process!'

The team members look at each other. This is far more complex than they thought.

April

Bulelwa starts the meeting by saying that she wants to concentrate on understanding the flow of products. 'The former businesses had two very diverse methods of doing logistics. We may have to keep both of these, or we may be able to make sense of the flows and synchronise them. Tenda has prepared some data which he handed out to everyone yesterday, so we have had time to think about what the data means.'

Tenda motions that he wants to add something. 'The data is the best we can get at this moment,' he says. 'The finance department spent considerable time finding corresponding information about the two firms. Unfortunately, the financial systems are not identical, and the majority of the information about deliveries is unavailable. We had to dig for the information with the assistance of Saaid and Peter.'

Bulelwa resumes the review of the data. 'What does the data tell us?' she asks Saaid and Peter.

'Saaid and I have looked at the data. Each distribution centre or DC has different standards and costs,' offers Peter.

'The problem has been that each DC was seen as an isolated entity, not part of a total supply chain,' says Saaid. 'Our standards are also very different. Where sixteen per cent of the deliveries of Sports Professionals in Durban are late, there are no late deliveries at the Active Wear warehouse in Cape Town.'

Bulelwa interposes: 'That is true, but the cost to achieve this is very high – the warehouse has the highest stockholding and the highest transport cost of all the facilities. Is this the performance we want to reward? Anyone can achieve high service levels by spending a large amount of money. However, we want to be effective and efficient while supporting the marketing and sales efforts. Perhaps we should first address the service level that is required and then look at what it costs to achieve this. These figures show that if one adds up the inventory, warehouse, and transport costs, this Cape Town warehouse actually costs eight per cent of sales more than the next warehouse. The question is whether this is acceptable and necessary for satisfying the customers.'

Everyone looks at Lulama, the team member from the marketing department, for an answer.

	Order cut-off time	Percentage of late deliveries	Stock-holding as percentage of sales	Transport costs as percentage of sales	Warehouse cost for staff and facility as percentage of sales	Quantities distributed per month (m^3)	Total of warehouse stock and transport as percentage of sales
Active Wear							
Cape Town	next day [1]	0	7	10	9	60	26
Johannesburg	next day [2]	5	5	7	6	180	18
Durban	next day [2]	7	5	6	5	60	16
Sports Professionals							
Cape Town	next day [2]	12	3	8	6	64	17
Johannesburg	next day [1]	15	4	7	5	192	16
Durban	next day [1]	16	2	6	5	64	13
	next day [1]	An order placed before 14:00 will be delivered on the next working day.					
	next day [2]	An order placed before 12:00 noon will be delivered on the next working day.					

Table 19.1 Warehouse performance

'We are not certain,' she says, 'but in anticipation of this question we have done some calculations and we believe that if you can deliver on time ninety-eight per cent of the time and ensure that the late delivery is done by the next day, you will have achieved the best balance between cost and service level.'

There is consensus among the team members that this will change the way the warehouses operate. Saaid raises a further issue: 'How do we cope with the different deadlines or cut-off times required by which each warehouse for the placement of orders? I see that some warehouses require the orders to be placed before 14:00, while the other warehouses require the orders to be placed before noon. This doesn't make sense.'

'We will have to standardise these,' Peter replies. 'We can't have one standard for some and another standard for the rest. Perhaps we should just choose the average and make the cut-off time for all of them 13:00. This is a realistic compromise for everyone!'

There is a quick smatter of noise, as everyone seems to agree with Peter's proposal. Bulelwa, however, protests: 'I think we are falling into a trap here. The issue isn't the average or a compromise. The issue is what is necessary for the stores to ensure the customers get the products they require. We are ignoring the basic requirement of what we are doing – servicing the needs of the customer.'

Lulama seems a little rueful. 'I nearly got swayed by Peter's argument. I am now beginning to see how the logistics decisions can have a great impact on the stores and on our customer service. From this perspective, we need the orders to be open until 18:00 when we shut the stores. I realise this may not be realistic. I think it is best to set the order cut-off time at 14:00 at present. This improves the situation for three of the warehouses and doesn't affect the customers of the rest. I predict that we may want to set this time even later in future.'

Bulelwa takes stock of their progress. 'We now know what delivery standard we aim to achieve and we can begin to balance the demands of the internal functional departments. However, our focus is on supporting the marketing requirements as defined in the delivery requirements Lulama has given us. As we all know, these are specific delivery requirements. This means we need to scrutinise the inventory, how we acquire the inventory, and our ability to store and deliver the product. Then we can look at the cost and find the most cost-effective means to achieve these standards.'

'Our next tasks will be to decide what facilities we need and where,' Bulelwa added. 'The network is too complex and I can't see how we can continue to operate six warehouses. There must be a better arrangement. Peter and Saaid, will you please investigate the best strategic choice of warehouses and the location of these facilities? Bear in mind that we want to be more efficient and effective and that we want to reach the service level suggested by Marketing.'

May

Peter and Saaid have called a meeting to look at the network of warehouses and the strategic need for each warehouse. There is a high level of interest, as it is known that each of them wants to retain the warehouses from their previous operations. There has been considerable discussion and Bulelwa has assisted with reviewing the information they now present.

Saaid opens the meeting saying that they spent some time arguing the merits and demerits of each facility. To get past this discussion they have prepared a table of the data (see Tables 19.2 and 19.3) for the team to review. This they present with something of a flourish, as it took much effort to make it accurate.

'We decided to ignore the individual ware-houses that we currently own and ask ourselves what we require,' Peter explains. 'What we can see is the source of the goods that each warehouse receives, the total that must be sent to the other warehouses and the total that must be delivered to customers. We have assumed that the suppliers deliver to the nearest warehouse, as we believe this is the cheapest method. We need to review this assumption later but, as this is our current practice, we decided not to introduce added complexity that will cloud our judgement when we decide on the fate of the warehouses. We know we sell twenty per cent of our goods in the Cape Town region, twenty per cent of the goods in the Durban region, and sixty per cent of the goods in the Gauteng region. If you look at the second table, you will see the Johannesburg warehouse receives 108 m³ of goods from Cape Town, 144 m³ of goods from the Johannesburg suppliers, and 120 m³ of goods from overseas. The deliveries from the warehouse constitute 372 m³ of goods to customers and 48 m³ of goods to each of the Durban and Cape Town warehouses.'

Peter sits down and Saaid continues the presentation: 'For our review of the warehouses, the

Source of the products by geographical region				
Products	**Paid by**		**Source**	**Quantity (m³ per month)**
clothing	Active Wear		Cape Town	180
shoes	Active Wear		overseas	120
shoes	Sports Professionals		overseas	80
racquets	Sports Professionals		Johannesburg	140
cricket bats	Sports Professionals		Johannesburg	100

Table 19.2 Product origin and volumes

			Cape Town	**Johannesburg**	**Durban**
Percentage consumed in the region =			**20 %**	**60 %**	**20 %**
Source of products	**Warehouse received**	**Volume**	**Cape Town**	**Johannesburg**	**Durban**
Cape Town	Cape Town	180	36	108	36
Johannesburg	Johannesburg	240	48	144	48
Overseas	Durban	200	40	120	40
Total sent to customers		**620**	**124**	**372**	**124**
Total received by warehouse			**268**	**468**	**284**

Table 19.3 Warehouse and products

total product into and out of the warehouse needs to be considered. The Johannesburg warehouse receives a total of 468m³ each month. This helps define the size of Johannesburg warehouse and similar calculations have helped to define the size of warehouses we need in the other regions. The Active Wear warehouse in Cape Town is large enough. In Durban, the Sports Professionals warehouse is large enough. It is in Johannesburg that we have a problem. Neither facility is large enough. We must therefore either operate two facilities or we must build a new larger one to provide for the new volumes of the business.'

Test yourself

Chapter 3: Logistics channel strategy

19.9 Peter and Saaid also consider the source of the product. If they only considered the quantities of the products that need to be delivered, would this produce the same conclusions? Explain your reasoning. The information can be presented in a different form than a table. Create a diagram to depict the flows, with arrows showing the inbound flows and the outbound flows from each warehouse.

19.10 Show how the 468m³ received by Johannesburg warehouse is calculated from the figures in Tables 19.2 and 19.3.

June

Tenda and two purchasing managers meet at Bulelwa's office. 'We need to talk about the procurement and the inventory management,' they say.

Initially, the purchasing managers have a somewhat hostile attitude. After a while, Bulelwa understands the problem. They feel uncertain about how the logistics chain will affect their work. They are particularly worried about their ability to source products. She turns to the purchasing managers and says, 'Please understand that the focus on the customer is not a slight to your work. If the wrong or insufficient inventory is held, we cannot deliver ninety-eight per cent of the goods on time, as the marketing department

requested. Of course, if we carry too much inventory, Finance will ask us why we have this excess inventory.' After some discussion, they decide that very little will change, except that the timescales will be very different.

'If we have to order footwear from overseas, it takes thirty-five days to get a container to the Durban warehouse. If we purchase the product from local sources, it takes approximately six days to get the goods to the nearest warehouse. How do we maintain the appropriate inventory for the two different products when we don't know what will be sold in the future?' one of the purchasing managers asks.

The question is a good one, muses Bulelwa. The answer is not simple. The budget merely takes into account the expected sales in a year. This is no answer.

She decides to consult other colleagues. After talking to a former colleague, Bulelwa returns to the purchasing people with Tenda. 'We need to be able to plan or forecast the future purchases with sufficient accuracy to ensure there are no stock shortages in the store. This means the warehouses must have sufficient stock levels. We can replenish stock in the stores from the warehouses. Once the stock level in the warehouse falls to below a certain point, we must order additional stock. It is essential that there is stock in the warehouse to support the stores at all times. We just need to agree on the criteria for reordering. One of my colleagues says there is a formula to calculate the order quantity, called the 'Economic Order Quantity' or EOQ. Initially, I think we need to simply use this and add the more sophisticated techniques later.'

There is some heated discussion. The concept of an automatic reordering process sounds like a vast improvement, but the managers keep finding products and situations where the process will not work. As one manager says, 'For the products we sell continuously each week and month of the year, this process sounds like a good idea. Unfortunately, it is of limited value for stock that is not sold on a regular basis. The sales of many products vary according to the season or are subject to special offers.'

The team members discuss this and then Bulelwa summarises their needs: 'If our stock needs to be in the store to make sales, we need to know the future sales the stores expect to make.'

The purchasers look astounded. 'Are you saying that Marketing has to tell us what to order for future sales?' they ask.

'The marketing department can't give us a service target unless they are willing to tell us the future needs in time to source the goods. Otherwise we will buy too much and too early to protect ourselves. That will remove the focus from the needs of our customers and will raise our cost significantly. Finance will have every right to complain that we do not abide by the aim of logistics, which is to do the work effectively,' Bulelwa replies.

A few days later, Bulelwa calls another meeting. After spending much time discussing this requirement with Lulama, the head of marketing, Lulama agreed that Marketing cannot ask for a service target without a plan of the goods required. Once Lulama understood and agreed that the future needs should be planned, she committed her marketing team to creating a plan of sales by product category. The question now is how far into the future the plan should extend. The debate centres around the purchasing department, who want a month to 'shop around for the best deal' before committing to an order. Lulama compromises and offers to plan four weeks ahead for locally sourced product and eight weeks ahead for products sourced overseas, by means of a forecast. She undertakes to set up weekly review sessions with Marketing, Purchasing, and Logistics to update and review the forecast plan.

'If purchasers find a very good opportunity to purchase a product, they need to bring it to the planning committee. We can see if it fits into our sales plan and then incorporate the purchase into our planning system. This will help increase our sales, and procurement will then add value above the traditional function of obtaining products at the lowest cost. All the other purchases will be planned ahead for the agreed periods and will be discussed weekly,' Lulama emphasises.

Test yourself

Chapter 4: Planning Systems

19.11 The business will now plan the quantities of products needed in the stores in future. Do you agree with this idea? What are the advantages and the disadvantages of this process?

19.12 The business will plan ahead four weeks for locally sourced products and eight weeks for products sourced overseas. Are these periods realistic? Should the periods for promotions be the same as those for regularly purchased products?

19.13 What type of planning system would you use?

Chapter 5: Procurement Management

19.14 The stock that is handled regularly will be purchased based on the reorder point and the re-order quantity set at the warehouse. It is also part of the planning process. Do you think it should be?

19.15 The reorder process is the purchase of a fixed quantity of a product when the stock level falls to a specified value. Many warehouse operations use this to automatically purchase stock. Can you think of reasons why the stock reorder level and the quantity ordered need to be regularly reviewed?

July

'We have come to the conclusion that the inventory needs to be investigated,' says Bulelwa while talking to Peter, Saaid, and Tenda. 'Each warehouse has its own idea of what levels of inventory are required. In the information you produced (Table 19.1), the inventory levels vary from seven per cent of sales for the Cape Town Active Wear warehouse to two per cent of sales for the Durban warehouse of Sports Professionals. Two per cent of sales would be ideal, but the consequences are that the service level is affected. Sixteen per cent of the deliveries from this warehouse are late, which is unacceptable. We also cannot choose the highest levels, as this would not be the most effective use of resources. We must decide how to set the levels of inventory in such a way that we can achieve the required delivery standard at the lowest cost. The transport costs may rise if we have to rush out to get products from suppliers because we carry too little stock. We need to accept that this will also increase our warehouse costs. We therefore need to set the inventory levels and then make the transport and the warehouse operations as effective as possible. I am unclear about the method of setting the inventory level. Will you please look into the problem and advise how to deal with the inventory of the regularly sold items and the promotions respectively?' she asks, looking at Tenda.

Tenda thinks for a few moments. 'Sure, I can do that, but I just wonder if the inventory should be set before considering the delivery. I don't know of a better way, but give me a few days and I will try to get an answer for you. I must also think about whether we should set the average inventory cost to sales as a target, or if there is some other method.'

Test yourself

Chapter 6: Inventory management

19.16 The method of setting a financial target to sales is discussed above. Is this the best method for setting the inventory in this case? Take into consideration that there have been many changes in the business. The data dates from the period before the merger and may not be suitable for the new business and the team's approach to logistics.

19.17 Calculate the average inventory you would hold for a specific line of socks, sold throughout the country. Assume one hundred pairs are sold per month and the store requires that at least ten pairs be in stock at any time. The reorder quantity is one hundred pairs.

19.18 If the reorder quantity is fifty pairs, what should the average inventory be?

19.19 If the sales of these socks were doubled for six months of the year because the socks are used for the seasonal sports, how would you alter the re-order point, the reorder quantity, and the frequency of ordering?

August

Tenda walks into Bulelwa's office one day. 'I have been looking at the costs for some of our suppliers. One of them charges us for the product and additionally for the boxes in which they deliver the product. I assume that this is a more expensive box than what we had previously. I have asked around and no one seems to know why we want a special box.'

Bulelwa looks surprised. 'I didn't even know we had the special box requirement. I will see if I can make sense of the matter.' After investigations with the procurement and logistics staff, Bulelwa reports to Tenda. 'You won't believe what I have found out about your box costs. It appears that about ten years ago the clothes were damaged in the original box, a store display box that was not suitable for transporting. We forced the manufacturer to use a stronger box. We also decided to put eight of the individual boxes into a larger box to make it easier to transport them to the DCs. This came about because the transporter complained of problems with the small display boxes. At the DC, we dispose of the large outer box, as we supply to the stores in the smaller boxes. The stores discard the smaller box and display the clothes in the display package.'

Tenda starts muttering about costs and waste of money, but Bulelwa smiles and adds that she has instructed the manufacturer to eliminate the outer box immediately. This will save some cost. Bulelwa thanks Tenda for his input and asks if he will assist some of the logistics team members to look at alternatives for the current packaging. 'There seems to be three choices here,' she summarises. 'We can supply the clothes in the smaller boxes and the stores can continue to discard these. We can place the clothes in their display packaging in a large box and deliver them to the warehouse, eliminating the smaller box. The final alternative is to replace the large box with a plastic container that can be used to carry the products to the store, returned from the store to the manufacturer, and reused.'

Tenda agrees to help with the investigation.

Chapter 8 Packaging

Assume eight items with display packaging fit into one of the smaller boxes, and four of the smaller boxes fit into the larger box. The smaller box costs R4,00 and the larger box costs R12,00. A returnable plastic container costs about R18,00 per trip and holds thirty display packages.

19.20 Define the packaging alternatives. Which is the better choice from a financial point of view? Which alternative is more suitable for handling through the logistics chain and why?

19.21 The average cost of the round trip for the plastic container is R18,00. If the volume the container occupies in the transport can be reduced on the return journey when the containers are empty, so that they take less space, the cost is reduced to R14,00. Does this change the answers to the above questions and, if so, how and why? Give two methods to reduce the size of the container in order to decrease the space required for the return transport.

September

Saaid and Peter advise Bulelwa that they are ready to talk about the new warehouse they will need in Johannesburg. They are very excited as they unroll plans from a variety of architects. After poring over the plans for an hour, Bulelwa asks them, 'Why have the architectural firms come up with such different designs? Surely, they should have similar designs for the same building?'

Peter and Saaid explain that they had asked three different firms for designs based on land the firms knew to be available. This meant that the firms, rather than Saaid and Peter, looked for the land. One firm used a site that was square in shape, a second chose a site that was on a slope, and a third had a site that was level with the only feasible access road in the middle of the site. The buildings and layouts are therefore very different for each site.

Bulelwa thinks this over while Saaid and Peter begin to talk about the marvellous features that

each plan offers. She carefully phrases her answer: 'They all sound really superb. I understand the great features they offer and I can see you are really excited. What I don't understand is which of these will give you the most efficient and effective operation. There must be a specific design that will suit our products, and while different firms may design the facility with different layouts and features, the principles of the design must be similar. What requirements did you specify to these designers, and what data did you give them?'

After a long silence, Peter answered: 'We gave them the expected distribution quantities from our original investigation. We explained how we operate, but we never specified the exact operation or any of our requirements in writing. I guess the excitement of a new warehouse blinded us. We got carried away and assumed the architects would build us the perfect warehouse.'

Bulelwa laughs: 'I understand your excitement, after working in the old facilities for years. However, we have only one chance to get the operation right. Once we commit to a building, it must be the best we can design or specify, and it must give us the most value for the money we spend on it. I think you should sit down and list everything you want from the facility, specify how you want to store the various products, and describe the total operation of the facility. Look at it with a fresh view, don't just copy what is in the existing facilities or use what a firm offers you. Record all the valuable features in these designs in a Request for Proposal (RFP). Issue this RFP to firms to see who comes closest to matching your specifications.'

Chapter 9 Warehouse design

19.22 What would the design requirements be for the warehouse in the case study? To answer this question, specifically refer to the types of products and how they will be stored and/or transported.

19.23 Would you expect to see the same or similar designs for the storage and the assembly areas from each of the architectural firms?

19.24 Where would you place the manager's office and administration space – in a separate building, an adjacent building, or in the warehouse?

19.25 If you were instructed to place the administration space in the warehouse, where in the building would you place it to be the most cost-effective and efficient?

Chapter 7 Materials handling and equipment

19.26 Define how each of the products in Tables 19.2 and 19.3 should be stored and why.

19.27 In a table, summarise the storage required. Add the materials handling equipment most suited for picking and storing the products in the warehouse, the equipment needed to unload containers, and the equipment needed to load trucks.

October

Peter and Saaid have a new problem. 'We have seen tremendous improvement in the levels of the inventory handled by each warehouse,' says Saaid.

'The inventory levels, as a ratio to sales for each warehouse, are all starting to approach the same value,' agrees Peter.

Saaid continues: 'We now need to address the transport costs, as these vary tremendously, especially when compared to sales. I have been looking at the warehouses and the way the transport is done. All the warehouses have a fleet of trucks, which they use to deliver all products. The exception is the Active Wear warehouse in Cape Town. They have trucks dedicated to the different products and the transport costs are significantly more than for any other warehouse.'

After some debate they agree that individual trucks for specific products do not make sense. As Saaid says, 'One store may be visited by two trucks per day to deliver goods. Not only are two trucks travelling the same route inefficient, but the store has to manage two trucks when it could manage one.'

'We should insist that the transport fleet is used for all the goods,' says Peter. 'This is even more important as we continue to integrate the two businesses. The transport function may be more complicated to manage, but it will result in operations that are more effective.'

'There is still one more issue we need to think about,' says Saaid. 'In Johannesburg, the transport cost of the Sports Professionals warehouse is lower than that of the Active Wear warehouse. I think this is because they deliver to the stores for longer hours every day.'

Peter looks surprised. 'I thought all the trucks from all the warehouses worked from 8:00 to 16:00?'

'This warehouse has managed to reduce its costs while still meeting its delivery targets,' Saaid answers. 'It has done this by making some of the trucks work for longer periods. The trucks leave early in the morning so they get to the stores before peak hour morning traffic. The stores pay two people to come in early, but the truck is unloaded between 7:30 and 8:00, and the goods are on the shelves before the store is opened. The store benefits and the trucks are used more efficiently.'

Peter thinks about this and then says: 'This makes sense. The value of the trucks is far higher than the small amount of overtime that is incurred to allow them to operate for a few extra hours. I think we should investigate whether it is sensible to do deliveries in the evening if the stores are open until 18:00. We should also think about doing deliveries on weekends, as we currently only deliver on weekdays.'

Test yourself

Chapter 12: Transport management

19.28 Is it generally better to dedicate separate vehicles to each type of product, or is it better to use the transport available for all the products and find ways to load the truck to provide for the different products?

In this case study, the gym equipment is handled differently from the boxes of clothes and shoes. Look at the volumes of the products in Table 19.2 to answer the following questions and motivate your answers.

19.29 Scheduling the trucks to be at the store while the peak morning traffic occurs seems to improve the transport effectiveness. Should the business pursue both the scheduling and the extended hours? Motivate your answer and try to devise a simple calculation to show the value thereof, based on the information in the case study.

19.30 How much value does the receipt of products outside the usual store receiving times (08:00 to 16:00) add? Consider the impact on customers if display areas are continuously being replenished while they shop.

November

'Bulelwa, we need some advice,' Saaid says one morning. 'We established the basis for the design and issued it to architectural firms. It really does make more sense now and we are much clearer about what we want. The problem is the operation and the information systems that we need in order to make a facility of this size work. The information system affects the speed of the flows, the number of steps required, the administrative paperwork and, to a certain extent, the size of the facility. We have issued the size requirements for a one-shift operation using Active Wear's old warehouse management system, which is still better than the Sports Professionals system. If we are to finalise the warehouse design and prepare staff to use the new facility, we need to decide the operational process flows, both for physical products and for the administration. This means we need to identify the system for managing our facility and define the physical and administration process flows. We have also realised that we need a decent system for the transport management. There are optimisation packages that tell you how to use your trucks, but capturing the data manually is too complex and time-consuming. By the time the data is in the system, the trucks are loaded and have left.'

Bulelwa agrees that they need to consider these issues and undertakes to set up a meeting with Anne and the training staff. She points out that, if a transport optimisation package is used, there will be a single fleet for each warehouse as the fleets cannot be segregated according to different products or routes.

Bulelwa summarises the situation: 'A new warehouse is being specified in Johannesburg. It needs to be designed around the products and the handling practices. We know the products, but the processes are not clear. What we do know is that the facility is too big for the existing Warehouse Management Systems (WMS). We would like to investigate some other systems, such as transport optimisation, but this can only be done if we have accurate information available quickly. This means we need a system to manage the facility.' Bulelwa looks to Anne to answer.

'We have looked at the WMS systems available and we have identified three that we think are suitable for our business. I suggest that you design your warehouse on the principle that we will use a new warehouse system that will not use bar code scanning technology. Our costing shows that with the current volumes the use of scanning is not justified as it only speeds up the physical process. This means that the processes in the system will be similar to the current ones. These processes have not been recorded, but the staff members know them from experience. The system will be faster and more flexible than both the old systems. We can add the scanning capability at a later stage.'

Test yourself

Chapter 10: Warehouse management

19.31 It is proposed that the new warehouse adopt processes that are the same as the ones currently in practice. Should Saaid and Peter accept this or can you foresee future problems? Motivate your answer.

19.32 The new warehouse will carry the stock for the new business and will handle the full range of the products of the two former businesses. Will the processes have to be altered? Discuss your answer.

19.33 The processes are not recorded, but Anne believes the staff know the processes and do not need special training on the processes in the new system. Is this a valid conclusion? Try to find an operation that does not have written or documented procedures, and see whether the various staff members do the same job in the same way every time. Is it necessary that all the staff members do the same job in the same way?

December

Some time later, Tenda goes to see Bulelwa. 'We have to discuss the products from the overseas suppliers,' he says. 'We previously used the service of a clearing and forwarding agent as we never filled a container. We filled approximately fifty per cent of a container each time. We now can fill the container each time. I see there are two competing lines that can handle our full containers. The first sails every week and takes twenty-two days to reach Durban. The second sails every two weeks but takes twenty days to reach Durban. We now need to choose one, but I am not sure how to make the choice.'

Bulelwa looks at the figures she scribbled while Tenda was talking. 'I can see what your problem is,' she says. 'The choice between the shipping lines will be interesting. One piece of information that we will need is the total value of products in a container.'

Tenda smiles. 'That is one of the values for which I have managed to get data. The average value is R250 000,00 per container containing 25m³ of products.'

'We really need to ask the shipping lines to tell us why their times and routes are the best for us,' Bulelwa suggests. 'Let us draft an RFP that asks them to tell us which line will offer the cheapest rate for transporting the products. This must include the cost of the inventory during the transportation.'

January

'We have come a long way from the first days of the merger,' Bulelwa says at the end of one of the management meetings. 'If I look at what we were capable of when we started we were a poor imitation of the value we deliver today. We currently deliver our products to the marketing specification of ninety-eight per cent the next day and the remaining two per cent on the following day. Our new warehouse in Johannesburg serves the Gauteng region extremely effectively. We have improved our transport and our imports. We have a new warehouse system that gives us more information than we had before. We have eradicated some silly practices like the use of one box in another, which is just a waste of money and adds no value. All these have been great achievements.'

She pauses. 'There is one area that still concerns me tremendously. We have a very large administration staff to ensure the orders are captured from the stores on our WMS. This seems to me to be the biggest bottleneck that we have in the entire process.'

The other team members begin to comment on this. Some suggest the biggest problem is the operations staff, who are now working an hour overtime most evenings to finish the picking and dispatch of the products. The debate rages on for a while before Bulelwa interrupts. 'The symptoms are the size of the administration staff and perhaps the hour of overtime for the operations staff. We need to find the causes of these problems and eliminate them. Peter and Saaid, will you look at our total operation and advise us what the primary cause of the problem is?' Peter and Saaid look at each other. These are common occurrences in the warehouses and they are sceptical about identifying causes. As Saaid comments to Peter as they walk out of the meeting, 'Surely these are just operational issues that occur in every warehouse?'

After spending days looking at the operations, Peter and Saaid are very careful to say nothing to their colleagues about their findings before the next meeting. Everyone is intrigued to hear if they have found a cause for the problems and if they have a solution.

Saaid begins the presentation: 'We all know that warehouses work overtime. We all know that it takes a large amount of administration to make a warehouse work smoothly. Peter and I approached this problem with these thoughts in our minds. We were right when we suggested that warehouses often have these problems, but we were very wrong in our assumption that nothing could be done about this. There are underlying problems that account for most of the overtime and the administrative load. In this case, both the overtime and the administration load are caused by the time we need to take an order – whether it is faxed or telephoned to us – and capture it on the WMS. It takes about an hour to capture the orders in the peak activity period between mid-morning and the afternoon cut-off time of 14:00. This hour is critical to us. This is how long the staff works overtime. The administration department needs to have additional staff to capture the orders. If we can eliminate the process of capturing the details of the orders, we can save an hour. We will also eliminate the additional work caused by an error rate that increases as the administration personnel work under increasing pressure during this peak period.'

Peter takes the floor and summarises, 'We have found the cause of two of our most common problems. It lies in the data capturing of orders. We need to find a new way of receiving orders into our WMS that removes these delays and eliminates the errors. This will give us more time to pick, and will reduce the administrative workload. Anne will now do a presentation on e-commerce. We agree that this is the way we should go to eliminate these problems.'

Anne rises and says, 'E-commerce is a very complex subject to discuss in a short period. What I want to present is a simple concept. We will give our stores a software programme that will present all their sales as a list of products that require replacement. They may add or subtract additional items to arrive at what they think are the appropriate quantities needed in the store. This list will be sent electronically to our WMS. The WMS will read the information and make it into an order for the store. As long as this is done before the 14:00 cut-off time, the store will receive its products the next day in ninety-eight per cent of the cases. Of course, this is a very simple description of a complex software and hardware process. We can save you the hour in the processing time that delays the issuing of the order to the picking staff, as well as the effort of capturing the orders into the WMS.'

The team members now start to see the value of the integrated computer systems. 'Are you sure the store staff can handle the additional work on their computers?' one of the store representatives asks.

'We have looked at the stores ordering process,' replies Anne. 'Currently, they do most of the work manually by writing the order and faxing it. If we make the software user-friendly, the stores will see an immediate benefit.'

Test yourself

Chapter 16: E-business in logistics

19.41 What type of e-business is Anne advocating – B2B or B2C?

19.42 If the process of getting the order into the WMS is reduced by an hour, there will be a saving of one hour in the picking. The new e-business process will introduce other improvements. Name a few.

19.43 The business delivers products from the warehouse to the stores. Currently the stores sign a Proof of Delivery (POD). Could the business introduce an improvement on the POD using e-business? Describe in a short paragraph what would be required to achieve this.

Chapter 6: Inventory management

19.44 How frequently should the stores order and why? (Look at the store inventory and the cost of delivering the goods.)

Bibliography

Adendorff, S.A. and De Wit, P.W.C. 1997. *Production and operations management: A South African perspective,* second edition. Cape Town: Oxford University Press.

APICS: The performance advantage. February 2001(a). 'The ITX shakeout: re-invent and survive'. Vol. 11, no. 2.

APICS: The performance advantage. February 2001(b). 'Making the case for supply chain management — it's high time to buy in'. Vol. 11, no. 2.

Ballou, R.H. 1987. *Basic business logistics,* second edition. Englewood Cliffs, New Jersey: Prentice-Hall.

Ballou, R.H. 1993. 'Reformulating a logistics strategy: A concern for the past, present and future' in *International Journal of Physical Distribution and Logistics Management.* Vol. 23, no. 5. England: MCB University Press.

Ballou, R.H. 1999. *Business logistics management,* fourth edition. Upper Saddle River, New Jersey: Prentice-Hall.

Bentley, J. 1995. 'Designing for the future' in *CAR Magazine.* May 1995.

Bowersox, D.J. and Closs, D.J. 1996. *Logistical management: the integrated supply chain process.* Singapore: McGraw-Hill.

Branch, A.E. 1994. *Export practice and management,* third edition. London: Chapman & Hall.

Bramel, J. and Simchi-Levi, D. 1997. *The logic of logistics: Theory, algorithms, and applications for logistics management.* New York: Springer-Verlag Inc.

Braziers (Pty) Ltd. *Systems for palletised loads.* Durban: Braziers.

Braziers (Pty) Ltd. *Systems for un-palletised loads.* Durban: Braziers.

Button, K.J. 1993. *Transport economics,* second edition. Aldershot, Hants: Edward Elgar.

Bytheway, A. and Goussard, Y. 2000. *Electronic commerce strategies for small, medium and large businesses. Promoting electronic commerce in South Africa: Some academic perspectives.* http://www.ecomm-debate.co.za

Chopra, S. and Meindl, P. 2001. *Supply chain management: Strategy, planning, and operation.* New Jersey: Prentice-Hall.

Christensen, D.E. 2001. 'Dot-com: the channel, the challenge' in *Annual conference proceedings for CLM, September 2000.* Oak Brook, Illinois: CLM.

Christopher, M. 1990. *The strategy of distribution management.* Oxford: Heinemann Professional Publishing.

Christopher, M. 1998. *Logistics and supply chain management,* second edition. Great Britain: Prentice-Hall.

Christopher, M.G. and Ryals, L. 1999. 'Supply chain strategy: its impact on shareholder value' in *The International Journal of Logistics Management.* Vol. 10, no. 1.

Colliers, P.F. 1993. 'Logistics' in *Colliers Encyclopedia.* Vol. 14. New York: Colliers Inc.

Cooper, M.C., Innis, D.E. and Dickson, P.R. 1992. *Strategic planning for logistics.* Oak Brook, Illinois: CLM.

Council of Logistics Management. 1993. *What's it all about?* Oak Brook, Illinois: CLM.

Council of Logistics Management. 1998. *What it's all about.* Oak Brook, Illinois: CLM.

Council of Logistics Management. 2001. http://www.CLM1.org.

Coyle, J.J., Bardi, E.J. and Langley, C.J. (Jr). 1996. *The management of business logistics,* sixth edition. Minneapolis/St. Paul: West Publishing Company.

Coyle, J.J., Bardi, E.J. and Novack, R.A. 2000. *Transportation,* fifth edition. Cincinnati, Ohio: South-Western College Publishing.

Crown product information, provided by Goscor Industrial Corporation (Pty) Ltd. Munich, Germany: Crown.

Daewoo product catalogue. Inchon, Korea: Daewoo.

Department of Water Affairs and Forestry. 1998. *Minimum requirements for waste disposal by landfill.* Pretoria: Government Printer.

De Villiers, G. 1997. 'Third-party logistics' in *Logistics News.* June/July 1997. Johannesburg: Bolton Publications.

Durlinger, P.P.J. and Bemelmans, R.P.H.G. 1999. *Logistieke Technieken,* third edition. Posterholt, Netherlands: Durlinger Publishing.

E-centreUK. Association for Standards and Practices in Electronic Trade – EAN UK Ltd. http://www.e-centre.org.uk

Fair, M.L. and Williams, E.W. 1981. *Transportation and logistics,* second edition. Plano, Texas: Business Publications.

Fairplay. March 1, 2001. 'Box portals set to open'.

Fawcett, P., McLeish, R.E. and Ogden, I.D. 1992. *Logistics management.* London: Pitman Publishing.

Fawcett, P., McLeish, R.E. and Ogden, I.D. 1992. *Logistics management: Frameworks.* Harlow, England: Prentice-Hall.

Fortune, March 2001. 'Edison's curse'. Vol. 143, no. 5.

Gattorna, J.L. 1998(a). 'Effective logistics management' in *International Journal of Physical Distribution and Materials Management.* Vol. 18, no. 1. England: MCB University Press.

Gattorna, J.L. 1998(b). *Strategic supply chain alignment.* Aldershot: Gower Publishing Company.

Gitman, L.J. 2000. *Principles of managerial finance,* ninth edition. New York: Addison Wesley Publishing Company.

Goetsch, D.L. and Davis, S. 1995. *Implementing total quality.* Englewood Cliffs, New Jersey: Prentice-Hall.

Hadamitzky, M.C. 2000. 'eBusiness – Strategische Herausforderungen und Entwicklungstendenzen' in *Konstanz.* November 24, 2000.

Harmon, R.L. 1993. *Reinventing the warehouse.* The Free Press.

Heyns, G.J. 2001. *Co-ordinating incoming traffic.* Department of Logistics, University of Stellenbosch. (Working paper, January 2001.)

Hinkelman, E.G. 2000. *Dictionary of international trade: Handbook of the global trade community,* fourth edition. Novato, California: World Trade Press.

Huff, S.L., Wade, M., Parent, M., Schneberger, S. and Newson, P. 2000. *Cases in electronic commerce.* Boston: Irwin/McGraw-Hill.

Hugo, W.M.J., Van Rooyen, D.C. and Badenhorst, J.A. 1997. *Purchasing and materials management,* third edition. Pretoria: J.L. van Schaik.

INTTRA. http://www.inttra.com

Johnson, J.C., Wood, D.F., Wardlow, D.L. and Murphy, P.R. 1999. *Contemporary logistics,* seventh edition. Englewood Cliffs, New Jersey: Prentice-Hall.

Keenan, F. 2000. 'Logistics gets a little respect' in *Business Week.* November 11, 2000.

Lambert, D.M., Cooper, M.C., and Pagh, J.D. 1998. 'Supply chain management: implementation issues and research opportunities' in *The International Journal of Logistics Management.* Vol. 9, no. 2.

Lambert, D.M. and Stock, J.R. 1993. *Strategic logistics management,* third edition. Homewood: Irwin.

Lambert, D.M., Stock, J.R. and Ellram, L.M. 1998. *Fundamentals of logistics management.* Singapore: Irwin McGraw-Hill.

Lambert, D.M. and Burduroglu, R. 2000. 'Measuring and selling the value of logistics' in *The International Journal of Logistics Management.* Vol. 11, no. 1.

Marx, S., Radermeyer, W.F., and Reynders, H.J.J. 1993. *Business economics: Guidelines for business management.* Pretoria: J.L. van Schaik.

McCarthy, E.J. and Perreault, W.D. (Jr). 1984. *Basic marketing,* eighth edition. Illinois: Richard D Irwin Inc.

Morreale, R. and Prichard, D. 1995. *Logistics rules of thumb, facts and definitions III.* Southern California Round Table/Council of Logistics Management.

Morris, D.R. 1966. *The washing of the spears.* Johannesburg: Jonathan Ball Paperbacks.

Muller, G. 1995. *Intermodal freight transportation,* third edition. Lansdowne, Virginia: Eno Transportation Foundation.

Nix, N.W. 2001. 'The consequences of supply chain management: creating value, satisfaction and differential advantage' in Mentzer, J.T. 2001. *Supply chain management.* London: Sage Publications.

Occupational Health and Safety Act of 1993, Republic of South Africa. Pretoria: Government Printer.

Peck, B. 2000. 'Buy-side pays the bills' in *The e-commerce handbook 2000: Your guide to the Internet revolution and the future of business.* Cape Town: Trialogue.

Pienaar, W.J. 2001. *Business logistics management as academic discipline: a South African perspective.* Paper presented at the International Conference on Integrated Logistics, Nanyang Technological University, Singapore.

PricewaterhouseCoopers. 1999. *South African value chain analysis: Final report.*

Ramberg, J., Rapatout, P., Reynolds, F. and Debattista, C. 2000. *Incoterms 2000: A forum of experts.* Paris: International Chamber of Commerce. (ICC Publication Number 617.)

Ramsdell, G. 2000. 'The real business of B2B' in *The McKinsey Quarterly*. No. 3.

Rushton, A. and Oxley, J. 1989. *Handbook of logistics and distribution management*. London: Kogan Page.

Rushton, A. and Saw, R. 1992. 'A methodology for logistics strategy planning' in *The International Journal of Logistics Management*. Vol. 3, no. 1. Florida: International Logistics Research Institute.

Schonberger, R.J. and Knod, E.M. 1992. *Operations management: Improving customer service,* fourth edition. Plano, Texas: Business Publications.

Schumer, L.A. 1974. *Elements of transport,* third edition. Sydney: Butterworths.

Slater, A. 2000. 'Should third-party logistics service providers compete or co-operate?' in *Logistics and Transport Focus*. November 2000, Vol. 2, no. 9.

South African Income Tax Act No. 58 of 1962 (as amended). Pretoria: Government Printer.

Spamer, J.S. and Pienaar, W.J. 1998. 'Riglyne vir die implementering van 'n eienaar-drywerstelsel' in *South African Journal of Business Management*. Vol. 26, no. 4.

Special interest group on supply chain inventory management. *Glossary of inventory and materials management definitions*. Institute of logistics and transport: www.iolt.org.uk/sig/scim-glossary.htm.

Stavrou, A., May, J. and Benjamin, P. 2000. *E-commerce and poverty alleviation in South Africa: An input paper to the Government Green Paper*. Paper prepared for input into E-Commerce Green Paper Process.

Stock, J.R. 1998. *Development and implementation of reverse logistics programs*. Oak Brook, Illinois: CLM.

Symbol Technologies, Inc. 1999. *Bar coding for beginners*.

The e-commerce handbook 2000: Your guide to the Internet revolution and the future of business. Cape Town: Trialogue.

The global logistics research team of Michigan State University. 1995. *World class logistics: The challenge of managing continuous change*. Oak Brook, Illinois: CLM.

TradeWorld. http://www.tradeworld.net

Visagie, S.E. 2001. *Operations research in physical distribution*. Department of Logistics, University of Stellenbosch. (Workbook LB 348.)

Van den Berg, M. 2000. 'Development of EDI over VANS' in *The e-commerce handbook 2000: Your guide to the Internet revolution and the future of business*. Cape Town: Trialogue.

Van Vuuren, J.P. 1996. *Effective exporting: a South African guide*. Pretoria: Institute for International Marketing.

Wells, A.T. 1999. *Air transportation: A management perspective,* fourth edition. Belmont, California: Wadsworth.

Wood, D.F. and Johnson, J.C. 1996. *Contemporary transportation,* fifth edition. Upper Saddle River, New Jersey: Prentice-Hall.

World Cargo News. Various months. New Jersey: WCN Publishing.

Zeithaml, V.A. 1988. 'Consumer perceptions of price, quality and value: a means-end model and synthesis of evidence' in *Journal of Marketing*. Vol. 52.

Index